THE COMPLETE BOOK
OF INTERNATIONAL INVESTING

Books on the Foreign Securities Markets by Rainer Esslen

A Guide to Marketing Securities in Europe 1971-1972, copyright ©
1972, 1971 by Wall Street Reports Publishing Corporation. Published
by Wall Street Reports Publishing Corporation, New York, N.Y.

How to Buy Foreign Securities, copyright © 1974 by Rainer Esslen.
Published by Columbia Publishing Company, Inc., Frenchtown, N.J.

The Complete Book of International Investing, copyright © 1977 by
Rainer Esslen. Published by McGraw-Hill Book Company, New York,
N.Y., by arrangement with Columbia Publishing Company, Inc., French-
town, N.J.

THE COMPLETE BOOK OF INTERNATIONAL INVESTING

How to Buy Foreign Securities

and

Who's Who on the International Investment Scene

RAINER ESSLEN

McGRAW-HILL BOOK COMPANY
New York   St. Louis   San Francisco   Auckland   Bogota
Dusseldorf   Johannesburg   London   Madrid   Mexico
Montreal   New Delhi   Panama   Paris   Sao Paulo
Singapore   Sydney   Tokyo   Toronto

Library of Congress Cataloging in Publication Data

Esslen, Rainer.
    The complete book of international investing.

    Includes index.
        1. Investments, Foreign—Handbooks, manuals, etc.
    2. Investments, American—Handbooks, manuals, etc.
    3. Securities—Handbooks, manuals, etc. I. Title.
    HG4538.E758   332.6'73   77-9108
    ISBN 0-07-019665-6

70387

This is an updated and completely rewritten version of a previous book by Rainer Esslen on the foreign securities markets:

How to Buy Foreign Securities, copyright © 1974 by Rainer Esslen. Published by Columbia Publishing Company, Inc. Frenchtown, N.J.

Contents

Introduction

Why Buy Foreign Securities?

Who Buys Foreign Securities?

In the investment world, what's expected by the many hardly ever happens.

On January 30, 1974, the Federal government removed the Interest Equalization Tax payable on the purchase price of most foreign stocks and bonds bought by residents of the United States. For almost ten years, this tax had effectively kept American investors out of foreign stock markets and closed the American capital market to foreign borrowers.

With the removal of the IET, American investors were expected to rush far afield to taste of the fruits that had been denied them for so long. Many of these fruits at that time looked tastier than the domestic variety. A number of foreign stock markets, including Japan, the United Kingdom, Canada, Spain, Denmark, Norway, and Israel, had outperformed the American market in the years 1968 to 1973. In addition, an investor in many of the foreign markets would have had a currency gain of about 30% *vis-à-vis* the dollar since the dollar devaluation in August 1971. Several American brokerage houses and foreign-owned securities firms established in the United States geared up to service this new demand. Some of the largest American banks made plans to create foreign portfolio management services. Conferences were held to educate American institutional investors in foreign securities. Articles on world-wide investment strategy and reports on specific foreign stock markets began to appear regularly in American financial publications.

vii

International Investing

A Non-Event

However, for almost two years, the removal of the Interest Equalization Tax proved to be a non-event in American investment history. Except for gold stocks, investments in foreign securities remained almost zero. American professional and individual investors had been out of touch with foreign markets for too long. The information gap was tremendous. Execution ability had been reduced to a handful of traders.

Taking a second, more sober look, most American brokerage houses came to the conclusion that the cost and effort required to rebuild the research and trading expertise in foreign securities was out of proportion to the potential business. Thus, the vast majority of registered representatives serving the individual investor remained unable to provide information on foreign securities to their customers. Neither could they offer good execution in foreign securities, except for a limited number of American Depositary Receipts of foreign stocks actively traded on United States stock exchanges or over-the-counter. Foreign securities firms established in the United States primarily to buy American stocks and bonds for their parent companies and to participate in American underwriting syndicates found it impractical to service the American individual investor. American institutional investors, with better access to information on foreign stocks than individuals had, were at first reluctant to wet their feet in waters that had been closed to them for so long. They browsed but didn't buy.

By the same token, foreign borrowers were slow in coming back into the American capital market where they had to reeducate the American institutional investor and go through the pains of SEC registration. During the life of the Interest Equalization Tax, they had found a convenient substitute in the Eurobond market, which required no registration with any government.

Then, early in 1974, when most of the foreign bull markets seemed to have run their course and the dollar appeared undervalued, foreign investors began to look to the American market for the next run for their money—a year too early, as some of them found out to their chagrin. But there seemed less reason than ever for American investors to look the other way.

A New Turnaround

In 1975 and early 1976, the influx of foreign investment money into the United States became a veritable flood. Net purchases of American se-

Introduction

curities by foreign investors amounted to $4.4 billion in 1975, up from $540 million in 1974. The buying spree continued during the first months of 1976. Apart from the fact that the United States market looked more promising to most foreign investors than their own, it also had far greater depth and liquidity. Huge sums of flight money from Italy and France accumulated in the hands of international money managers over and above the regular flow of Arab oil money and other funds seeking neutral havens. The continental European markets were too thin to absorb even a fraction of these sums. They had two main markets to turn to: the United States market and the Eurobond market. New issues in the Eurobond market amounted to $7 billion in 1975, up from $1.18 billion in 1974, and reached $12 billion in 1976.

As with so many events in nature, investment trends move in cycles: Flight money and even Arab oil money can dry up; depressed currencies can rise from the abyss if a spendthrift government is replaced by a fiscally conservative one; economic recessions give way to booms, and vice versa; interest rates fluctuate; investment fashions change. Seasoned international investors have observed that the United States economy usually leads economic trends in other industrial countries, both up and down, by six to 12 months. When the American economy seems to be well on its way to a peak, these investors begin to look at other markets. And this time around some American investors joined them.

By 1976, many American institutional investors had become serious about foreign securities. They had discovered attractive opportunities in the Eurobond market. They had become more receptive to new offerings by foreign borrowers in the American capital market. Some of them had begun to include a few well-known foreign stocks in their portfolios. A few farmed out a small portion of their assets to foreign money managers for investment in foreign securities. A number of American banks and brokers organized international research and portfolio management capabilities to compete with foreign money managers. Multinational corporations shopped for international portfolio management expertise for their foreign pension funds and unrepatriated working capital. Thus, in 1976, international portfolio management was no longer an esoteric and theoretical subject in the United States. A new, updated edition of this book appeared justified.

Why Internationalize a Portfolio?

There are a number of good reasons for an international, rather than a purely national, portfolio: 1. better performance; 2. greater diversification; 3. better industry selections; 4. investment opportunities not existing in the United States; 5. more cyclical play; and 6. availability or need of funds in foreign countries.

1. Enough evidence exists to show that an American portfolio with anywhere from 10% to 30% of foreign content would have performed better during the last ten years than a purely American portfolio (see the chart at the end of this introduction). This is true even if the investments were made on a random walk basis.

2. A portfolio manager who believes in diversification adds several dimensions by going abroad. Stock markets tend to move in different cycles, and industry trends vary among countries.

3. A security analyst or portfolio manager considering the best bets in an industry is not doing his homework if he ignores *Siemens, Hitachi,* or *Philips* in the electrical industry; *Sony* and *Pioneer* in consumer electronics; *L'Oréal* in cosmetics; *Petrofina* in petroleum; *Michelin* in tires and rubber; *Carrefour* in retailing; *Carlsberg-Tuborg* and *Heineken* among breweries; *Swissair* among airlines; and *Unilever, Ciba-Geigy,* and a host of others among multinationals.

4. Some investment opportunities abroad are not available in the United States, either because there is no such industry of consequence, such as gold mining, or because the industry has exhausted most of its growth potential in the United States. Supermarkets and discount chains, mature industries in the United States, are still in their early youth in France and Japan. Nation-wide banking, as it exists in Germany, Switzerland, Canada, Australia, and other countries, has no equivalent in the United States. World-wide trading companies are almost unique to Japan. Many nonferrous mining and production facilities are concentrated in foreign hands, notably Australian and Canadian. While none of these may be good investments at all times, they and others are worth watching.

5. Some American portfolio managers have achieved good performance by playing the cycles of American cyclical industries. Many foreign portfolio managers have learned to play additional cycles successfully: those of entire national economies (often easier to predict than the cycles of individual industries or companies); the cycles of currency fluctuations; and the interest rate cycles in various countries.

6. Finally, anyone accumulating or needing funds abroad may benefit from seasoned international portfolio management expertise — pension fund managers, insurance companies, finance officers of multinational corporations, authors and artists, and individuals who want to retire in the homelands of their ancestors or in otherwise inviting foreign retirement havens such as Mexico or the south of France.

Introduction

Four Objectives

The book should also be of use to many people who may not want to buy foreign securities, but who have to deal with international securities firms for a number of other reasons — to raise money abroad, to search for acquisition candidates or other business opportunities abroad, or to communicate with foreign investors who buy American securities.

Thus, this book was prepared with four main objectives in mind: 1. to give the reader an over-all view of foreign investment markets; 2. to provide him with the best possible sources of information; 3. to help him find the best international portfolio managers for world-wide investments or for investments in a specific country; and 4. to provide him with a foreign view of international portfolio strategy for an all-round perspective.

This book is conceived as a guide and is in no way intended to offer investment advice—a task left to the professional investment advisor.

Acknowledgements

More than 100 investment professionals in Europe and the United States were interviewed during the research for this book, and I would like to thank all of them for their time, patience, and cooperation.

I am particularly grateful to the members of a number of investment firms, banks, and stock exchanges who went to great trouble to review parts of the manuscript and provided valuable critiques to assure the greatest possible accuracy. I hasten to add, however: if errors remain, these are entirely my responsibility. In many cases, more than one member of an organization offered comments and it is therefore difficult to do justice to each and every one. These are the organizations that were particularly helpful in reviewing individual chapters.

Australia: *Bank of New South Wales* and *The National Bank of Australasia*

International Investing

Austria: *Wiener Börsekammer*
Belgium: *Banque Bruxelles Lambert* and *Peterbroeck, Van Campenhout & Cie.*
Brazil: *Vickers, da Costa & Co., Ltd.*
Canada: *The Toronto Stock Exchange*
Denmark: *Københavns Fondsbørs*
Eurobonds: *Fiduciary Trust Company of New York*
France: *Crédit Commercial de France, Crédit Lyonnais,* and *Banque de l'Indochine et de Suez (Suez-American Corporation)*
Germany: *ADIG-Investment, Frankfurter Wertpapierbörse,* and *Gesellschaft für Vermögensanlagen*
Israel: *Leumi Securities Corporation* (New York)
Italy: *Borsa Valori di Milano*
Japan: *Daiwa Securities Co.* and *Nomura Securities Co.*
Mexico: *Allen W. Lloyd y Asociados, Fondo Industrial Mexicano,* and *The Mexican Investor*
The Netherlands: *Algemene Bank Nederland, Robeco,* and *Vereniging voor de Effectenhandel*
Sweden: *Skandinaviska Enskilda Banken* and *Svenska Handelsbanken*
Switzerland: *Bank Julius Bär & Co., Swiss Credit Bank,* and *Swiss Reinsurance Co.*
United Kingdom: *Kleinwort, Benson Ltd., S.G. Warburg & Co., Ltd.,* and *Vickers, da Costa & Co. Ltd.*

Many members of the now internationally thundering herd of *Merrill Lynch, Pierce, Fenner & Smith, Inc.* in New York, Toronto, and a number of overseas offices provided information, opened doors, and helped in many other ways to facilitate my task.

My sincere thanks also to many members of the various *Burson-Marsteller* offices throughout the world who helped the project along — but above all to Toni Bensen of the New York office who worked far beyond the call of duty to assemble the manuscript and keep control of the flood of information pouring in.

Finally, I'd like to give particular recognition to two friends who gave me invaluable counsel on the over-all concept of the book as well as critiques on specific chapters — André Sharon of *Drexel Burnham Lambert* and David Darst of *Goldman, Sachs & Co.*

Rainer Esslen

Introduction

Returns from the Six Largest Equity Markets in the World

"Most likely" rate of return (compounded annually) for any randomly selected investment period of one year or longer. Foreign market figures are based on Capital International indices; United States market on S&P 500.

10 Years 1966-1975	Capital Appreciation	Dividends	Gains vs. U.S.$	Total
Japan	13.4	4.3	3.2	20.9
Germany	2.1	4.1	5.4	11.6
Canada	3.7	3.8	1.1	8.6
U.K.	4.1	5.0	-3.0	6.1
France	0.9	4.5	0.7	6.1
U.S.	0.1	3.4	—	3.5

5 Years 1971-1975				
Japan	17.6	3.3	4.9	25.8
Germany	2.8	4.2	7.9	14.9
France	-1.9	4.8	4.4	7.3
Canada	0.3	3.8	-0.1	4.0
U.K.	0.8	5.1	-4.4	1.5
U.S.	-2.4	3.5	—	1.1

Effect of Injecting Increasing Percentages of Foreign Indices into S&P 500 Index

Percentage of improvement on "most likely" rate of return, compounded annually. Foreign indices=combined Capital International indices equally weighted and randomly selected. Improvement over 3.5% total return from S&P 500 for 5 and 10 years.

10 Years 1966-1975	Capital Appreciation	Dividends	Gains vs. U.S. $	Total
5%	0.28	.05	0.07	0.4
10%	0.56	.09	0.15	0.8
15%	0.84	.13	0.05	1.2
20%	1.11	.18	0.31	1.6
25%	1.39	.22	0.39	2.0
100%	5.10	.09	1.60	7.6

5 Years 1971-1975	Capital Appreciation	Dividends	Gains vs. U.S. $	Total
5%	0.34	.03	0.13	0.5
10%	0.67	.08	0.25	1.0
15%	1.00	.12	0.38	1.5
20%	1.33	.25	0.52	2.0
15%	1.66	.19	0.65	2.5
100%	6.30	.07	2.50	9.5

Table courtesy InterSec Research Corp.

CORRELATION* BETWEEN OVERSEAS MARKETS AND S&P 500

1967-1976

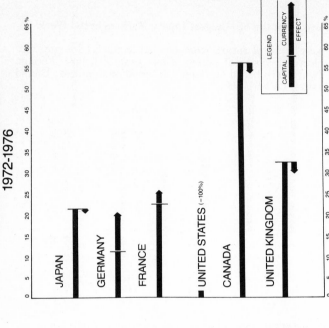

*R² (Correlation Coefficient Squared) = Percentage of overseas market movement
explained by movement of S&P 500.
Countries are shown in order of total return. U.S. $ adjusted.

Source: InterSec Research Corp., New York

CORRELATION* BETWEEN OVERSEAS MARKETS AND S&P 500

1972-1976

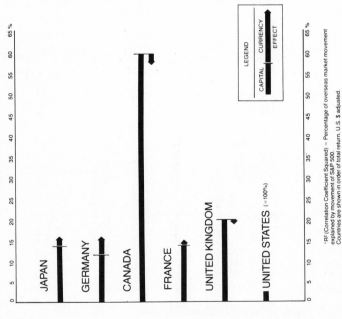

*R² (Correlation Coefficient Squared) = Percentage of overseas market movement
explained by movement of S&P 500.
Countries are shown in order of total return. U.S. $ adjusted.

Source: InterSec Research Corp., New York

xiv

"MOST PROBABLE"* RATES OF RETURN
COMPOUNDED ANNUALLY   1967-1976

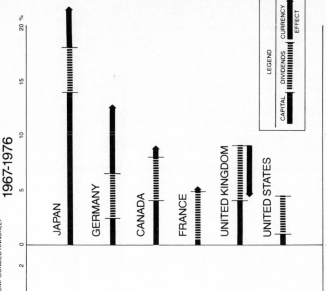

JAPAN

GERMANY

CANADA

FRANCE

UNITED KINGDOM

UNITED STATES

LEGEND

CAPITAL   DIVIDENDS   CURRENCY EFFECT

*"Most Probable" returns are for any randomly selected investment interval, I.E., the arithmetic mean return of all intervals beginning each January 1st and ending each subsequent December 31st.

Source: InterSec Research Corp., New York

"MOST PROBABLE"* RATES OF RETURN
COMPOUNDED ANNUALLY   1959-1976

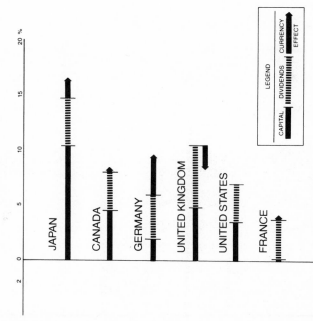

JAPAN

CANADA

GERMANY

UNITED KINGDOM

UNITED STATES

FRANCE

LEGEND

CAPITAL   DIVIDENDS   CURRENCY EFFECT

*"Most Probable" returns are for any randomly selected investment interval, I.E., the arithmetic mean return of all intervals beginning each January 1st and ending each subsequent December 31st.

Source: InterSec Research Corp., New York

These are, of course, theoretical figures, based on the average capital appreciation and dividends of a great number of stocks in each market as well as on currency adjustments. Nevertheless, it has to be remembered that most United States portfolio managers during these years performed worse than the averages.

For more elaborate studies of comparative stock market returns, the reader is referred to "A New Route to Higher Returns and Lower Risks" by Gary L. Bergstrom in the Fall 1975 issue of *Journal of Portfolio Management* and to "World, Country, and Industry: Relationships in Equity Returns" by Donald R. Lessard, Sloan School Working Paper, January 1975, pp. 766-775.

Notes to the Reader

The information presented in this book was collected from the very best available sources during April to December 1976. Every effort was made to have the facts in each chapter checked by investment professionals in the country described. Nevertheless, the author is not infallible, and regulations and other facts affecting the investment scene change frequently in almost all countries. Thus, the reader is cautioned to check any facts that might influence his investment decisions when the moment of decision is reached.

Where dollar equivalents of foreign currency figures are given, these were converted at an approximate round figure representative of exchange rates in 1975 and 1976. All dollar amounts are US$ unless otherwise indicated. Because of the wide currency fluctuations since 1971, there is no practical way of providing precise dollar equivalents for most of the statistics covering several months or years.

All stock exchanges publish indices to reflect the average price action of the stocks traded on the exchange. However, all of these indices are composed of different elements and, therefore, they are not truly comparable with each other. *Capital International Perspective*, an international investment information and chart service in Geneva, has devised a formula to bring all major stock exchange indices on to a common denominator and plot the performance of each stock exchange relative to a world index. A number of their charts are reproduced at the end of this book by permission.

International Investing

Most of the technical investment terms used in this book, as well as some other commonly-used investment terms, are defined in brief in the glossary. The leading stocks, principal brokers and banks, as well as other information, can be found at the end of each chapter.

Taxes

Most foreign governments withhold a tax on dividends and interest from securities held by non-residents of their countries. Withholding taxes vary from country to country and are discussed in general in the respective chapters of this book. If he files IRS Form 1116 with his Form 1140, a United States citizen or resident can offset the taxes withheld abroad against his taxable income, subject to certain limitations.

An increasing number of countries levy a capital gains tax on security transactions, but this applies normally only to residents of the country and is not withheld. In a few rare instances, such as investment trusts subject to a capital gains tax, a foreign owner of the shares of the trust may indirectly pay a capital gains tax. It appears that such indirect payment of a foreign capital gains tax cannot be recovered or deducted from Federal income taxes. A United States citizen or resident filing a Federal income tax return must, of course, pay tax on capital gains made from foreign stock transactions at the same time he pays for domestic transactions.

1. Shopping at Home

Anyone wanting to venture into foreign securities for the first time will find a wide choice available in the United States — enough to build up a diversified international portfolio. International investment favorites not traded in the United States, but actively traded on foreign exchanges, can normally be traded through a United States brokerage house with foreign trading capabilities. Foreign-owned securities firms will usually deal only with institutional investors.

In 1976, 36 foreign companies were listed on the New York Stock Exchange, and 72 on the American Stock Exchange. Several hundred were traded over-the-counter, 75 of them quoted on NASDAQ, the central electronic quotation system of the National Association of Securities Dealers Inc. used in every American brokerage office. A number of foreign stocks are also listed on regional exchanges, but most of these duplicate the New York and American Stock Exchange listings.

Most foreign stocks are traded in the form of American Depositary Receipts (ADRs). Others are traded in the form of American Depositary Shares or of original foreign shares. As far as trading and receipt of dividends are concerned, there is no practical difference between the three. However, original foreign shares and American Depositary Shares of certain countries may be subject to foreign death duties and probate. ADRs usually are not.

International Investing

What are ADRs?

American Depositary Receipts are issued by an American custodian bank in the United States in lieu of the original shares held in custody abroad whenever there is sufficient American investor interest in the stock. ADRs may be issued in two ways — under Form S-1, registered with the Securities and Exchange Commission under the requirements of the Securities Act of 1933, or with Form S-12, a simpler method supported by the latest financial reports of the foreign company, and not registered with the SEC.

One ADR may represent one underlying foreign share or several. The custodian bank usually tries to issue an ADR in a price range with which the American investor is accustomed. Many Japanese shares sell within a price range of 30¢ to $3 in Japan, and one of their ADRs may represent anywhere from 2 to 100 underlying Japanese shares.

All ADRs are registered in the name of the owner, or in the name of the brokerage house in case of a street name holding, even if the underlying shares are not registered shares. An investor can trade and transfer ADRs in exactly the same way he does American stock certificates. However, if it is advantageous for him, an investor can sell the underlying stock abroad in foreign currency and surrender the ADRs to the American custodian bank. Or, if he moves abroad or opens an account abroad, he can take possession of the underlying shares abroad and surrender the ADRs in the United States.

The American investor will automatically receive dividends due from the custodian bank if he has the ADRs registered in his own name, or he gets a credit for them from his broker if he has left them in street name. The ADR bank sells the foreign currency in which it receives dividends and pays it in dollars minus the foreign withholding tax, if any. This withholding tax can be reclaimed by the American investor on his Federal income tax return with Form 1116. The bank also takes care of rights offerings, stock splits, and stock dividends that arise with the underlying shares. If a foreign rights issue is not registered in the United States with the SEC (and it rarely is), the subscription cannot be legally offered to United States shareholders by American brokers or banks. In such a case, the ADR bank sells the rights and transfers the proceeds to the holders of the ADRs, unless the American investor who does not want to lose the rights gives instructions to the ADR bank to deliver the rights to a foreign bank or broker and exercises his rights abroad.

The custodian bank charges a small fee for the issue, transfer, and surrender of ADRs, as well as for dividend payments and other services required in connection with stock splits, rights offerings, etc. In addition, the investor loses small amounts in the currency conversions in connection with purchases, sales, and dividend payments, not counting the basic currency fluctuations inherent in floating exchange rates, from which the investor can gain as well as lose.

The number of ADRs on the over-the-counter market increased sharply during the first half of the 1970s. In early 1976, new listings of foreign stocks, on the other hand, lagged, because of the rather cumbersome listing requirements. However, in May 1976, the SEC approved new listing requirements for foreign stocks on the New York Stock Exchange which make it easier for large foreign corporations with a minimum of 5000 round-lot shareholders world-wide to list. *Bell Canada*, in August 1976, was the first foreign company to list under these new rules, followed by *Kubota*, a Japanese manufacturer of agricultural and industrial machinery. The American Stock Exchange was at that time also trying to get simpler listing requirements for foreign securities approved by the SEC.

Up-to-date lists of all listed, NASDAQ quoted, and other over-the-counter ADRs and foreign securities can be obtained from the stock exchanges, the National Association of Securities Dealers, and the ADR custodian banks: *Morgan Guaranty Trust Company, Citibank, Irving Trust Company, Chemical Bank, Chase Manhattan Bank,* and *Bankers Trust,* all in New York City. *Shields Model Roland* publishes an ADR guide from time to time.

Actively Traded Issues

During the gold rush of the early 1970s, South African gold mining shares were the most actively traded foreign issues in the United States, but by 1976 this market had become rather quiet. Other groups of foreign shares actively traded include Canadian, Japanese, and Israeli shares. These are discussed in more detail in the respective chapters.

One of the most popular foreign stocks on the New York Stock Exchange is *Sony*, which has almost as many shareholders in the United States as it has in Japan. Its somewhat less well-known competitor in certain product lines, *Matsushita Electric Industrial* (maker of Panasonic products, among others), was getting increasing attention from professional investors in 1976. *Plessey*, a British electronic equipment manufacturer, was for a while the plaything of traders because of its very low per-share price under which it was listed. By 1976, after a reverse split of its ADRs, it was largely ignored. The British and the Dutch *Unilever* companies are both listed on the New York Stock Exchange. In view of their world-wide significance in food and household products, their sizable capitalization and their relatively good stock market performance since the 1974 slump, they are well represented in American mutual fund portfolios. *British Petroleum* and *Royal Dutch Petroleum,* comparable in size and performance to the large American oil companies, are also widely held by American mutual funds.

Schlumberger, originally a French company but now registered in the Netherlands Antilles and managed from New York, is one of the most actively traded issues on the New York Stock Exchange. Doing much of its business with American oil companies, it can hardly be still considered foreign.

Among the more sizable non-Canadian foreign companies traded on the American Stock Exchange are several British companies: *British American Tobacco* (which owns *Gimbels,* among others), *Imperial Chemical Industries, Imperial Group* (food, tobacco, breweries), and *F.W. Woolworth U.K.* With the British economy being what it was in 1976, they did not arouse American investors.

In the over-the-counter market the British *Rank Organisation* (film production, *Xerox* office machines in the U.K.) and *Fisons* (agricultural chemicals, pharmaceuticals) were at times very actively traded. *Rank* is in many mutual fund portfolios. Several of the Japanese stocks have a relatively good following in the United States, including *Tokio Marine and Fire Insurance, Hitachi* (electrical equipment), and *Toyota Motor*, and so does the Dutch *Philips Lamps.* The Japanese *Pioneer Electronics* and *Honda Motor* made public offerings of 2 and 2.3 million ADRs, respectively, in the United States in the latter part of 1976, and subsequently listed on the New York Stock Exchange.

Much of the trading in ADRs and foreign securities is done by arbitragers. This helps to keep the market liquid and narrows the price differentials between underlying foreign shares and ADRs to a minimum.

ADRs and other foreign stocks quoted on the New York and American Stock Exchanges are included in the daily stock tables published in all major American newspapers. Both *The New York Times* and the *Wall Street Journal* print daily trading volumes and prices for a number of ADRs traded over-the-counter; and in *Barron's* they can be found on a weekly basis.

Prices or quotes for over-the-counter ADRs not found in the news media can be checked in the daily "pink" sheets available in all brokerage houses.

Investment Funds

A relatively simple way for an investor to internationalize his holdings is to buy shares of a fund that has foreign securities in its portfolio. He has the choice between two basic varieties: 1. funds that invest more or less exclusively in a foreign industry or in a single country, and 2. mixed funds that have part of their assets in foreign securities.

The first variety includes the gold and precious metal funds — *ASA*, traded on the New York Stock Exchange, and *International Investor* and *Precious Metals,* sold through brokerage houses with a front-end-load sales commission. Specialization by country is offered by *Japan Fund, Nomura Capital Fund of Japan, Israel Investors Corporation, Israel Development Corporation,* and *Canadian Fund* (which includes foreign securities other than Canadian). Funds with the majority or a significant portion of their holdings in foreign securities include *Scudder International Investors, New Perspective Fund, Putnam Growth Fund,* and *Transatlantic Fund.* Performance records of these funds are available from the managements.

In 1976, foreign funds managed and headquartered abroad, and not registered with the SEC, could not be offered to residents of the United States (although, of course, a United States investor could, at his own initiative, buy foreign fund shares directly from the foreign fund management or from a foreign bank or broker). Under new SEC guidelines that would relax registration requirements for foreign-based funds, several foreign funds in 1976 were planning to apply to the SEC for permission to sell their shares in the United States.

How to Buy Foreign Earnings

Some American investors are already diversified internationally without knowing it. Others know that they can diversify internationally without buying a single foreign security. Both groups are investors in American multinational companies with much of their earnings coming from abroad.

For instance, whenever pork and beans and ketchup are discussed in England, *H.J. Heinz* comes up as *the* household word, and many a Britisher who is confronted with the irrefutable evidence that *Heinz* is not as British as plum pudding but is an American company headquartered in Pittsburgh seems to feel like a child who discovers for the first time that Santa Claus is really the handyman in disguise. The company has been operating in England since before World War I. During the early 1960s, when its United States operations were less profitable, the British earnings accounted for more than 75% of the total and helped the company's stock weather a difficult spell. Today, foreign earnings from England and other countries still account for almost 50% of the total, and the steady *Heinz* earnings record testifies to the benefits of multinational diversification.

A multinational can be defined as a company that has major production and/or marketing operations in several foreign countries and allows them to operate as relatively or completely independent profit centers.

Thus, major bank holding companies, such as *Citicorp, J.P. Morgan,* and *BankAmerica Corporation,* deriving anywhere from 30% to 50% of their earnings from foreign operations, are obviously multinational. The large Japanese trading companies, on the other hand, such as *Mitsubishi* and *Mitsui,* under this definition are not, even though they derive most of their income from abroad. They are exporters and traders, not producers and marketers. By the same token, oil companies that only explore and produce abroad but have no, or only limited, foreign marketing capabilities abroad are not truly multinationals.

Among the large American corporations that derive 30% to 50% of their earnings, and sometimes more, from foreign operations are *Burroughs, CPC International, Caterpillar Tractor, Coca-Cola, Colgate Palmolive, Gillette, W.R. Grace, Hoover, IBM, International Harvester, IT&T,* and *Xerox.* Anyone interested in the latest foreign earnings percentages of New York Stock Exchange-listed companies can find them in the company reports published quarterly by *Standard & Poor's* or *Value Line.*

A word of caution, however. It is earnings that count, not foreign sales. Many United States companies that ventured abroad in the 1960s did worse than those that stayed at home. The learning curve for starting foreign operations can be a deep and long one in the red, as many corporations discovered when they rushed into foreign countries expecting to do business there as it is done in the United States. Untold millions were lost by such seasoned giants as *General Electric, Westinghouse, Raytheon,* and *Deere.* Many of the foreign companies that were snapped up by American companies were the ones that were in trouble. And there are still quite a number of American corporations with foreign lemons on their hands, which, in the 1975 recession, they were desperately trying to unload. Moreover, it must be realized that, in contrast to the popular intellectual fairy tale, foreign governments and their citizens are not at the mercy of the multinationals, but rather the multinationals are at the whim of even the weakest nation through potential overnight expropriation or nationalization. Thus, the risk factor in multinationals is always high, no matter whether the company operates in a fully industrialized democratic country where the rule of law applies (and nationalization can be accomplished by a majority vote), or in a dictatorship at the lowest rung of economic development. The safest investment bets in multinationals are those companies that, like *Heinz* in England, understand how to become accepted as national institutions rather than remain foreign elements. Apart from good citizenship, good communications, and the use of local managerial personnel, the cause of national identification can be furthered by leaving a minority interest in the foreign subsidiary in the hands of local investors and by listing the parent company's stock on the national stock exchange. Many multinationals resist the recommendations of the European Economic Community and the United Nations to report their financial results by country. Neither organization has much enforcement power. However, such reporting may not only be good public relations in defense of nationalization threats, it may also be good investor relations by establishing a better understanding of the company and building greater credibility.

The emergence of multinationals has created the need for a new discipline in security analysis. With very few exceptions, this discipline is still in its infancy in the United States. When considering whether to recommend a corporation with a high percentage of foreign earnings, an analyst does not do all of his homework if he talks only to domestic management and looks at the consolidated figures in the financial reports. If he is conscientious, he should also be familiar with all of the major markets in which the company operates — know the economic and fiscal trends there, assess foreign managements, and know the market performance and profitability of each subsidiary. American companies are beginning to encourage security analysts to visit their foreign operations.

More than in any other industry, an analyst looking at a multinational company should know the comparable foreign multinationals. Many foreign companies, notably the Dutch, Swiss, Swedish, and British internationals, have been multinationals far longer than their American counterparts, and they may be a good deal more seasoned in the game. Before recommending *Merck, Pfizer,* or *Schering-Plough,* an analyst should probably also know *Hoffmann-La Roche,* the German *Schering,* and a few other pharmaceutical companies abroad. *Electrolux* is at least as multinational as *Hoover* but a good deal bigger. Does *Colgate Palmolive* compare favorably or unfavorably with *Unilever?*

A research report of *Drexel Burnham Lambert* states: "The multinational corporation is a natural, healthy, and normal response to overcome an unnatural, unhealthy, and abnormal man-made impediment to the free flow of resources — the nation state."

An investor who believes that, in spite of frequent setbacks, the

International Investing

Western world is moving more and more towards an integrated economy, will want to keep an eye on multinationals. But, by and large, he needs a good deal more information than is available now on this subject.

Foreign Fixed-Income Securities

Foreign fixed-income securities can be divided into three main categories: 1. domestic issues sold in the home country of the issuer in domestic currencies (and discussed in the respective country chapter); 2. Eurobond issues sold to international investors outside the country of the issuer (discussed in Chapter 20); and 3. issues offered in only one foreign country. Thus, for instance, the Mexican and Australian governments have sold bond issues in Japan. Japanese firms have sold convertible bond issues on the German market. But most important, many foreign borrowers have come back into the United States capital market.

Before the Interest Equalization Tax was imposed in 1963, the United States was a large market for foreign bond issues. During the existence of the tax, Canadian issues, which were exempt from the tax, were practically the only types of foreign issues sold in the United States. When the tax was removed in 1974, foreign borrowers were at first slow to return to the United States capital market. They were held back by the complications of SEC registration and the initial reluctance of American institutional investors who could find unusually attractive terms in domestic bonds and had been out of touch for too long with foreign bond issues.

In 1975, however, $3.4 billion of dollar-denominated non-Canadian foreign bond issues (so-called Yankee bonds) were sold in the United States, and in 1976, new foreign issues amounted to $4.3 billion.

The main attraction of a foreign issue denominated in dollars is a higher yield than that of comparable United States issues. For instance, issues of various government agencies of Canada, Australia, New Zealand, and Norway pay a better interest rate than comparable United States government issues. By the same token, several international organizations, such as the European Economic Community or the World Bank, backed by a host of governments, offer attractive yields. Foreign borrowers come to the United States market when they get a lower interest cost than in their domestic markets even if they have to pay a somewhat higher interest rate than a comparable American borrower.

Such offerings are to a large extent placed with institutional investors. Most retail brokers are not sufficiently informed to alert individual investors to special opportunities in this field. However, a yield-conscious investor can ask his broker to receive advance notification of upcoming new issues, including all foreign issues, with an indication of the expected yield.

Risks in foreign government bonds denominated in dollars are primarily political. What are the chances of Canada, New Zealand, France, or Norway being embroiled in wars, going communist, or defaulting on their obligations? Or of the EEC or World Bank collapsing?

Such risks are not entirely theoretical, as a large number of defaulted foreign dollar-denominated bonds of foreign governments testifies, including issues from Russia, China, Cuba, and several Balkan states. Surprisingly, none of these defaulted issues is entirely without market price, which may fluctuate substantially in response to the changing political climate. One brokerage house specializing in making a market for defaulted foreign bond issues is *Deltec Securities* in New York.

Foreign bonds or other fixed-income vehicles, denominated in foreign currencies have, of course, also a currency risk. The devaluation of the Mexican peso in 1976, wiped out the equivalent of three or four years of interest income for American investors in peso fixed-income securities and deposits.

Sources of Information

Information on foreign securities has improved since the removal of the Interest Equalization Tax, but it still remains scanty. All foreign issues on the New York Stock Exchange, most of those traded on the American Stock Exchange, and a few traded over-the-counter are covered by the regular stock report services of *Standard & Poor's, Moody's,* and *Value Line.* In addition, *Standard & Poor's* has an *International Stock Report Service* which covers about 75 foreign issues at regular intervals. An investor can also subscribe to a foreign service, such as *Capital International Perspective* of Geneva, which in monthly and quarterly editions publishes statistics and charts on about 1100 companies outside North America.

Several American brokerage houses have increased their coverage of foreign stock markets, notably *Drexel Burnham, Arnhold and S. Bleichroeder, Oppenheimer,* and also *Merrill Lynch, Pierce, Fenner & Smith.* Others have established affiliations with foreign investment and research firms to provide regular information on foreign securities primarily to their institutional customers. *E.F. Hutton* distributes the research information of *Iris* of Geneva. *Becker Securities* is now part of the *Warburg-Paribas* liaison. *Drexel Burnham & Co.,* through its merger with *Lambert Brussels Witter, Inc.,* became affiliated with *Banque*

International Investing

Bruxelles Lambert to form *The Drexel Burnham Lambert Group Inc.* And *Mitchell Hutchins* has a working arrangement with *James Capel* of London. *Goldman, Sachs*, together with the British merchant banker *Kleinwort, Benson*, formed a New York-based investment management company, *Kleinwort, Benson, McCowan.*

Institutional investors can also get information on specific stock markets from the foreign-owned securities firms established in the United States.

The foreign analysts group of The New York Society of Security Analysts has come back to life since the removal of the Interest Equalization Tax. Anyone interested in its activities should contact its president or program chairman through the business manager of the society.

An American owner of a foreign stock or of an ADR will in most cases find it difficult to get regular information on his holding. By writing to the company directly, he may be able to get on its mailing list. As an owner of an ADR, he can also ask the ADR bank to be put on the mailing lists for the stocks he owns. In the past, many foreign companies disclosed far less information than American companies, but disclosure practices improved greatly in the years 1973 to 1976, notably in Switzerland and France. In fact, some of the foreign annual reports have such an overwhelming mass of information that an American investor used to more compressed reports is likely to be confused rather than enlightened. Accounting practices vary greatly from country to country, and it requires international auditing training to know the differences. In general, it can be stated that many foreign companies — notably German, Japanese, Swiss, and French — keep substantial open or hidden reserves in their balance sheet and understate their earnings per share by American standards.

Thus, even if an American investor subscribes to many foreign investment information services and is on the mailing list of many foreign corporations, he requires seasoning before he can make his own investment decisions. For the individual investor the better solution is probably to open an account with an American brokerage house that provides research reports on foreign securities and rely on these recommendations. If his total portfolio is $100,000 or more, he can avail himself of the portfolio management services of institutions that have international expertise, as a number of institutional investors have done. The oldest with such expertise in the United States are *Morgan Guaranty Trust, Fiduciary Trust Co. of New York*, and *U.S. Trust Company.* Other large American banks are developing this expertise, mostly through offices abroad, including *Citibank, Bank of America, Chemical Bank*, and *Continental Illinois Bank.* An increasing number of banks are offering clients international diversification through commingled funds.

Shopping at Home

Some fund management companies are now also offering international management services, including *Capital Research and Management, Putnam Management,* and *Fidelity Management & Research.*

An American investor, whether he is a United States resident or not, may find it advantageous to employ the services of a seasoned international portfolio manager abroad, either for a completely international portfolio or for investments in a specific country. The leading managers are reviewed in each chapter. An American resident subject to American income tax must report the use of a foreign investment manager or of a foreign bank account on his Federal income tax return.

A broker or bank will in most cases charge a custodial fee, in addition to the commission for each transaction. Portfolio management usually involves payment of a management fee. Commissions vary greatly from country to country and with the size of the transactions involved, but many foreign commissions are comparable to or even lower than commissions charged in the United States. Nevertheless, when negotiating a foreign stock transaction or the management of a foreign portfolio with a broker or bank, the investor should reach a clear understanding about all fees and commissions involved before he starts doing business.

International Investing

Alcan Aluminium (Canada)
ASA (financial; South Africa)
Bell Canada (telephone)
Benguet Consolidated (mining; Philippines)
British Petroleum
Campbell Red Lake Mines (Canada)
Canadian Breweries
Canadian Pacific (railroad)
Canadian Southern Railway
Deltec International (foods, commodities; Canada)
Distillers Corp.-Seagrams (Canada)
Dome Mines (Canada)
EMI (electronics, records, entertainment; United Kingdom)
Genstar (building; Canada)
Honda Motor (Japan)
Hudson's Bay Mining and Smelting (Canada)
Inco (nickel; Canada)
International Diversified (gambling casinos; Panama)
KLM Royal Dutch Airlines
Kubota (machinery; Japan)
Massey-Ferguson (agricultural machinery, diesel engines; Canada)
Matsushita Electric Industrial (Japan)
McIntyre Porcupine Mines (Canada)
Norlin (holding company; Panama)
Northern Telecom (telephone equipment; Canada)
Northgate Exploration (mining; Canada)
Pacific Petroleums (Canada)
Pioneer Electronics (audio equipment; Japan)
Plessey (electronic equipment, systems; United Kingdom)
Royal Dutch Petroleum
Schlumberger (petroleum production equipment; Netherlands Antilles)
"Shell" Transport and Trading (petroleum; United Kingdom)
Sony (radios, recorders, televisions; Japan)
Unilever Ltd. (foods, commodities; United Kingdom)
Unilever N.V. (foods, commodities; the Netherlands)
Hiram Walker-Gooderham & Worts (distilleries; Canada)
West Coast Transmission (natural gas distributor; Canada)

Canadian Issues Traded on the American Stock Exchange
*Securities "admitted to unlisted trading privileges"

Aquitaine Company of Canada (oil exploration)
Asamera Oil
Ashland Oil Canada
Bow Valley Industries (oil and gas exploration)

Shopping at Home

Brascan* (holding company with Canadian and Brazilian properties)
Campbell Chibougamau Mines
Canadian Export Gas & Oil
Canadian Homestead Oils
Canadian Hydrocarbons (petrochemicals)
Canadian International Power (utility)
Canadian Javelin (mineral exploration)
Canadian Marconi* (telecommunications)
Canadian Merrill (minerals, oil, gas)
Canadian Occidental Petroleum
Canadian Superior Oil
Chieftain Development (oil and gas exploration)
Cominco* (zinc, lead, fertilizers)
Commodore Business Machines
Dome Petroleum
Domtar* (forest products)
Ford Motor Co. of Canada*
Giant Yellowknife Mines
Gulf Oil Canada*
Hollinger Mines*
Home Oil
Hudson's Bay Oil & Gas
Husky Oil
Imperial Oil*
Kilembe Copper Cobalt (mining)
Lake Shore Mines*
Neonex International (consumer businesses)
North Canadian Oils
Numac Oil & Gas
Pato Consolidated Gold Dredging (mining)
Placer Development Company (mining)
Prairie Oil Royalties
Preston Mines
Quebecor (oil)
Ranger Oil (Canada)
Revenue Properties Co. (real estate)
Rio Algom Mines
Scurry-Rainbow Oil
Supercrete (building products)
Total Petroleum (North America)
Union Gas Co. of Canada*
United Asbestos Corp.
Wainoco Oil
Western Decalta Petroleum
Wright-Hargreaves Mines*

International Investing

Foreign Issues Other than Canadian
Traded on the American Stock Exchange
*Securities "admitted to unlisted trading privileges"

Alliance Tire and Rubber (Israel)
American Israel Paper Mills (Israel)
Anglo Company (holding company; Bahamas)
Atlas Consolidated Mining and Development (Philippines)
*British-American Tobacco** (United Kingdom)
*Courtaulds** (synthetic fibers; United Kingdom)
*Dunlop Holdings** (tires and rubber; United Kingdom)
Etz Lavud (wood products; Israel)
*Imperial Chemical Industries** (United Kingdom)
*Imperial Group** (chemicals; United Kingdom)
Interpool (rental and leasing of shipping containers; Bahamas)
Kesko (retail buying and distribution service; Finland)
Komatsu (machinery; Japan)
Marinduque Mining & Industrial (Philippines)
Mitsui Co. (trading; Japan)
Mortgage Bank and Financial Agency of the Kingdom of Denmark
O'okiep Copper (South Africa)
Philippine Long Distance Telephone
Republic of Peru
San Carlos Milling (sugar; Philippines)
Syntex (pharmaceuticals; Panama)
Tubos de Acero de Mexico (steel)
F.W. Woolworth (retail; United Kingdom)

ADR Securities Traded Over-the-Counter and
Quoted on the NASDAQ System

Anglo American Corp. of South Africa (natural resources holding
    company)
Anglo American Gold Investment (fund; South Africa)
Bank Leumi le-Israel
Bayer (chemicals; Germany)
Beecham Group (pharmaceuticals; United Kingdom)
Blyvooruitzicht Gold Mining (South Africa)
Botswana RST (mining; Botswana)
Bowater (paper; United Kingdom)
British Petroleum
Broken Hill Proprietary (steel, heavy manufacturing, oil; Australia)
Buffelsfontein Gold Mining (South Africa)
Burmah Oil (United Kingdom)

Shopping at Home

Canon (photographic equipment; Japan)
Dai'Ei (retail; Japan)
DeBeers Consolidated Mines (diamond mining; South Africa)
Dresdner Bank (Germany)
Fison's (chemicals; United Kingdom)
Free State Geduld Mines (South Africa)
Glaxo Holdings (drugs, foods; United Kingdom)
Gold Fields of South Africa (mining)
Hitachi (industrial machinery; Japan)
Honda Motor (Japan)
IDB Bankholding (Israel)
Japan Air Lines
Kansai Electric Power (Japan)
Kirin Brewery (Japan)
Kloof Gold Mining (South Africa)
Kyoto Ceramics (Japan)
Matsushita Electric Works (lighting equipment, wiring devices; Japan)
Minerals & Resources (mining; Bermuda)
Mitsui Co. (trading company; Japan)
Nippon Electric (Japan)
Nissan Motors (Japan)
Palabora Mining (South Africa)
Philips Gloeilampenfabrieken (lamps, electrical equipment; Holland)
Potgietersrust Platinums (South Africa)
President Brand Gold Mining (South Africa)
President Steyn Gold Mining (South Africa)
Rank Organisation (leisure-time industry; United Kingdom)
Royal Dutch Petroleum
St. Helena Gold Mines (South Africa)
Shiseido (cosmetics; Japan)
Telefonos de Mexico
Tokio Marine & Fire (insurance)
Tokyo Shibaura Electric (equipment)
Toyota Motor (Japan)
Union Corp. (gold mining; South Africa)
Vaal Reefs Exploration & Mining (gold mining; South Africa)
West Dreifontein Gold Mining (South Africa)
Western Deep Levels (gold mining; South Africa)
Western Holdings (gold mining; South Africa)

Foreign Securities Quoted on the NASDAQ System

Abitibi Paper (Canada)
Agnico-Eagle Mines (Canada)
Alcan Aluminium (Canada)

American International Reinsurance (Canada)
Consumer Distributing (catalogs; Canada)
Denison Mines (Canada)
Elscint (medical equipment; Israel)
L.M. Ericsson Telephone (Sweden)
Falconbridge Nickel Mines (Canada)
Investors Group (investment fund; Canada)
Liberian Iron Ore (Sweden)
Interprovincial Pipeline (Canada)
Macmillan Bloedel (forest products; Canada)
Moore (business forms; Canada)
Na-churs International (fertilizer; Canada)
Overseas Inns (Luxembourg)
Sunlite Oil (Canada)
Universal Gas & Oil (Panama)
United Canso Oil & Gas (Canada)
Velcro Industries (textile fasteners; Canada)
Westcoast Petroleum (Canada)

*Selected United States Multinational Companies with
an Estimated 25% or More in Foreign Earnings*

AMF
AMP
Addressograph-Multigraph
BankAmerica
Black & Decker
Burroughs
CPC International
Caterpillar Tractor
Cheesebrough-Pond's
Coca-Cola
Colgate-Palmolive
Dow Chemical
du Pont
Eastman Kodak
Engelhard Minerals & Chemicals
Ferro
Firestone Tire & Rubber
First National City
Gillette
Goodyear Tire & Rubber
W.R. Grace
Grolier
Halliburton

Shopping at Home

H.J. Heinz
Honeywell
Hoover
IBM
International Flavors & Fragrances
International Harvester
IT&T
Eli Lilly
Merck
Minnesota Mining & Mfg.
J.P. Morgan
National Cash Register
Pfizer
Proctor & Gamble
Richardson-Merrell
Schering-Plough
Schlumberger
Squibb
Sterling Drug
Sunbeam
Tektronix
Union Carbide
Uniroyal
Warner-Lambert
F.W. Woolworth
Xerox

Investment Funds Available in the United States With Substantial Foreign Securities Portfolios

ASA Ltd. / 54 Marshall Street / Johannesburg, South Africa and P.O. Box 1724, F.D.R. Station / New York, New York 10022 / closed end; gold mining shares; traded on the New York Stock Exchange

Canadian Fund, Inc. / 1 Wall Street / New York, New York 10005 open end; primarily Canadian securities

International Investors Inc. / 122 East 42nd Street / New York, New York 10017 / open end; primarily gold mining shares

Israel Development Corp. / 75 Rockefeller Plaza / New York, New York 10019 / closed end; Israeli securities

Israel Investors Corp. / 850 Third Avenue / New York, New York 10022 / closed end; Israeli securities

Japan Fund / 1 Rockefeller Plaza / New York, New York 10020 closed end; Japanese securities; traded on the New York Stock Exchange

International Investing

New Perspective Fund (Capital Research Co.) / 611 West 6th Street /
  Los Angeles, California 90017 / open end; about 30% in foreign
  securities; diversified
Nomura Capital Fund of Japan Inc. / 100 Wall Street / New York,
  New York 10005 / open end; Japanese securities
Scudder International Fund Inc. / 345 Park Avenue / New York, New
  York 10022 / closed end; diversified Canadian and international
  portfolio
Partial lists of foreign funds and foreign securities holdings of United
States funds are available from *Vickers Association* / 226 New York
Avenue / Huntington, New York 11743

Partial List of United States Brokerage Houses With
Research and/or Trading Ability in Foreign Securities

Arnhold and S. Bleichroeder, Inc. / 30 Broad Street / New York,
  New York 10004
Becker Securities Corporation / 55 Water Street / New York, New
  York 10041
Drexel Burnham Lambert / 60 Broad Street / New York, New York
  10004
Goldman, Sachs & Co. / 55 Broadway / New York, New York 10004
Lazard Frères & Co. / 1 Rockefeller Plaza / New York, New York 10020
Loeb, Rhoades & Co. / 42 Wall Street / New York, New York 10005
Carl Marks & Co. / 77 Water Street / New York, New York 10005
Merrill Lynch, Pierce, Fenner & Smith Inc. / 1 Liberty Plaza, 165
  Broadway / New York, New York 10006
Mitchell Hutchins Inc. / 1 Battery Park Plaza / New York, New
  York 10004
Oppenheimer & Co., Inc. / 1 New York Plaza / New York, New York
  10004
Salomon Brothers / 1 New York Plaza / New York, New York 10004
Shields Model Roland Inc. / 44 Wall Street / New York, New York
  10005
Smith Barney, Harris Upham & Co. Inc. / 1345 Avenue of the Ameri-
  cas / New York, New York 10019

Partial List of International Portfolio Managers
in the United States

Bank of America N.T. & S.A. / 555 California Street / San Francisco,
  California 94104
Capital Research Co. / 611 West Sixth Street / Los Angeles, California
  90017

Shopping at Home

Carrett & Co. Inc. / 200 Park Avenue / New York, New York 10017
Chase Investors Management Corp. / 1211 Avenue of the Americas / New York, New York 10036
Citibank / 399 Park Avenue / New York, New York 10022
Dreyfus Corporation / 767 Fifth Avenue / New York, New York 10022
Fiduciary Trust Co. of New York / 2 World Trade Center / New York, New York 10048
Keystone Securities Co. Inc. / 99 High Street / Boston, Massachusetts 02104
Morgan Guaranty Trust Company of New York / 23 Wall Street / New York, New York 10015
Putnam Management Co. / 265 Franklin Street / Boston, Massachusetts 02110
U.S. Trust Co. of New York / 45 Wall Street / New York, New York 10005
Wellington Management Company / 28 State Street / Boston, Massachusetts 02109

*United States Broker-Dealers
Wholly Owned by Foreign Interests*

ABD Securities Corp. / 1 Battery Park Plaza / New York, New York 10004 owned by *Algemene Bank Nederland* (Amsterdam); *Banque Bruxelles Lambert* (Brussels); *Bayerische Hypotheken- und Wechsel-Bank* (Frankfurt); *Dresdner Bank* (Frankfurt)
Baer Securities Corp. / 489 Fifth Avenue / New York, New York 10005 owned by *Julius Bär & Co.* (Zurich)
Basle Securities Corporation / 120 Broadway / New York, New York 10005 owned by *Swiss Bank Corporation* (Basel)
James Capel Inc. / 20 Exchange Place / New York, New York 10005 owned by *James Capel & Co. Ltd.* (London)
Cazenove Incorporated / 67 Wall Street / New York, New York 10005 owned by *Cazenove & Co. Ltd.* (London)
Daiwa Securities America Inc. / 1 Liberty Plaza / New York, New York 10006 owned by *Daiwa Securities Co. Ltd.* (Tokyo)
Deltec Securities Corporation / 1 Battery Park Plaza / New York, New York 10004 owned by *Deltec Banking Ltd.* (Bahamas)
EuroPartners Securities Corporation / 1 World Trade Center / New York, New York 10048 owned by *Banco di Roma* (Rome); *Commerzbank* (Frankfurt); *Crédit Lyonnais* (Paris); *Bank Leu* (Zurich); *Nordic Bank Ltd.* (London)
Robert Fleming, Inc. / 100 Wall Street / New York, New York 10005 owned by *Robert Fleming & Co. Ltd.* (London)

37

French American Capital Corporation / 40 Wall Street / New York, New York 10005 owned by *Banque Nationale de Paris*

Hill, Samuel Securities Corporation / 375 Park Avenue / New York, New York 10022 owned by *Hill, Samuel & Co. Ltd.* (London)

Kleinwort, Benson Incorporated / 100 Wall Street / New York, New York 10005 owned by *Kleinwort, Benson Ltd.* (London)

New Court Securities Corporation / 1 Rockefeller Plaza / New York, New York 10020 owned by *Arcan N.V.* (owned by *Banque Lambert* of Brussels); *Banque Rothschild* (Paris); *Pierson, Heldring & Pierson* (Amsterdam); *N.M. Rothschild & Sons* (London)

New Japan Securities International / 80 Pine Street / New York, New York 10005 owned by *New Japan Securities Co. Ltd.* (Tokyo)

The Nikko Securities Co. / 140 Broadway / New York, New York 10005 owned by *Nikko Securities Co. Ltd.* (Tokyo)

Nomura Securities International, Inc. / 100 Wall Street / New York, New York 10005 owned by *Nomura Securities Co. Ltd.* (Tokyo)

North American Securities Corp. / 8810 Frost Avenue / St. Louis, Missouri 63134 owned by *North American Fund Management Corp.* (London)

Rowe & Pitman, Inc. / 111 Pine Street / San Francisco, California 94111 owned by *Rowe & Pitman, Hurst-Brown* (London)

Joseph Sebag Incorporated / 523 West Sixth Street / Los Angeles, California 90014 owned by *Joseph Sebag & Co. Ltd.* (London)

SoGen-Swiss International Corporation / 20 Broad Street / New York, New York 10005 owned by *Amsterdam-Rotterdam Bank N.V.*; *Crédit Suisse* (Zurich); *Société Générale* (Paris); *Société Générale Alsacienne de Banque* (Strasbourg); *Société Générale de Banque* (Brussels); *Sofina S.A.* (Brussels)

Suez American Corporation / 77 Water Street / New York, New York 10005 owned by *Banque de l'Indochine et de Suez* (Paris); *Compagnie Financière de Suez* (Paris)

Swiss American Securities Inc. / 100 Wall Street / New York, New York 10005 owned by *Swiss American Corporation* which is owned by *Swiss Credit Bank* (Zurich)

UBS-DB Corporation / 40 Wall Street / New York, New York 10005 owned by *Deutsche Bank* (Frankfurt); *Union Bank of Switzerland* (Zurich)

Ultrafin International Corporation / 63 Wall Street / New York, New York 10005 owned by *La Centrale Finanziaria Generale* (partly owned by *Banco Ambrosiano* of Milan); *Investco S.A.* (which owns *Kredietbank N.V.* of Brussels)

Yamaichi International (America), Inc. / 1 World Trade Center / New York, New York 10048 owned by *Yamaichi Securities Co. Ltd.* in turn owned by *Fuji Bank of Japan, Industrial Bank of Japan,* and *Mitsubishi Bank*

2. Canada

The historically amiable relationship between the United States and Canada became strained in the 1970s. American control of much of Canada's industry was a growing political irritant. Canada's dependence on the United States for almost 70% of its foreign trade remains an uncomfortable reminder to Canadians of their neighbor's powerful economic force of gravity. American businessmen have become convinced that "U.S. investment in now unwelcome in Canada and will be increasingly discriminated against in the future," said a 1976 report of the *Canadian-American Committee*, established to study the problematic relationship between the two countries. "The momentum for positive, forward-looking bilateral agreements between Canada and the United States appears spent, at least for the present," the report continued. Some American businessmen were critical of what they considered punitive taxation, anti-business sentiment, and high-handed provincial government measures.

These cooled-off feelings are reflected to some extent in the portfolio investments of the two countries in each other's equities, as these figures show:

Note: C$1 = US$1

International Investing

	Trading in Canadian Stocks			Trading in U.S. Stocks		
Year	U.S. Purchases	U.S. Sales	Net	Canadian Purchases	Canadian Sales	Net
1971	327.1	367.9	-40.8	1,609.8	1,846.1	-236.3
1972	419.0	565.5	-146.5	1,412.7	1,683.5	-270.8
1973	756.7	764.0	-7.3	1,376.7	1,450.9	-74.2
1974	673.5	727.5	-53.9	928.1	964.7	-36.6
1975	584.7	557.8	+ 26.9	1,320.0	1,337.7	-17.7

Source: Statistics Canada, Balance of Payments and Financial Flows Division, Balance of Payments Section, Cat. No. 67002.

Apart from the United States bear markets in the early 1970s, two other factors have reduced Canadian purchases of United States shares: 1. Canadian employee benefit funds must invest at least 90% of their assets in Canadian securities, and 2. the first $1000 in dividends from Canadian stocks are tax free to a Canadian investor but he pays tax on all dividends received from foreign stocks.

The energy crisis and the interest in gold stocks sparked a temporary interest in Canadian stocks but, on balance, United States investors have been net sellers of Canadian stocks.

On the other hand, the United States market has absorbed huge amounts of new Canadian bond issues — $3 billion in 1975, an all-time record, up from $1.5 billion in 1974. During the first six months of 1976, the total was $4 billion. Lenders, obviously, continue to have confidence in Canada's future.

Going Its Own Way?

Canadians have always wished that the hackneyed phrase "when the United States sneezes, Canada catches cold" were no longer true. Since 1973, their wish may have come true. The Arab oil embargo and runaway natural resources prices seemed to make Canada an isolated tower of strength. The subsequent recession was not as severe in Canada as in the United States (although Canadian stock prices plunged to comparable depths). On the other hand, when in 1976 the United States emerged from the recession with an unexpected vigor, Canada seemed to be headed for economic and fiscal trouble, and the Canadian stock markets recovered less than the United States markets.

Canada

In 1975, the Canadian real gross national product showed zero growth. Inflation ran at a rate of 12% in 1974 and of close to 11% in 1975, almost exclusively sparked by an increase in the money supply and government deficits. In 1975, currency and demand deposits (M1) increased by 22.9% and currency, demand, and time deposits (M2) increased by 17.2%. Deficits of all Canadian federal and provincial governments combined amounted to $4.4 billion in 1975. The balance of payments on all current accounts showed a deficit of $5.3 billion in 1975 with another huge deficit in sight for 1976. As often happens with government-created inflation, the Canadian government put the screws on the innocent victims. In October 1975, it published anti-inflation guidelines, putting a lid on increases in prices, wages, corporate profits, and dividend payouts. Wherever such measures have been tried in the past, they have usually created distortions in the economy. The Canadian dollar showed a deceptive strength in 1975 and for the first six months of 1976, due to an almost staggering increase of foreign borrowing abroad. This influx of foreign loans boosted the Canadian dollar to the detriment of Canadian exports, and contained a hidden time bomb. Continued trade and budget deficits resulted in a retarded decline of the Canadian dollar at the end of 1976, creating serious concern about the future of the Canadian economy and its stock markets. The election of the separatist party in Quebec added to the uncertainties.

Industry Groups

The attraction for foreign portfolio investors in Canadian stocks in the past has always been the country's vast and largely unexplored natural resources — riches which cannot be depleted for centuries by a population of 22 million. Thus, foreign investors have been primarily interested in the stocks of companies involved in mining, oil, natural gas, forest products, and, occasionally, banking.

Canadian metal and mining stocks best known to American investors are *Alcan Aluminium, Inco,* and *Hudson's Bay Mining and Smelting.* During the gold rush of the early 1970s, gold mining stocks were added to this list, with *Campbell Red Lakes Mines* and *Dome Mines* leading the group. These five are among the Canadian stocks traded on the New York Stock Exchange. (Two stocks were recently listed on the New York Stock Exchange — *Bell Canada,* listed in 1976, immediately developed a very active trading volume. *Northern Telecom,* its successful, 60%-owned subsidiary making telecommunications equipment, was listed a year earlier.) Another 50 Canadian issues are listed

41

on the American Stock Exchange and 16 issues traded over-the-counter are quoted on the NASDAQ system (see the end of Chapter 1 for complete lists). On the over-the-counter list, the most actively traded Canadian mining stock is *Noranda Mines*, a major producer of copper. Other major mining stocks include *Denison Mines* and *Placer Development*.

The Arab oil embargo focused attention on Canada as an oil exporter and possessor of huge untapped reserves, including the Athabasca tar sands. In fact, Canada was an exporter in the west and an importer in the east in 1976, and the export surplus, as a result of government policy, was relatively small. In May 1976, the Canadian government allowed an increase in the wellhead prices of oil and natural gas and proposed complex legislation to encourage oil exploration. If passed, this proposal would, among other things, require a minimum of 25% Canadian participation. This would favor Canadian-controlled oil companies, such as *Dome Petroleum* and *Home Oil*. Other large oil producers are *Aquitaine Company of Canada, Pacific Petroleums,* and *Husky Oil. (Petro-Can,* government owned, is not traded.)

Canadian forest products depend to a large extent on the United States construction level and paper demand, and with the upturn in the United States economy in 1975 and 1976, there was cautious optimism for this group, dampened by the Canadian government's inflation controls affecting earnings. The largest Canadian forest products company is *Abitibi Paper*, followed by *Macmillan Bloedel* and *Domtar*.

Theoretically, Canadian pipelines have a tremendous growth potential because of the immense distances that oil and natural gas are being carried and will have to be carried from the new exploration areas. However, it is a regulated industry, subject to fluctuating money costs, and earnings prospects are likely to remain clouded. Among the leading Canadian pipelines are *Transcanada Pipelines, Interprovincial Pipeline*, and *Alberta Gas Trunk Line*.

The ten chartered Canadian banks occupy a somewhat unique position. In contrast to the United States, where commercial banks can operate only within a limited geographical area (and in some cases, such as Texas, not have any branch offices at all), the Canadian chartered banks operate nation-wide. Their extensive network of branches have put the leading Canadian banks among the largest banks of the world. Canadian chartered banks provide roughly the same services that American commercial banks provide, except for trust services. Trusts are managed by specialized trust companies which also handle savings accounts.

Canada

The five largest Canadian banks are *Royal Bank of Canada, Canadian Imperial Bank, Bank of Nova Scotia, Bank of Montreal,* and *Toronto Dominion Bank.*

The largest trust and loan companies are *Montreal Trust, National Trust,* and *Royal Trust.* The anti-inflation regulations and a proposed new bank act had depressed the stocks of bank and trust companies in 1976.

Investors can get a double play on two foreign economies — Brazil and Canada — by buying *Brascan,* a Canadian holding company, traded on the American Stock Exchange. Its main holding in Brazil is *Light,* an electric utility which, together with the Brazilian economy, has grown at a rapid rate. In Canada, *Brascan* holds 33% of *John Labatt,* a leading brewery, and in 1973 it acquired *Great Lakes Power,* a utility.

Foreign Ownership

A special feature of the Canadian stock markets is the fact that many of the largest corporations are partially or wholly owned by United States or other foreign interests. Of the 25 largest Canadian companies listed on the *Fortune* "Directory of the 500 Largest Industrials Outside the United States," 11 show more than one-third ownership by United States parent companies. *General Motors of Canada,* second among the 25, and *Chrysler Canada,* fifth, are 100% owned by their parent companies, thus offering no opportunities for Canadians to invest directly in them. *Ford Motor of Canada,* the largest Canadian corporation, is 88% owned by the parent, leaving 12% for public trading by investors. It is listed on both the Toronto and Montreal exchanges. Other large companies with substantial United States ownership include *Imperial Oil* (69.5%), *Massey-Ferguson* (35.4%), *Alcan Aluminium* (38.4%), *Gulf Oil Canada* (68.2%), *Inco* (37%), *Texaco Canada* (68.2%), and *Canadian General Electric* (91.9%). On an industry basis, United States interests control 36% of Canada's paper and pulp industry, 43% of its mining and smelting industry, 45% of manufacturing, and 58% of the oil and natural gas industry. As *Fortune,* in its August 1976 issue, points out, Canadian control is even less than these figures indicate, since they do not show the holdings of private United States investors nor of investors who are neither Canadian nor United States citizens.

The Canadian government has taken steps to slow down or reduce foreign control of Canadian enterprises. In 1974, the government

43

created the Canadian Foreign Investment Review Agency to examine take-over proposals of Canadian-owned companies and deny those which it deems to be not in the national interest. Under the agency's rule, a proposed foreign holding of 5% or more is considered to be establishing control and must be reported to the Review Agency, which may request either a reduction of the holding or may disallow the proposed transaction altogether. Copies of the Foreign Investment Review Act may be obtained from the Commissioner of the Canadian Foreign Investment Review Agency, Ottawa.

New Issues and Rights Offerings

In 1975, about $1 billion was raised in the form of common or preferred shares in Canada, up from 1974, when the amount was $570 million. United States investors cannot participate in these new offerings unless the issues are registered with the SEC, and few are. However, when a new issue is considered "settled" — usually 90 days or more after the initial or primary distribution — it may be sold to United States residents. The same applies to the rights issues which some Canadian companies occasionally offer their shareholders. A broker cannot "offer" them to United States shareholders unless they have been registered with the SEC. However, if a United States owner of a Canadian stock becomes aware of a rights offering, he can, on his own initiative, inform the Canadian distributor that he wants to exercise his rights, or he can sell the rights through a Canadian broker.

Fixed-Income Securities

Many new Canadian fixed-income issues are SEC-registered and are sold in the United States. In addition, Canadian borrowers have used the Eurobond and other foreign capital markets, while their borrowings in Canada declined.

As a natural resources supplier, not only for its own expansion but also for the increasing needs of the world at large, Canada will require a tremendous amount of new financing during the next two decades. It is estimated that the energy industries alone will need more than $100 billion of new capital in the next 15 years. This includes some $10 billion for a number of new oil and gas pipelines to connect the Arctic fields with the population centers of Canada and several billion dollars more

Canada

for vast hydroelectric projects, such as the James Bay and Nelson River developments.

The general policy is to use debt as much as possible in the construction and development stages, and then try to retire these debt issues with equity issues when the projects begin to operate and produce income. Such huge financing cannot, at this time, be done in Canada alone.

There are four main types of fixed-income securities in Canada: federal government, provincial governments and agencies, municipals, and corporates. The interest rates for these different types of bonds rise in the same order with a spread of 1% to 1.5% between federal government and corporate bonds. There are no tax-exempt bonds in Canada.

Frequently, Canadian bonds offer more attractive terms than United States bonds of comparable ratings. However, yields and prices on both sides of the border are in continuous flux, sometimes in unrelated trends. It takes an experienced bond trader or knowledgeable investor to know when a Canadian bond is particularly attractive. A yield-conscious investor will find it worth his while to keep an eye on the Canadian bond market.

New Canadian issues offered in Canada or the Eurobond market, and not registered with the SEC, cannot be offered to United States residents until they have "settled."

Taxes

There is no withholding tax on interest received by non-residents from Canadian federal, provincial, and municipal government bonds. As of June 23, 1975, corporate bonds with maturities of five years or more are also exempt from withholding tax for non-resident investors. A withholding tax of 15% applies to older corporate bonds as well as to all dividends from Canadian common stock. For certain common stock, at least 25% Canadian owned, the withholding tax may be reduced to 10%, and there are other exceptions.

Tax laws affecting Canadian investors are very complex. The *Canadian Securities Institute* has an excellent publication on the subject, and information can also be obtained from any Canadian Federal District Taxation office.

Investment Funds

Canada has a thriving investment fund industry. At the end of 1975, there were about 200 open-end funds with total assets of about $3.3 bil-

45

lion, plus 22 closed-end funds with assets of about $593 million. Most closed-end funds sold at considerable discount from net asset value.

Canadian funds cannot be offered in the United States if not registered with the SEC. However, United States investors dealing through Canadian brokers in Canada, or directly with the fund management, can buy fund shares at their own initiative.

Canadian funds offer a convenient way to invest broadly in Canada or in specific sectors of the Canadian economy. There are funds specializing in securities of the metal and mining, oil and gas, utility, and paper industries, for example. Many Canadian funds have broad international portfolios. Canadian trust companies offer investment funds which are sold through their own offices, at a relatively low commission charge. However, asset values for most of them are established only once a month, which means that shares can only be bought or sold once a month. Life insurance companies offer pension plans based on common stock funds. Such funds must consist of at least 90% Canadian securities.

Mutual funds, life insurance companies, trust companies, and banks now also offer funds registered as retirement savings plans into which a self-employed individual may contribute a percentage of his income and claim the contribution as a deduction from his taxable income.

Canadian investment funds and their portfolios are reviewed yearly in the *Survey of Funds* published by *The Financial Post*.

Canadian Fund Inc. is a United States-based fund with a predominantly Canadian portfolio.

Where to Buy Canadian Securities

All Canadian stocks actively traded on United States exchanges or the over-the-counter market can be bought through any registered United States broker. The purchase of a Canadian security traded only in Canada may prove a little more difficult, at least for the individual investor.

Canadian brokers established in New York will accept business from institutional investors and United States brokers, but practically none of them handle retail business unless it involves a sizable portfolio. Six United States brokers have subsidiaries in Canada which are members of either the Toronto or Montreal exchange or both. This enables them to carry on retail business in both countries. The most active among them are *Merrill Lynch, Pierce, Fenner & Smith* and *Bache Halsey Stuart*. If a United States broker has to go through a Canadian broker to buy Canadian shares for a customer he will often add an override to the regular commission charged by the Canadian. Some United

Canada

States investors have accounts with Canadian brokers in Canada. They must report this information on their IRS returns.

Some of the larger Canadian brokers have United States correspondent brokerage houses. Correspondent brokers reciprocate in their business referrals and exchange research materials.

Stock Exchanges

The services provided by Canadian brokers are comparable to those provided by United States brokers. They include institutional and retail business, research, investment banking, and other financial services.

All broker-dealers, as well as anyone else connected with selling or recommending securities, must be registered with their provincial securities commissions. Regulations vary somewhat between the provinces, but efforts are underway to make them more uniform. An excellent summary of provincial securities legislation is found in the textbook of the Canadian Securities Course published by the *Canadian Securities Institute*.

Canadian brokers operate as floor brokers and make markets on their stock exchanges. There are no floor specialists like those on United States exchanges. The Canadian exchanges are auction markets where the sale is made to the highest bidder.

Many Canadian stocks have multiple listings on at least two of the exchanges — usually Toronto and Montreal — and often also on one of the United States exchanges. An astute Canadian broker will execute the order on whichever exchange he gets the best price. Arbitrage keeps the prices of a multiple-listed stock pretty much in line on all exchanges. But the Toronto exchange does not allow arbitrage with Montreal.

With the shift of financial weight from Montreal to Toronto since the 1950s, Toronto has become the largest exchange in Canada. Value of all trades in 1975 was $4.1 billion, compared with $133 billion on the New York Stock Exchange and $5.7 billion on the American Stock Exchange. At the end of 1975, there were 1,279 stock listings on the Toronto exchange, about 75% of them industrial shares, underscoring the increasing importance of The Toronto Stock Exchange in the industrial development of Canada.

Second is the Montreal Stock Exchange, with a total trading volume of $1.3 billion in 1975 and 866 listings. In 1973, the Montreal exchange absorbed the Canadian Exchange, where less seasoned issues were traded.

47

International Investing

The third largest exchange is in Vancouver, with a 1975 trading volume of $314 million. At the end of 1975, more than 600 companies were listed on the Vancouver Stock Exchange, many of them oil and mining stocks which do not meet the listing requirements of the Toronto exchange. Smaller exchanges of local significance are in Calgary and in Winnipeg.

Trading volume of all Canadian stock exchanges in 1975 was down sharply from 1973 and 1974 levels.

Both Toronto and Montreal operated option markets in 1976, with 18 underlying securities in Montreal and 10 in Toronto — six of them the same stocks. Trading in them, however, is not interchangeable because the option markets of the two exchanges operate on different clearing cycles.

United States Listings in Canada

At the end of 1975, some 70 United States stocks were listed on The Toronto Stock Exchange and some 50 in Montreal (many of them duplicate listings). Only a few, notably those of the big automobile manufacturers, were actively traded. The Toronto exchange does not actively promote the listing of foreign stocks and actually discourages those that are unlikely to develop much trading volume. Nevertheless, it does not refuse a listing application of any company that puts forward good reasons for listing, and the Montreal exchange takes the same attitude. One of the most cogent reasons for a natural resource company to list is the fact that a listing on a Canadian exchange is necessary to qualify for holding exploration leases in certain areas of Canada. Other companies with stock options or employee stock purchase plans like to provide their employees with a local market for their stock. Companies selling consumer products often feel that a listing helps to promote their names and demonstrates good citizenship. Listing of a Canadian subsidiary can be good public relations if a sufficient number of shares is left in Canadian public hands to provide a ready market for the stock in Canada. Listing of a United States stock on a Canadian exchange rarely does much for creating additional investor interest or trading volume. Canadian brokers almost always buy a stock where it has the most active market and the most competitive price. This, in most cases, is on the home exchange of the stock.

Listing is relatively simple by direct application to the stock exchanges at fees ranging between $10,000 and $15,000. Even though

Canada

each Canadian province has its own requirements for disclosure, these are usually waived if an American company complies with SEC disclosure requirements.

Sources of Information

All leading Canadian brokerage houses provide investment research service for their customers and make them available in the United States through their United States offices or their correspondent brokerage houses. The six United States brokerage houses established in Canada also provide Canadian investment information.

The leading independent investment information service, comparable to *Standard & Poor's*, is *The Financial Post Corporation Service*. It provides complete information on most of the publicly traded Canadian companies, plus special supplements, dividend records, new issue reports, and warrant reports. A somewhat more limited information service is provided by *Canadian Business Service*.

There are two Canadian chart services: *Canadian Industrial Stock Charts* and *Canadian Analyst*.

The leading English-language financial newspapers in Canada are *The Financial Times of Canada* and *The Financial Post*. *The Globe and Mail* has a special financial section which can be subscribed to separately. *Investor's Digest of Canada* is a bi-monthly financial publication.

The Toronto and Montreal exchanges publish excellent annual reports, as well as monthly reviews which provide valuable information on the activities of the exchanges and the Canadian economy.

Good reference books include the securities textbook mentioned earlier and *Management of Change in the Canadian Securities Industry* and *The Supply Of, and the Demand For Canadian Equity*, both available from The Toronto Stock Exchange.

International Investing

Canadian Stock Exchanges

Alberta Stock Exchange / 201, 500-4th Avenue S.W. / Calgary, Alb.
Montreal Stock Exchange / 800 Victoria Square / Montreal, Que.
The Toronto Stock Exchange / 234 Bay Street / Toronto, Ont.
Vancouver Stock Exchange / 536 Howe Street / Vancouver, B.C.
Winnipeg Stock Exchange / 167 Lombard Avenue / Winnipeg, Man.

Canadian Brokers in New York City

A.E. Ames & Co. / 2 Wall Street / New York, New York 10005
Bell, Gouinlock & Co., Inc. / 74 Trinity Place / 10006
Burns, Fry & Timmins Inc. / 100 Wall Street / 10005
Dominion Securities Harris & Partners, Inc. / 100 Wall Street / 10005
Equitable Canada Incorporated / 27 William Street / 10005
Greenshields & Co., Inc. / 70 Pine Street / 10005
McLeod, Young, Weir, Incorporated / 63 Wall Street / 10005
Midland Doherty, Inc. / 20 Exchange Place / 10005
Nesbitt Thomson Securities, Inc. / 1 Battery Park Plaza / 10004
Pittfield, Mackay & Co., Inc. / 30 Broad Street / 10004
Richardson Securities, Inc. / 40 Wall Street / 10005
Wood Gundy Incorporated / 100 Wall Street / 10005

United States Brokers With Canadian Affiliates

Bache Halsey Stuart / 100 Gold Street / New York, New York 10038.
Affiliate: *Bache Halsey Stuart Canada Ltd.* / 18 King Street / To-
ronto and 1 Westmount Square / Montreal
Dominick & Dominick, Inc. / 55 Water Street / New York, New York
10041. Affiliate: *Dominick Corporation of Canada Ltd.* / P.O.
Box 272, Royal Trust Tower, Toronto Dominion Centre / To-
ronto and Suite 3434, 1 Place Ville Marie / Montreal
Merrill Lynch, Pierce, Fenner & Smith Inc. / 1 Liberty Plaza / New
York, New York 10006. Affiliate: *Merrill Lynch, Royal Securities
Ltd.* / 20 King Street West / Toronto and Suite 300, 800 Dorches-
ter Boulevard West / Montreal
L.F. Rothschild & Co. / 99 William Street / New York, New York
10038. Affiliate: *L.F. Rothschild & Co.* / Suite 500, 800 Dorches-
ter Boulevard West / Montreal
Shearson Hayden Stone Inc. / 767 Fifth Avenue / New York, New
York 10022. Affiliate: *Shearson Hayden Stone (Canada) Inc.* /
Suite 3304, Stock Exchange Tower / Montreal
All Canadian brokers are listed in *Security Dealers of North America*

Canada

published by *Standard & Poor's Corp.* / 345 Hudson Street / New York, New York 10014.

Stocks That Make Up the Indices of The Toronto Stock Exchange

Banks
Bank of Montreal
Bank of Nova Scotia
Canadian Imperial Bank
Royal Bank
Toronto Dominion Bank

Beverages
Carling O'Keefe
Crush International
John Labatt "A"
Molson "A"
Seagram Co.
Hiram Walker-Gooderham "A"

Chemicals
Canadian Industries
Celanese Canada
duPont of Canada
Union Carbide Canada

Communications
Maclean-Hunter "A"
Selkirk Holdings "A"
Southam Press "A"
Standard Broadcasting
Thomson Newspapers "A"
Western Broadcasting "A"

Construction & Materials
Canada Cement Lafarge
Dominion Bridge
Lake Ontario Cement
St. Lawrence Cement "A"

Food Processing
B.C. Sugar Refinery "A"
Burns Food
Canada Malting "A"
Canada Packers "C"

Jannock
Redpath Industries "A"
Schneider Corp. Pref. "B"
George Weston

General Manufacturing
C.A.E. Industries
Canron
Canadian Corp. Mgmt. "A"
Canadian Marconi
Emco
Ford Motor of Canada
Hayes-Dana "A"
Interprovincial Steel & Pipe
I.T.L. Industries
Ivaco Industries "A"
Leigh Instruments
Versatile Manufacturing "A"
Wajax "A"
Westinghouse Canada

Industrial Mines
Alcan Aluminium
Brunswick Mining
Cominco
Denison Mines
Falconbridge Nickel
*Hudson's Bay Mining &
    Smelting "A"*
Inco "A"
Mattagami Lake Mines
Noranda Mines "A"
Rio Algom
Sherritt Gordon Mines "A"

Merchandising
Canadian Tire "A"
Dominion Stores
Hudson's Bay Co.
Koffler Stores "A"

51

Loblaw's "B"
M. Loeb
Metropolitan Stores "A"
Oshawa Group "A"
Silverwood Industries "A"
Simpson's
Simpsons-Sears "A"
Steinberg's "A"
Woodward Stores "A"
Zellers

Oil Refining
Gulf Oil Canada
Imperial Oil "A"
Petrofina Canada
Shell Canada "A"
Texaco Canada

Paper & Forest Products
Abitibi Paper
British Columbia Forest Products
Consolidated Bathurst Cl.
Domtar
Fraser "A"
Great Lakes Paper
Maclaren Power & Paper "A"
Macmillan Bloedel
Price

Pipeline
Alberta Gas Trunk Line "A"
Interprovincial Pipeline
Transcanada Pipelines
Trans Mountain Pipe Line
Westcoast Transmission
Westcoast Petroleum Pref. "A"

Real Estate
Abbey Glen Property
Block Bros. Industries
Bramalea Cons. Develop.
Cadillac Fairview
Campeau "A"
Consolidated Building
S.B. McLaughlin
Trizec

Steel
Algoma Steel
Dominion Foundries & Steel "A"
Steel Co. of Canada "A"

Trust and Loan
Canadian Permanent Mortgage
Guaranty Trust
Huron & Erie Mortgage "A"
IAC
Investors Group "A"
Laurentide
Montreal Trust
National Trust
Royal Trust "A"
Victoria & Grey Trust

Utility
Bell Canada
British Columbia Telephone
Calgary Power "A"
Canadian Utilities
Consumers' Gas
Inland Natural Gas
Maritime T&T
Norcen Energy Resources
Union Gas "A"

Miscellaneous Industrials
AGF Management Pref. "B"
Algoma Central Railway
Argus "C"
Canadian Cablesystems
Canadian General Investments
Canadian Pacific
R.L. Crain
Dominion Textile
Federal Industries "A"
Genstar
Great West Life Assurance
Greyhound Lines of Canada
Harding Carpets "A"
Hawker Siddeley
Imasco "A"
IU International
Kaps Transport

Canada

Massey-Ferguson
McIntyre Mines
Moore
Neonex International
OSF Industries
Power Corporation of Canada
Reed Shaw Osler
Rothmans of Pall Mall Canada
Slater Steel Industries
United Corp "B"
Westburne Int'l. Industries

Gold Index
Agnico-Eagle Mines
Camflo Mines
Campbell Red Lake Mines
Dickenson Mines
Dome Mines
East Malartic Mines
Giant Yellowknife Mines
Little Long Lac Gold Mines
Pamour Porcupine Mine "A"
Sigma Mines (Quebec)
Upper Canada Resources

Base Metal Index
Advocate Mines
Asbestos Corporation
Bethlehem Copper "A"
Campbell Chibougamau
    Mines "A"
Cassiar Asbestos
Conwest Explorations
Craigmont Mines
Cyprus Anvil Mining
East Sullivan Mines "A"
Falconbridge Copper
Gibraltar Mines

Granduc Mines
Hollinger Mines "A"
International Mogul Mines
Kerr-Addison Mines "A"
Labrador Mining & Exploration
Northgate Explorations
Orchan Mines "A"
Patino N.V.
Pine Point Mines
Placer Development
Roman Corporation
Steep Rock Iron Mines
Teck "A"
United Asbestos
United Keno Hill Mines
United Siscoe Mines
Yellowknife Bear Mines

Western Oil Index
Alberta Eastern Gas
Alminex
Aquitaine Co. of Canada
Bow Valley Industries
Canadian Export Gas & Oil
Canadian Homestead Oils
Canadian Hydrocarbons
Canadian Occidental Petroleums
Canadian Superior Oil
Dome Petroleum
Home Oil "A"
Hudson's Bay Oil & Gas
Husky Oil
Numac Oil & Gas
Pacific Petroleums
PanCanadian Petroleum
Union Oil Co. of Canada
United Canso Oil & Gas
Western Decalta Petroleum

Financial Publications

The Financial Post (weekly) / 481 University Avenue / Toronto, Ont.
The Financial Times of Canada (weekly) / 1885 Leslie Street / Don
    Mills, Ont.

International Investing

Globe and Mail Report on Business (daily Tuesday through Saturday) /
444 Front Street West / Toronto, Ont.
Investor's Digest of Canada (bi-monthly) / 481 University Avenue /
Toronto, Ont.

Sources of Information

Annual Review of the Canadian Equity Market and Canadian Economy
from *The Toronto Stock Exchange* / 234 Bay Street / Toronto,
Ont.
Canadian Business Service / 133 Richmond Street / Toronto, Ont.
Canadian Daily Stock Charts (weekly) and *Graphoscope* (bi-monthly)
from *The Canadian Analyst Ltd.* / 32 Front Street West / To-
ronto, Ont.
Canadian Mining & Oil Stock Charts (weekly) and *Canadian Industrial
Stock Charts* from *Independent Survey Co. Ltd.* / 1706 West First
Avenue / Vancouver, B.C.
Conway, G. *The Supply Of, and the Demand For Canadian Equities*
from *The Toronto Stock Exchange* / 234 Bay Street / Toronto,
Ont.
The Financial Post Corporation Service and *The Financial Post Survey
of Industrials, Oils, Mines, Markets, and Investment Funds* from
Maclean-Hunter Ltd. / 481 University Avenue / Toronto, Ont.
How to Invest Your Money and other publications from *The Canadian
Securities Institute* / P.O. Box 225, Commerce Court South /
Toronto, Ont.
Management of Change in the Canadian Securities Industry from *The
Toronto Stock Exchange* / 234 Bay Street / Toronto, Ont.
Montreal Stock Exchange (monthly) from *Montreal Stock Exchange* /
800 Victoria Square / Montreal, Que.
The Toronto Stock Exchange Review (monthly) from *The Toronto
Stock Exchange* / 234 Bay Street / Toronto, Ont.

3. United Kingdom

From the downfall of Napoleon to the rise of Hitler, London was the financial center of the world. Then things began to slip. Most of England's wealth was sacrificed in the defense of the free world during World War II. A good deal was spent on efforts to establish social equality and economic security for all. Some was just dissipated in low productivity. Today, The Stock Exchange in London ranks third behind New York and Tokyo in terms of the total value of transactions (though first in the total number of securities listed). In terms of portfolio assets managed, the United Kingdom as a whole probably ranks third behind the United States and Switzerland. As a source of new capital for worldwide use, the United Kingdom has practically dried up. Stringent currency restrictions in the form of a "dollar premium" on foreign investment by residents have severely cramped Britain's traditional role in international finance. The plight of the "City" reached abysmal depths in

Note: No dollar equivalents for the pound Sterling are given due to the wide fluctuation of this currency. For approximate comparisons consider its value at $2.00.

International Investing

1974 with a disastrous decline of the market index and trading volume; and this was followed by precipitous slippage of the pound Sterling through 1975 and 1976. Many brokerage houses went out of business or merged and a number of smaller merchant banks and investment managers disappeared from the scene.

In view of this decline in Britain's financial fortunes, it is all the more surprising and noteworthy that the London financial community has lost little or none of its leadership in international investment expertise — in versatility and new ideas for world-wide portfolio management and underwriting ventures. British merchant bankers "invented" the Eurodollar bond issue — the sale of dollar bonds to dollar-owning investors domiciled outside the United States (see Chapter 20). London brokers and merchant banks were among the first to take advantage of the emerging stock markets in Japan, Hong Kong, Singapore, and Australia. With their historical expertise in South African, Australian, and Canadian mining stocks, London brokers were the first to promote gold stocks before the devaluation of the dollar.

When gold became unpopular late in 1975, London merchant banks and brokers launched offshore funds in other metals and commodities to provide investors with an alternative inflation hedge. London and Scottish investment firms developed the first and most thorough expertise in the stocks of companies involved in North Sea oil exploration. London brokers were the first to devise a way of making portfolio investments in the emerging economy of Brazil (see Chapter 17). Thus, anyone seeking international investment sophistication would certainly want to make London one of his first shopping stops. A number of United States institutional investors who have been trying to get their feet wet in international portfolio investments since the removal of the Interest Equalization Tax in 1974 are using either British merchant banks for this purpose or have established their own international investment departments in London. Only in London can they find an adequate supply of seasoned international investment professionals.

Old City Tradition

London's continuing lead role as an international investment center in spite of the sadly slipping British economy is based on centuries-old traditions and business ethics. (An Act of 1697 established regulations for stock brokers that to some extent still apply today.) A relationship of personal trust among the "in" members of the City has been built up.

United Kingdom

Personal contacts and the word of a member of the fraternity were as important in making investment decisions as the analysis of a balance sheet. "Research" on foreign stocks, in past decades, consisted often of a conversation with trusted brokers and bankers throughout the world. British investment professionals still make frequent trips abroad. In the United States, for instance, they pay regular visits to trusted regional brokers in Cleveland, Chicago, Dallas, Atlanta, and other cities to get first-hand information from people who are intimately familiar with local publicly-held companies. Even today, when extensive research reports are available from many sources, these personal contacts still play an important role in making investment recommendations and decisions.

The flush of success in the heyday of the "City" of London also created a certain tradition of what a report of the British Cabinet Office some years ago called sluggishness and complacency, excessively rewarded in relation to the services offered. The City has never been communicative about itself, and as a result, according to the same report, "The City is not generally well regarded by industry, by educated and professional people, or by the populace at large." The decline of the British economy, the diminishing role of The Stock Exchange in London and the tough international competition have eliminated much of this "sluggishness and complacency" — largely by the elimination of the less successful firms. The leading brokers and merchant banks that have remained in business are today as competitive, sophisticated, and unsluggish as the best in any other part of the world.

In relation to the British economy as a whole, the British financial community, including the insurance industry with its world-wide services and investment portfolios, probably provides more jobs and earns more foreign exchange than any other financial community does in relation to its own national economy. In 1974, the City produced £905 million in foreign earnings, up from £397 million in 1967, according to *Investor's Chronicle*. Nevertheless, in 1976, this fact had apparently not penetrated far into government circles or the general populace, mired in their money-losing nationalized industries. The City continues to have some domestic public relations problems.

The Stock Exchange

The regional British exchanges were combined with the London exchange in 1973, and the combined exchange became the United Stock Exchange. Nevertheless, the exchange in London, which moved into a

57

spanking new skyscraper in 1972, is still called The Stock Exchange, as thought it is the only one in the world.

At the end of 1975, 9,037 securities were listed on The Stock Exchange. This included 1,103 domestic and Commonwealth fixed-income securities and 411 foreign stocks and bonds, of which 104 were United States stocks. Total market valuation of all listed securities was £250 billion, including foreign securities. Total value of British securities was about £90 billion, of which £30 billion were equities.

The trading volume in fixed-income securities greatly exceeded that of equity issues, and while equity trading peaked in 1972, value of the trading in fixed-income securities rose to record levels in 1975:

	Fixed Income (in billions)	Equity (in billions)
1970	£ 29.9	£ 8.8
1971	£ 50.8	£ 13.3
1972	£ 36.4	£ 20.0
1973	£ 38.7	£ 17.0
1974	£ 44.1	£ 12.6
1975	£ 76.5	£ 17.5
1976	£ 92.3	£ 14.1

Since both sales and purchases are recorded, these figures must be halved to make them comparable to those of other exchanges.

There is practically no over-the-counter market in the United Kingdom. A computerized service, *Ariel*, provides a limited third market for subscribing institutions, making it possible to bypass The Stock Exchange, but in 1975 this service accounted for only about 1% of the institutional volume.

In 1971 and 1972, the individual investor still accounted for more than 40% of the trading volume. In addition, clearing banks (the commercial checking account banks) serving small investors contributed additional volume on behalf of individual investors. However, the poor market performance in 1973 and 1974 drove many small investors out, and few seem to have returned. In addition, brokers encourage their smaller accounts to put all of their investments into unit trusts (mutual funds). This impairs the liquidity of many equity issues with smaller capitalization.

Ireland

The United Stock Exchange also includes Irish companies, and some investors feel that the Irish economy, much less fettered than the British by government regulations, has a better growth potential. Irish stocks with the largest market capitalization include *Bank of Ireland, Allied Irish Banks, Waterford Glass,* and *Irish Distillers Group.*

New Issues

The market for new equity suffered from the poor market performance of 1973 and 1974 and from the disappearance of the small individual investor. In addition, the threat of a wealth tax may discourage smaller companies from going public, since wealth is more easily assessed in terms of marketable securities than in shares privately held in a business. In any case, practically no company went public in 1974 and 1975. On the other hand, the British government, in 1975, was able to finance a large portion of its huge budget deficit by selling £7.2 billion of fixed-income securities. Public companies, through rights offerings, took advantage of the improved market performance in 1975 to do £1.2 billion of equity financing versus only £230 million in bond financing.

Shares of companies coming to the market for the first time are sold directly to the public through advertisements and a prospectus. An investor normally subscribes by sending his check directly to a clearing bank appointed by the selling syndicate to allocate and distribute the new shares. In the past, a very popular new issue was often over-subscribed, and a subscriber would receive only a small percentage of the number of shares he requested. As soon as such popular shares were traded on the exchange, they commanded a premium over the subscription price, permitting a handsome profit for an investor who received shares at the subscription price.

A listed company can raise additional equity capital only through a rights offering to its existing shareholders. A shareholder who does not want to exercise the rights can sell them on the open market. To raise equity capital directly from outsiders, a public company requires shareholder approval.

Trading Practices

Trading traditions on The Stock Exchange are colorful and complex. Only jobbers and brokers can be members of the exchange; not banks. Jobbers make the "book" (market) for individual stocks by establishing a selling and buying price. They do not deal directly with the public, only with brokers. Brokers deal with the public, including banks and other institutional investors.

International Investing

Many jobbers specialize in certain types of stocks or sectors of the market. Several jobbers may make book for the same stock. Some jobbers may make a book for several hundred stocks. The largest jobber reportedly makes a book for about 80% of the securities listed on The Stock Exchange. Different jobbers may quote different prices for the same stock. There is no central reporting system for prices. A broker wanting to buy or sell a stock on behalf of a customer sends a "blue button" around — a clerk apprentice whose job it is to obtain price quotations and collect other information. While his services are nowadays supplemented by two-way short-wave radio communications among jobbers and brokers on the floor, the "blue button" is likely to remain around for a while if only because of the British love of tradition and the fact that, while working, the apprentice is learning to become a jobber or broker. Since jobbers do not know whether an inquiring broker wants to buy or sell, they always quote two prices, comparable to the bid and ask prices of over-the-counter dealers in the United States. Like competing bazaar merchants, jobbers often shout their prices at the tops of their voices to be heard above the din of the trading floor.

Options Dealing

Options on The Stock Exchange are always for a fixed period of time, usually three months. They are bought on the exchange like other securities, but they cannot be traded. There are call options which allow an investor to buy a certain security at an agreed on price within the life span of the option; put options permitting the investor to sell a certain security at an agreed on price within a specified period of time; and double options, which are put and call options.

Options trading became slow on the London market after the bear market of 1974 and perhaps also as a result of option trading on the Chicago Option Exchange and the American Stock Exchange offered by United States brokers and some British brokers. Chicago and Amex option trading can be done without restriction on behalf of investors who are not residents of the United Kingdom. British investors must pay the dollar investment premium as they do for the purchase of all other foreign securities (see below) and new restrictions in 1976 made it prohibitive for them to play this field.

In 1976, there were discussions between the Amsterdam Stock Exchange and The Stock Exchange to develop a double-tiered option trading system on both exchanges for a limited number of international stocks.

United Kingdom

Listing of Foreign Stocks in London

Under a special rule of The Stock Exchange, members of the exchange can trade securities listed on any other recognized stock exchange of the world on the floor. For instance, when the Australian *Poseidon* nickel mine became a hot issue, hectic trading in its stock took place on The Stock Exchange even though the stock was not listed. British institutional investors make extensive use of foreign brokers to buy and sell foreign securities in their national markets. Practically all trading in United States securities is handled through American brokers in the United States or through their branch offices in London. Certain listed foreign securities that have traditionally had an active market in London, notably foreign mining stocks, still develop some trading volume in London. But trading in most other foreign securities listed in London is negligible, including the more than 100 United States securities listed on The Stock Exchange.

Most experts agree that a new listing of a foreign security in London is primarily of publicity value. Financial news reporting of the actual listing can be extensive if adequately prepared. In addition, coverage of financial news about a listed foreign company is usually better than for unlisted companies. Such publicity is meaningful for foreign companies with major operations in the United Kingdom, especially if they are selling consumer products or have dealings with the government.

Listing in London is easiest for United States companies traded on the New York or American Stock Exchanges because The Stock Exchange in London accepts the disclosure requirements of these two exchanges. A company wanting to list is usually sponsored jointly by a British merchant bank and a broker, who handle all of the formalities. Admission to the exchange can be accomplished within two to four weeks from application. Listing fees are graduated according to capitalization, but most American companies would be in the top bracket of £8,500. The total costs, including sponsor's fee and advertising, may range up to $50,000. Yearly fees to maintain a listing of a large company is £750. *The Financial Times* charges an annual fee of $650 for daily quotation of an inactive stock in its stock tables.

Costs for an American over-the-counter company and all other foreign companies are considerably higher. A special prospectus must be prepared and reprinted in full in an advertisement in *The Financial Times* and one other national paper. For a company preparing its financial reports in a language other than English, translation costs are involved. Thus, total costs for listing on The Stock Exchange in such a case may run from $150,000 to $200,000.

International Investing

Brokers

The British brokerage business is comparable to that in the United States. British brokers handle most of the business for individual investors. They tend to encourage discretionary accounts. Small accounts are often referred to the commercial clearing banks or put into unit trusts. Research has become an important sales tool, especially when competing for the institutional business. A number of brokers are involved in the management of pension funds, investment funds, and other institutional portfolios, but as one broker pointed out, such portfolio management may represent competition to customers such as the institutional money managers, and therefore cut into his execution business.

There are three types of orders under which a broker may operate: "discretion," giving him freedom to use his own judgment in executing an order; "best," instructing him to execute the order immediately at the best possible terms; and "limit," defining the price within which he may execute the order.

By all accounts, *Cazenove* is recognized as the largest British broker with special prowess in new issue work and with an effective world-wide network of branch offices, including offices in New York and San Francisco. Its expertise on United States securities is highly regarded.

Other leading British brokers with overseas branches include *Vickers, da Costa; James Capel; W.I. Carr, Sons; Joseph Sebag;* and *Rowe & Pitman, Hurst-Brown.*

Vickers, da Costa has built a reputation for its special expertise in Japanese and Southeast Asia stocks. It pioneered the first portfolio investments in Brazil through investment funds and is usually found in the forefront of new international investment ideas.

James Capel has entered into a working arrangement with a leading United States institutional broker, *Mitchell Hutchins,* and offers this firm's highly regarded institutional research services on United States securities to all of its United Kingdom customers. The two firms have also organized among themselves the research for other important investment markets, to which *Capel* contributes, among other things, its recognized expertise in metal and mining shares and the United Kingdom market.

On the domestic scene, *Wood McKenzie*, based in Edinburgh and with an office in London, has established an outstanding reputation for imaginative investment ideas and strategy and specialized research expertise in specific industries, including pharmaceuticals, banks, and North Sea oil exploration. *Grieveson Grant* is cited for good investment performance and *L. Messel* is renowned for its special expertise on investment funds. The firm publishes one of the best guides on British closed-end investment trusts, including performance. ratings. There are many other brokers with excellent reputations for performance or specialized expertise. Many individual investors outside the United Kingdom, especially those in offshore tax havens or in countries with limited local investment expertise, are using the services of British brokers. Even though British brokers dropped their rule against advertising or promoting their services in 1975, there was little promotion visible in 1976. An investor wanting to select a British broker must rely on the recommendation of a friend, banker, or other knowledgeable person, or go shopping among a number of them to find one that suits his specific investment requirements. The minimum funds handled varies with each brokerage house, but a reasonable lower limit is about £50,000.

Merchant Banks

Great international investment sophistication also exists among the British merchant banks or their investment management companies. The merchant banks have played a unique role in the history of international finance. Starting out as skilled financiers of international trade and shipping and as providers of what today is called ventury capital, they now offer a wide variety of services, including underwriting of domestic and international issues, private placements and loans, portfolio management for large amounts of money (usually £100,000 to £500,000 minimum), foreign exchange and bullion dealing, mergers and acquisitions, and other services typical of investment banking. They do not handle checking and savings accounts.

Even though most merchant bankers may offer a full range of services, many of them are recognized for special expertise. By all accounts, *Robert Fleming* is the largest in portfolio management, with about $2.5 to $3 billion in managed assets in 1976. Between 25% to 30% of the total was in United States securities. Through its Hong Kong affiliate, *Jardine Fleming Securities*, it has a strong position in Southeast Asia, both for research expertise and portfolio management. It is involved in the management of the largest unit trust (open-end mutual fund) operation, the *Save and Prosper Group*.

No official rank list for portfolio managers exists, but those rated among the largest in total assets managed, behind *Fleming*, include *J. Henry Schroder Wagg; Kleinwort, Benson; Hill, Samuel; Morgan Grenfell;* and *Hambros Bank*. Because of their international expertise, British merchant bankers are competing for the pension fund management of multinational corporations, of international organizations, and of United States institutions that want international securities in their portfolios. *Robert Fleming*, in 1976, advised 30 United States institutions on their international investments. *S.G. Warburg* and *N.M. Rothschild* have been given portions of the *Ford Foundation* portfolio to be invested in non-United States securities. *Warburg* is affiliated with *Paribas*, the leading French private bank, and both banks together have bought an interest in *A.G. Becker*, a Chicago-based brokerage house strong in research, commercial paper, and corporate finance. *Warburg*, among the British merchant banks, is the leading underwriter of Eurobonds (see Chapter 20). It has been a pioneer in this market since its inception in the early 1960s, and it is recognized for its many new ideas and its sophistication in this field. Other British merchant banks particularly active in the Eurobond market are *N.M. Rothschild; Kleinwort, Benson; Robert Fleming; Hill, Samuel;* and *Hambros Bank.*

In the domestic money market, the leading issuing houses (underwriters) include *Kleinwort, Benson; Morgan Grenfell; J. Henry Schroder Wagg; S.G. Warburg; Lazard Brothers;* and *N.M. Rothschild.*

An interesting new financing method for United States corporations needing operating funds in the United Kingdom was pioneered by *Kleinwort, Benson* — a Sterling issue convertible into the common stock of the corporation. It provides money at low fixed rates to the corporation while giving the investor a play of the United States market. He does not pay the usual dollar premium due on the purchase of foreign stock until conversion. *Kleinwort, Benson* has also been the most active sponsor for foreign corporations seeking to list their securities on The Stock Exchange.

The leading merchant banks belong to the exclusive Accepting Houses Committee — a distinction which means that bills (debt notes) endorsed by a member of the committee are discounted by the *Bank of England* at the most favorable rate. A somewhat less illustrious club is the Issuing Houses Association, to which any bank that has ever been involved with new issues or flotation (underwriting) can belong.

Clearing Banks

A third bankers association is the Clearing Houses Association, to which the so-called clearing (which "clear" checks) banks belong. These banks have a large network of branch offices throughout the country, originally catering primarily to commercial banking and the retail customer. After a number of mergers, only five remain: *Barclays Bank, Lloyds Bank, Midland Bank, National Westminster Bank,* and *Williams &*

Glyn's. In addition, the *Co-Operative Bank* and the *Central Trustee Savings Bank* have become members of the association.

Clearing banks have become increasingly involved in the investment business. They serve the individual investor whose portfolio is too small for the brokerage houses. They execute transactions through brokers, splitting the commission with the brokers, so that the investor does not pay a higher commission. Brokers are willing to handle the small-investor business because of the other business they receive from the banks. The clearing banks actively promote and sell unit trust shares (open-end mutual funds) and are involved in the management of many of them. They also have begun to compete with the traditional business of the merchant banks, notably in the areas of corporate finance and portfolio management. In 1976, these merchant bank activities were still relatively small. There is naturally some concern among merchant banks as to whether they can compete in the long run against the clearing banks which have far greater capital funds at their disposal. The question is: Will the concept of all-inclusive banking of the continental European banks win out in England or can merchant banks maintain their traditional business on the strength of their special entrepreneurial talents and great flexibility.

Investment Funds

Two types of investment funds exist in the United Kingdom: the investment trusts, which are closed-end funds listed on The Stock Exchange, and unit trusts, which are open-end mutual funds.

Investment trusts were started in the 1800s in Scotland. They are usually managed by a merchant bank or an independent management company. In 1976, there were about 200 investment trusts with approximately £5 billion in assets. Most of them were selling at discounts of up to 30% of their net asset value. They lost much of their popularity during the bear market of the 1970s. They also lost ground *vis-à-vis* unit trusts since they are not actively advertised and promoted.

Unit trusts are comparable to United States open-end mutual funds. The first unit trusts were launched in the 1930s by *M&G Group*, 38% owned by *Kleinwort, Benson*, but it wasn't until the late 1950s that unit trusts became popular with the public. At the end of 1975, there were about 400 unit trusts, managed by 94 different management groups, with total assets of about £2.5 billion. Managers include merchant banks, independent management companies, clearing banks, insurance companies, and brokers. Trust shares are sold directly to the public by the manager or through the branch offices of clearing banks.

Both investment trusts and unit trusts offer the investor an almost infinite variety of investment opportunities and the greatest possible diversification. A trust may specialize in growth, income, growth plus yield, world-wide international securities, specific geographical areas (such as the United States, Canada, Japan, the Far East in general, etc.); mixed domestic and international securities, and particular industries such as oil and energy, gold, mining, metals, banking, and special situations. There are even several unit trusts that have only investment trusts in their portfolios.

Other Institutional Investors

Insurance companies as a group are among the largest investors in the United Kingdom, with at least £ 20 billion under management. Most of the funds are invested in British common stocks and fixed-income securities. United States securities holdings may amount to more than $2 billion — only a small percentage of the total assets.

Another large investment group is represented by the self-managed pension funds, including the Post Office fund and the funds of a number of nationalized industries, such as the Coal Board and the Electricity Council. Among the largest private self-managed pension funds are *Barclays Bank, British Petroleum Company,* and *British American Tobacco.* Most smaller pension funds are managed by merchant banks and a few are handled by brokers and independent management companies.

The primary business of the independent investment companies is the management of investment trusts and unit trusts. The largest among them have between $500 million to over $1 billion under their management, including *Touche Remnant, F&C Management, Ivory & Sime, Gartmore Investment,* and *Henderson Administration.* Several, including *Ivory & Sime,* are headquartered in Scotland, the original home of some of the oldest merchant banks and investment trusts. Today the Edinburgh investment community still plays a somewhat independent and important role in international portfolio management.

Investment Regulations

A very important and somewhat distorting factor in the United Kingdom investment scene is the investment currency that a United

United Kingdom

Kingdom investor must use when he buys foreign securities. The investment currency sells at a premium above the commercial rate which may vary with supply and demand and the value of the pound Sterling. In 1976, the premium was quoted in relation to a fictitious exchange rate of £1 = $2.60. If the pound Sterling sells below the $2.60 rate, as it did in 1976, the effective premium is reduced accordingly. In mid-1976, the effective premium was about 50% above the commercial rate of exchange.

When a British investor sells a foreign security he must surrender 25% of the proceeds to the *Bank of England* for conversion into pounds Sterling at the regular rate of exchange. He may reinvest the remaining 75% in foreign securities without premium, but if he wants to invest the full 100% he must buy back the 25% in investment currency at the dollar premium rate. If the effective premium is 50%, such a switch costs the British investor about 10% of the total value of the transaction.

The investment currency premium is a serious deterrent for the United Kingdom citizen to invest in foreign securities. At the same time, it is a prop under British stock prices because it channels funds into the British stock market that otherwise might have gone into foreign markets.

British institutional investors can avoid paying the premium for investment currency by borrowing dollars or other foreign currency, with special permission of the *Bank of England*, to pay for their portfolios of foreign securities. They also avoid surrender of 25% of the sales proceeds when they make switches in their portfolios. However, such investment loans became very unpopular in the bear markets of the early 1970s when the value of the securities bought with foreign loans fell greatly below the 115% cover required by the *Bank of England*, and British institutions had to buy the difference with investment dollars at a premium, thereby magnifying their portfolio losses.

One way for a British investor to avoid the 25% surrender whenever a portfolio change is made in foreign security holdings is to buy shares of an offshore fund with a legal seat in such offshore havens as Bermuda or Luxembourg. A British investor pays the dollar premium when he buys the fund shares and he must surrender 25% of the proceeds when he sells them, but the fund itself is outside the United Kingdom exchange control and usually operates tax free. It pays no investment premium when buying foreign shares and does not surrender 25% of the proceeds when selling shares. Some British offshore funds are also established in the Channel Islands, which are given special status under United Kingdom exchange control regulations. Channel Islands funds are exempt from dollar premiums and surrender regulations.

67

International Investing

Domestic British investment and unit trusts with foreign securities in their portfolios can be bought by a British resident investor without paying the dollar premium since the trusts themselves must pay the premium when buying foreign securities. Nor does a British resident pay a premium when he buys a foreign stock on The Stock Exchange. The prices of foreign stocks traded in London reflect the premium.

A non-resident buying foreign stock in the United Kingdom does not pay the premium as long as he pays for the stock in foreign currency or Sterling converted from such currency. There are no impediments for the foreign investor to buy British stocks, with the exception of a very few companies that restrict foreign ownership.

Transfer of ownership of stocks and bonds is not quite as simple in London as it is in those European countries which have central clearing agencies for stock transfers or deal primarily in bearer shares (which are not registered in the name of the owner and can be handled like cash).

In the United Kingdom, practically all shares are registered in the name of the owner. When the stock is sold, the seller must sign a stock transfer form. For an investor living outside the United Kingdom, or travelling widely, the only practical way is to have his shares registered in the name of a nominee or trustee, often a legal entity especially created for this purpose by the bank or brokerage house through which the investor deals. A stockholder can instruct his nominee how to vote at the annual shareholders meeting.

Investment Strategy

The expertise of the London financial community and the world-wide trading range of The Stock Exchange in London may persuade a foreign investor to entrust management of his portfolio to a London firm, but it is not necessarily an inducement to invest in British securities. The sagging economy and the weakness of the pound Sterling in 1976 were not encouraging, to say it with British understatement. In any case, a foreign investor interested in the United Kingdom market may be more inclined to play it on its cycles rather than on the merits of long-term growth of a specific industry or company. The British market went into one of its worst tailspins in 1973 and 1974. *The Financial Times* Industrial Ordinary Index fell from about 500 at the beginning of 1973 to 150 at the end of the following year. By early 1976 it had recovered to 400, a nice ride for anyone who put his money in near the bottom, even if one allows for currency loss in the pound Sterling *vis-à-vis* many other currencies. Towards the end of 1976 it was back down to 300.

United Kingdom

A United Kingdom broker managing a portfolio for a non-resident in 1976 had very few, if any, United Kingdom securities in a growth-plus-yield portfolio. These few included North Sea oil stocks, companies with large export content, commodity stocks, selected banks and insurance companies shares, and some retail stocks. About 50% of the portfolio was in United States stocks and about 20% in Japanese, Southeast Asian, and Australian stocks. Eurobond issues in United States dollars and Deutschmarks provided a touch of yield.

Investment strategy of British portfolios with international content and subject to the investment currency premium and/or the 25% surrender in switches are to a great extent governed by these restrictions. Such portfolios are thus not a good reflection of what a British portfolio manager would do if he had a free hand. Portfolios managed for foreign investors show a great deal more flexibility, taking into account the trends in currency exchange rates, money costs, and inflation rates in various countries in addition to the normal fundamental analysis of industries and individual stocks.

Fixed-Income Securities

In terms of value, fixed-income securities in 1974 and 1975 accounted for about four times as much trading volume as equity issues. Yields by American standards have been high, with government bonds yielding up to 13% in 1976, and high-grade corporate bonds up to 14%. Under normal circumstances the sagging pound Sterling would discourage investment in fixed-income securities by a foreign investor. However, at certain times an alert and sophisticated United States investor could have bought high-yielding government bonds while hedging the exchange rate and thereby obtain a yield about 2% higher than for comparable United States Treasury securities. Many British government bonds, including the British War Loan, are, on application, exempt from withholding tax if purchased by a non-resident. The War Loan is not redeemable, it is a perpetual government stock without maturity. The majority of United Kingdom fixed-income securities owned by non-resident investors is subject to a 30% withholding tax.

Taxes

A new tax law, effective since April 1973, changed the system of withholding tax on dividends. Formerly, companies withheld the appropriate rate of tax from the dividends paid to residents and non-residents alike. Under the new law, tax on dividends is no longer withheld at the source. A company pays a higher corporation tax than before — in 1976, it was 52% as compared to 40% in 1973. This is due on all profits, whether distributed or undistributed. When dividends are paid, the company pays an "advance corporation tax," which amounted to 35% of the gross amount of the dividend paid in 1976. This tax is offset against the company's corporation tax on its eligible profits for the year. The recipient of the dividend is entitled to a corresponding tax credit on his own income tax. A non-resident can claim part or all of this 35% advance corporation tax back from the British tax authorities, depending on the terms of the double taxation agreement that his country had with Great Britain. Tax on interest from fixed-income securities is deducted at the source (35% in 1976). Depending on the terms of the double taxation agreement between the investor's country of residence and Great Britain, the tax can be wholly or partially reclaimed.

Approved investment trusts pay no income tax on dividends but let the dividend and tax credit flow through to their shareholders. However, they pay a corporate tax on interest received from government securities on which there is no withholding tax.

United Kingdom residents pay a 30% capital gains tax on all profitable transactions irrespective of the length of time the securities are held. Government securities held for more than one year are exempt. Approved investment trusts pay 17½% effective capital gains tax and the shareholder may elect to pay half of his own rate of tax or 30%. In either case, the 17½% paid by the trust is counted as a tax credit. It is impossible for a non-resident owner of investment trust shares to reclaim this capital gains tax from the British tax authorities (and most likely not from his own tax authorities).

Sources and Channels of Information

Under the most recent Companies Act of 1967, standards of company accounting and disclosure were improved in England, but they still fall short of practices in the United States. Quoted companies publish at least a semi-annual report in addition to the annual report and pay two dividends per year.

Security research of United Kingdom companies by British investment firms is generally organized by industry. Research on foreign securities is organized by country or geographical region. Some industries, such as oil, energy, or electrical equipment, are researched across border lines. Most British merchant banks obtain information on United States securities from American brokers or research services.

United Kingdom

This is supplemented by personal visits to the United States and published material received from the companies. Visits by United States company officers or group meetings with them are welcomed by the British as long as the chief executive officer or the chief financial officer are involved and the company has something meaningful to say. There has been an overdose of visiting company executives who wanted a good excuse for a trip to Europe, and their visits are likely to have negative results. Group meetings are most effective when started with a business-like information session late in the morning followed by lunch. It requires "in" knowledge to assemble a quality audience, preferably under the sponsorship of, or in consultation with, a London merchant bank or broker. The British Society of Investment Analysts is large and active and holds regular meetings with company officials, mostly British, but foreign companies with enough local investment appeal are not necessarily excluded. The society has done excellent work in professionalizing security analysis and is improving disclosure practices of British firms.

Most of the brokerage houses and merchant banks with institutional and private customers publish investment information for their customers, often on a world-wide basis. A number of brokerage houses offer their research on a subscription basis, usually payable in commission dollars, sometimes in hard currency. *Datastream*, a computerized information retrieval system originated by *Hoare & Co., Govett*, makes it possible for subscribers to have up-to-date information at their fingertips on several thousand companies. After *Moodies Investor Services* went our of business in the bear market of 1974, only *Extel Statistical Services* remains to provide regular information sheets on several thousand British and several hundred foreign companies. It also publishes a quarterly handbook providing company information by industry grouping. Chart service is provied by *Chart Analysis* and *Investment Research*. *Reuters* and *Extel* offer news ticker service and instant stock quotations from about a dozen stock markets all over the world. *Universal Services* operates a news ticker for corporate news, comparable to *P.R. Newswire* in New York. It is also used by some brokers and merchant banks.

The leading financial newspaper is *The Financial Times*, comparable in stock market coverage to the *Wall Street Journal*, but far more internationally oriented in its news and feature articles. *Investor's Chronicle* is the most widely read weekly investment publication; it also publishes a weekly newsletter with investment advice. The renowned *Economist* has changed its editorial content over the years, putting less stress on economic and business features, and becoming more like *Time* or *Newsweek* in its world-wide news coverage. Some of the daily newspapers provide extensive business coverage, notably the *Daily Tele-*

graph, The Guardian, and *The Times.* So do the three leading Sunday papers, the *Sunday Times,* the *Sunday Telegraph,* and the *Observer.* The *Evening Standard* and the *Evening News,* much briefer in their financial reporting, nevertheless find a good readership among homeward bound City commuters.

United Kingdom

Stock Exchange

The Stock Exchange / Old Broad Street / London

Partial List of British Brokers Doing International Business

James Capel & Co. / Winchester House, 100 Old Broad Street / London. Affiliate: *James Capel Inc.* / 20 Exchange Place / New York, New York 10005

W.I. Carr, Sons & Co. / Ocean House, 10-12 Little Trinity Lane / London

Cazenove & Co. / 12 Tokenhouse Yard / London. Affiliate: *Cazenove Inc.* / 67 Wall Street / New York, New York 10005

De Zoete & Bevan / 25 Finsbury Circus / London

Fielding, Newson-Smith & Co. / Garrard House, 31 Gresham Street / London

Greene & Co. / 1 Copthall Chambers / London

W. Greenwell & Co. / Bow Bells House, Bread Street / London

Grieveson, Grant & Co. / 59 Gresham Street / London

Hoare & Co., Govett Ltd. / Atlas House, 1 King Street / London

L. Messel & Co. / Winchester House, 100 Old Broad Street / London

Montagu, Loebl, Stanley & Co. / 2 Throgmorton Avenue / London

Myers & Co. / 16th & 17th Floors, The Stock Exchange / London

Panmure Gordon & Co. / 9 Moorfields Highwalk / London

Phillips & Drew / Lee House, London Wall / London

Rowe & Pitman, Hurst-Brown / City Gate House, 39-45 Finsbury Square / London. Affiliate: *Rowe & Pitman, Inc.* / 111 Pine Street / San Francisco, California 94111

J. & A. Scrimgeour Ltd. / Mansion House Place / London

Joseph Sebag & Co. / Bucklersbury House, 3 Queen Victoria Street / London. Affiliate: *Joseph Sebag Inc.* / 523 West Sixth Street / Los Angeles, California 90014

Sheppards & Chase / Clements House, Gresham Street / London

Simon & Coates / 1 London Wall Buildings / London

Strauss, Turnbull & Co. / 3 Moorgate Place / London

Vickers, da Costa & Co. Ltd. / Regis House, King William Street / London

Wood, Mackenzie & Co. / Erskine House, 68-73 Queen Street / Edinburgh and 62-63 Threadneedle Street / London

Leading Merchant Banks

Arbuthnot Latham & Co. Ltd. / 37 Queen Street / London

Baring Brothers & Co. Ltd. / 88 Leadenhall Street / London

73

International Investing

Brown, Shipley & Co. Ltd. / Founders Court, Lothbury / London
Charterhouse Japhet Limited / 1 Paternoster Row, St. Paul's / London
Robert Fleming & Co. Ltd. / 8 Crosby Square / London. Affiliate:
    Robert Fleming & Co. Ltd. / 100 Wall Street / New York, New
    York 10005
Antony Gibbs & Sons, Ltd. / 23 Bloomfield Street / London
Guinness Mahon & Co. Ltd. / 3 Gracechurch Street / London
Hambros Bank Limited / 41 Bishopsgate / London
Hill, Samuel & Co. Ltd. / 100 Wood Street / London. Affiliate: *Hill,*
    Samuel & Co. Ltd. / 375 Park Avenue / New York, New York
    10022
Kleinwort, Benson Limited / 20 Fenchurch Street / London. Affiliate:
    Kleinwort, Benson Limited / 100 Wall Street / New York, New
    York 10005
Lazard Brothers & Co. Ltd. / 11 Old Broad Street / London
Samuel Montagu & Co. Ltd. / 114 Old Broad Street / London
Morgan Grenfell & Co. Limited / 23 Great Winchester Street / London
Rea Brothers Limited / 36-37 King Street / London
N.M. Rothschild & Sons Limited / New Court, St. Swithin's Lane /
    London
J. Henry Schroder Wagg & Co. Ltd. / 120 Cheapside / London
Singer & Friedlander Limited / 20 Cannon Street / London
S.G. Warburg & Co. Limited (incorporating *Seligman Brothers*) /
    30 Gresham Street / London

Clearing Banks (*Commercial and Retail*)

Barclays Bank Ltd. / 54 Lombard Street / London
Lloyds Bank Ltd. / 71 Lombard Street / London
Midland Bank Ltd. / Poultry / London
National Westminster Bank Ltd. / 41 Lothbury / London
Williams & Glyn's Bank Ltd. / 1 King William Street / London

Partial List of Actively Traded British Stocks

Albright & Wilson (chemicals)
Allied Breweries
Associated British Foods
Barclays Bank
Bass Charington (alcoholic beverages)
Beecham Group (pharmaceuticals)
Boots (pharmaceuticals)
Bowater‡ (paper, packaging)
C.T. Bowring (banking, finance)

United Kingdom

British American Tobacco† (tobacco, paper products)
British Home Stores
British Insulated Callender's Cables (engineering, cables)
*British Petroleum**
BSR (electronics)
Burmah Oil‡
Cadbury Schweppes (food, beverages)
Carrington Viyella (textiles)
Coats Patons (textiles)
Courtaulds† (synthetic fibers)
Curry's (retailing)
Delta Metal (non-ferrous metals)
Dickinson Robinson Group (paper products)
Distillers (alcoholic beverages)
Dunlop Holdings† (tires and rubber goods)
Eagle Star Insurance
*EMI** (records, electronics)
Fison's‡ (food, pharmaceuticals)
Freemans London (mail order)
General Accident Fire and Life Assurance
General Electric
Glaxo Holdings‡ (pharmaceuticals, foods)
Grand Metropolitan (hotels, catering)
Great Universal Stores
Guest, Keen & Nettlefolds (automotive, industrial equipment)
Arthur Guinness (breweries)
Hambros Bank
Hawker Siddeley Group (aerospace engineering)
Imperial Chemical Industries†
Imperial Group† (tobacco, food, paper)
Kleinwort, Benson (banking)
Lloyds Bank
Lucas Industries (automotive, aircraft equipment)
Marks & Spencer (retailing, apparel)
Midland Bank
National Westminster Bank
Peninsular and Oriental Steam Navigation (shipping)
Phoenix Assurance
Pilkington Brothers (glass)
*Plessey** (telecommunications)
Rank Organisation‡ (leisure time)
Ranks Hovis McDougall (foods)
Reckitt & Colman Holdings (food, household products)
Reed International (paper products)
Rio Tinto-Zinc (mining, chemicals)
Sears Holding (textiles, apparel, shows)

75

*Shell Transport and Trading** (petroleum products)
W.H. Smith (news dealers)
Standard Chartered Banking Group
Tarmac (building materials)
Tate & Lyle (food, shipping)
Thomson Organisation (publishing)
Thorn Electrical Industries (radios, televisions, appliances)
Trust Houses Forte (hotels, catering)
Tube Investments (tubes, bicycles, engineering)
Turner & Newall (automotive parts, building materials)
*Unilever Ltd.** (foods, soaps, cosmetics)
F.W. Woolworth & Co.† (retailing)

* Also traded on the New York Stock Exchange
† Also traded on the American Stock Exchange
‡ Also traded over-the-counter in the United States

Unit Trust Management Companies

Abbey Unit Trust Managers Ltd. / 72-80 Gatehouse Road / Aylesbury, Bucks
Alben Trust Managers Ltd. / 14 Finsbury Circus / London
Allied Hambro Group / Hambro House, Rayleigh Road / Hutton, Brentwood, Essex
Anderson Unit Trust Managers Ltd. / 158 Fenchurch Street / London
Ansbacher Unit Management Co. Ltd. / 1 Noble Street, Gresham Street / London
Arbuthnot Securities Ltd. / 21 Leven Street / Edinburgh
Archway Unit Trust Managers Ltd. / 24 St. Mary Axe / London
Barclays Unicorn Ltd. / Unicorn House, 252 Romford Road / London
Bishopsgate Progressive Unit Trust Management Co. Ltd. / 9 Bishopsgate / London
Bridge Talisman Fund Managers Ltd. / Plantation House, 5-8 Mincing Lane / London
British Life Office Ltd. / Reliance House / Tunbridge Wells, Kent
Cabot Unit Trust Management Co. Ltd. / The Bristol & West Building, Broad Quay / Bristol
Canada Life Unit Trust Managers Ltd. / 6 Charles II Street / London
James Capel and Co. Unit Trust Management Ltd. / Winchester House, 100 Old Broad Street / London
Carliol Unit Fund Managers Ltd. / A Floor, Milburn House / Newcastle upon Tyne
Charterhouse Japhet Unit Management Ltd. / 1 Paternoster Row, St. Paul's / London
College Hill Unit Trust Managers Ltd. / 6 Wardrobe Place / London

United Kingdom

Confederation Funds Management Ltd. / 120 Regent Street / London
Cosmopolitan Fund Managers Ltd. / 56 Copthall Avenue / London
Coyne Investment Management Ltd. / Fairhill Courthouse / Hildenborough, Kent
Crescent Unit Trust Managers Ltd. / 4 Melville Crescent / Edinburgh
Discretionary Unit Fund Managers Ltd. / Finsbury House, 22 Bloomfield Street / London
Emblem Fund Management Co. Ltd. / 20 Copthall Avenue / London
Equitas Securities Ltd. / 5 Rayleigh Road, Hutton / Brentwood, Essex
Equity & Law Unit Trust Managers Ltd. / Amersham Road / High Wycombe, Bucks
Founders Court Management Services Ltd. / Founders Court, Lothbury / London
Framlington Unit Management Ltd. / Framlington House, 5-7 Ireland Yard / London
Friends' Provident Unit Trust Managers Ltd. / Pixham End / Dorking, Surrey
G and A Unit Trust Managers Ltd. / 5 Rayleigh Road, Hutton / Brentwood, Essex
Gartmore Fund Managers Ltd. / 2 St. Mary Axe / London
Antony Gibbs Unit Trust Managers / 23 Bloomfield Street / London
Glenfriars Unit Trust Management Ltd. / 25 Austin Friars / London
Grieveson Management Co. Ltd. / 59 Gresham Street / London
John Govett Unit Management Ltd. / Winchester House, 77 London Wall / London
GT Unit Managers Ltd. / 6th Floor, 16 St. Martins-le-Grand / London
Guardian Royal Exchange Unit Managers Ltd. / The Royal Exchange / London
Hill Samuel Unit Trust Managers Ltd. / 45 Beech Street / London
Henderson Unit Trust Management Ltd. / 11 Austin Friars / London
Intel Funds (Management) Ltd. / 15 Christopher Street / London
Ionian Unit Trust Management Ltd. / 64 Coleman Street / London
Key Fund Managers Ltd / 25 Milk Street / London
Kleinwort Benson Unit Managers Ltd. / 20 Fenchurch Street / London
L & C Unit Trust Management Ltd. / The Stock Exchange / London
Lawson Securities Ltd. / 63 George Street / Edinburgh
Lazard Brothers & Co. Ltd. / 21 Moorfields / London
Legal & General-Tyndall Fund Managers Ltd. / 18 Canynge Road / Bristol
Leonine Administration Ltd. / 28 Throgmorton Street / London
Lloyds Bank Unit Trust Managers Ltd. / 71 Lombard Street / London
Lloyd's Life Unit Trust Managers Ltd. / 72-80 Gatehouse Road / Aylesbury, Bucks
London Wall Group of Unit Trusts Ltd. / 1 Finsbury Square / London
M & G Group Ltd. / Three Quays, Tower Hill / London
ManuLife Management Ltd. / ManuLife House, St. George's Way / Stevenage, Herts

77

Mayflower Management Co. Ltd. / Clements House, Gresham Street / London

Mercury Fund Managers Ltd. / St. Albans House, Goldsmith Street / London

Metropolitan Exempt Fund Managers Ltd. / 28 Haymarket / London

Midland Bank Group Unit Trust Managers Ltd. / Courtwood House, Silver Street Head / Sheffield

Minster Fund Managers Ltd. / Minster House, Arthur Street / London

Mutual Unit Trust Managers Ltd. / Throgmorton House, 15 Copthall Avenue / London

National Provident Investment Managers Ltd. / 48 Gracechurch Street / London

National Westminster Unit Trust Managers Ltd. / 41 Lothbury / London

NEL Trust Managers Ltd. / Milton Court / Dorking, Surrey

New Court Fund Managers Ltd. / New Court, St. Swithin's Lane / London

Norwich General Trust Ltd. / Surrey Street / Norwich

Oceanic Unit Trust Managers Ltd. / 15 Great St. Thomas Apostle / London

Pearl Trust Managers Ltd. / 252 High Holborn / London

Pelican Units Administration Ltd. / Fountain House, 81 Fountain Street / Manchester

Perpetual Unit Trust Management Ltd. / 48-50 Hart Street / Henley-on-Thames, Oxon

Piccadilly Unit Trust Managers Ltd. / 65 London Wall / London

Practical Investment Co. Ltd. / Europe House, World Trade Centre / London

Provincial Life Investment Co. Ltd. / 222 Bishopsgate / London

Prudential Unit Trust Managers Ltd. / Holborn Bars / London

Quilter Management Co. Ltd. / Gerrard House, 31-35 Gresham Street / London

Raphael Unit Trust Managers Ltd. / 10 Throgmorton Avenue / London

Reliance Unit Managers Ltd. / Reliance House / Tunbridge Wells, Kent

Remigium Management Ltd. / 1st Floor, City-Gate House, 39-45 Finsbury Square / London

Rothschild & Lowndes Management Ltd. / New Court, St. Swithin's Lane / London

Rowe & Pitman Management Ltd. / 1st Floor, City-Gate House, 39-45 Finsbury Square / London

Royal Trust Co. of Canada Fund Management Ltd. / Royal Trust House, 54 Jermyn Street / London

Schlesinger Trust Managers Ltd. / 19 Hanover Square / London

Save and Prosper Group Ltd. / 4 Great St. Helens / London

J. Henry Schroder Wagg & Co. Ltd. / 120 Cheapside / London

United Kingdom

Scottish Equitable Fund Managers Ltd. / 28 St. Andrew Square / Edinburgh

Sebag Unit Trust Managers Ltd. / Bucklersbury House, 3 Queen Victoria Street / London

Security Selection Ltd. / 8 The Crescent Minories / London

Stewart Unit Trust Managers Ltd. / 45 Charlotte Square / Edinburgh

Stratton Trust Managers Ltd. / 88 Leadenhall Street / London

Slater, Walker Trust Management Ltd. / Leith House, 47-57 Gresham Street / London

Sun Alliance Fund Management Ltd. / 1 Bartholomew Lane / London

Target Trust Managers Ltd. / Target House, 7-9 Breams Buildings / London

Trades Union Unit Trust Managers Ltd. / 100 Wood Street / London

Transatlantic and General Securities Co. Ltd. / 91-99 New London Road / Chelmsford

Trustee Savings Banks Unit Trust Managers Ltd. / White Bear House, 21 Chantry Way / Andover, Hants

Tyndall Managers Ltd. / 18 Canynge Road / Bristol

Ulster Bank Unit Trust Managers Ltd. / Waring Street, Belfast

Unit Trust Accounting & Management Ltd. / Plantation House, 5-8 Mincing Lane / London

Investment Trust Managers (Not Including Merchant Banks)

Baillie, Gifford & Co. / 3 Glenfinlas Street / Edinburgh

Edward Bates & Sons / 88 Leadenhall Street / London

Black, Geoghegan & Till / 10 Lefebvre Street / St. Peter Port, Guernsey

Britannic Assurance / Moor Green House, Moor Green Lane / Moseley

Brodies / 7 Rothesay Terrace / Edinburgh

Chatsworth Management Services / Hesketh House, Portman Square / London

City Financial Administration / Plantation House, Mincing Lane / London

City Investment Trust Managers / 11 Austin Friars / London and 12-16 Booth Street / Manchester

Coggan Smith & Co. / 20 Fenchurch Street / London

Cripps Warburg / 20 Birchin Lane / London

Martin Currie & Co. / 29 Charlotte Square / Edinburgh

Dawnay Day / 31 Gresham Street / London

Dawson & Fornes / 38 Queen Street / London

Debenture Corporation / Winchester House, London Wall / London

Drayton Montagu Portfolio Management / 117 Old Broad Street / London

International Investing

East of Scotland Investment / 10 Queens Terrace / Aberdeen
Edinburgh Fund Managers / 4 Melville Crescent / Edinburgh
Electra Group Services / Electra House, Victoria Embankment / London
F & C Management / Winchester House, London Wall / London
Fleming & Murray / Bucklersbury House, 83 Cannon Street / London
James Finlay Investment Management / 52-56 Osnaburgh Street / London
Gartmore Investment / 2 St. Mary Axe / London
John Govett & Co. / Winchester House, London Wall / London
G.T. Management / 16 St. Martins-le-Grand / London
Guinness, Mahon & Co. / 32 Mary at Hill / London
Hambros Investment Management Services / 41 Bishopsgate / London
T.G. Harrison & Co. / 37 Queen Street / London
Harrisons & Crosfield / 1-4 Great Tower Street / London
Heenan Beddow Securities / 15-17 King Street / London
Henderson Administration / 11 Austin Friars / London
Philip Hill (Management) / 8 Waterloo Place / London
Industrial & Commercial Financial Corporation / 7 Copthall Avenue / London and 29 Charlotte Square / Edinburgh
Investment Trust Services / Bucklersbury House, 11 Walbrook / London
Ionian Bank / 64 Coleman Street / London
Ivory & Sime / 1 Charlotte Square / Edinburgh
Jardine, Fleming & Co. (Hong Kong) / 3 Lombard Street / London
Leopold Joseph & Sons / 31-45 Greshem Street / London
Keyser, Ullman / 25 Milk Street / London
London & Yorkshire Trust / 87 Eaton Place / London
M & G Securities / Three Quays, Tower Hill / London
Murray, Johnstone & Co. / 175 West George Street / Glasgow
Normandie Securities / 6 New Street / St. Peter Port, Guernsey
Paull & Williamsons / 6 Union Row / Aberdeen
Robertson & Maxtone Graham / 34 Charlotte Square / Edinburgh
Scottish United Management / 37 Renfield Street / Glasgow
Seton Trust / 20 Copthall Avenue / London
W.H. Stentiford & Co. / 25-35 City Road / London
Stewart Fund Managers / 45 Charlotte Square / Edinburgh
Talisman Fund Managers / 5-8 Mincing Lane / London
Tay & Thames / Royal Exchange / Dundee
Thomson, McLintock & Co. / 216 West George Street / Glasgow
Touche, Remnant & Co. / 3 London Wall Buildings / London
Turner Hutton & Lawson / 90 Mitchell Street / Glasgow
Whitbread & Co. / Brewery, Chiswell Street / London
Wilsone & Duffus / 7 Golden Square / Aberdeen

80

United Kingdom

United States Brokers in London

Alexander & Company / 63 Fenchurch
Bache Halsey Stuart / 5 Burlington Gardens
Baker, Weeks & Co., Inc. / Winchester House, 77 London Wall
Becker Securities Corporation / 10-11 Lincoln's Inn Fields
Brown Brothers Harriman & Co. / 34 Lime Street
Dominick & Dominick Incorporated / 32 Lombard Street
Donaldson, Lufkin & Jenrette Securities Corporation / 1 Cornhill
Drexel Burnham & Co. Incorporated / Winchester House, 77 London Wall
Fahnestock & Co. / 2 Broad Street Place, Finsbury Circus
First Boston Corporation / 16 Finsbury Circus
First Regional Securities Inc. / 4 Tokenhouse Building, King's Arm Yard
Goldman, Sachs & Co. / 40 Basinghall Street
Hornblower & Weeks-Hemphill, Noyes Inc. / 21 Mincing Lane
E.F. Hutton & Co. Inc. / Cereal House, 58 Mark Lane
Jessup & Lamont Inc. / 44 High Street
Kidder, Peabody & Co. Inc. / Bucklersbury House, Cannon Street
Lehman Brothers Inc. / P & O Building, Leadenhall Street
Loeb, Rhoades & Co. / 16 Moorfields, High Walk
Merrill Lynch, Pierce, Fenner & Smith Inc. / 153 New Bond Street
Moseley, Hallgarten & Estabrook, Inc. / 80 Bishopsgate
Paine, Webber, Jackson & Curtis Inc. / 3 Tokenhouse Building, King's Arm Yard
Roulston & Co., Inc. / 55 New Bond Street
Salomon Brothers / 1 Moorgate
Shearson Hayden Stone Inc. / 1 Maltravers Street
Shields Model Roland Inc. / River House, 119;121 Minories
Smith Barney, Harris Upham & Co. / 9 Basinghall Street
Thomson & McKinnon Auchincloss Kohlmeyer Inc. / 55 London Wall
White, Wedl & Co. Inc. / St. Helens 1 Undershaft, Commerce Union Building
Dean Witter & Co., Inc. / 7 Cleveland Row

Investment Information Services

Chart Analysis Ltd. / 194 Bishopsgate / London
Extel Statistical Services / 37-45 Paul Street / London
Investment Research / 36 Regent Street / Cambridge

International Investing

Leading Financial Publications

The Financial Times / Bracken House, Cannon Street / London
Investor's Chronicle / 30 Finsbury Square / London

Other Business and Financial Publications

The Banker / Bracken House, Cannon Street / London
City Press / 4 Moorfields / London
The Economist / 25 St. James's Street / London
Euromoney / Tallis House, Tallis Street / London
Money Management / 30 Finsbury Square / London

National Daily Newspapers with Financial Coverage

Daily Telegraph / Bracken House, 112 Queen Victoria Street / London
The Guardian / 829 Salisbury House, Finsbury Square / London
The Times / New Printing House Square, Grays Inn Road / London

National Sunday Newspapers with Financial Coverage

The Observer / 160 Queen Victoria Street / London
Sunday Telegraph / Bracken House, Queen Victoria Street / London
The Sunday Times / New Printing House Square, Grays Inn Road /
    London

4. Switzerland

Cuckoo clocks, watches, perforated cheese, and innkeeping may once have been Switzerland's main claim to international business fame. No longer. Money management and international banking have completely overshadowed, and to some extent even choked, other sectors of the Swiss economy. The country's mounting attraction as a money haven has driven the Swiss franc to heights that have priced Swiss goods out of some export markets and reduced the occupancy rates of Swiss resort hotels. Lack of space and labor have put limits on domestic growth of Swiss industry. In 1975, most export industries and the construction trade were in a deep recession. Yet, the lines to deposit money in Switzerland or to come and live there remained as long as ever.

Freedom Tradition

Switzerland's role as a financial and retirement haven is based on its long tradition of fiercely defended freedom and democracy. The first three cantons (comparable in constitutional rights to the States of the Union) formed a defense alliance against the autocratic and arbitrary

Note: 1 SFr. = $0.40

rule of the Hapsburg Empire in 1291. (The Wilhelm Tell legend has its origin in that time.) In the course of the centuries, 19 other cantons joined the original three, including French- and Italian-speaking areas. Switzerland received its status of neutrality after the Napoleonic Wars during which it had been occupied by both sides. The neutrality was preserved in both World Wars. The fact that every adult Swiss male carried arms and every Swiss mountain was spiked with fortifications and modern weaponry probably helped during World War II.

Democracy is practiced to such an extent that most matters affecting the pocketbook, life style, and principles of the citizens are decided by plebiscite rather than by elected officials.

Nest Egg Haven

Neutrality, bank secrecy, stable government, and the rule of law have made Switzerland, since the 1800s, the haven for the nest eggs of the rich, and often their retirement haven or second home as well. Until World War II, these rich were only a happy few, and Switzerland could cope with their number and their money. While the Swiss did not make it easy for foreigners to reside in their country and become citizens, anyone with enough money, perseverance, and a clean past could usually settle there.

After World War II, the situation changed radically. Switzerland had again proven that its neutrality worked. It emerged as one of the few countries where savings had been preserved without serious devaluation. As Europe recovered from the devastations of the war and became prosperous again, and as other nations came into money, notably those that had oil or other treasures in the ground, the happy few taking their nest eggs to Switzerland became a stampeding crowd. The influx swelled to a veritable flood late in the 1960s, when the dollar became increasingly unstable. Bank deposits of the leading Swiss banks trebled from 1967 to 1974.

The influx of money and people created an industrial and construction boom in Switzerland. In addition to retirement and second homes for foreigners, the Swiss built second homes for themselves in the choicest scenery. There were not enough Swiss workers to cope with the increasing manufacturing and construction output, so the Swiss, like several other European countries, admitted foreign workers, many of them from nearby Italy, until foreigners·represented about 20% of the total population. These foreign workers needed places to live, too, further fanning the construction boom. Soon it became obvious that

Switzerland

Switzerland was running out of space, its beautiful streams and lakes were being polluted, its services and resources became strained, and the financial institutions were being drowned in money.

So the Swiss took drastic steps. They restricted further immigration of foreign workers in 1973, and the number actually decreased in the recession of 1975. It has become very difficult, even for the wealthiest, to settle in Switzerland. Non-residents can no longer freely buy real estate. Foreign companies operating in Switzerland find it extremely difficult, if not impossible, to get work permits for their nationals, even on a temporary basis. And it is just as difficult for them to hire qualified Swiss personnel. The Swiss have taken several steps to stem the tide of foreign bank deposits. They charge a negative interest rate (40% per annum in 1976) on Swiss franc deposits by non-residents. They have limited the importation of foreign bank notes (more a political than a practical move, since Swiss bank notes can be bought freely in several foreign financial markets). And they are trying to operate a gentleman's agreement with major multinational companies to develop an orderly flow of corporate funds into and out of Switzerland without playing havoc with the exchange rates. Temporary restrictions on the purchase of Swiss stocks and fixed-income securities by non-residents, however, were no longer in force in 1976, and as always, foreign investors of any type and size who wanted their portfolios managed in Switzerland were welcomed by the banks.

How to Choose a Swiss Money Manager

There are no official figures on the total securities assets under management in Switzerland. Estimates in 1976 ranged from $120 to $200 billion. If one deducts the official Swiss market capitalization of about $20 billion in 1976 and domestic Swiss bond capitalization of about $30 billion, one is left with an impressive amount in foreign securities. In 1976, many of the Swiss banks had around 50% of their portfolios in United States securities.

With such a large amount in foreign securities under control, Switzerland obviously ranks among the leaders in international portfolio management. It also explains the fact that Switzerland has by far the largest number of banks per capita of any country in the world (about one for each 1200 of the 6 million Swiss residents, or about 5000 banks if one counts each branch office). However, it must be remembered that, traditionally, Switzerland catered to the private foreign customer. Much of the money was in flight from political instability, inflation, or the tax collector. Many foreign depositors were quite satisfied when their capital was preserved in Swiss francs under Swiss bank secrecy with a minimum of "performance" or accumulating interest. Moreover, most of the Swiss themselves are savers rather than investors, and with the strong Swiss currency throughout the ages, there was never much incentive for them to invest in foreign securities. Thus, anyone shopping for international portfolio management in Switzerland will find that he can limit his search to a relatively small number of banks and a handful of portfolio management companies independent of banks. There are perhaps no more than 20 institutions that have formal investment organizations, with original research in depth, portfolio managers with clearly defined responsibilities, and investment and review committees. All others accepting money management rely on second-hand information. Some of the leading banks have only recently established separate departments for institutional investors.

In spite of its small size, Switzerland has clearly defined regional differences in investment tradition. Zurich is the largest investment center, with two of the Big Three banks headquartered there and the most active stock exchange. It has traditionally catered to the North European countries, and the investment policy of Zurich banks has been on the conservative side. Basel, headquarters for the third of the Big Three banks, also has a northerly orientation. It was instrumental in financing much of the industrial growth of Switzerland, notably that of the chemical companies. Geneva, with its satellite Lausanne, owes much of its banking role to the large French fortunes that have been managed there since before the French Revolution. Because of linguistic and temperamental affinities, many of the South American and Middle Eastern investors have also come to Geneva (although the new Arab oil money seems to stay short-term with the Big Three banks). Geneva has a concentration of foreign banks and brokers because of simpler cantonal regulations than Zurich. Investment policy of the Geneva banks has reportedly been more aggressive and internationally oriented than that of the German Swiss banks. Lugano has recently gained importance as a depositary and investment center for Italian flight money. In addition, it serves many Germans who have selected the Tessin canton for retirement because it offers all that Italy has to offer without an Italian government. However, Lugano banks rely on their head offices or outside sources for investment information and policy.

An investor shopping for money management has the choice of three distinct types of banks: the large Swiss commercial banks, the Swiss merchant banks, and foreign banks established under Swiss banking law. Competition for business is keen, and when it comes to describing the available investment services, Swiss banks apply none of the Swiss bank secrecy, except perhaps for performance records. There is, of course, some indication of performance for banks that also manage investment trusts. But this would have only limited application since the investment objectives and availability and disposition of funds may vary greatly among the infinite number of different private and institutional portfolios. A good procedure for the selection of a Swiss bank for portfolio management purposes is to question a number of authorities who are not themselves involved in the business of money management — other investors, commercial banks, or brokers. One shopper who had been given the names of three private banks comparable in reputation decided to apply his own criterion. He visited each one unannounced to see how long it would take to meet a responsible partner. It took two hours in one bank, half an hour in the second, and two minutes in the third. He picked the third.

Swiss banks normally do not charge a management fee. Their income comes from commissions and custodial fees. These may be on the high side when compared to some other countries.

Commercial Banks

It is estimated that about one-half of the total assets managed in Switzerland are in the hands of the Big Three: *Schweizerische Bankgesellschaft* (*Union Bank of Switzerland*) and *Schweizerische Kreditanstalt* (*Swiss Credit Bank*) in Zurich; and *Schweizerischer Bankverein* (*Swiss Bank Corporation*) headquartered in Basel, with strong investment management representation in Zurich. In terms of total assets, *Union Bank* and *Swiss Bank Corporation* are about equal in size; *Swiss Credit Bank* is somewhat smaller. As in several other European countries, the Big Three are all things to all men — they are deposit banks for retail and commercial customers, they provide commercial and industrial loans, they are lead underwriters for both domestic and international issues; they are the main dealers in foreign exchange and gold bullion; they are members of the stock exchanges and are the largest traders; and they are investment advisors, portfolio managers, and custodians. They manage investment funds and sell the shares through their branch office systems. All three have investment subsidiaries in New York through which they place part of their United States brokerage business and participate in underwritings. The *Union Bank* shares this subsidiary (*UBS-DB*) with the Frankfurt-based *Deutsche Bank*. *Swiss Credit Bank*, represented in New York by *SoGen Swiss International*, has a financial interest in *White, Weld*. The two operate a joint underwriting subsidiary, *Crédit Suisse, White Weld*. *Basel Securities* is the New York subsidiary of *Swiss Bank Corporation*. All three banks are represented throughout the world with branches or representative offices.

Also counted among the big commercial banks, but considerably smaller than the Big Three in terms of total assets, are *Schweizerische Volksbank* in Bern and *Bank Leu* in Zurich. *Schweizerische Volksbank*, founded as a retail bank for the small depositor, has become a major manager of investment funds. *Bank Leu* is a member of an affiliation of five European banks cooperating in investment research and management.

Private Banks

With their origins in the financing of international trade, the private banks in Switzerland have become a major factor in international portfolio management and investment banking.

One of the largest Swiss private banks, *Julius Bär* in Zurich, incorporated at the end of 1974 without changing its nature as a leading manager of private fortunes and institutional funds. Through its subsidiaries, *Baer Securities* in New York and *Julius Baer International* in London, it participates in major United States and international underwritings. Three other Zurich private banks strongly involved in money management are *Guyerzeller Zurmont Bank* (owned by *Samuel Montagu & Co.* of London), *J. Vontobel & Co.*, and *Rahn & Bodmer*.

Geneva has a concentration of private banks. The four largest today (in alphabetical order rather than in the order of the unknown size of assets which they manage) are: *Ferrier Lullin & Cie., Hentsch & Cie., Lombard, Odier & Cie.*, and *Pictet & Cie. Ferrier Lullin*, founded in 1795, has the distinction of being the oldest of the four. *Hentsch* has built up a reputation for special expertise in United States securities and investment fund management. *Lombard, Odier* is the most prolific publisher of excellent investment reports and studies. *Pictet* prides itself on the personal involvement of its partners in all accounts. All operate research departments drawing on world-wide information sources. *Lombard, Odier* and *Pictet* have established separate departments for institutional portfolios and pension fund management. Together with three other Geneva banks — *Bordier & Cie., Darier & Cie.*, and *De L'Harpe, Leclerc & Cie.* — they formed the *Groupement des Banquiers Privées Génèvois* as an underwriting syndicate and to sponsor listings on the Geneva exchange.

Switzerland

Basel also has a number of respected private banks specializing in portfolio management, including *Dreyfus Söhne & Cie., E. Gutzwiller & Cie., LaRoche & Co.,* and *A. Sarasin & Cie.*

Foreign Banks

Many foreign banks have established Swiss subsidiaries in order not to lose their own customers who want investment and other financial services in Switzerland. The oldest foreign bank in the country is the *Banque de Paris et des Pays-Bas,* which established an office in Geneva in 1872. Two other French banks of long standing in Switzerland are *Crédit Lyonnais* and *Société Générale Alsacienne de Banque. First National City Bank,* now *Citibank,* was the first of the American banks to establish a firm foothold in Switzerland. It provides international portfolio management from its Geneva office. Many others followed, including *Bank of America, Morgan Guaranty Trust Company,* and *Chase Manhattan. Dow Banking Corporation,* established in 1965 in Zurich by *Dow Chemical,* is one of several banks in Switzerland created by foreign industrial interests to finance international operations and expansion. Italians find the services of several of their own banks in Switzerland, including the *Banca di Roma per la Svizzera, Lavoro Bank,* and *Banca del Gottardo.*

Important to the Swiss financial system, but involved in securities investments only to a limited extent, are the Swiss cantonal banks, the savings banks, and the loan associations.

Investment Management Companies

Investment management companies for private and institutional accounts are rare in Switzerland, and a few smaller ones cater primarily to individuals. They charge a management-fee in addition to the broker commission and custodian fee. Of institutional stature is *Capital International* in Geneva, owned jointly by *The Capital Group* of Los Angeles and an affiliate of *The Chase Manhattan Bank.* It can draw on the world-wide original research of *Capital International Perspective. Rhoninter* is the Swiss portfolio management arm of four foreign banks cooperating in international investment research and management: the French *Crédit Lyonnais,* the German *Commerzbank,* the Italian *Banca di Roma,* and the Spanish *Banco Hispano Americano.* It uses the *Iris Institutional Research* services established in Geneva by these four banks.

International Investing

Investment Funds

At the end of 1975, there were 131 open-end investment funds in Switzerland with total assets of about $5.6 billion. Of these, 37 were real-estate investment funds, and 11 were in liquidation. In addition, 54 foreign securities investment funds were admitted for distribution in Switzerland.

The most widely sold funds are those managed by the investment fund subsidiaries of the Big Three banks, as well as those sold by *Schweizerische Volksbank, Handelsbank in Zürich, Julius Bär,* and *Hentsch.* By far the largest fund management company is *Intrag* of Zurich, a subsidiary of *Union Bank of Switzerland,* with assets of over $1.2 billion. *Swiss Credit Bank* and *Swiss Bank Corporation,* which formerly operated a fund management company jointly, have separated the management and sale of their securities funds. All domestic and foreign funds are sold through banks and their branch offices directly to the public at per-share net asset value quoted on the stock exchanges. By far the largest funds are fixed-income funds — *Bond Invest* (international bonds, managed by *Intrag* with SFr. 2.4 billion [$960 million] in assets at the end of 1975), *Crédit Suisse Fonds-Bonds* (with SFr. 1.3 billion [$520 million] in assets), and *Universal Bond Selection* (sold by *Swiss Bank Corporation,* with SFr. 1.1 billion [$440 million] in assets). *AMCA,* managed by *Intrag,* is the largest fund for American and Canadian securities, with assets of SFr. 300 million ($120 million) at the end of 1975.

A complete list of Swiss and foreign funds sold in Switzerland is published at the end of each year by *Eidgenössische Bankenkommission, Kammer für Anlagefonds* in Bern. The list includes the address and sponsoring bank of each fund management company, total asset value of each fund, and the nature of the portfolios.

In addition, Switzerland has a number of large investment and holding companies, organized under the Swiss banking law rather than the investment fund law. The leading ones, with world-wide portfolios and direct investments, are in the utility field — *Electro-Watt, Indelec,* and *Motor-Columbus.* Their shares are actively traded on the Swiss stock exchanges.

Other Institutional Investors

Insurance companies and pension funds are a major factor on the Swiss investment scene, but their portfolios are heavily weighted in favor of fixed-income securities, mortgages, and real estate investments. Life insurance companies are limited by law in the percentage of their assets that can be invested in equity. Even though this limit has been raised from 5% to 8%, in practice the average holding in equity of life insurance portfolios has remained as low as 1.5%. Casualty insurance companies and reinsurance companies are less restricted and invest much more heavily in equity, including foreign stocks — notably those doing a great amount of international business. The two largest investors in foreign securities are *Swiss Reinsurance Company* and *Zurich Insurance Company*. Both have investment affiliates in the United States and highly professional investment research and investment management organizations.

The pension fund business in Switzerland received a boost through a law approved by plebiscite in 1972, establishing compulsory private group insurance to provide a "reasonable standard of living" for retirees. Formerly such group insurance was voluntary, over and above a compulsory national insurance scheme providing old age and survivor's insurance, as well as disability insurance and workmen's compensation. Most of the pension funds are managed by the banks. Equity content of portfolios is very small. Pension fund administration in Switzerland is complicated by the fact that regulations may vary among the 22 different cantons. An excellent study of Swiss pension schemes has been published by *Lombard, Odier*.

Investing in Switzerland

Through the limits on the size of its labor force, the Swiss have put a limit on the growth of their domestic industry. Exports have also suffered because of the strength of the Swiss franc. Thus, growth must come primarily from the banks and other service industries and the industrial companies that make direct foreign investments through acquisitions and plant construction. However, foreign earnings are generally consolidated in a Swiss franc balance sheet. With the Swiss franc gaining in relation to most foreign currencies, it is difficult for most multinational Swiss companies to show a continuing growth record in terms of Swiss francs. Nevertheless, a number of European investors in 1975 and 1976 invested in Swiss equity and bond issues as a currency hedge as much as for growth and income.

Foremost among the international money earners are the Swiss banks, notably the Big Three — *Union Bank of Switzerland, Swiss Bank Corporation,* and *Swiss Credit Bank* — which rank in the top five Swiss companies in terms of market capitalization. All three have been increasing their total capitalization through new stock and convertible issues.

Also in the service industry category are the three largest insurance companies — *Swiss Reinsurance, Zurich Insurance,* and *Winterthur.*

First in terms of market capitalization and the largest industrial corporation in the country is *Nestlé.* Through the acquisition of *Libby, Stauffer, Crosse & Blackwell,* and other medium-sized food companies throughout the world, it has become one of the largest multinational food companies.

Hoffmann-La Roche, with more than SFr. 5 billion ($2 billion) in world-wide sales, is the largest pharmaceutical company in the world. *Ciba-Geigy,* a chemical producer, with 1975 sales of SFr. 9 billion ($3.6 billion), is the second largest industrial company in Switzerland and one of the largest multinational companies in the world. Less than 5% of its sales are made in Switzerland. *Sandoz,* with about SFr. 4 billion ($1.6 billion) in 1975 sales, is the third largest chemical producer in Switzerland, with a slightly higher percentage of Swiss sales than *Ciba-Geigy.*

An exceedingly efficient operation, heavily dependent upon foreign income and known to many travellers, is *Swissair.* In contrast to most other international airlines, and in spite of the recession, higher oil prices, the rising Swiss franc, and chaotic pricing conditions on the transatlantic market, *Swissair* has continued to make money every year.

For believers in the future of electrical equipment manufacturing as a result of the high oil prices, *Brown Boveri,* with 1975 sales of over SFr. 7.7 billion ($3 billion) is an interesting consideration. About 22% of its sales are within Switzerland, making it less vulnerable than other Swiss multinationals to foreign currency weaknesses.

Sulzer, with 1975 sales of SFr. 3.3 billion ($1.32 billion), derives some two-thirds of its income from exports. It is one of the world's largest manufacturers of diesel engines and also makes textile machinery, heating and air conditioning equipment, and a range of other machinery.

Aluminium Suisse is the world's sixth largest aluminum producer and it controls *Conalco* in the United States. It had a loss in 1975.

Types of Shares

In Switzerland, three types of shares are traded and it is important to know the difference: *Inhaberaktie* — bearer share; *Namensaktie* — registered share; and *Partizipationsschein* — participation certificate. Few companies have issued all three, but many have issued at least two.

Switzerland

Bearer shares show no name. They are as good as cash. They carry dividend coupons which must be detached when due (usually once a year) to collect the dividend. The shares can be voted and the owner can take advantage of any rights offering if he claims his rights.

Registered shares are registered in the owner's name, and the dividends are usually paid directly to the owner or his custodian bank. Most companies restrict the sale of registered shares to residents to prevent control from passing into foreign hands. Swiss nationals and bona fide Swiss residents usually can buy most registered shares and vote them.

To further limit outside control, some companies have also issued participation certificates, which have no voting rights, but usually carry all other benefits of the other types of shares, including dividends and rights offerings.

With a company that has issued two or three types of shares, dividend rates may be the same for all, or they may differ with each type. Where the dividend rate is the same, the bearer certificate usually sells at a premium, often a substantial one. Thus, when the *Ciba-Geigy* registered share sold at SFr. 600 in 1976, the bearer share was selling at SFr. 1500. Both paid dividends of SFr. 22 per share. The differential reflects the anonymity value and cash nature of the bearer share. The yield, on the other hand, is better on registered shares. Increasing premiums for bearer shares often reflect purchases by foreign investors since they can buy only bearer or non-voting shares.

The division of the equity of many Swiss companies into two or three different types of shares decreases the liquidity of many Swiss issues. There are only about 15 issues considered liquid enough for sizable institutional holdings.

Stock Trading

Switzerland has seven stock exchanges. By far the largest is Zurich, followed by Geneva and Basel. Regional exchanges are in Bern, Lausanne, Neuchâtel, and St. Gall, trading mostly local issues. Zurich, Geneva, and Basel, for all practical purposes, function as a single exchange since execution is made wherever terms are most favorable.

Total market capitalization is about $20 billion, but this does not include *Hoffmann-La Roche*, with 70,400 voting and participating shares (traded over-the-counter, in May 1976, at about SFr. 100,000 per share). *Hoffmann-La Roche* is also excluded from trading volume figures. Moreover, trading volume is estimated only for the Zurich exchange, about SFr. 84 billion ($33.6 billion) in 1975 without separation for stocks and bonds. The latter account for the largest percentage of the trades. A good deal of trading is carried on outside the exchanges over the telephone among the banks that are members of the exchange, as well as among non-member banks and brokerage houses that have been licensed to deal in securities. Licenses for banking and brokerage businesses are issued by cantonal authorities and are valid only in the canton in which they are issued.

All trading on the Swiss exchanges is in the hands of the member banks, but licensed non-member banks and brokers can deal outside the exchange over-the-counter. Membership on the three leading exchanges is somewhat exclusive. In addition to the Big Three banks, only a limited number of, other banks are members of the Zurich exchange. Total membership in 1976 was 25, including one foreign bank, *Société Générale Alsacienne de Banque*.

Of the more than 1500 securities listed on the three leading exchanges in 1976, about 210 were Swiss shares and about 140 were foreign securities. The balance were fixed-income securities. Switzerland offers a wide variety of fixed-income securities, including bonds of the federal government, cantons, communes, electric utilities, corporations, and banks. The new issue market was particularly active in 1975, when a total of SFr. 5.8 billion ($2.32 billion) was sold. Interest rates for federal bonds had come down to about 5½%, while borrowers with lower ratings paid up to 1¼% more. These low rates reflect the low inflation rate in Switzerland (slightly over 2% in 1975 and 1976) and the strength of the Swiss franc.

Switzerland, as most other European countries, has a central agency for the transfer of stock, called *Schweizerische Effekten Giro* (*SEGA*), which makes it possible to register change of share ownership without physical exchange of stock certificates. *SEGA* cooperates with *SICOVAM* in France and the *Kassenverein* in Germany, its equivalents in those countries, in the international transfer of ownership on the basis of bookkeeping records.

A non-resident investor is well advised not to take physical possession of a Swiss stock certificate but leave it in the custody of the Swiss bank through which he deals. There are a number of good reasons: ownership is more promptly established through bookkeeping record rather than physical possession of the certificates, and it is safer; the bank will maintain the confidential nature of the account; and the bank will collect the dividends and take care of rights offerings or other actions connected with the stock ownership.

94

Switzerland

Listing on Swiss Stock Exchanges

New listings of Swiss issues are relatively rare on Swiss exchanges, partly because of a lack of suitable candidates, and possibly because of a threatened "wealth tax" which would tax the market capitalization of a publicly-held company. A notable exception was *Oerlikon-Bührle*, with a 1975 sales volume of SFr. 2 billion ($800 million), which listed both registered and bearer shares in December 1973. As a leading arms manufacturer, also producing machinery and textiles, the company may have found it an advantage from a public relations point of view to be publicly rather than privately owned. Other new listing candidates in 1976 were *Maag-Zahnräder und Maschinen*, a gear and machinery manufacturer, and the famous chocolate producer *Lindt & Sprüngli*.

Foreign listings were far more prevalent in the 1970s. In mid-1976, the Zurich exchange traded 140 listed foreign stocks, of which 70 were United States securities. New listings in 1976 included *Norton Simon, Owens-Illinois, Deutsche Bank, Dresdner Bank, Algemene Bank Nederland, Amsterdam-Rotterdam Bank,* and *United Technologies.*

Swiss banks encourage the listing of foreign stocks in which they have an interest to save commission rates on the foreign exchanges. Trading costs are generally lower on the Swiss exchanges than on most foreign exchanges. Prerequisites for listing on a Swiss exchange are that the stock be widely held by Swiss institutions, that it be traded actively, and that unhampered arbitrage be possible between the Swiss exchanges and the home exchange of the stock. While the research departments of the Swiss banks will not put out a stock recommendation on the basis of whether or not a foreign stock is listed on a Swiss exchange, listing no doubt increases investor interest in Switzerland, and with other things being equal, Swiss investors are likely to give preference to a listed stock over an unlisted stock. Listing in Switzerland may also facilitate financing in the Eurobond market since a great portion of Eurobond issues are placed in Switzerland. If a foreign company finds that not enough shares of its stock are in Swiss hands, bank sponsorship and an active investor relations program prior to listing is helpful.

Listing on the Zurich exchange is always sponsored by all of the Big Three, with one of them acting as the lead bank. In Geneva, sponsorship is by the *Groupement des Banquiers Privées Génèvois*, the affiliation of the seven leading private banks in the city. Total listing costs — including sponsor's fee, preparation of documents, advertising, and publicity — may range from $50,000 to $75,000.

International Investing

Sources and Channels of Information

All major Swiss commercial and private banks provide investment information, generally with a world-wide viewpoint rather than strictly focused on Swiss securities.

Particularly useful for Swiss securities are *Schweizer Aktienführer* (published by *Union Bank of Switzerland*) and *Kleines Handbuch der Schweizer Aktien* (published by *Swiss Bank Corporation*). *Lombard, Odier* has published, in English, *Switzerland: The Economic and Stock Market Scene*, with a selection of Swiss issues. An independent guide to Swiss securities, without investment recommendations, is *Handbuch der Schweizerischen Anlagewerte* (*Guide des Valeurs Suisses de Placement*) published by *Editions Cosmos*. A number of specialized Swiss financial publications report in detail about Swiss markets and companies, leading among them are *Finanz und Wirtschaft, Finanz-Revue, AGÉFI*, and *Schweizerische Handelszeitung*. The leading newspapers in Zurich, Basel, and Geneva also provide good financial coverage.

Within the span of a few years, Swiss companies have gone from almost complete secrecy in financial disclosure to reports that are more comprehensive than those required by the SEC. The Swiss Association of Security Analysts has done an outstanding job of promoting better disclosure, and it establishes annual ratings of corporate investor information. Top marks in 1976 were given to *Magazine zum Globus*, a department store and real estate company, *Swissair*, and *Landis & Gyr*, an electrical and electronics manufacturer and a pioneer in good disclosure practices. Swiss security analysts now have easy access to Swiss corporate management and they also conduct field trips to Swiss plants and corporate headquarters, including trips for foreign analysts. Private banks have also sponsored visits of foreign institutional investors to Swiss companies, notably *Pictet*. The analysts society regularly invites executives to address its members, including some executives of foreign companies listed on Swiss exchanges. Research on foreign securities is generally organized by geographical region, with strong reliance on information provided by foreign brokers, research services, and affiliated banks. This is supplemented at the larger commercial and private banks with visits by their own security analysts to foreign corporations. Most of the larger banks operate with investment committees and an approved list of stocks. Portfolio managers, especially at the private banks, often have some leeway in managing individual portfolios.

Visits of corporate executives with Swiss analysts and portfolio managers, as well as privately sponsored presentations to Swiss investment professionals, are welcome as long as they are made by the chief executive or top financial officer and the information provided is timely and factual. Some Swiss banks have complained about an overdose of visits during summer vacations and the skiing season and about presentations with more promotional than factual content. A canvass prior to a trip to Switzerland to establish interest in a personal visit or a presentation is usually advisable.

Most Swiss banks will request annual reports and other financial literature from companies in which they have an interest. However, if a major Swiss bank is not on the mailing list of a company interested in developing investor interest in Europe, it should be added. Where no specific name is available, it is adequate to address the mail to *Finanzanalyse* for German-Swiss banks and *Études Financières* for French-Swiss banks.

Two international research services located in Geneva provide valuable investor information on a world-wide basis. *Capital International Perspective* produces both a monthly and a quarterly publication, providing charts, financial figures, stock market performance, comparative market valuation figures, and other information on some 1700 companies in 33 industries, 18 stock markets, and gold shares. Quarterly company charts and statistics are organized world-wide by industry rather than country. Charts on the performance of individual stock markets are related to a world index developed by *Capital International*.

Iris Institutional Research and Investment Services sells for hard or soft dollars an investment advisory service that includes a weekly market review by Telex of the leading stock markets of the world, a monthly report on international investment policy, and individual company reports. This service is distributed through *E.F. Hutton* in America.

Instant television transmission from Swiss stock exchanges as well as world-wide instant stock quotation systems are well developed in Switzerland. Thanks to Telekurs or Reuters, a Swiss portfolio manager can get immediate quotations from New York, London, Paris, Milan, Amsterdam, Brussels, Tokyo, Sydney, and the Swiss stock exchanges, as well as quotes on Eurodollar bonds, European commodity prices, and United States bonds.

International Investing

Principal Stock Exchanges

Börsenkammer des Kantons Basel-Stadt / Freistrasse 3 / Basel
Chambre de la Bourse de Génève / 8 rue Petitot / Geneva
Effektenbörsenverein Zürich / Bleicherweg 5 / Zurich

Partial List of Swiss Banks Handling Investment Business

The Big Three
Schweizerische Bankgesellschaft / Bahnhofstrasse 45 / Zurich. Affiliate: *UBS-DB Corp.* / 40 Wall Street / New York, New York 10005
Schweizerische Kreditanstalt / Paradeplatz 8 / Zurich. Affiliate: *SoGen Swiss International Corp.* / 20 Broad Street / New York, New York 10005
Schweizerische Bankverein / Aeschenvorstadt 1 / Basel. Affiliate: *Basel Securities Corp.* / 120 Broadway / New York, New York 10005

Other Banks — Zurich
Bank für Handel und Effekten / Talacker 50
Bank Leu A.G. / Bahnhofstrasse 32
Bank of America / Börsenstrasse 16
Julius Bär & Co. / Bahnhofstrasse 36. Affiliate: *Baer Securities Corp.* / 67 Wall Street / New York, New York 10005
Chase Manhattan Bank (Schweiz) / Genferstrasse 24
Dow Banking Corporation / Limmatquai 4
Guyerzeller Zurmont Bank A.G. / Genferstrasse 8
Handelsbank in Zürich / Talstrasse 59
Morgan Guaranty Trust Co. / Stockerstrasse 38
Rahn & Bodmer / Talstrasse 15
Schweizerische Volksbank / Bundesgasse 26
Société Alsacienne de Banque / Bleicherweg 1
J. Vontobel & Co. / Bahnhofstrasse 3

Other Banks — Geneva
Banque de Paris et des Pays Bas / 6 rue de Hollande
Bordier & Cie / 16 rue de Hollande
Citibank / 16 Quai Général Guisan
Crédit Lyonnais / 2 place Bel-Air
Darier & Cie / 4 rue Saussure
De L'Harpe, Leclerc & Cie / 2 boulevard Théâtre
Ferrier Lullin & Cie / 15 rue Petitot
Hentsch & Cie / 15 rue de la Corraterie
Lombard, Odier & Cie / 11 rue de la Corraterie
Pictet & Cie / 29 boulevard Georges-Favon

Switzerland

Other Banks — Basel
Dreyfus Söhne & Cie A.G. / Aeschenvorstadt 16
E. Gutzwiller & Cie / Kaufhausgasse 7
La Roche & Co. / Rittergasse 25
A. Sarasin & Cie / Freie Strasse 107

Other Banks — Lugano
Banca del Gottardo / via Canova 8
Banca della Svizzera Italiana / via Magatti 2
Banca di Roma per la Svizzera / Piazetta San Carlo

Other Banks — St. Gall
Wegelin & Co. / Bohl 17

Leading Swiss Fund Management Companies

A.G. für Fondsverwaltung / Poststrasse 9 / Zug sponsored by *Handelsbank in Zürich*
Julius Bär Fondsleitung A.G. / St. Peterstrasse 10 / Zurich sponsored *Julius Bär & Co.*
Hentsch & Cie / rue de la Corraterie 15 / Geneva sponsored by *Hentsch & Cie*
Ifag Fondsleitung A.G. / Bundesplatz 8 / Bern sponsored by Swiss cantonal banks
Interfonds / Aeschenvorstadt 1 / Basel sponsored by *Schweizerische Bankverein*
Intrag S.G. / Bahnhofstrasse 45 / Zurich sponsored by *Schweizerische Bankgesellschaft*
Kafag A.G. / Bahnhofstrasse 53 / Zurich sponsored by *Schweizerische Volksbank*
Schweizerische Kreditanstalt Fonds / Paradeplatz 8 / Zurich sponsored by *Schweizerische Kreditanstalt*
Each management company manages several funds. A complete list of Swiss-based funds, as well as of foreign funds admitted for sale in Switzerland, is available from *Eidgenössische Bankenkomission, Kammer für Anlagefonds,* Bern

American Brokers in Switzerland

Basel
Dominick & Dominick Inc. / Aeschengraben 10
Shearson Hayden Stone Inc. / St. Jakobstrasse 3

99

Coppet
Baird, Patrick & Co., Inc. / En Savoyan, 1296

Geneva
Bache Halsey Stuart Inc. / 40 rue du Rhône
Baird, Patrick & Co., Inc. / 18 avenue Dumas
Baker, Weeks & Co., Inc. / 7 rue Versonnex
Bear, Stearns & Co. / 42 rue du Rhône
Becker Securities Corporation / 16 avenue Eugène-Pittard
Blyth Eastman Dillon & Co., Inc. / 3 place St. Gervais
Drexel Burnham Lambert / P.O. Box 290
F. Eberstadt & Co., Inc. / 24 avenue de Champel
Harris, Upham & Co. Inc. / 14 rue de la Corraterie
Herzfeld & Stern / 14 avenue Ernest Hentsch
Hornblower & Weeks-Hemphill, Noyes Inc. / 15 rue du Jeu de L'Arc
E.F. Hutton & Co. Inc. / 9 place du Bourg-de-Four
Kidder, Peabody & Co. Inc. / 11 Cours de Rive
Merrill Lynch, Pierce, Fenner & Smith Inc. / 65 rue du Rhône, 31 rue
   du Rhône, 62 rue du Rhône
Moseley, Hallgarten & Estabrook, Inc. / 5 rue Petitot
Paine, Webber, Jackson & Curtis Inc. / P.O. Box 89, 11211 Geneva 3
C.B. Richard, Ellis & Co. / 15 rue Pierre Fatio
L.F. Rothschild & Co. / 21 rue du Rhône
Shearson Hayden Stone Inc. / P.O. Box 1211
Smith, Barney & Co. Inc. / 6-8 rue de Candolle
Stralem & Co. Inc. / 6 avenue de Frontenex
White, Weld & Co. Inc. / 1 quai du Mont-Blanc, P.O. Box 899
Dean Witter & Co., Inc. / 34 avenue de Frontenex

Lausanne
Dominick & Dominick Inc. / 7 rue St. Martin
Droulia & Co. / 2 place St. François
Faulkner, Dawkins & Sullivan, Inc. / 10 place de la Gare
Loeb, Rhoades & Co. / Galeries Street, François A.
James H. Oliphant & Co. Inc. / 10 place de la Gare
Reynolds Securities Inc. / 10 place de la Gare
Thomson & McKinnon Auchincloss Kohlmeyer Inc. / 5 rue Centrale
Tucker, Anthony & R.L. Day, Inc. / 11 Chemin du Frene

Lugano
Bache Halsey Stuart Inc. / Piazza Monte Ceneri 9
E.F. Hutton & Co. Inc. / Via S. Balestra 9
Loeb, Rhoades & Co. / Via Besso 31, 6900 Lugano-Besso
Merrill Lynch, Pierce, Fenner & Smith Inc. / Via Balestra 27
Paine, Webber, Jackson & Curtis Inc. / Via Pioda 8

Switzerland

Reynolds Securities Inc. / Via Pretorio 20
Thomson & McKinnon Auchincloss Kohlmeyer Inc. / Via Cantonale 16

Zurich
Amivest Corp. / Zelweg 48
Bache Halsey Stuart Inc. / Bahnhofstrasse 106
D.H. Blair & Co., Inc. / Dornenstrasse 27
Brown Brothers Harriman & Co. / Stockerstrasse 38
First Boston Corporation / Stockerstrasse 38
Goldman, Sachs & Co. / Limmatquai 4
Harris, Upham & Co. Inc. / Ourlindenstrasse 59
E.F. Hutton & Co. Inc. / Kuttelgasse 4
Merrill Lynch, Pierce, Fenner & Smith Inc. / Muehlenbachstrasse 25
White, Weld & Co. Inc. / Schmelzbergstrasse 56

Partial List of Actively Traded Swiss Stocks

Aluminium Suisse (aluminum)
C.F. Bally (shoe manufacturing and retail shoe stores)
Bank Leu
Brown Boveri (electric and electronic equipment)
Ciba-Geigy (pharmaceuticals)
Electrowatt (electric utility and industrial holding company)
General Shopping (retail holding company)
Helvetia Schweizerische Feuerversicherungsgesellschaft (insurance)
Hoffmann-La Roche (pharmaceuticals)
Interfood (food and household products)
Jelmoli (retailing)
Landis & Gyr (electric and electronic equipment)
Lonza Elektrizitätswerke und Chemische Fabrik (chemicals)
Motor-Columbus (electric utility)
Nestlé (food and household products)
Oerlikon-Bührle (armaments, machinery)
Sandoz (pharmaceuticals)
Saurer (machinery and engineering)
Schweizerische Bankgesellschaft
Schweizerische Kreditanstalt (banking)
Schweizerische Rückversicherungsgesellschaft (insurance)
Schweizerische Volksbank
Schweizerischer Bankverein
Sulzer (machinery and engineering)
Swissair (airline)
Winterthur (insurance)
Zürich Versicherungsgesellschaft (insurance)
Zyma (pharmaceuticals)

International Investing

Sources of Information

Investment information in Switzerland comes almost exclusively from banks. All banks listed above provide investment information in greater or lesser detail, much of it in English. Particularly useful are *Schweizer Aktienführer*, published by *Schweizerische Bankgesellschaft*, and *Kleines Handbuch der Schweizer Aktien*, published by *Schweizerischer Bankverein*. An independent guide to Swiss securities is *Handbuch der Schweizerischen Anlagewerte (Guide des Valeurs Suisse de Placement)*, published by *Editions Cosmos, S.A.* / Aarbergergasse 46, Case postale 2637 / Bern. The classic book on Swiss banks is *The Banking System of Switzerland* by Hans J. Bär, published by *Schulthess Polygraphischer Verlag* of Zurich.

International Research Organizations

Capital International S.A. / 15 rue du Cendrier / Geneva
Iris Institutional Research and Investment Services / 5 rue des Alpes / Geneva

Leading Swiss Newspapers with Financial Coverage

Basler Nachrichten / Dufourstrasse 40 / Basel
Journal de Génève / 5-7 rue Général Dufour / Geneva
Neue Zürcher Zeitung / Falkenstrasse 11 / Zurich

Financial Publications

Agence Économique et Financière / Limmatquai 2 / Zurich and 3 rue de la Vigie / Lausanne
Finanz-Revue / Löwenstrasse 11 / Zurich
Finanz und Wirtschaft / Werdstrasse 11 / Zurich
Schweizerische Finanzzeitung / St. Alban Anlage 14 / Basel
Schweizerische Handelszeitung / Postfach 434 / Zurich

5. France

Many Americans trying to do business in France find the French exasperating — uncooperative, unbending in their ways, and unappreciative of American know-how. These negative feelings are often reciprocated. To many Frenchmen, Americans appear dull witted, insensitive to the true values of life, and singularly untalented to learn the only language worth speaking.

Several joint American-French ventures have been spectacular failures, notably *General Electric's* aborted liaison with *Machines Bull* and *Westinghouse's* costly involvement in the French elevator industry. Many other American companies have closed down their French operations or abandoned Paris as a European headquarters seat in favor of Brussels or London. Many American tourists complain about the high prices in Paris and the unloving way in which they are treated by the natives.

Yet, as with most antagonistic feelings, those between the Americans and the French may be based partly on poor communica-

Note: 1 FFr. = $0.20

tions and a lack of understanding. Frenchmen who have taken the trouble to overcome the language barrier have fared much better in the United States, witness *Schlumberger's* world-wide operations headquartered in New York, the purchase of *Certain-Teed Products Corporation* by *Saint-Gobain-Pont-à-Mousson* and of *Howmet Corporation* by *Péchiney-Ugine Kuhlmann,* and *Michelin's* new tire manufacturing plants in the Carolinas. The two largest French merchant banks bought major interests in American brokerage houses — *Compagnie Financière de Suez* into *Blyth Eastman Dillon* and *Paribas,* together with *S.G. Warburg* of London, into *A.G. Becker.* Of course, these French companies in the United States have been hamstrung far less by government bureaucracy than an American company encounters in France.

Nevertheless, to any traveler with even a minimum of fairmindedness, it becomes obvious that Paris, among the superstars of world cities — with New York, London, Rome, and Tokyo — is the only one that has rigidly upheld the quality of life while coping with the needs of industrial growth by constructing new subways, roadways, underground parking, office buildings, and satellite towns. Many Americans, as well as other foreigners, have found that for retirement purposes a small farm in France, preferably with a vineyard attached, is one of the best investments they have ever made. Apart from the overcrowded French Riviera and the industrial northeast, France has been able to preserve the beauty of its countryside better than any other industrial nation. Until 1976, when the shock waves of the Italian political situation spilled into France and inflation continued at a high rate, the French economy and the French franc were among the soundest in the world. Obviously, the French must have been doing something right.

Revival of the Stock Market

The French stock market also began to gain world stature in the 1970s. Traditionally, the French despised and distrusted their market, having been made cautious by regular financial scandals in the course of several centuries. Repeated spurts of inflation have induced many Frenchmen to hoard their savings in the form of gold.

Frenchmen never seem to sell gold. They may stop buying it for a time when the currency is firm, the inflation rate is low, and the political situation stable, but they are back in the gold market again when times look troubled.

Another distraction from the French stock market is the long-time

France

custom of many Frenchmen to invest through Swiss banks. It is estimated that there are about 400,000 French accounts in Switzerland with total assets of FFr. 300 billion ($60 billion).

Thus, it is all the more surprising that the French market has become quite active in the 1970s, with the total market capitalization of equity issues having increased from about FFr. 90 billion ($18 billion) in 1967 to about FFr. 163 billion ($32.6 billion) in 1975, even though the number of listed stocks decreased from about 1400 to about 740. Trading volume increased from about FFr. 30 billion ($6 billion) to FFr. 58 billion ($11.6 billion). In evaluating the total market capitalization it must be remembered that large sectors of French industry are nationalized utilities, railroads, air transport, major banks, insurance companies, and automobile manufacturers.

Much of the stimulation apparently came from foreign investors who seemed to have more confidence in the French market and economy than the Frenchmen themselves and who are buying and selling French securities on market cycles. The revitalization of the Paris Bourse is the result of a conscious effort by the French government to make Paris an international financial center. A special commission was appointed in the late 1960s — the Baumgartner Commission — which, in 1971, published a comprehensive report on what ailed the market, with recommendations for improvements. All restrictions against portfolio purchases of French securities by non-residents were lifted in 1971, except that foreign ownership of French companies is limited to 20%.

One of the more important steps forward has been the strengthening of the role of the official brokers — the only agents who can trade on the floor of the exchange. They have been allowed to merge to reduce their number and strengthen the remaining firms. They now can advertise and open branch offices to compete with the banks for the investment business of the public. They are organized in an association, *Compagnie des Agents de Change*, which has embarked on an active public relations campaign to educate the public on the operations of the stock market and investment procedures. Together with government bodies, the association has also started a program aimed at encouraging French companies to provide more meaningful information to shareholders and potential investors. French brokers do not buy for their own accounts, as the specialists in New York do. They merely establish a price for a traded stock and act as commission agents between buyers and sellers. In addition to Paris, there are six other stock exchanges in the country, in Lyon, Marseille, Lille, Nantes, Bordeaux, and Nancy. However, well over 90% of all transactions are executed in Paris.

105

International Investing

Cash and Forward Market

There are two types of markets on the Paris Bourse: "cash" and "forward." All officially admitted securities can be traded on the cash market, which requires immediate settlement. It is primarily used for purchases of odd lots of stocks and for the trading of most bonds, although larger equity blocks are also traded to some extent.

Only actively traded common stocks — 192 in 1976 — and the most actively traded government bond issues — *Rente Giscard* (formerly *Rente Pinay*) and *Caisse Nationale de l'Énergie* — are admitted to the forward market. *Rente Giscard*, which is indexed to the price of the Napoleon 20 franc gold piece, was by far the most popular issue with the French public, accounting for 10% to 20% of all forward transactions, but volume declined in 1976 with the declining price of gold. Napoleons are no longer struck and now sell at premiums of 100% or more above the bullion price.

Settlement of all transactions on the forward market takes place once a month. Forward market transactions can be margined, which means that the buyer puts up only a part of the total purchase price until he decides to take delivery of the shares. The percentage of the required margin, determined by the exchange, varies with the industry and the issue.

There are two types of forward trades: the "firm trade" under which the buyer commits himself to take delivery at a firm price and the "conditional trade."

The firm trade provides for three options: 1. the buyer pays the full price of the securities on the settlement day and takes delivery; 2. the deal is cancelled by a reverse trade in which the buyer sells the securities before the settlement day and collects the net profit from the operation or pays for the loss; and 3. the deal is extended to the next settlement day.

The conditional forward market is comparable to option trading in the United States. Two types of options are offered to the investor: 1. *option*, a put-or-call option which gives the buyer the right either to buy or sell a certain number of securities for the duration of the contract (up to nine months) at the last price paid on the forward market on the day the option was purchased; and 2. *prime*, which is a one-, two-, or three-month call. The buyer pays the price of the option only if he does not take delivery of the securities at the price which was agreed upon when the deal was made (a price substantially above the current price on the forward market).

106

France

Option trading is somewhat limited in France, but a few enterprising French investors were playing the Chicago option board in 1976.

French Common Stocks

Many French stocks have a thin float and this can lead to erratic price movements. The thin float, even with some large companies, may be the result of several factors: close family control, part ownership by the government, holding companies, banks, or interlocking ownership with other companies. Interlocking ownership is widespread throughout France and occurs even within the same industry.

For instance, *Peugeot*, the leading French automobile maker, owns 90% of *Citroën*. *Michelin* has a major holding in *Kléber-Colombes*, a smaller French tire maker. *Michelin* pioneered the steel-belted radial tire which is now used on practically all European cars and has made considerable inroads in the United States. To participate in the American business, *Michelin* has built plants in Canada and the United States. It is a closely-held family company whose tradition of limited communications with its shareholders is in stark contrast to the wealth of information which it imparts to tourists in its red and green guide books. Nevertheless, *Michelin B* (the publicly-traded holding company) is popular with investors and often is the most actively traded issue.

Another actively traded stock is that of *Carrefour*, the originator of the "hypermarket." A land of small shopkeepers, France bypassed the supermarket stage and went straight from the corner grocery to the hypermarket — an oversized supermarket combined under one roof with a giant Sears-Roebuck-type store that is set in the countryside at comfortable driving distance from several population centers. In spite of dire predictions of failure at its outset, *Carrefour* has established one of the most spectacular growth records of any stock in the world. Carrying its concept beyond the French border, *Carrefour* was seen in Brazil in 1976. Also ranking high on the active list with good performance records are *Moulinex*, a manufacturer of small electrical appliances; *L'Oréal*, a cosmetic firm second only to *Avon*; and *Air Liquide*, a producer of industrial gases which has established itself in the United States through *Liquid Air Corporation of America*, traded here over-the-counter. Dear to the hearts of both its consumers and stockholders has been *Moët-Hennessy*, producers of excellent champagne, cognac, and perfumes. In 1973, the company bought vineyards in California to make French California "champagne." Other companies with major stakes in the United States are *Saint-Gobain-Pont-à-Mousson*, a diversified glass maker,

107

about 20% owned by the leading French holding company, *Compagnie Financière de Suez; Péchiney-Ugine Kuhlmann*, a major producer of aluminum and other nonferrous metals and chemicals; and *Bic*, a maker of ballpoint pens, pencils, and cigarette lighters, which went public in 1972 (its American subsidiary is traded on the American Stock Exchange). Truly international in its earnings is the *Club Méditerranée*, which spices its vacation services with matchmaking opportunities.

Among the stocks high on the trading volume list in 1976 are the two largest French oil companies — *Société Nationale des Pétroles d'Aquitaine (SNPA)*, 51% government owned, and *Compagnie Française des Pétroles*, 35% government owned — and *Rhône-Poulenc*, a large producer of chemicals, synthetic fibers, pharmaceuticals, and photographic film (with its market price on the skids for several years).

Bank stocks, while not actively traded, nevertheless feature in many investment trust portfolios, including *Compagnie Bancaire, Crédit Commercial de France,* and *Crédit du Nord*, as well as finance holding companies such as *Financière de Paris et des Pays-Bas* and *Financière de Suez.*

The Paris Bourse, in contrast to other stock exchanges on the Continent, has attracted a number of new companies going public. In addition to *Bic*, new issues in the early 1970s include *Skis Rossignol* (skis), *Jacques Borel International* (tourism), *Maisons Phenix* (construction and real estate), *Legrand* (electrical equipment), and *SEB* (small appliances).

Fixed-Income Securities

Reforms of the stock exchange have also been beneficial to the French bond market. About 40% of the trading volume is in fixed-income securities. About 80% of the total outstanding quoted bonds are issues of the government or quasi-government organizations, such as the mail and telecommunications office, the government broadcasting corporation, utilities, toll roads, municipalities, overseas territories, credit institutions, and government-owned banks. Sometimes a number of smaller municipalities jointly sell a bond issue. In the private sector, only financially strong and well-known companies are successful in the bond market.

A number of convertible issues have also been sold. It is noteworthy that in 1976, in spite of a high inflation rate, long-term bonds, up to 15 years, could still be sold. This may be partly the result of the sweeteners that issuers often include in new issues to overcome the Frenchman's traditional reluctance to put his savings into the stock or bond market.

France

A popular sweetener in the past, for instance, but falling into disuse in the mid-1970s, were lottery bond issues. Among the bonds of each issue drawn yearly for redemption are a few big lottery winners, with the *grand prix* for a nominal FFr. 250 ($50) bond having been as high as FFr. 1 million ($200,000). Or a railroad bond holder, for example, could win a certain number of miles of free travel.

More frequently used now are indexed bonds (although, in 1976, this sweetener was no longer permitted for new issues in the private sector). The most famous among them was the *Rente Pinay*, indexed to the average price of a 20 franc gold piece, which was exchanged in 1973 for the *Rente Giscard*, officially called the *4½% 1973 Emprunt d'État*. The new issue has lost one of the most attractive features of the old one — dispensation from inheritance tax. Another government issue — the *7% 1973 Emprunt d'État* — has a complex index related to the European "currency basket" — the median combined par value of nine European currencies — with a back-up index of the bullion price of gold. One of the most popular issues is that of the *Caisse Nationale de l'Énergie*, which is indexed to the combined price average of gas and electricity as well as to the total revenues of the gas and electric utilities. This means that the investor has a protection against inflation as well as an opportunity to participate in economic growth.

Many of the older French bond issues sold at very low coupon rates in the 1950s and 1960s were traded in the mid-1970s at considerable discount. They are of particular interest to private investors since capital gains realized at maturity are tax free. Because of the complexities of the French bond market, and the illiquidity of some of the issues, the services of an experienced French bond trader and analyst are essential to trade in French bonds.

Listing of Foreign Securities

The revival of the French stock market has also stimulated the listing and trading of foreign securities. In 1976, 160 foreign issues were listed on the *Bourse de Paris*, including 37 United States stocks. In addition, a number of foreign securities are traded on the *hors côte* (over-the-counter) market, which is often the first step towards listing. Trading volume of foreign securities has been as high as 15% of the total trading volume. The five most active foreign stocks in 1975 were *Schlumberger, IBM, Norsk Hydro, Petrofina,* and *Royal Dutch Petroleum.*

For several foreign corporations, listing in Paris has increased the French investor's interest in their stocks. Thirteen foreign stocks were among the 100 most actively traded stocks in 1975. French insurance companies, even though modest investors in foreign securities, can invest only in securities listed on a French stock exchange. For companies with large operations in France, listing is a good public relations move. A listed company may find it easier to raise money in France or in the Eurobond market.

Listing is a somewhat complex procedure that takes about three months. All of the necessary formalities are handled by the sponsoring bank. Total costs, including bank fees, auditing, translating and printing of the prospectus, and obligatory advertising may range from $75,000 to $100,000. In addition, sponsoring banks usually insist on substantial advertising above and beyond the government's requirements. Sponsoring banks include the three nationalized banks — *Banque Nationale de Paris, Crédit Lyonnais,* and *Société Générale* — as well as *Banque de Paris et des Pays-Bas, Banque de l'Indochine et de Suez, Crédit Commercial de France,* and *Morgan Guaranty Trust Company of New York*, which has played an important role on the French investment scene for well over 100 years.

French investors buying foreign securities must leave their stock certificates under the control of an *intermédiaire agréé* (approved intermediary), which is usually a bank. The association of French brokers, *Compagnie des Agents de Change*, can also act as an *intermédiaire agréé.* In practice, stock certificates remain on deposit with the French central clearing agency, *SICOVAM*. Transfer of ownership is by bookkeeping entry on the basis of a *virement*, a check-like document given by the seller to the buyer. Even though most French securities are in the form of bearer certificates, many French investors, notably the institutions, also leave their certificates on deposit with *SICOVAM*.

Banks

Changes in the French banking laws in the 1960s have greatly strengthened the French banking system and produced a number of bank mergers, primarily between the *banques de dépôts*, the commercial retail banks, and the *banques d'affaires*, the merchant banks.

Practically all investment portfolios in France are managed or controlled by banks — private portfolios, institutional portfolios, investment funds, and employee benefit funds. The three largest banks are the nationalized ones — *Banque Nationale de Paris, Crédit Lyonnais,* and *Société Générale*. Their total assets represent about 50% of the French banking industry. They hold about 70% of all deposits with commercial banks. All three provide investment advisory service through their large branch systems, manage investment portfolios, and sell investment fund shares managed by subsidiaries. All three have an international network of affiliated banks and subsidiaries for pooling of research, portfolio management, underwriting, and execution of securities transactions.

Each has about $2 billion or more in assets under management, including investment funds, employee benefit funds, and private funds. Portfolios of *Crédit Lyonnais* seem to have more of an international orientation than those of the other nationalized banks, which are more than 80% invested in French securities.

Another 30% of the total assets of the French banking industry is controlled by the two large publicly-owned finance and holding companies — *Compagnie Financière de Paris et des Pays-Bas* and *Compagnie Financière de Suez*. The two main banking operations of the *Compagnie Financière de Paris et des Pays-Bas* are the merchant and investment bank *Banque de Paris et des Pays-Bas (Paribas)* and the commercial and deposit bank *Crédit du Nord. Paribas* is affiliated with *S.G. Warburg* of London, and together with *Warburg* it has bought an interest in a leading United States brokerage house, *A.G. Becker*, and formed a United States securities affiliate, *Warburg-Paribas-Becker. Paribas* has also been established in Geneva for over 100 years and it operates a banking subsidiary in Brussels.

Compagnie Financière de Suez organized itself after the nationalization of the Suez Canal, using the proceeds to enter the banking and underwriting business and assemble a wide-ranging investment portfolio, which in 1976 amounted to about FFr. 2 billion ($400 million), one-third of it in portfolio investments and two-thirds in direct investments. Its original banking subsidiary, *Banque de Suez et de l'Union des Mines*, merged in 1975 with the *Banque de l'Indochine* to form the *Banque de l'Indochine et de Suez. Crédit Industrial et Commercial* is a deposit bank subsidiary of *Suez*. In 1976, *Suez* bought a 20% interest in *Blyth Eastman Dillon* (of which *INA Corporation* of the United States owns 60%) to establish a firmer foothold in the United States. Through subsidiaries and affiliates, *Suez* has a far-flung banking and investment network throughout the world.

Paribas and *Banque de l'Indochine et de Suez* each manage investment portfolios of about $1 billion, of which perhaps 75% represent investment funds. The foreign securities content of their portfolios is higher than that of the nationalized banks. Both merchant banks are major participants in international underwriting syndicates.

Next in order of total assets, and also very active in private and institutional portfolio management, is *Crédit Commercial de France*. As a member of the *Inter-Alpha Group* — an affiliation of seven banks in as

111

many countries — *Crédit Commercial* stresses its international investment research and management expertise.

Even though a good deal smaller in capitalization than the larger banks, a number of other French merchant banks are important in international portfolio management and underwriting, including *Lazard Frères, Banque Rothschild, Banque Worms,* and *Banque de Neuflize, Schlumberger, Mallet.*

As of 1976, foreign institutional investors were using French managers mainly for portions of their portfolios to be invested in French securities, but there is no reason to assume that the international investment sophistication of the larger banks with their world-wide research operations is not on a level with those of comparable banks and money managers in other countries. Theoretically, a foreign investor could place his order for French securities directly with a French broker, but since execution ability can vary greatly among the many French brokers for the different types of securities, an intimate knowledge of the Paris exchange is essential and found among banks dealing daily on the *bourse.*

Investment Funds

France has had a long history of closed-end investment funds, which were the only funds permitted until 1964, when open-end mutual funds were authorized by the government. With the rapid rise in popularity of open-end funds and their active promotion by the selling banks, closed-end funds lost ground and, by 1976, only 12 remained. All of them were traded on the Paris exchange considerably below asset value.

Most of the open-end funds (*SICAVs* — *Sociétés d'Investissement à Capital Variable*) are managed by bank subsidiaries and sold through the branches of the deposit banks. Efforts to set up direct sales forces have not been very effective, with perhaps one or two exceptions, including the *Banque de l'Indochine.* Some *SICAVs* are sold by insurance companies in conjunction with life insurance.

At the end of 1975, there were 90 *SICAVs* with total assets of around FFr. 23 billion ($4.6 billion). About half of them were fixed-income funds, some of which include equity holdings. The common stock funds must also, by law, hold about 30% of their assets in bonds. As a result, French bonds constitute well over 50% of all *SICAV* holdings. Foreign securities range between 15% to 20% of all *SICAV* holdings, depending on the appeal of foreign stock markets.

Financial reports of *SICAV* performance records and composition of portfolios can be picked up at the various bank offices which sell them, but each bank, naturally, promotes only its own funds. An investor who wants a choice from among the full range of funds should consult a stock broker, or obtain the yearbook of the French investment companies association, *l'Association des Sociétés et Fonds Français d'Investissement.*

Other Institutional Investors

A special feature of the French market is profit sharing funds, established by law in 1967. Mainly managed by banks, they enjoy certain tax advantages. Contributions remain frozen for the first five years. These funds cannot invest in foreign securities, but may invest in *SICAVs* with foreign securities in their portfolios. The yearbook of the investment companies association contains a list of these funds and their managers. Regular pension funds are confined to French securities, usually bonds. Most of them are managed by banks.

Caisse de Dépôts et Consignations plays a dominant role on the French stock market as it administers investment portfolios of close to FFr. 200 billion ($40 billion). It acts as a central depository for the nation-wide savings banks network. It is a manager of public and private pension funds and mutual funds. And it acts as a finance institution for the French *départements* (political subdivisions), communities, labor unions, and a number of public institutions. Investments are primarily in French bonds.

Insurance companies are also major investors, but in the past, 50% of their portfolios had to be in government issues or government-guaranteed bond issues. Now this 50% may also include bonds of private industry, but the change has had little effect on the composition of portfolios. About 25% of the portfolios are in French common stock and less than 10% in foreign securities. Insurance companies can buy only securities listed on the Paris exchange.

Sources and Channels of Information

Many formerly close-mouthed French companies have in the last few years suddenly opened the floodgates of financial communications, with detailed, colorful annual reports, press releases, conferences, public relations campaigns, and meetings with security analysts. While most French companies formerly did not release their yearly figures until publication of the annual report in May or June, some companies now release their figures a few weeks after the end of the year, including *Peugeot* and *Saint-Gobain-Pont-à-Mousson*. Several companies have begun to translate their annual reports into English.

Two official bodies have established reference libraries where investors can get comprehensive information on all publicly-traded companies. One is the information center of the stock brokers association, *Centre de Documentation et d'Information de la Chambre Syndicale des Agents de Change*, which has information files on over 2000 French and foreign companies, and the other is the *Centre d'Information* of the *Commission des Opérations de Bourse*, a government watchdog operation, comparable to the SEC, which has complete information files on all listed French companies.

The most widely used investment information sources are the *fiches* (sheets on French companies) prepared regularly by *SEF* (*Société d'Éditions Économiques et Financières*). These can be bought individually at many French book stores. *SEF* also publishes weekly bulletins with company information and general stock market news.

SEF has been acquired by *DAFSA* (*Société de Documentation et d'Analyses Financières*), a securities research organization established by most of the leading banks. *DAFSA* publishes a great amount of investment information that is made available to the member banks as well as to outsiders on subscription. The material includes information sheets, comparable to *Standard & Poor's* cards, on more than 1000 French and foreign companies, as well as quarterly information on French mutual funds. It also provides detailed research reports on all leading French companies as well as on a number of foreign companies and it prepares studies on specific industries. Together with similar organizations in other European countries, it is developing a unified "European method" of security analysis that is aimed at making it possible for investors to compare performances of different companies in different countries.

Eurofinance, an independent organization, specializes in research reports in depth for portfolio investments and acquisitions searches. These reports are available to subscribers.

All major banks involved in portfolio management have large research departments, which are also available to the *SICAV* management companies. *Crédit Lyonnais*, for instance, employs about 60 security analysts who follow all main industries on a world-wide basis with regional specialists for major markets, such as the United States and Japan. *Crédit Commercial*, with about 12 analysts, uses the same approach. Others, such as the *Banque de l'Indochine et de Suez*, follow European stocks by industry and have regional specialists for the United States and Japan. *Paribas* has established its research department as an independent subsidiary, called *SAFE* (*Société des Analyses Financières et Économiques*), and it sells some of its reports to outsiders. *Banque Industrielle et Mobilière Privée* also sells its research.

The French society of financial analysts sponsors company meetings and general educational seminars, but foreign companies are relatively rare on its programs. Paris investment professionals seem less responsive than those in other countries to privately-sponsored company meetings. The senior people appear particularly disinterested. Because of Paris as a tourist attraction, there may have been an abuse of "business" visits with French investment professionals. Unsolicited financial mail seems to get less readership in Paris than in other financial centers. A good knowledge of who is who and of French practices is particularly helpful for good communications in France.

This also applies to press relations. French financial publications are numerous, maintained to a large extent by financial and corporate advertisers who pay not only for their advertisements but also for the editorial coverage of their news. This is not quite as nefarious as it sounds, since the better publications separate the "company news" from the copy prepared by the editorial staff. Nevertheless, it is possible for a company to get its news releases printed as written if the space is bought.

Some of the weekly publications, such as *La Vie Française, Investir*, and *Le Journal des Finances*, present stock recommendations and analyses in addition to regular financial news. The leading daily financial papers are *AGEFI, Côte Desfossés, Les Échos*, and *Le Nouveau Journal*. They publish extensive company and general financial and economic news as well as detailed stock market reports. The two leading general Paris dailies, *Le Figaro* and *Le Monde*, also carry good stock market coverage in addition to general business and economic news. Both publish comprehensive economic supplements once a week.

Taxes

French companies pay a 50% corporate tax. In order to avoid double taxation, French tax authorities permit investors to use 50% of their dividends as a tax credit (*avoir fiscal*) against their income tax. For a non-resident investor there is a 25% withholding tax on dividends. A United States citizen or resident filing a Federal income tax return can apply the 25% withholding tax as well as the 50% *avoir fiscal* against his taxable income.

The first FFr. 3000 ($600) in interest from French fixed-income securities is tax free. Beyond that amount, the French taxpayer has the choice of either adding the interest income to his other taxable income or paying tax on the interest at a flat rate of 25%.

International Investing

Bourse de Paris / 4 place de la Bourse / Paris

French Nationalized Banks in Paris

Banque Nationale de Paris / 16 boulevard des Italiens. Affiliate: *French American Capital Corporation* / 40 Wall Street / New York, New York 10005

Crédit Lyonnais / 19 boulevard des Italiens. Affiliate: *EuroPartners Securities Corporation* / 1 World Trade Center / New York, New York 10048

Société Générále / 29 boulevard Haussmann. Affiliate: *SoGen-Swiss International Corporation* / 20 Broad Street / New York, New York 10005

Partial List of Other French Banks Active in Investment Business
All in Paris unless otherwise indicated

Banque Française du Commerce Extérieur / 21 boulevard Haussmann

Banque Française de Dépôts et de Titres (BFDT) / 142 boulevard Haussmann

Banque de l'Indochine et de Suez / 96 boulevard Haussmann. Affiliate: *Suez American Corporation* / 77 Water Street / New York, New York 10005

Banque Industrielle et Mobilière Privée / 22 rue Pasquier

Banque Louis-Dreyfus / 6 rue Rabelais

Banque de Neuflize, Schlumberger, Mallet / 3 avenue Hoche

Banque Rothschild / 21 rue Laffitte. Affiliate: *New Court Securities Corporation* / 1 Rockefeller Plaza / New York, New York 10020

Banque de Paris et des Pays-Bas / 3 rue d'Antin. Affiliate: *Warburg-Paribas-Becker Inc.* / 55 Water Street / New York, New York 10041

Banque de la Société Financière Européenne / 20 rue de la Paix

Banque de l'Union Européenne / 4 rue Gaillon

Banque Worms / 45 boulevard Haussmann

Crédit Commercial de France / 103 avenue des Champs-Élysées

Crédit Industriel et Commercial (CIC) / 66 rue de la Victoire

Crédit du Nord / 6-8 boulevard Haussmann (also 28 place Rihour / Lille)

Hottinguer & Cie / 38 rue de Provence

Lazard Frères et Cie / 5 rue Pillet-Will

Morgan Guaranty Trust Co. of New York / 14 place Vendôme

Union des Banques Arabes et Françaises (UBAF) / 4 rue Ancelle / Neuilly-sur-Seine

France

A complete list of banks in France is available from *Association Professionelle des Banques* / 18 rue Lafayette / Paris.

United States Brokers in France

Cannes
Merrill Lynch, Pierce, Fenner & Smith Inc. / Carlton Hotel

Paris
Bache Halsey Stuart Inc. / 6 rue Royale
Bear, Stearns & Co. / 12 avenue Montaigne
Blyth Eastman Dillon & Co. Inc. / 1 rue François 1er
Drexel Burnham Lambert / 23 place Vendôme
F. Eberstadt & Co., Inc. / 6 place Vendôme
Fahnestock & Co. / 5 rue Gaillon
E.F. Hutton & Company, Inc. / 43 avenue Marceau
Kidder, Peabody & Co. Inc. / 420 rue Saint-Honoré
Loeb, Rhoades & Co. / 4 rue Saint-Florentin
Merrill Lynch, Pierce, Fenner & Smith Inc. / 25 avenue des Champs-Élysées, 4 rue Saint-Florentin, and 96 avenue d'Iena
Mitchell Hutchins, Inc. / 21 rue Royale
Moore & Schley, Cameron & Co. / 120 avenue des Champs-Élysées
Paine, Webber, Jackson & Curtis Inc. / 23 rue Royale
Shearson Hayden Stone Inc. / 16 place Vendôme
Shields Model Roland Inc. / 370 rue Saint-Honoré
Smith, Barney & Co. Inc. / 20 place Vendôme
Stralem & Co. Inc. / 30 avenue Marceau
Thomson & McKinnon Auchincloss Kohlmeyer Inc. / 15 rue de la Paix
Tucker, Anthony & R.L. Day Inc. / 9 rue de la Paix
Wertheim & Co. / 4 place de la Concorde
White, Weld & Co. Inc. / 142 boulevard Haussmann

Partial List of Most Actively Traded French Stocks

Air Liquide (industrial gasses)
BIC (ballpoint pens and cigarette lighters)
Jacques Borel (tourism)
BSN-Gervais Danone (glass, beverages, food)
Carrefour (retailing)
Ciments Français (cement)
CIT-Alcatel (electrical products and electronics)
Club Méditerranée (tourism)
Compagnie Bancaire (credit, financing)
Compagnie Financière de Paris et des Pays-Bas (banking)
Compagnie Financière de Suez (financial holding company)
Compagnie Française des Pétroles (petroleum)

117

International Investing

Compagnie Générale des Eaux (utility)
Compagnie Générale d'Électricité (electrical manufacturing)
Crédit Commercial de France (banking)
Crédit Foncier de France (mortgage banking)
Crédit du Nord (banking)
Denain Nord-Est Longwy (steel)
Économiques du Casino (retailing)
Imetal (nickel)
Kléber-Colombes (tires)
Legrand (electrical equipment)
Librairie Hachette (publishing)
Locafrance (equipment leasing)
Machines Bull (electrical products and electronics)
Maisons Phenix (construction and real estate)
Le Matériel Téléphonique (electrical products and electronics)
Michelin (tires)
Moët-Hennessy (champagne, cognac, perfume)
L'Oréal (cosmetics)
Paris-France (retailing)
Péchiney-Ugine Kuhlmann (aluminum, electrometallurgy)
Pernod-Ricard (distillery)
Peugeot (automobiles)
Printemps (retailing)
Rhône-Poulenc (chemicals, synthetic fibers, drugs, film)
Roussel-Uclaf (pharmaceuticals)
Saint-Gobain-Pont-à-Mousson (glass)
SEB (small appliances)
Skis Rossignol (skis)
Société Nationale des Pétroles d'Aquitaine (petroleum)
La Télémécanique Électrique (electrical products and electronics)
Thomson-Brandt (radios, televisions, appliances)
Usinor (steel)

Partial List of French Mutual Funds

Diversified Funds
Élysées-Valeurs
Épargne Mobilière
Épargne Unie
Épargne-Valeur
France-Investissement
France-Placement
Gestion Mobilière
Livret-Portefeuille

Optima
Rothschild-Expansion
Séléction Croissance
Slivam
Sogevar
UAP Investissements
Univalor
Valorem

France

Foreign Securities Funds
Épargne Inter
Séléction Mondiale
Slivinter
Soginter

Bond Funds
Épargne Obligations
France Obligations
Fructidor
Séléction Rendement
Slivarente
Sogépargne

A complete list of funds, including addresses and sponsors, is available from *l'Association des Sociétés et Fonds Français d'Investissement* / 1 rue d'Astorg / Paris

Partial List of Investment Trusts and Investment Companies Traded on the Paris Bourse

Investment Trusts
Nationale d'Investissement
Investissement et Gestion
Investment Companies
Denain Nord-Est Longwy
France S.A.

Industrielle de l'Abeille
Paternelle S.A.
Préservatrice S.A.
Pricel
Providence S.A.
Schneider

Sources of Investment Information in Paris

Centre de Documentation et d'Information (Chambre Syndicale des Agents de Change) / 4 place de la Bourse
DAFSA / 125 rue Montmartre
Eurofinance / 9 avenue Hoche
SAFE / 41 avenue de l'Opéra
SEF / 31 rue de Rome

Daily Parisian Newspapers With Extensive Financial Coverage

Le Figaro / 14 Rond-Point des Champs-Élysées
International Herald-Tribune (English language) / 21 rue de Berri
Le Monde / 5 rue des Italiens

Specialized Daily Financial Publications in Paris

AGEFI (l'Agence Économique et Financière) / 108 rue de Richelieu
Côte Desfossés / 42 rue Notre-Dame-des-Victoires
Les Échos / 37 avenue des Champs-Élysées
Le Nouveau Journal / 108 rue de Richelieu

International Investing

Other Financial and Business Publications in Paris

L'Actionnaire / 21 boulevard Montmartre
L'Économie / 26 rue du Bouloi
L'Expansion / 10 rue Lyautey
Le Hors-Côte / 2 rue du Pont Neuf
Investir / 31 rue des Geuners
Le Journal des Finances / 122 rue Réaumur
Le Journal de Tirage Financiers / 5 rue du Faubourg-Montmartre
Le Moniteur du Commerce International / 5 avenue Pierre 1 de Serbie
Le Nouvel Économiste / 17 rue d'Uzes
Perspectives / 55 rue de Châteaudun
Valeurs Actuelles / 14 rue d'Uzes
La Vie Française / 2 rue du Pont Neuf

6. Germany

Completely prostrate at the end of World War II, the Federal Republic of Germany, within two decades, became the *Wirtschaftswunder*, the economic wonder, of the world, staging an economic recovery that was perhaps less of a miracle than the result of hard work. Subsequently, West Germany became a money haven, comparable to Switzerland, with a veritable flood of flight and speculative capital pouring into the country in the early 1970s. In spite of this surplus of money, the economic boom, the spurt in oil prices, real estate speculation, and some deficit spending, Germany in the 1970s maintained one of the lowest inflation rates of the world. In the first half of 1976, when the first signs of economic recovery became visible in the United States, when England and Italy were in serious trouble and France looked shaky, Germany was clearly one of the few strong industrial nations in the world, with its currency firmer than ever — an attractive feature for investors.

Yet, in comparison to this industrial and financial strength, the German stock markets, at least as far as equities are concerned, continued to play a minor role in the German capital market, with a capitalization only one-third of that of Tokyo, which serves an economy comparable in size, and a much lower trading volume. German portfolio management, in the mid-1970s, was only beginning to become a factor on the international investment scene, primarily for the management of

Note: 1 DM = $0.40

121

the German portion of foreign institutional portfolios and of some Arab money. A number of reasons are responsible for this lag.

Germany's economic growth was accomplished practically without equity financing. Most of the capital, apart from internally generated funds, came from liberal commercial bank credits and the issue of corporate notes (*Schuldscheine*), sold largely to insurance companies, and rarely traded. Thus, the German stock markets saw very little action as the result of economic growth and the number of publicly-traded companies decreased over the years. Only about 470 stocks were listed in 1976, of which no more than 25 or 30 were considered to have sufficient float and liquidity for institutional trading. Corporate bonds play a minor role in comparison to public authority, communal, and mortgage bonds.

Traditionally, Germans have shunned their stock markets. It is not clear whether they stayed away because the markets offered such limited investment opportunities and were considered play pits for the banks, or whether the stock markets played such a small part in capital formation because Germans, by nature, are not speculators. If the latter, they changed their nature almost overnight in the late 1960s when a speculative investment frenzy broke out, sparked by the high-powered sales methods of Bernard Cornfeld's *IOS*, which was banned in the United States. *IOS* salesmen and other security peddlers "educated" the Germans about investments. As a result, many German investors ventured into the stock markets on their own, providing a temporary land office business for foreign brokers, mushrooming investment counselling firms and tip sheet publishers.

After the collapse in 1969 of *IOS* and *Gramco* (another questionable investment fund operation that appealed to many Germans), followed by the United States bear market in the early 1970s, the sobering awakening swung the pendulum in the opposite direction. Most German investors fled back into the cover of safe fixed-income securities, and German banks began to steer the small investor into investment funds. In 1976, the individual investor accounted for perhaps less than 20% of the trading on all German stock exchanges; the balance was institutional trading by the banks, investment management companies, insurance companies, and foreign investors. German investment trusts and portfolio management companies, many of them controlled by the banks, have become major factors on the German stock markets and are substantial buyers of foreign securities, notably United States stocks. Both have grown rapidly since 1970. The relatively new portfolio management companies, operating special investment funds for large institutional investors (and discussed below) should be of particular interest to institutions and corporations shopping for international investment expertise in Germany.

Banks

There is probably no country in the world where the banks occupy such a dominant role in both finance and industry as in Germany. The banking system is complex and diversified. In addition to the visible multiple-purpose banks with their many branches, there are savings banks, mortgage banks, regional banks, merchant banks, rural cooperative banks, and banks catering to special sectors of the economy, such as housing, agriculture, and small business.

There is no separation between commercial banking and investment banking in Germany. The multi-purpose banks provide both private and commercial loans, they are major underwriters, they act as stock brokers with the public, they are members of the stock exchanges and are active floor traders and major market makers. They invest for their own accounts and they act as investment advisors. They own the management companies of most of the investment funds and of special institutional funds. They have major investments in German industry.

The Big Three multi-purpose banks are *Deutsche Bank, Dresdner Bank,* and *Commerzbank,* all headquartered in Frankfurt. All three provide investment advisory service to individual investors and execute trades through their extensive nation-wide branch systems. Large portfolios are managed by central and regional offices.

The private banks are comparable to the English merchant banks, with specialized expertise in corporate finance and portfolio management. Generally cited for excellent international portfolio expertise is *Schröder, Münchmeyer, Hengst.* Others active in international investments include *Sal. Oppenheim Jr., Georg Hauck, C.G. Trinkaus & Burkhardt,* and *Merck, Finck.*

Among the regional and special-interest banks particularly active in international underwriting and portfolio management are *Berliner Handels-Gesellschaft-Frankfurter Bank (BHF-Bank), Westdeutsche Landesbank-Girozentrale, Bayerische Hypotheken- und Wechsel-Bank, Bayerische Vereinsbank,* and *Bank für Gemeinwirtschaft.*

Portfolio Management Companies (Special Funds)

Under German investment law, as it applies to mutual funds, several banks have created "special funds," managed by separate investment companies, to handle large institutional portfolios, primarily for pension funds and small- and medium-size insurance companies. A separate fund is established for each portfolio and managed very much in the same way as a publicly-sold mutual fund. New money can be added to the fund as it accrues, or shares liquidated as cash is needed. These funds benefit from the same tax advantage as the publicly-sold mutual funds and are subject to the same regulations. Transactions are not subject to a sales tax, as other stock market transactions are, and the fund can receive dividends and interest without withholding tax, both for income derived from domestic sources as well as from foreign sources. Where foreign withholding tax has been levied, the fund can usually reclaim it under double taxation relief agreements. The funds operate under a few restrictions. They may invest only in securities listed on approved stock exchanges (this includes most major stock exchanges of the world but excludes over-the-counter stocks) and all funds under one management may not hold more than 5% of all outstanding shares of one company. The assets of the funds must be totally segregated from those of the management company and are not liable for any claims against the latter.

Started in 1968, these funds have been exceptionally successful. At the end of 1975, their total assets amounted to DM 4.8 billion ($1.92 billion). An estimated 20% of this amount was in foreign securities, mostly United States securities. Management fees are relatively low, ranging from 0.2% to 0.4% of assets invested. The leading management companies are *Gesellschaft für Vermögensanlagen Kapitalanlagegesellschaft (Dresdner Bank), Deutsche Gesellschaft für Fondverwaltung (Deutsche Bank), Commerzbank Fondverwaltungsgesellschaft, Oppenheim Kapitalanlagegesellschaft*, and special funds operated by *Westdeutsche Landesbank Girozentrale, Bayerische Vereinsbank, Vereins- und Westbank, Georg Hauck*, and a few other banks.

While originally aimed at German institutional investors, such funds are now also available to foreign investors for investments in German securities or for international portfolio management. Minimum portfolio size at the larger management companies is about DM 10 million ($4 million).

Pension Funds and Insurance Companies

These special funds have a great growth potential because of a change in the German pension law. Many corporate pension funds in the past were not funded, but paid from corporate reserves as the obligation arose, with the benefits determined by management at retirement. Such unfunded pension funds without specific benefits will lose their tax privileges so they will be converted into funded obligations. Many of these new pension plans are most likely to be managed by outside management companies. It is estimated that total pension obligations in 1976 amounted to about DM 50 billion ($20 billion), much of it still in corporate hands.

The special fund management companies also have taken over many insurance company portfolios, though the largest German insurance companies manage their own portfolios, including *Allianz Lebensversicherung, Münchener Rückversicherung, Victoria Feuer-Versicherung,* and *Hamburg-Mannheimer.* More than 90% of these portfolios are in German fixed-income vehicles; only about 8% in common stock, including a small percentage in foreign issues. In the past, German insurance companies could buy only securities listed on a German exchange, but since 1975 they can buy securities on any approved stock exchange in the world.

Investment Funds

German investment funds had a slow start in the 1950s. It wasn't until the late 1960s that German funds, sparked by the promotional efforts of foreign funds, experienced an upturn in sales. In 1969, sales of foreign funds were regulated by a new law, and thereafter the German funds had the field mostly to themselves. German funds increased from 28 in 1966, with total assets of about DM 3 billion ($1.2 billion), to 104 in 1975, with total assets of about DM 18 billion ($7.2 billion). This includes a handful of real estate funds with assets of about DM 2.3 billion ($920 million). Common stock funds accounted for about 55% of the security funds. Total assets of foreign equity funds at the end of 1975 were DM 1.4 billion ($560 million). All German funds are open-end funds and most of them are sold through banks directly to the investor. Many funds have automatic investment plans and dividend reinvestment plans. A number of German funds are sold outside Germany. Practically all funds are managed by special management companies owned by one or several banks. The largest fund management company is *Deutsche Gesellschaft für Wertpapiersparen (DWS),* a subsidiary of *Deutsche Bank,* followed by *Deutsche Investment-Trust-Gesellschaft für Wertpapieranlagen (DIT),* a subsidiary of *Dresdner Bank,* and *Allgemeine Deutsche Investment-Gesellschaft (ADIG),* owned by a group of banks with *Commerzbank* and *Bayerische Vereinsbank* as the lead banks. Another important investment fund management is *Union-Investment-Gesellschaft*, which sells its funds mostly through communal and savings banks. It has also successfully introduced its leading funds — *Unifonds* with German equity 1975 assets of DM 1.6 billion ($640 million) and *Unirenta* with German fixed-income 1975 assets of DM 397 million ($159 million) — outside Germany. The largest fund is *Concentra*, a German equity fund managed by *DIT*. The largest foreign equity fund, with 1975 assets of DM 229 million ($91.6 million), is *Fondis*, managed by *ADIG*.

German Stock Exchanges

Germany has an abundance of stock exchanges. There are a total of eight: Frankfurt, Düsseldorf, Hamburg, Munich, Berlin, Hanover, Bremen, and Stuttgart. Frankfurt and Düsseldorf are the largest exchanges, with Frankfurt claiming an edge in fixed-income securities and international issues and Düsseldorf being oriented more towards industrial issues. Frankfurt, as the seat of the *Deutsche Bundesbank* (the German central bank), headquarters of the Big Three banks, and a concentration of other banks and financial institutions, must be considered the financial capital of Germany. The Hamburg and Munich exchanges are of secondary importance, while the other four play regional roles. Before World War II, Berlin was the focal German exchange. The German banks distribute their trading among the leading exchanges, and a good deal of arbitrage is carried on between the exchanges.

The number of German equity issues has been declining steadily over the last decade or two. It was down to 471 at the end of 1975, from 627 ten years earlier. New issues have been rare; the most notable ones in the 1960s and 1970s included *Volkswagenwerk, Lufthansa,* and *Horten* (a department store). Total market value of all listed German equity issues at the end of 1975 was DM 134 billion ($53.6 billion). Total value of all fixed-income securities at the end of 1975 was DM 317 billion ($126.8 billion). Total reported trading volume on all German exchanges in 1975 was DM 65 billion ($26 billion).

A good deal of trading among German banks does not take place on the exchanges, including much of the bond trading. In addition to the official market, there exists a "regulated over-the-counter" market for which admission requirements are simpler than for the official trading floor. There is a voluntary agreement among traders to trade all equity issues on the floor of the exchange unless the customer requests otherwise. Put and call options for two-, three-, or six-month duration are traded on the exchanges, and trading volume picked up significantly in 1975.

Three groups can trade on the exchanges: 1. the member banks acting as commission agents for customers or for their own accounts, 2. official brokers appointed by the government to establish prices for the securities assigned to them but not permitted to trade for their own accounts, and 3. unofficial floor brokers who can trade with anyone admitted to the trading floor and who can buy and sell for their own accounts. A number of foreign banks and brokers are members of the Frankfurt exchange, including *Chemical Bank, Citibank, Morgan Guaranty, Chase Manhattan, Hill Samuel,* and *Bank of Tokyo,* but they do not participate in trading.

Most German shares, excluding insurance company shares, are bearer shares. When an investor does not want physical possession of his stock certificates, transfer of ownership is accompanied by simple bookkeeping entry through a clearing house (*Kassenverein*) operated by the banks. A separate clearing house (*Girosammelverkehr Auslandskassenverein*) has been set up for foreign stocks and bonds, which has clearing arrangements with similar organizations in some other countries, including *SICOVAM* in France and *CEDEL* in Luxembourg for the clearance of Eurobonds.

Listing of Foreign Securities

Until about 1970, foreign securities were a rarity on German stock exchanges, and their trading volume was negligible. In the 1970s, an increasing number of foreign issues appeared. At the end of 1975, 140 foreign equity issues were listed on the Frankfurt exchange, including 37 United States issues and 30 Japanese issues. Trading volume in 1975 for the most popular issues was more than nominal — *Philips* at DM 160 million ($64 million), *IBM* at DM 127 million ($50.8 million), *Royal Dutch Petroleum* at DM 114 million ($45.6 million), and *Chase Manhattan* at DM 106 million ($42.4 million). Only 22 of the 471 German issues traded more than DM 100 million ($40 million) in 1975. Thus, listing on a German exchange can have more than public relations value. However, unless a company is well known, a good deal of publicity work is necessary to popularize a stock with German investors. Japanese firms have been particularly active in this respect.

International Investing

Most listings are sponsored by one of the Big Three banks, but any member bank can be a sponsor. Preparations and formalities take about three months. Costs are rather high — $100,000 or more in 1976, not including a follow-up public relations program.

German Stocks

The German equity market offers limited opportunities to the investor. Only 25 to 30 issues have enough trading value for institutional investments. Another 40 to 50 stocks may be suitable for individual investors or small institutional holdings. All others have a very small float or are regional issues. A large number of German companies are controlled by family groups, banks, holding companies, or investment companies to such an extent that only a small percentage of the outstanding shares is available for public trading. There is no mystery about the control of German companies. *Commerzbank* regularly publishes a widely-used directory, *Wer Gehört zu Wem* (Who Belongs to Whom), which provides precise ownership information about 8000 publicly- and privately-owned German companies.

The stock most widely traded on the Frankfurt exchange is *Deutsche Bank*, with a reported trading volume of about DM 1 billion ($400 million) in 1975. *Dresdner Bank* was third, with a trading volume of DM 545 million ($215 million), and *Commerzbank* was number nine, with a trading volume of DM 395 million ($158 million). Investment in any one of the three banks is a fairly representative investment in the German economy as a whole since all three have large holdings in various industrial sectors. *Commerzbank* holdings in department stores are particularly prominent.

The second most active stock is *Siemens*, with 1975 sales of DM 19 billion ($7.6 billion), one of the leading electrical and electronics manufacturers of the world, and generally praised for its excellent management. The second largest German manufacturer in this industry, *AEG*, with sales of about DM 10 billion ($4 billion), was operating at a loss in 1975. Some analysts considered it a turnaround candidate. Another turnaround situation in 1975 was *Volkswagenwerk*, with world-wide sales of DM 19 billion ($7.6 billion). It had been a great disappointment to those who bought the stock when the company went public in 1971.

Among other giants in German industry are the three *I.G. Farben* successor companies — *BASF, Bayer,* and *Hoechst* — all world-wide chemical giants with sales in the range of DM 18 billion ($7.2 billion) to

128

Germany

DM 20 billion ($8 billion). Other leading issues are the steel companies *Mannesmann* with DM 13 billion ($5.2 billion) in 1975 sales, *Thyssen-Hütte* with DM 21 billion ($8.4 billion) in 1975 sales, and *Daimler-Benz* with DM 15 billion ($6 billion) in 1975 sales. German breweries are often appealing, including *Löwenbräu* and *Dortmunder Union-Schultheiss.*

Many German utilities are publicly owned, several of them issuing both common and preferred stock. Among the most actively traded are *VEBA* (partly government owned) and *RWE*. Department stores are also popular with German investors. The leading ones are *Karstadt, Horton,* and *Kaufhof.*

In 1976, there were no restrictions on the purchase of German common stocks by non-residents. There is a 25% withholding tax on dividends and interest for foreign investors. United States residents can reclaim 10% of this tax from the German authorities under the double taxation agreement and the balance can be set off against their United States income tax.

German Fixed-Income Securities

Non-residents can buy German fixed-income securities with maturities of four years or more. For short-term bonds of less than four years maturity, a special *Deutsche Bundesbank* permit was required in 1976.

German fixed-income securities have been popular with many foreign investors because of the strength of the currency and the great safety of the securities. Thanks to a quality control system operated by the banks and the federal supervisory office for insurance companies and savings banks, there have been no defaults of German domestic bond issues since World War II. These controls are not applied to Euro-DM bond issues.

A great number of long-term instruments are available in Germany. Some of the older issues had maturities of up to 40 years, but, in the mid-1970s, it was difficult to sell bonds with maturities much in excess of ten years. Among the public authority bonds are those of the federal government, the post office, the federal railroad, and individual states and municipalities. In addition, there are the so-called *Schatzbriefe* sold by the *Bundesbank* to absorb excessive liquidity in the money market. The *Bundesbank* also supports the market for public authority bonds in times of unsettled market conditions to prevent sharp price fluctuations.

The mortgage and communal banks have issued a great number of mortgage and communal bonds. The latter are floated in the name of

129

the issuing bank to refinance loans made to communities, which guarantee these loans. A number of specialized banks issue bonds for special purposes, such as the *Landwirtschaftliche Rentenbank* (Agricultural Loan Bank), *Kreditanstalt für Wiederaufbau* (Reconstruction Credit Corporation), and *Deutsche Siedlungs- und Landesrentenbank* (German Settlers and Land Financing Bank).

Industrial bonds are relatively few in number, including some convertible issues. German industry prefers to finance itself with commercial bank loans, private placements (*Schuldscheindarlehen*), and internally generated funds.

Sources and Channels of Information

The German accounting profession has developed very elaborate financial reporting methods, which go a good deal beyond what is customary in the United States and require special expertise to be properly interpreted. German firms have the tendency to set aside large reserves and understate their earnings. Abuse of inside information was considered a problem in Germany in the past, and in 1975 a stock exchange commission published new guidelines to cope with this problem.

A large amount of investment information is available about German securities. The Big Three banks, as well as some of the other banks listed at the end of this chapter, publish ample information on the German market, some of it in English. *Deutsche Bank* has established a separate investment information and counselling service — *Deutsche Gesellschaft für Anlageberatung* — whose services are made available through the branch system to customers of the bank and to affiliated banks in other countries. The service, also sold to outsiders, includes reports on German and foreign companies, industry reports, and statistical material. *Commerzbank* and *Dresdner Bank* publish investment information under their own names. Among the regional and private banks publishing comprehensive investment information are *BHF Bank*, *Georg Hauck*, and *Schröder, Münchmeyer, Hengst*. Some English brokers have published good information on the German market, including *Vickers, da Costa* and *Hoare & Co., Govett*.

By far the largest German independent publisher of investment information as well as of other business and financial reference books, information services, and directories, is *Verlag Hoppenstedt* in Darmstadt. Publications include company fact sheets comparable to those published by *Standard & Poor's*, a fixed-income guide, chart service, a *Vademecum* (guide) on German and foreign investment funds sold in

Germany

Germany, and statistical data. Another publisher of various investment publications is *Hans Holzmann* in Bad Wörishofen. *Institut für Bilanzanalysen* sells in-depth studies on German companies.

Research on foreign stocks plays a somewhat lesser role in Germany than in some other countries such as England, Switzerland, and the Netherlands, where the foreign content of portfolios is higher. The large German banks use their United States securities affiliates as listening and sifting posts for information on United States stocks and rely to a large extent on the research of United States brokerage houses. They seem to prefer ready-made investment policy and market strategy from trusted sources to a flood of undigested information they would have to interpret for themselves. Nevertheless, they welcome financial reports mailed directly from United States companies, as well as American visitors and company presentations since they are not deluged with such attention to the same extent as some other countries. Frankfurt, whatever its other merits, is less of a tourist attraction than Paris, Amsterdam, or London.

The German press has a tradition of bending over backwards not to be the vehicle of *Schleichwerbung* (sneak advertising) in the form of publicity releases. Nevertheless, it has come around to using legitimate corporate financial news, although still to a more limited extent than the press of most other countries. The *Handelsblatt* is the leading German financial and business paper, comparable to the *Wall Street Journal*. The *Börsen Zeitung*, with a smaller circulation, specializes in stock market news. *Blick durch die Wirtschaft* deals with general economic matters and carries no advertising. The three leading national dailies with good business sections are *Die Welt, Frankfurter Allgemeine Zeitung*, and *Süddeutsche Zeitung*.

International Investing

Major German Stock Exchanges

Bayerische Börse / Lenbachplatz 2a / Munich
Frankfurter Wertpapierbörse / Börsenplatz 6 / Frankfurt
Hanseatische Wertpapierbörse Hamburg / Börse, Zi. 151 / Hamburg
Rheinisch-Westfälische Börse zu Düsseldorf / Berliner Allee 10 / Düsseldorf

The Big Three Banks

Commerzbank A.G. / Neuer Mainzer Strasse 32-36 / Frankfurt. Affiliate: *EuroPartners Securities Corporation* / 1 World Trade Center / New York, New York 10048
Deutsche Bank A.G. / Grosse Gallusstrasse 10-14 / Frankfurt. Affiliate: *UBS-BD Corporation* / 40 Wall Street / New York, New York 10005
Dresdner Bank A.G. / Gallusanlage 7-8 / Frankfurt. Affiliate: *ABD Securities Corporation* / 1 Battery Park Plaza / New York, New York 10004

Other German Banks Active in the Securities Business

Bank für Gemeinwirtschaft A.G. / Mainzer Landstrasse 16-24 / Frankfurt
Bankhaus B. Metzler seel. Sohn & Co. / Neue Mainzer Strasse 40-42 / Frankfurt
Bayerische Hypotheken- und Wechsel-Bank / Theatinerstrasse 11 / Munich
Bayerische Vereinsbank / Kardinal-Faulhaber-Strasse 14 / Munich
Joh. Berenberg, Gossler & Co. / Neuer Jungfernstieg 20 / Hamburg
Berliner Bank A.G. / Hardenbergstrasse 32 / Berlin
Berliner Handels-Gesellschaft und Frankfurter Bank / Bockenheimer Landstrasse 10 / Frankfurt
Delbrück & Co. / Gereonstrasse 15-23 / Cologne
Deutsche Girozentrale-Deutsche Kommunalbank / Taunusanlage 10 / Frankfurt
Deutsche Länderbank A.G. / Bockenheimer Landstrasse 23 / Frankfurt
Effectenbank-Warburg A.G. / Kaiser Strasse 30 / Frankfurt
Georg Hauck & Sohn Bankiers / Kaiser Strasse 24 / Frankfurt
Hessische Landesbank-Girozentrale / Junghofstrasse 18-26 / Frankfurt
Merck, Finck & Co. / Pacellistrasse 4 / Munich
Norddeutsche Landesbank-Girozentrale / Georgsplatz 1 / Hanover
Sal. Oppenheim, Jr. & Cie / Unter Sachsenhausen 4 / Cologne

Germany

Schröder, Münchmeyer, Hengst & Co. / Friedenstrasse 6-10 / Frankfurt
Trinkaus & Burkhardt / Königsallee 21-23 / Düsseldorf
Vereins- und Westbank A.G. / Alter Wall 20-32 / Hamburg
M.M. Warburg-Brickmann, Wirtz & Co. / Ferdinandstrasse 75 / Hamburg
Westdeutsche Landesbank Girozentrale / Friedrichstrasse 56 / Düsseldorf
Westfalenbank A.G. / Huestrasse 21-25 / Bochum

German Investment Fund Management Companies

ADIG-Investment / Von-der-Tann-Strasse 11 / Munich
AGI / Frankfurter Strasse 50 / Wiesbaden
Allfonds / Brienner Strasse 14 / Munich
DEGI / Niddastrasse 16-22 / Frankfurt
DEKA / Mainzer Landstrasse 37 / Frankfurt
DESPA / Mainzer Landstrasse 37 / Frankfurt
DG-Invest / Konrad-Adenauer-Ufer 79-81 / Cologne
DIT / Biebergasse 6-10 / Frankfurt
DWS / Grüneburgweg 113-115 / Frankfurt
FT / Bockenheimer Landstrasse 10 / Frankfurt
Hansainvest / Alter Weg 20-32 / Hamburg
III / Leopoldstrasse 28a / Munich
Inka / Königsallee 19 / Düsseldorf
Kapitalfonds / Unter Sachsenhausen 6 / Cologne
SMH / Friedensstrasse 6-10 / Frankfurt
Union / Neue Mainzer Strasse 33-35 / Frankfurt
Universal / Buchgasse 11 / Frankfurt

Portfolio Management and Advisory Services

Anlage- und Vermögensberatung / Metzer Strasse 5 / Saarlouis
CRM Vermögensberatung GmbH / Jacobistrasse 3 / Düsseldorf
Deutsche Gesellschaft für Anlageberatung mbH / Postfach 26 43 / Frankfurt
Gesellschaft für Vermögensanlagen Kapitalanlagegesellschaft mbH / Niddastrasse 5 / Frankfurt
Mathematischer Beratungs- und Programmierungsdienst GmbH / Kleppingstrasse 26 / Dortmund
Münchner Kapitalanlage A.G. / Marstallstrasse 8 / Munich
PM Portfolio Management / Postfach 9 60 / Munich
Portfolio Management / Färbergraben 1/IV / Munich

International Investing

American Brokerage Offices in Germany

Düsseldorf
Bache Halsey Stuart Inc. / Taubenstrasse 22 1 Stock
Hornblower & Weeks-Hemphill, Noyes, Inc. / Königsallee 61
Merrill Lynch, Pierce, Fenner & Smith Inc. / Königsallee 30, KOE
Center Building
Dean Witter & Co. Inc. / Königsallee 88

Frankfurt
Bache Halsey Stuart Inc. / Wiesenhüttenstrasse 18
Dominick & Dominick Inc / Westendstrasse 28
Hornblower & Weeks-Hemphill, Noyes, Inc. / Unterlindau 76
E.F. Hutton & Co. Inc. / Bockenheimer Landstrasse 51-53, Rhein-
Main Center
Loeb, Rhoades & Co. / Wesenhüttenplatz 26
Merrill Lynch, Pierce, Fenner & Smith Inc. / Ulmenstrasse 30
Roulston & Co., Inc. / 17 Unterlindau
Thomson & McKinnon Auchincloss Kohlmeyer Inc. / Hochstrasse 43

Hamburg
Bache Halsey Stuart Inc. / Neuer Wall 10
E.F. Hutton & Co. Inc. / Gaensmarkt 21-23
Merrill Lynch, Pierce, Fenner & Smith Inc. / Jungfernstiegl Reesen-
damm 3

Munich
Bache Halsey Stuart Inc. / Ludwigstrasse 8
Fahnestock & Co. / Frauenplatz 11
Hornblower & Weeks-Hemphill, Noyes, Inc. / Burgstrasse 2
E.F. Hutton & Co. Inc. / Odeonplatz 18
Merrill Lynch, Pierce, Fenner & Smith Inc. / Dienerstrasse 21

Selected List of Actively Traded German Stocks
*ADRs traded over-the-counter in the United States

Automotive
Bayerische Motorenwerke (BMW)
Continental Gummiwerke
Daimler-Benz
Volkswagenwerk *

Banking and Insurance
Aachener & Münchener Versicherungs-Gesellschaft
Allianz Versicherung

Germany

Bayerische Hypotheken- und Wechsel-Bank
*Bayerische Vereinsbank**
*Commerzbank**
*Deutsche Bank**
*Dresdner Bank**
Frankfurter Hypothekenbank
Münchener Rückversicherung

Building Materials
DLW
Dyckerhoff Zementwerke
Gerresheimer Glashüttenwerke
Heidelberger Zement
Philipp Holzmann

Chemical Manufacturing
*BASF**
*Bayer**
DEGUSSA
*Hoechst**
Schering

Electrical Manufacturing
*AEG**
Brown Boveri Mannheim
*Siemens**
Varta

Machinery
Deutsche Babcock
Gutehoffnungshütte
Klöckner-Humboldt-Deutz
Linde
MAN

Retailing
Horten
Karstadt
Kaufhof
Neckermann

Steel
Hoesch
Mannesmann
Thyssen-Hütte

Utilities
Nordwest Kraftwerke
RWE
VEBA
Vereinigte Elektrizitätswerke Westfalen

Miscellaneous
Lufthansa (airline)
Dortmunder Union-Schultheiss (brewery)
Girmes-Werke (textiles, shoes, apparel)
Harpener (holding company)
Löwenbräu (brewery)
Metallgesellschaft (non-ferrous metals)
Preussag (diversified metals and other raw materials)

Sources of Information on German Securities

Bundesverband für Anlageberatung und Vermögensplanung / Oberlindau 3 / Frankfurt
Deutsche Gesellschaft für Anlageberatung mbH / Postfach 2643, Reuterweg 51 / Frankfurt
Hans Holzmann Verlag K.G. / Postfach 460 / Bad Wörishofen
Institut für Bilanzanalysen / Corneliusstrasse 28 / Frankfurt
Verlag Hoppenstedt & Co. / Postfach 4006, Havelstrasse 9 / Darmstadt
In addition, all major German banks offer information.

National Dailies With Financial Coverage

Frankfurter Allgemeine Zeitung / Hellerhofstrasse 2-4 / Frankfurt
Süddeutsche Zeitung / Sendlingerstrasse 80 / Munich
Die Welt / Kölnerstrasse 99 / Bonn-Bad Godesberg

Leading Financial Publications

Blick durch die Wirtschaft / Hellerhofstrasse 2-4 / Frankfurt
Börsen Zeitung / Düsseldorferstrasse 16 / Frankfurt
Handelsblatt / Martin-Luther-Platz 27 / Düsseldorf

Partial List of Other Financial and Business Publications

Die Aktiengesellschaft / Ulmenallee 96-98 / Cologne
Capital / Eupener Strasse 70 / Cologne

Germany

Effekten Spiegel / Untere Marktstrasse 9 / Bochum
Frankfurter Börsenbriefe / Grüneburgweg 69 / Frankfurt
Geld Magazin / Malmedyerstrasse 18 / Cologne
Wertpapier / Humboldtstrasse 9 / Düsseldorf
Wirtschaft und Investment / Hermann-Aust Strasse 4 / Bad Wöris-
   hofen
Wirtschaftswoche / Martin-Luther-Platz 23 / Düsseldorf

7. The Netherlands

With the British and the Swiss, the Dutch share the reputation of being seasoned international investment managers. They have a long tradition of international trade and finance. The Amsterdam exchange claims to be the oldest in the world where stocks were traded. The first shares admitted were those of the East India Company, founded in 1602. Shareholders received some of their first dividends in the form of spices rather than cash.

The Dutch have always taken a global view of investments — out of necessity, because their own small country does not offer enough investment outlets for the vast sums that the Dutch have always earned through international trade, shipping, insurance, and finance. Investments in the leading Dutch international companies — *Royal Dutch Petroleum, Philips Gloeilampenfabrieken,* and *Unilever N. V.* — represent an international investment rather than an investment in the Dutch economy since the majority of their earnings comes from outside the country.

A Model Investment Trust

The best illustration of Dutch portfolio management, and the most dominant factor on the Dutch investment scene, is the *Robeco (Rotterdamsch Beleggingsconsortium)* investment trust.

Note: 1 Fl. = $0.37

139

International Investing

Robeco is not a mutual fund in the American sense, but rather a publicly-held corporation whose business consists of investing money. It has no separate management company and no sales force; hence no sales commissions or front-end loads.

An investor wanting to develop a truly international portfolio could benefit from studying the trust's investment policy — or much more simply, buying *Robeco* shares. In 1976, they were not traded in the United States, and a United States resident would have to go to an American broker dealing in foreign securities to buy *Robeco* shares on a foreign exchange. In 1976, *Robeco* shares were listed on 19 exchanges — Amsterdam, Antwerp, Basel, Berlin, Brussels, Dublin, Düsseldorf, Frankfurt, Geneva, Hamburg, Hong Kong, Lausanne, London, Luxembourg, Munich, Paris, Stockholm, Vienna, and Zurich — thereby establishing an all-time record for multiple listings. Technical aspects have so far prevented a listing in New York, but it is quite possible that *Robeco* will one day have its ticker symbol on the Big Board.

At the end of 1975, total assets of *Robeco* were Fl. 4,339 billion ($1.6 billion). Composition of portfolio by industries and countries was:

Investments by Industry (%)		*Investments by Country (%)*	
financial institutions	18.11	United States	34.61
oil	12.43	Japan	13.84
public utilities	8.49	Dutch internationals	9.96
commercials, transport.	7.29	Germany	8.76
chemicals, glass	7.23	Dutch nationals	6.46
electrical equipment	6.75	Canada	3.96
engineering	5.99	Australia	2.77
foods	5.35	Belgium	2.03
office equipment	3.26	Hong Kong	1.90
pharmaceuticals	3.04	Switzerland	1.60
property shares	1.77	France	1.57
mines	1.57	Great Britain	1.10
other industries	8.51	Brazil	0.37
Sophia-Jacoba		Sweden	0.24
(coal mining subsidiary)	1.73	Denmark	0.21
property	1.04	Singapore	0.14
cash or equivalent	7.44	Austria	0.13
		Philippines	0.08
		Spain	0.04
		Netherlands Antilles	0.02
		Cash and other assets	10.21

The Netherlands

Up to 1972, *Robeco*, when allowing for its dividend and stock distribution, had an almost unparalleled performance record, which looks even better in terms of United States dollars when allowing for the devaluation of the dollar. Net asset share value declined steeply in 1973 and 1974 but had recovered some of its losses by the end of 1975, and was headed further upwards in 1976, with the rise in the United States market. On September 1, 1976, total net assets were Fl. 4.413 billion ($1.63 billion). *Robeco* management sees to it that the market price of its shares stays close to the net asset value per share. It sets a price every day at the Amsterdam Stock Exchange at which it is prepared to buy if selling pressures tend to drive the market price below net asset value. It sets another price, about Fl. 1.50 higher, at which it is willing to sell additional shares if buying pressures drive the market price above net asset value. Prices on other stock exchanges where *Robeco* is traded follow suit thanks to the arbitragers. The market price on the exchanges is the same for both sellers and buyers. The price of the shares includes the cost of issuing new shares (about 4% to 5%). Management costs are exceptionally low — .26% of assets in 1975. (The average figure in the United States is about four or five times higher.)

Robeco management also operates two other trusts: *Rolinco*, aiming at capital appreciation, and *Rorento*, seeking high income from fixed-interest securities and based legally in the Netherlands Antilles. *Rolinco's* portfolio composition is comparable to that of *Robeco,* but with a somewhat larger United States content and more stress on energy and growth stocks. With rapidly rising assets, reaching Fl. 3.006 billion ($1.112 billion) by the end of August 1976, it has lost some of its original flexibility advantage over the *Robeco* funds. *Rorento,* started in July 1974, when interest rates were at their peak, had run up an excellent performance record by the end of February 1976, with an appreciation of 30%, including re-invested dividends. Originally started with Dutch and German fixed-income securities, the fund in 1975 added many US$ and DM Eurobonds. *Rorento* dividends are not subject to withholding tax in the Netherlands.

For all three trusts, *Robeco* offers an attractive feature for the small investor — a "shareholder's account" either in Rotterdam or Geneva, where an investor can make deposits as in a bank and direct his money to be invested in any one, two, or all three of the funds. Dividends can be reinvested automatically. He can withdraw any sum of money not exceeding his total holding at any time, as he would withdraw money from a bank.

141

International Investing

Other Dutch Investment Funds

Robeco has been so successful that in the early 1970s it bought three major Dutch investment funds that were losing ground and selling much below their asset value. The three larger funds, other than *Robeco*, that remain are *ABN-Beleggingspool*, managed by *Algemene Bank Nederland*, with total assets on March 31, 1976, of Fl. 314 million ($116 million); *Amro Pierson Fund*, managed jointly by the merged *Amsterdam-Rotterdam Bank* and *Pierson, Heldring & Pierson*, with total assets, on January 31, 1976, of Fl. 361 million ($134 million); and *Amsterdams Belegging Depot*, managed by *Hollandsche Belegging en Beheer Maatschappij*, with assets of Fl. 207 million ($77 million) on April 14, 1976. Portfolios of these funds are completely international, with the United States content, at the end of 1975, being around 40% of the total. *Algemene Bank Nederland* and *Hollandsche Belegging en Beheer Maatschappij* also operate a number of smaller funds, including an income fund and *America-Fund*, consisting entirely of United States and Canadian securities. United States content at the end of March 1976, was $32 million, Canadian content about $4 million.

At the end of 1975, total assets of all Dutch securities, investment trusts, and funds listed on the Amsterdam Stock Exchange were Fl. 8.3 billion ($3.1 billion) plus about Fl. 930 million ($344 million) of in-house funds. *Robeco* managed about 90% of this grand total.

Institutional Money Management

Another dominant role in the Dutch securities market, not seen to this extent in any other country, is played by the self-managed Dutch pension funds. Of the about 1500 company pension funds, an estimated 500 manage their own portfolios. The largest, with some portfolios exceeding Fl. 1 billion ($370 million), include the Dutch international companies — *Royal Dutch Shell Petroleum, Unilever N.V., Philips, AKZO, Hoogovens,* and *KLM Royal Dutch Airlines.* The international content of their portfolios tends to be lower than that of the investment trusts, and the United States portion is likely to be around 20%, or less. Fund management is usually very efficient, with professional portfolio managers and research staff. There are no government rules concerning the types of investments to be made by pension funds, and portfolio performance is left to the investment sophistication of the fund management.

Insurance companies, hardly more restricted than pension funds in their investment strategy, are also a major factor on the investment scene and play a role that is large in relation to the size of the market. With a population of about 13 million, the Netherlands probably has the largest number of insurance companies per capita in the world — about 350 companies covering every type of risk. The leading ones are large multinational operations, including *Nationale-Nederlanden* and the *AMEV Group* holding companies. All Dutch insurance portfolios combined are estimated to exceed $5 billion, but a large percentage is in fixed-income securities, and perhaps only 5% in foreign stocks.

Banks

Many individual investors in the Netherlands are as independent in their investment decisions as the institutional investors. They rely on banks for investment information, advice, and execution but they manage their own portfolios. To strengthen their positions in both the domestic and foreign capital markets, the two largest commercial banks merged with the two leading merchant and investment banks in 1975 — *Amsterdam-Rotterdam Bank (Amro)* with *Pierson, Heldring & Pierson;* and *Algemene Bank Nederland* with *Bank Mees & Hope.* According to the official announcements all four banks will continue to operate as separate entities in their fields of special expertise. Nevertheless, opportunities for efficiencies through consolidation of some operations are likely to present themselves. *Morgan Guaranty* established a foothold in the Netherlands by buying a 50% interest in an investment banking subsidiary of *Amro* and operating it under the name *Bank Morgan Labouchère. First National Bank of Chicago* has an interest in *Slavenburg, Oyens & van Eeghen,* which represents an earlier merger of the commercial *Slavenburg's Bank* with the investment banking firm of *Oyens & van Eeghen.* The only other Dutch bank with sizable investment interest is *Nederlandsche Middenstandsbank.* The largest Dutch bank in terms of assets, *Coöperatieve Centrale Raiffeisen-Boerenleenbank,* is primarily a retail and credit bank for rural communities and is not yet involved in major investment activities.

Investment in Management

Security analysts who evaluate a company for a recommendation of its stock usually try to assess one factor that is not spelled out in the financial statements — the effectiveness of management. Effective management, efficiency, and individuality are Dutch characteristics that have impressed many outsiders who have worked with the Dutch on common projects — an efficiency that does not run rampant for its own sake and seems singularly free from status seeking, pretensions, and showmanship. It is an efficiency that was born in long, hard struggles against hostile men and elements in which no movement could be wasted and everyone had to pitch in, irrespective of rank, whenever needed.

The Dutch won their freedom from the then powerful Spaniards during the second half of the 16th century. They have conducted a never-ending struggle against the sea. Disastrous floods in the Middle Ages, notably the one in 1421 which wiped out 72 villages and more than 100,000 lives, spurred the Dutch into developing their sophisticated dike building techniques and other methods of controlling the sea. Taking the offensive, they have reclaimed lost areas from the sea, the largest and most recent of these projects being the gigantic Delta Plan under which many of the wide arms of the Rhine-Maas-Schelde estuaries are filled in and the islands connected to the mainland.

Twice during their history the Dutch had their economic base completely wiped out by foreign wars fought on their soil — first during the Napoleonic Wars when the French occupied the country and, to spite the British, cut Holland off from all of its international trade routes, and the second time during World War II, when in the very last months of the war fierce battles were fought in Holland and the retreating Germans left nothing behind but destruction and bare cupboards.

Soon after World War II, the Dutch lost their Indonesian possessions with a population of 70 million — then seven times greater than the home country — and a source of great natural wealth.

The Dutch rebuilt Holland with amazing speed. As soon as it was practicable, they returned to the principles of free trade and free flow of capital. Having, over the centuries, developed particular skills in shipping, finance, trading, insurance, and marketing, they earn almost as much money from these service industries as they do from manufacturing. Today, the Dutch are also major participants in the exploration of the North Sea gas and oil fields. In 1976, budget deficits and inflation weakened the Dutch economy and guilder.

The Dutch Internationals

Efficiency, drive, and the need to seek growth outside the confining borders of the Netherlands have made the six largest Dutch corporations multinational rather than domestic operations — *AKZO, Hoogovens, KLM, Royal Dutch-Shell, Philips,* and *Unilever N.V.* Domestic efficiency is, of course, not enough to recommend these companies for investment purposes since, like all multinational companies, they are vulnerable to the economic, social, and political climates of those countries wherein they have major operations (and the inefficiencies that may be present there). As a result, their stock performances have followed world-wide economic trends rather than those of the local market.

KLM, even though efficiently managed, suffers from the same problems that plague all transatlantic air carriers — overcapacity and chaotic, not to say questionable, pricing and marketing practices.

Royal Dutch-Shell, the second largest integrated oil company in the world and a large chemical producer, is subject to the multifarious problems that all large multinational oil companies are exposed to. It is controlled by two holding companies — *Royal Dutch Petroleum* (Dutch), owning a 60% interest, and *Shell Transport & Trading* (British), owning a 40% interest. The stocks of both holding companies are traded on the New York Stock Exchange. The American *Shell Oil Company*, one of the largest United States integrated oil companies, is 69% controlled by *Royal Dutch-Shell* and is also traded on the New York Stock Exchange.

The Dutch *Unilever N. V.* and the British *Unilever Ltd.* are operated as one company. They have identical boards of directors. In general, any operation located in what was the former British Commonwealth is held by *Unilever Ltd.*, and the other interests are held by *Unilever N. V.*, including the two United States subsidiaries, *Lever Brothers* and *Thomas J. Lipton*. In terms of sales, the *Unilever* group is the ninth largest industrial enterprise in the world, operating in about 70 countries and producing fats and oils, soaps and detergents, processed food, animal feed, toilet preparations, and chemicals. It also operates plantations. Both *Unilever* companies are traded on the New York Stock Exchange.

Philips Lamp, owned 99% by the holding company, *Philips N. V.*, is the largest non-American manufacturer of light bulbs and electric and electronic equipment. *Philips* ADRs are traded in the United States on the over-the-counter market.

AKZO is a European giant in the man-made fiber, plastics, and chemical business, and *Hoogovens* is an iron and steel holding company. American Depositary Receipts of the shares of both companies are traded over-the-counter in the United States.

Dutch National Companies

An investor may sometimes find good performance among some of the Dutch national companies that derive most of their earnings from the

Dutch economy (although there are few that are completely isolated from international trade). The best known, and perhaps the only one known to most Americans, is *Heineken,* the Dutch brewery, which exports about 20% of its output and has some financial interests in non-Dutch breweries. Even though the annual growth rate of Dutch beer consumption has slowed down, the company has successfully introduced its beer into foreign markets and has also entered the soft drink, wine, and distillery markets.

Other companies that have aroused investor interest in the past include *Elsevier,* an international publishing house; *IHC Holland,* a maritime construction company heavily involved in the North Sea offshore drilling operations; and *Bredero,* a real estate financier and developer. Holdings of Dutch commercial and mortgage banks as well as of insurance companies feature large in Dutch institutional portfolios, including *Algemene Bank Nederland, Amro Bank, Pakhoed,* and *Nationale-Nederlanden.*

When looking at Dutch national stocks, it should be borne in mind that most of them have a small float. This makes it difficult to buy and sell shares at a given time and at a given place. Smaller Dutch companies have not been very communicative toward their stockholders in the past, but there are signs of improvement. Management is often controlled by a family or a few insiders. In fact, management control of many Dutch companies, including some of the very big ones, is by a few, including the government, banks, family, and preferential shareholders, rather than the many shareholders at large. It is reported, for instance, that *Philips,* a company with a sales volume of more than $10 billion, is effectively controlled by only ten registered priority shareholders. This close control may shield some managements from investment community pressure to perform for the benefit of the shareholders.

Non-residents can freely buy all Dutch common shares listed on a Dutch stock exchange (in addition to Amsterdam, there is a relatively inactive exchange in Rotterdam). However, they need a special permit, which any bank can obtain, to buy unlisted stocks. Unlisted stocks are usually those of smaller or closely-held companies, many of which do not want to conform to the reporting requirements of the stock exchange. Thus, they are not suitable investments, except for the initiated or someone advised by an initiate.

Fixed-Income Securities

The Netherlands market offers a fairly wide choice of fixed-income securities. There is no withholding tax for non-residents on interest received from Dutch fixed-income securities, although 25% is withheld on dividends paid by Dutch companies to non-resident investors. The most popular issues are those of the Dutch government and of the three main types of banks — commercial, mortgage, and communal. The *Rorento* fund, on August 31, 1976, was invested 36.7% in Dutch fixed-income securities, down from 94.8% in early 1975, representing a shift into United States and Canadian dollar and Deutschmark issues. The high inflation rate that had weakened the Dutch guilder may have influenced this shift.

Amsterdam Stock Exchange

The Amsterdam Stock exchange has had its ups and downs during its more than 300-year history. After a flourishing start, it was wrecked by the Napoleonic Wars and did not revive until the second half of the 19th century. At that time it became an important factor in the financing of American railroads, and by the turn of the 20th century Amsterdam had become the most important trading center for American securities outside the United States. After World War I, Amsterdam played a major role in financing the Dutch international companies. As these companies listed on other stock exchanges throughout the world, and as an increasing number of foreign stocks were listed on the Amsterdam exchange, Dutch brokers and bankers developed a very active arbitrage business.

World War II again wrecked the operations of the Amsterdam exchange, and it did not come to life again until the late 1950s. In 1975, total trading of all listed stocks and bonds was Fl. 24 billion ($8.88 billion), including a volume of Fl. 1 billion ($370 million) in foreign stocks and Fl. 386 million ($143 million) in foreign bonds. A total of 2120 issues were listed, including 1310 Dutch bonds, 168 foreign bonds, 72 Dutch and foreign investment trusts and funds, 275 Dutch common stocks, and 295 foreign stocks, of which 180 were United States stocks.

The Amsterdam exchange is considered to have one of the best standards in trading practices of any exchange in the world, and it is also the only exchange in the world charged with the protection of the shareholders, a function normally performed by a government agency.

Both banks and brokers can trade on the exchange, but as far as smaller individual investors are concerned the most practical relationship is with a Dutch bank oriented to retail business.

Most Dutch stock certificates are made out to bearer — they do not show the name of the owner. The owner must claim his dividends

147

and interest when due. The exchange has introduced a clearing system
with simplified certificates and centralized collection and distribution of
dividends and interest via the bank offices and brokers associated with
the system as depositors. Change of ownership of securities can be
accomplished by simple change of records.

Listing in Amsterdam

The Amsterdam exchange has always encouraged listings of foreign securities, but trading volume of most foreign issues was negligible or nil.
To make listing of foreign securities more meaningful, the Amsterdam
exchange, in 1975, introduced a new requirement according to which
an issue to be listed must develop a trading volume of at least Fl. 1 million ($370,000) shortly before being admitted to the exchange. In prac-
tice, this means that the sponsoring bank will try to create a certain
amount of investor interest in the stock while the listing application is
pending. The new requirement also changed the listing fee to Fl. 20,000
($7,400) for all listings irrespective of the capitalization of the applying
company. The annual fee thereafter is Fl. 2,000 ($740). Much higher
costs are the fees of the sponsoring bank, lawyers and auditors, the translation costs, and the supporting advertising and publicity. Total cost of
listing may run from $50,000 to $75,000. The banks most active in
sponsoring listings are *Pierson, Heldring & Pierson, Algemene Bank
Nederland*, and *Amsterdam-Rotterdam Bank*.

In 1976, it was too early to say whether these new requirements actually stimulated trading of foreign stocks on the Amsterdam exchange.
Nevertheless, it seemed that a listing would make sense only if a company would keep its financial news before investors by regular release of
its results through publicity and advertising. This is particularly important in the Netherlands where so many individual investors make their
own investment decisions.

Sources and Channels of Information

All banks listed at the end of this chapter provide stock market information, including stock reference booklets, general market letters, and individual stock recommendations. Some of the material is in English, including the very lively weekly newsletters *Amro Stock Market News,*
published by *Amsterdam-Rotterdam Bank,* and *Dutch Market Review,*
published by *Algemene Bank Nederland.*

The Netherlands

There is also a surprisingly large number of good independent stock information services in relation to the relatively small size of the country, reflecting the great public investment interest in Holland. They include: *Van Oss' Effectenboek,* a loose-leaf binder with descriptions of some 1000 companies, updated at regular intervals; *Gids bij de Prijscourant van de Vereniging voor de Effectenhandel te Amsterdam,* a reference book on about 2400 companies, grouped by industries; *Wegwijzer voor Nederlandse Effecten,* a publication appearing ten times a year providing information about the main companies traded in Amsterdam, classified by industry; and *Tabel van Laagste en Hoogste Koersen,* price information on all Dutch and foreign companies listed on the Amsterdam Stock Exchange over a period of eight years.

Dutch banks and other institutions obtain most of their information on United States and other foreign securities from the foreign brokers and banks with whom they do business. They evaluate this information through research analysts specialized by geographic regions rather than by industry. Investment group meetings are quite frequent in Amsterdam, either under the auspices of the Dutch security analysts society or sponsored by a broker or bank. About one in ten of the companies represented on the programs of the society is foreign. One of the problems with group meetings is the fact that many of the institutions that do their own research and make their own investment decisions are scattered throughout Holland. *Robeco,* the largest, is located in Rotterdam. This involves a two-hour roundtrip to attend a meeting in Amsterdam for *Robeco* personnel. Thus, if an institution such as *Robeco* has a substantial holding in a company's stock, it welcomes a visit to its office by a company officer. However, as almost all Dutch investment professionals stress, they prefer to see executives with corporate management responsibility in the off-season rather than tourists at tulip time.

Holland also has many financial publications in relation to the size of the country, leading among them *Het Financieele Dagblad.* Reporting standards are excellent, and financial public relations practices are good.

149

International Investing

Principal Stock Exchange

Vereniging voor de Effectenhandel / Beursplein 5 / Amsterdam

Dutch Securities Traded on the New York Stock Exchange

KLM Royal Dutch Airlines
Royal Dutch Petroleum
Unilever N. V.

Dutch Securities Traded Over-the-Counter in the United States

AKZO
Hoogovens
Philips

Partial List of Dutch Securities Actively Traded
on the Amsterdam Stock Exchange

Algemene Bank Nederland
Amsterdam-Rotterdam Bank
Lucas Bols (distillery)
Bredero (real estate)
Bührmann-Tetterode (paper, machinery, office equipment wholesaler)
Elsevier (publishing)
Gist-Brocades (pharmaceuticals and biochemical products)
Heineken (brewery)
Hollandsche Beton (construction and engineering)
IHC Holland (dredging and offshore drilling)
Internatio-Müller (wholesaler and international trading department stores)
Koninklijke Bijenkorf Beheer (department stores)
Koninklijke Nederlandsche Papierfabrieken (paper)
Nederlandsche Scheepvaart Unie (shipping, land and air transportation)
van Ommeren (tankers and coastal shipping)
Pakhoed Holding (tank storage and pipelines)
Rijn-Schelde-Verolme (shipbuilding and repair)
Scholten-Honig (starch and starch products)
Verenigde Machinefabriek (engineering)
Verenigde Nederlandsche Uitgeversbedrijven (printing and publishing)

150

The Netherlands

Partial List of Dutch Banks

Algemene Bank Nederland / Keizersgracht 573-575 / Amsterdam. Affiliate: *ABD Securities Corporation* / 1 Battery Park Plaza / New York, New York 10004 and 53 State Street / Boston, Massachusetts 02109

Amsterdam-Rotterdam Bank N.V. / Herengracht 595 / Amsterdam

Amsterdamse Crediet- en Handelsbank / Herengracht 553 / Amsterdam

Bank der Bondsspaarbanken / Singel 236 / Amsterdam

Bank Mees & Hope / Herengracht 548 / Amsterdam

Bank Morgan Labouchère / Tesselschadestraat 12 / Amsterdam

Banque de Paris et des Pays-Bas / Herengracht 539-541 / Amsterdam

Banque de Suez Nederland / Herengracht 320-324 / Amsterdam

H. Albert de Bary & Co. / Herengracht 450 / Amsterdam

Coöperatieve Centrale Raifeissen-Boerenleenbank / Beneluxlaan 33 / Utrecht

Kas-Associatie / Spuistraat 172 / Amsterdam

Nederlandsche Middenstandsbank / Herengracht 580 / Amsterdam

Nederlandse Credietbank / Herengracht 458 / Amsterdam

Pierson, Heldring & Pierson / Herengracht 206-214 / Amsterdam. Affiliate: *New Court Securities Corporation* / 1 Rockefeller Plaza / New York, New York 10020

Slavenburg, Oyens & van Eeghen / Keizersgracht 279-283 / Amsterdam

Partial List of Dutch Broker-Dealers

Barclays Kol & Co. N.V. / Herengracht 500 / Amsterdam

DeBeaufort & Kraaijenhagen N.V. / Dreikoningenstraat 4 / Amsterdam

Effectenkantoor A. Strating & Co. / Herengracht 130 / Amsterdam

Kempen & Co. N.V. / Dreikoningenstraat 4 / Amsterdam

Lind, Jarman en Westerouen van Meeteren N.V. / Herengracht 479 / Amsterdam

F. van Lanschot / Herengracht 199-201 / Amsterdam

van Haften & Co. / Rokin 113 / Amsterdam

van der Hoop, Offers & Zn. / Westersingel 88 / Rotterdam

W. Willems & Cie / Singel 540 / Amsterdam

Partial List of American Brokers in the Netherlands

Amsterdam

Bache Halsey Stuart Inc. / Geboaw Rivierstaete, Amsteldijk 166

Bear, Stearns & Co. / Singel 540

151

International Investing

Drexel Burnham Lambert / Singel 540
Herzfeld & Stern / Singel 160
Hornblower & Weeks, Hemphill, Noyes, Inc. / Hirsch Building
Merrill Lynch, Pierce, Fenner & Smith Inc. / Weesperstraat 107
Shearson Hayden Stone Inc. / Liedsegracht 11

Rotterdam
Merrill Lynch, Pierce, Fenner & Smith Inc. / Korte Hoogstraat 30

Dutch Investment Funds

ABN-Beleggingspool managed by *Algemene Bank Nederland* /
Keizersgracht 573-575 / Amsterdam
America Fifty managed by *Gilissen Jonker & Co. N. V.* / P.O. Box 586 /
Amsterdam
America-Fund managed by *Algemene Bank Nederland* / Keizersgracht
573-575 / Amsterdam
Amsterdam Belegging Depot managed by *B. V. Hollandsche Belegg-
ingen en Beheer Maatschappij* / P.O. Box 513, Keizersgracht
573-575 / Amsterdam
Amro-Pierson Fund managed by *Amro Bank N. V.* / P.O. Box 1220,
Herengracht 595 / Amsterdam
Beleggingsfonds van de 7 managed by *N. V. Beheermaatschappij Van
Het* / Amstelstraat 21 / Amsterdam
Beleggingsmaatschappij Obam N. V. / Herengracht 544 / Amsterdam
Converto (Beleggingsfonds von Converteerbare Obligaties) managed by
N. V. Hollandsche Belegging en Beheer Maatschappij / Keizers-
gracht 573-575 / Amsterdam
European Community Trust N. V. managed by *Trust en Administratie-
maatschappij Interland B. V.* / Tesselschadestraat 5 / Amsterdam
Holland Fund managed by *Labouchère & Co. N. V.* and *Bank Mees &
Hope N. V.* / P.O. Box 154, Tesselschadestraat 12 / Amsterdam
IKA (N. V. Beleggingsmaatschappij) Dual Fund managed by *Algemene
Bank Nederland N. V., H. Albert de Bary & Co. N. V.,* and *Van Der
Hoop, Offers & Zoon N. V.* / Keizersgracht 573-575 / Amsterdam
Interbonds managed by *Labouchère & Co. N. V.* and *Theodoor Gilissen
N. V.* / P.O. Box 154, Tesselschadestraat 12 / Amsterdam
Robeco, Rolinco, and *Rorento* managed by *Rotterdamsch Beleggings-
consortium N. V.* / P.O. Box 973, Heer Bokelweg 25 / Rotterdam

Dutch Investment Information Services

*Gids bij de Prijscourant van de Vereniging voor den Effectenhandel te
Amsterdam* / Herengracht 172 / Amsterdam
Tabel van Laagste en Hoogste Koersen and *Het Financieele Dagblad* /
Weesperstraat 85 / Amsterdam

The Netherlands

Van Oss' Effectenboek / Herengracht 172 / Amsterdam
Wegwijzer voor Nederlandse Effecten / Ruysdaelstraat 71-75 / Amsterdam

Specialized Financial Newspapers and Periodicals

Bank en Effectenbedrijf / Herengracht 136 / Amsterdam
Beleggers Belangen / Prinsengracht 770 / Amsterdam
Beursberichten / Lange Houtstraat 4-8 / The Hague
Beleggings Express / Huddestraat 7 / Amsterdam
Elseviers Weekblad Editie voor de Zakenman / Postbus 152 / Amsterdam
Feiten en Cijfers / Postbus 23 / Deventer
FEM / N.Z. Voorburgwal 94 / Amsterdam
Financiele Berichten / N. Doelenstraat 12-14 / Amsterdam
De Financiele Koerier / Postbus 3906 / Amsterdam
Handelsbelangen / Helmholtzstraat 61 / Amsterdam
Wall Street / Keizersgracht 215 / Amsterdam

General Interest Publications With Financial Coverage

Accent / Postbus 3038 / Utrecht
H.P. Magazine / Singel 136 / Amsterdam

Daily Newspapers With Extensive Financial Coverage

Algemeen Dagblad / Postbus 241 / Rotterdam
Haagsche Courant / Postbus 1050 / The Hague
NRC-Handelsblad / Westblaak 180 / Rotterdam
Het Parool / Postbus 433 / Amsterdam
De Telegraaf / N.Z. Voorburgwal 225 / Amsterdam
De Tijd / Postbus 348 / Amsterdam
Trouw / Postbus 859 / Amsterdam
De Volkskrant / Postbus 1002 / Amsterdam

8. Belgium and Luxembourg

The Belgians like to think they invented the word *bourse* for stock exchange. In the 14th century, traders in Bruges, then one of the leading cities of the Hanseatic League, conducted their business in front of the house of the Chevalier van der Buerse (who had three purses in his coat of arms). Going to the *buerse* began to mean going to the exchange, and from Bruges the name spread to other trading cities of the Hanseatic League, later becoming *bourse* in French, *beurs* in Dutch, *börse* in German, *bolsa* in Italian, and *börs* in Swedish.

Be that as it may, the historical name in the past did not spur the activities of the *Bourse de Bruxelles* (the main exchange of the country; there are smaller exchanges in Antwerp, Ghent, and Liège). For many years, Brussels was one of the most inactive of the European stock exchanges. It came to life in 1971 and 1972 when, in anticipation of the United Kingdom's entry into the EEC, English investors became more interested in Belgian stocks and trading volume began to exceed $1 billion per year. In 1976, trading volume was at an annual rate of close to $2 billion. Surprisingly, more than 50% of the trading represented foreign securities and foreign investment funds, including a score of United States securities. The most popular United States stocks are *Occidental Petroleum* and *Boeing*. At times, their trading volume in Brussels was comparable to that on the New York Stock Exchange. The volatility of the two stocks appealed to the speculative Belgian investor and the arbitrager. The latter do a high percentage of the trading in foreign stocks. Trading in Belgian stocks remained more limited. Twenty-five of 700 listed Belgian stocks account for about one-half of the trading volume in Belgian stocks.

Note: 1 BFr. = $0.025

International Investing

Foreigners Welcome

The revival of the Brussels exchange is the result of conscious efforts of the Belgian government and financial institutions to make Brussels an important international financial center. As the headquarters city for the European Economic Community, Brussels has ambitions to be regarded as the "Capital of Europe." Belgium, among all European countries, is the most hospitable to international organizations as well as to foreign companies wanting to invest in the country and to establish operations there. In fact, Brussels today is the most popular of the international headquarters cities, not only for Americans who represent their companies in Europe but even for many internationalized Europeans who work outside their own countries. In that respect, Brussels has decidedly won out over the two other cities frequently chosen for international headquarters — Geneva and Paris. The Swiss have made it increasingly difficult for foreigners to take up residence and work in their country, even temporarily, and in Paris many foreign firms have found it impossible to adapt to the French way of doing things.

Brussels, on the other hand, encourages foreigners to settle. Among the attractions it offers are an ample choice of modern offices and accommodations, tax breaks to individuals representing foreign companies, easy commuting, good international schools, and good restaurants. Belgians do not treat foreigners who do not speak their two languages like imbeciles, and they make every effort to be helpful.

Most importantly, there are no foreign exchange restrictions in Belgium. Money can be taken into and out of the country; residents can buy and sell foreign securities and gold; and non-residents can buy Belgian securities.

An interesting feature of the Belgian currency market is the fact that for many years the Belgian government has been able to maintain a two-tier market for the franc — a "commercial" rate for business transactions and a "financial" rate for all other transactions, including portfolio investments, tourist trade, and other capital movements. During heavy outflow of money, the Belgian free-market franc trades at a discount to the official rate. The theory is that the development of such a discount will have an automatic self-correcting effect, and it has worked well in practice. During periods of pressure on the Belgian franc, such as the 1975 recession, the free-market discount was 5%, after having been as low as 1%. In this range, the discount does not seem to have a deterring effect on Belgian investments in foreign securities, but may attract foreign investment in safe Belgian fixed-income securities if yields are high enough.

Belgium and Luxembourg

Economic Trends

Belgium has also freed itself recently from two bad economic heritages — early industrialization and a colonial empire. Early industrialization based on coal mining and steel created bad scars on the Belgian countryside, on the business traditions, and labor relations. It also left Belgium after World War II with antiquated production facilities. With the help of substantial foreign investments, Belgian industry in the 1960s has made great strides towards modernization.

The colonial empire of the Belgian Congo, huge in relation to the mother country, came to an abrupt end in 1960. This sent heavy shock waves through the population and its business establishment. Yet, in retrospect, this traumatic end to an era may have been a blessing in disguise. It accelerated the complete reorientation of Belgian business and the purposeful internationalization of its economy.

Belgium today exports almost 50% of its production. Of the more than $5 billion in capital investment since 1960, about 70% came from abroad, more than half of this sum from the United States alone. With Britain's entry into the European Economic Community on January 1, 1973, additional capital has flowed into Belgium. Many Belgian firms have been taken over by foreign companies. Brussels has become an important international banking center, and many international bond issues, notably Eurobonds, are managed here.

On the negative side is the fact that Belgium is a house divided against itself. Created as recently as 1830 as a somewhat artificial political unit, Belgium has developed a gaping rift between the Flemish-speaking population and the French-speaking Walloons. Both are very sensitive about the equal use of their own language and about proportional representation in all government, social, and educational organizations. The political scene is greatly fragmented because each of the three main political parties has a Walloon and a Flemish wing, and in addition there are a Walloon and a Flemish party, each concerned only with its own narrow ethnic interests. All factions want ministerial representation. Belgium, with a population of about 10 million, has three dozen ministers — per capita far more than any other country in the world. This makes for inefficiencies and delays in many governmental matters.

Another factor that may be considered negative from an investor's point of view is Belgium's heavy dependence on foreign trade, which makes many of its industries vulnerable to the economic trends of its main customers, primarily its Common Market partners and the United States. This was reflected in the severe recession of 1975, which showed very little improvement in the first half of 1976. A number of American companies closed·their Belgian operations in 1975 and 1976. The recession has intensified labor problems.

Holding Companies

If an investor wanted to make an over-all investment in the Belgian economy he could theoretically do this by buying just one stock — one of the larger holding companies. More than half of Belgium's national output is in the hands of holding companies, and there is a vast network of interlocking ownership in finance and industry. The largest holding company is *Société Générale de Belgique,* which controls an estimated 30% to 40% of the Belgian economy. It owns 20% of the largest Belgian bank, *Société Générale de Banque,* and it has a substantial stake in about 70 other companies, including financial institutions, insurance concerns, shipping lines, utilities, and industrial companies. It also has a 50% interest in three other holding companies, which in turn have a part-ownership in a total of 20 companies.

In addition to *Société Générale de Belgique,* there are some 40 other holding companies listed on the Brussels exchange. Some, like the *Société Générale,* are widely diversified, including the second largest, *Compagnie Bruxelles Lambert,* the result of a recent merger of four holding companies. Several have substantial foreign holdings among their assets and others are specialized in one industry.

Stock market performance of the holding companies varies greatly, with some of the smaller or specialized ones often doing better than the very large, diversified ones.

Many Belgian companies traded on the Brussels exchange are partly owned by holding companies, and often are not independent in their management. Others are partly owned by American or other foreign concerns. This does not necessarily recommend them as investments since some of the Belgian companies bought by foreign corporations were the ones in the most serious trouble.

Leading Corporations

The two largest Belgian companies are independent, however, and their stocks are among the most actively traded issues. They are *Petrofina,* the largest Belgian petroleum company, with 1975 sales of BFr. 193 billion ($4.8 billion), and *Solvay,* a large chemical concern, with an annual sales volume in 1975 of BFr. 80 billion ($2 billion). Business activities of both companies are world-wide. *Petrofina* is popular with foreign investors because of its strong involvement in North Sea oil exploration and its relative independence from the Arabs. It has shown one of the best market performances on the Brussels *bourse. Solvay,* on the other hand, has performed about as well or as badly as the market.

Other actively traded stocks include *Gevaert,* which, in a joint venture with the German *AGFA* (a division of *Bayer*), has become the second largest photographic supplier of the world after *Kodak,* and the largest Belgian retail merchandisers, *GB-INNO-BM* and *Delhaize.*

Utilities are publicly owned in Belgium rather than nationalized as in most other European countries. They are popular investments because of generous, steadily increasing dividends and a slow but steady appreciation of the stock price.

New Issues

An important event on the Brussels exchange was the 1972 public sale and listing of the large new issue of common shares of *Bekaert* accompanied by an issue of convertible bonds. *Bekaert,* with 1975 sales of BFr. 19 billion ($475 million), is a leading international wire manufacturer and supplier of steel wire for steel-belted radial automobile tires. It was hoped that this successful introduction would spark additional new public issues, and Belgian banks and brokers were casting their eyes hopefully at two large family-owned companies — *Eternit,* a building materials producer, and *Artois,* the largest Belgian brewery and one of the largest in Europe. But *Bekaert,* until 1976, has remained the one swallow. The only equity offerings on the Brussels exchange are the rights and convertible offerings of utilities and banks, which go regularly to the money market.

Fixed-Income Securities

Traditionally, Belgian investors lean towards fixed-income securities, both Belgian and foreign. Yields for Belgian government bonds in mid-1976 were about 10%, and for safe corporate bonds even more. For non-residents, there is a 20% withholding tax on the interest payments. However, there are a number of Belgian state bonds, as well as bonds of financial institutions, including convertible bonds, that are tax free for non-residents. Also exempt from the withholding tax payable by non-

159

residents are a number of international bond issues sold in Belgium, such as the bonds of the *International Bank for Reconstruction and Development*.

A somewhat unique institution among all fixed-income markets of the world is the Belgian *Fonds des Rentes,* an independent public institution that has been created to maintain a steady market in government bonds as well as in the bonds of public institutions, such as railroads, telephone and telegraph companies, national and regional finance institutions, and municipalities. By buying and selling bonds on the open market, the *Fonds des Rentes* influences the market price of the bonds, and thereby the yield. It also intervenes in the short-term money market. In 1976, the portfolio of the *Fonds des Rentes* contained about 25% of the about 250 listed and unredeemed Belgian bond issues, with an approximate market price of over $2 billion. Yearly transactions of the *Fonds des Rentes* are valued at close to $200 million.

Corporate bonds convertible into common stock have become popular with Belgian investors because they offer a fixed-income plus the possibility of an increase in the price of the convertible in line with the movement of the common stock. Yield of convertible issues in mid-1976 averaged slightly above 6%. About a dozen convertible bond issues are quoted on the Brussels *bourse.*

Investment Trusts

Belgium has a number of well-managed investment funds — some legally based in the country, others legally based in Luxembourg but promoted mainly in Belgium, such as *Renta Fund, Rentinvest,* and *KB Income Fund.* The banks also handle several foreign funds such as the popular German *Concentra* and *Unifonds* (the latter is traded on the Brussels exchange). The shares of the Dutch *Robeco* and *Rolinco* funds are also actively traded in Brussels. For the non-resident, the Luxembourg-based funds are of greater interest, since there is no withholding tax in Luxembourg. The portfolios of the Luxembourg funds are largely international.

Banks

Both banks and brokers handle individual and institutional investment accounts and offer discretionary and consulting accounts. However, the banks do the overwhelming proportion of business in medium and large accounts. In competition for the international portfolio management business, the Belgian banks stress their historical international orientation as a result of the fact that on a per-capita basis the Belgians are the leading international traders of the world. Moreover, Belgian investors have always invested to a far greater extent in foreign securities than in domestic issues. A typical 1976 Belgian portfolio, for instance, would consist of only 20% in Belgian stocks, 20% in United States stocks, 20% in German, Dutch, and French stocks, 10% in Japanese stocks, and the balance in fixed-income securities, gold, and cash.

In 1976, Belgium had three large banks — *Société Générale de Banque, Banque Bruxelles Lambert,* and *Kredietbank.* In addition, *Banque de Paris et des Pays-Bas Belgique,* affiliated with the French bank, did a good amount of business in Belgium.

Banque Bruxelles Lambert is the result of the 1975 merger of *Banque Lambert* with *Banque de Bruxelles* — a shotgun wedding, according to some. The latter, primarily a commercial bank, had management problems and was seriously hurt by currency dealings. *Banque Lambert* was primarily a merchant bank with an excellent reputation for portfolio management. *Kredietbank* is also strong in portfolio management, and through its partly-owned subsidiary, *Kredietbank S.A. Luxembourgeoise*, it plays a major role in Eurobond underwriting and the aftermarket. *Société Générale de Banque,* as the largest of the three, is renowned for its great conservatism.

Brokers

Belgian brokers handle, for the most part, individual accounts. They are the only ones who can execute orders on the floor of the Brussels exchange. Banks must place all of their stock orders for less than BFr. 10 million ($250,000) through a broker. Only for larger orders can they try to trade outside the exchange.

Even though there were still some 370 brokers in Brussels in 1976 (down from about 450 five years earlier), only two are involved in international business to any extent — *Dewaay, Sebille, Servais, Van Campenhout & Cie* and *Peterbroeck, Van Campenhout & Cie.* Both participate in international underwritings through subsidiaries. *Dewaay* stresses its expertise in international arbitrage, bond trading, and execution for institutional investors. *Peterbroeck* promotes its portfolio management abilities for both private and institutional accounts, and offers research expertise on Belgian securities.

American brokers may not accept orders from Belgian investors, but they do provide research information for them.

International Investing

Institutional Investors

Practically all Belgian pension funds are managed by the banks. The pension fund business has up to now not been significant in view of the relatively high level of social security pensions and certain tax provisions. As a result of new legislation, it is expected that pension funds and other benefit funds will develop quickly, as they have in other smaller European countries such as Holland and Switzerland. This is expected to have a major impact on the development of the Belgian capital market and of institutional savings.

The insurance business is widely diffused, with around 400 companies operating in the country. The two largest companies — *Royale Belge* and *Compagnie Belge d'Assurances Générales* — offering a full range of risk/life coverage are the largest institutional investors, but by Belgian law insurance companies may invest only up to 20% of their portfolios in foreign securities. In practice it has been less.

Listing on the Brussels Stock Exchange

In 1976, more than 150 foreign stocks, including about 40 United States stocks, were listed on the *Bourse de Bruxelles*. A great many are actively traded. Thus, the Brussels exchange is one of the few where a foreign listing can effectively stimulate local investor interest. It also is a good public relations move for companies doing business in Belgium. To maintain a continuing following among Belgian investors, it is advisable to advertise quarterly results in the leading financial pages and distribute earnings and dividend news releases. Listing application is a somewhat bureaucratic procedure and it takes at least three months or more from application to admission. Listing application must be approved by the *Commission Bancaire*, which has functions similar to those of the SEC. The sponsoring bank shepherds the applying company through the maze. *Banque Bruxelles Lambert* has been the leader in this field, claiming to have sponsored about 75% of all foreign stocks listed on the exchange. Total costs of listing in 1976, including costs of translations and fees, was about $50,000 to $75,000. In addition, some $5,000 to $10,000 is required for supporting publicity and advertising at the time of listing, plus a small continuing budget for announcements of quarterly results.

The Brussels *bourse* has both a cash and a forward market, operating very much in the same way as those on the Paris exchange. The cash market is primarily used for small equity transactions and bonds. The forward market, allowing 15 days for settlement, is used for

162

all larger trades and most of the trades in foreign securities. Practically all Belgian shares are traded as bearer shares, but the Brussels *bourse* also has a clearing system, *CIK*, through which many of the transactions of foreign securities are cleared. This requires a bookkeeping entry if the investor does not want to hold the certificates himself. Foreign shares can be traded either in the form of BDRs (Bearer Deposit Receipts) through *CIK*, or through a system combining *CIK* and BDRs.

Sources and Channels of Information

The standard information book on Belgian stocks is *Memento des Valeurs*, published yearly and distributed by most of the Belgian banks and brokers with their names imprinted on the cover. It provides basic information and financial figures for all actively traded Belgian companies, as well as the stock price ranges over a period of years. However, it does not recommend specific stocks or make projections for the earnings prospects of individual companies.

A much more detailed multi-volume work on Belgian stocks is *Recueil Financier*. This is primarily for professional use.

The Investment Research Group of *European Banks International* (*EBIC*) publishes a monthly European stock guide that includes a section on the most popular Belgian stocks. *Société Générale de Banque* is the Belgian member of this group and makes the book available to investors in Belgium.

Banque Bruxelles Lambert, through its subsidiary, *Eurosyndicat Investment Research Bureau*, provides an excellent international research service, including general economic reports on various countries and on individual industries and companies. This service is available by subscription.

Information on non-Belgian securities is largely obtained from foreign brokers and banks and is evaluated by the security analysts and portfolio managers of the Belgian banks and brokers.

The Belgian security analysts society has been active in improving disclosure practices of Belgian companies. It holds regular meetings with corporate executives, including a number of foreign corporations actively traded in Brussels. It has the good practice of sending a carefully prepared questionnaire to the speaker beforehand so that he can address himself to the topics of interest to the analysts.

For its size, Belgium has a surprisingly large number of media providing financial news and features both in French and Flemish. The leading papers with financial coverage are *Le Soir, La Libre Belgique,* and *La Dernière Heure.* The leading financial publications are *L'Écho de la Bourse, L'Agence Économique et Financière,* and *De Financieel-Ekonomische Tijd.* In addition to the financial bulletins printed by the large banks, two subscription weeklies cater to the individual investor, presenting stock market news and coverage of the markets for real estate, art, rugs, and jewelry. They are *Gestion Patrimoniale* and *Trends.*

Luxembourg — Investment Haven

The Grand-Duchy of Luxembourg, a country that came into independent existence in 1863, and with a population today of about 340,000, has only a handful of domestic stocks to offer investors, leading among them are *ARBED,* a steel company with a sales volume of about BFrs. 32 billion ($800 million) in 1975 and *Brasserie de Diekirch,* a brewery making good beer.

However, Luxembourg has become an important international banking center and legal seat for investment management firms, investment funds, and holding companies. The Luxembourg stock exchange is extensively used for listing Eurobond and investment company issues, even though trading may be directly between market makers. About 800 international bond issues were listed on the Luxembourg exchange in 1976, plus 40 international investment funds and 75 foreign common stock issues.

Luxembourg owes its popularity as a banking center to the fact that it imposes no compulsory reserve requirements for banks. It has no central bank. American and German banks in particular were attracted to participate in the Eurobond market from there when in the 1960s the United States imposed the Interest Equalization Tax and the German government imposed a tax on foreign holdings of domestic German bonds (both since repealed). *Citibank, Bank of America,* and *Compagnie Luxembourgeoise de Banque* (a *Dresdner Bank* subsidiary) were among the early arrivals. The Belgian *Kredietbank,* a leading managing underwriter of Eurobond issues, handles all of its Eurobond operations out of Luxembourg. *CEDEL,* a computerized clearing system for Eurobond and other international bond trading, is based in Luxembourg.

Foreign banks and brokers handle a substantial business for Belgian and other foreign investors. Luxembourg offers bank secrecy, as Switzerland does. The Luxembourg franc is linked to the Belgian franc, and money, gold, and securities can be moved in and out of the country as freely as they can in Belgium. There are also some tax advantages when investing through a bank or broker in Luxembourg. There is no withholding tax on dividends and interest earned from foreign investments, and foreign securities traded in Luxembourg are exempt from stamp duty and transfer tax. On the other hand, a non-resident investing in Belgian securities through a bank or broker located in Belgium pays 20% withholding tax on practically all interest and dividends received.

International Investing

Major Stock Exchanges

Beurs van Antwerpen / Klein Klarenstraat 1 / Antwerp
Bourse de Bruxelles / Palais de la Bourse / Brussels
Société de la Bourse de Luxembourg / 11 rue de la Porte Neuve / Luxembourg-Ville

Partial List of Brussels Banks Handling Investments

Banque de Bénélux S.A. / 40 rue des Colonies
Banque Bruxelles Lambert / 2 rue de la Régence
Banque de Commerce S.A. / 51-52 avenue des Arts
Banque Jean Degroof & Cie / 18 rue Guimard
Banque de Paris et des Pays-Bas Belgique / 31 rue des Colonies
Kredietbank N.V. / Arenbergstraat 7
Société Générale de Banque S.A. / 3 Montagne du Parc

*Partial List of Brussels Brokerage Houses
Accepting Business from Foreign Investors*

Dewaay, Sebille, Servais, Van Campenhout & Cie / 1 boulevard Anspach
Heinbergen, Pringiers, Valentyn & Cie / 34 rue de la Montagne
Peterbroeck, Van Campenhout & Cie / 19 place Ste. Gudule
Puissant Baeyens, Poswick & Cie / 36 rue Ravenstein
Remy Frères & Fils S.N.C. / 138 rue Royale
Van Moer-Santerre, S.N.C. / 49 rue de Ligne
Marcel Vermeulen & Fils, S.N.C. / 59 boulevard Anspach

American Brokerage Offices in Brussels

Dominick & Dominick Inc. / 2 rue de l'Aurore
Donaldson, Lufkin & Jenrette, Inc., S.A. / Tour-Porte de Namur, 5 place du Champ de Mars
Drexel Burnham Lambert / 5 boulevard de l'Empereur
First Manhattan Co. / 203 avenue Louise
Laidlaw-Coggeshall Inc. / 15 rue Blanche
Merrill Lynch, Pierce, Fenner & Smith Inc. / 221 avenue Louise
Shearson Hayden Stone Inc. / 368 avenue Louise
Thomson & McKinnon Auchincloss Kohlmeyer Inc. / 43 rue de Namur
Wood, Struthers & Winthrop Inc. / 497 avenue Louise

Belgium and Luxembourg

Partial List of Actively Traded Belgian Stocks

Banque Bruxelles Lambert
Bekaert (steel wire)
Cockerill (steel)
Compagnie Bruxelles Lambert (holding company)
Delhaize (retail merchandising)
EBES (utility)
Electrobel (electric utilities holding company)
GB-INNO-BM (retail merchandising)
Gevaert (photographic materials)
Intercom (utility)
Kredietbank
Petrofina (integrated oil company)
Société Générale de Banque
Société Générale de Belgique (holding company)
Société de Traction et d'Électricité (utility holding company)
Solvay (chemicals)
Union Minière (nonferrous metals)
Vieille-Montagne (zinc)
Wagons-Lits (sleeping and dining car operation)

Belgian Investment Funds

Managed by *Banque Bruxelles Lambert*
   Eurounion (European stocks and bonds); *Finance-Union* (international stocks); *Fonds Fiducem Internationale* (international stocks and bonds); *Fonds Prevoyance et Retraite* (fixed-income); *Patrimonial* (international stocks and bonds); *Renta Fund* (high yield distribution); *Renta Capital Fund* (high yield capital accumulation)
Managed by *Banque de Paris et des Pays-Bas Belgique*
   Benelfonds (Belgian and international stocks); *Paribas-Rente* (high yield)
Managed by *Kredietbank*
   Dépôt Américain (North American securities); *Dépôt Belge* (Belgian stocks and bonds); *Dépôt Intercontinental* (international stocks); *Dépôt d'Obligation International* (international bonds); *Euroinvest* (European stocks and bonds); *Institut Investors Fund* (international stocks); *Canadian Investment Fund; KB Income Fund; KB Kapital Fund* (growth); *Technology Fund.*
Managed by *Société Générale de Banque*
   Canafund (Canadian stocks); *Capital Rentinvest* (yield-capital accumulation); *North American Fund; Rentinvest* (yield distribution)

167

International Investing

Belgian Sources of Information

Eurosyndicat Investment Research Bureau / avenue Marnix / Brussels
Mémento des Valeurs / available from Belgian bankers and brokers
Recueil Financier / 65 rue de la Régence / Brussels

Belgian Financial and Business Press
All in Brussels unless otherwise indicated

AGÉFI / 5-7 quai Bois-à-Brûler
La Bourse de Bruxelles / 299 avenue Van Volxem
Courrier de la Bourse / 23 rue du Boulet
l'Écho de la Bourse / 47 rue du Houblon
De Financieel-Ekonomische Tijd / Tevernierkaai 4 / Antwerp
Gestion Patrimoniale / 382 avenue Louise
l'Informateur Économique et Financier / 23 rue du Boulet
Mercure / 135 boulevard M. Lemonnier
Moniteur des Intérêts Matériels / 23 rue du Boulet
Spécial / 31 rue des Drapiers
Trends / I.P.C.-Karel de Grotelaan 1
Trends-Tendances / 153 avenue de Tervueren

Belgian Daily Newspapers With Good Business Coverage
All in Brussels unless otherwise indicated

La Dernière Heure / 52 rue du Pont-Neuf
Gazet van Antwerpen / Katwilweg / Antwerp
Het Laatste Nieuws / Emil Jacqmainlaan 105
La Libre Belgique / rue Montagne-aux-Herbes-Potagères
Le Soir / 21 place de Louvain

Members of the Luxembourg Bourse
All in Luxembourg-Ville

Bank of America, S.A. / 35 boulevard Royal
Banque Commerciale, S.A. / 24 boulevard Royal
Banque Continentale du Luxembourg, S.A. / 3-5 boulevard Royal
Banque Générale du Luxembourg, S.A. / 27 avenue Monterey
Banque Interatlantique, S.A. / 28 boulevard Joseph II
Banque Internationale à Luxembourg, S.A. / 2 boulevard Royal

Belgium and Luxembourg

Banque Lambert-Luxembourg, S.A. / 11 boulevard Gr.-D. Charlotte
Banque Mathieu Frères, S.A. / 80 place de la Gare
Banque de Paris et des Pays-Bas Luxembourg, S.A. / 10a boulevard
Royal
Banque de Suez-Luxembourg, S.A. / 10 rue Aldringen
Caisse d'Épargne de l'État / 1 place de Metz
Chase Manhattan Bank Luxembourg S.A. / 47 boulevard Royal
Commerzbank International S.A. / 22-24 boulevard Royal
Compagnie Financière de la Deutsche Bank A.G. / 68 avenue de la
Liberté
Compagnie Luxembourgeoise de Banque S.A. / 26 rue du Marché-
aux-Herbes
Crédit Européen S.A. / 52 rue d'Esch
Crédit Industriel d'Alsace et de Lorraine / 103 Grand-rue
Crédit Lyonnais / 26a boulevard Royal
Dewaay Luxembourg S.A. / 47 boulevard Royal
Citibank (Luxembourg) S.A. / 16 avenue Marie-Thérèse
Eurocapital S.A. / 3 boulevard Royal
E.F. Hutton & Co. (Luxembourg) S.A. / 1 rue du Fort Elisabeth
Industrial Bank of Japan (Luxembourg) S.A. / 5 boulevard Royal
James Capel International S.A. / 103 Grand-rue
Kredietbank S.A. Luxembourgeoise / 37 rue Notre-Dame
Merrill Lynch Europe S.A. / 3 rue Aldringen
Nikko (Luxembourg) S.A. / 15 rue Notre-Dame
Société Générale Alsacienne de Banque / 15 avenue Emile Reuter
West LB International S.A. / 47 boulevard Royal

9. Scandinavia and Finland

Geography reflects to some extent the economic relationship of the four Nordic countries to the rest of Europe. Only Denmark has direct land connections with Western Europe. Denmark is also the only Nordic country to join the European Economic Community (EEC). Norway, Sweden and Finland are separated from Western Europe by the sea and Russia. The Norwegians, surprisingly to many of themselves and to other Europeans, voted down membership in the EEC in 1972. Sweden decided that membership in the EEC would not be compatible with its neutrality, which it has pursued since 1814. And Finland, as a result of its hapless wars with Russia (1939-1945), must maintain its own kind of neutrality under the giant wings of its neighbor.

From the viewpoint of a foreign investor, this situation is also reflected in the investment opportunities in the four Nordic countries. Only Denmark, since its entry into the EEC on January 1, 1973, has made it possible for foreign investors to buy stocks of its publicly-owned companies without restrictions and, since 1975, non-residents have also been able to buy Danish bonds. Both Norway and Sweden make it difficult for foreign investors to buy their securities, and foreign ownership in publicly-held companies is limited to varying degrees. Finland limits foreign ownership of its companies to 20%. Its stock market is the least active of the four.

Note: 1 DKr. = $0.17; 1 SKr. = $0.23; 1 NKr. = $0.18; 1 FMk. = $0.25.

International Investing

Free Enterprise "Socialism"

To some armchair conservatives, the Nordic countries, especially Sweden, are suspect because of their "rampant socialism," as it is often referred to, a socialism in the opinion of some that puts the Swedes into the category of state-controlled Marxist economies or near-communism. For anyone patient enough to look at the facts, however, economic enterprise in the four Nordic countries will appear as private and free as in most other countries of the non-communist world, and more private and freer than in some of them, although the programs of the socialist parties envision government control of banks, insurance companies, and other industries. What is loosely described as "socialism" are social services provided from tax income by democratically elected governments which ran on the platform of providing such social services. What is often overlooked is the fact that under their economic systems, whatever one may want to call them, the Nordic countries have reached the highest ranks in per-capita income among all countries of the world. In 1975, Sweden ranked second in the world, trailing Switzerland by a hair, Norway was third, Denmark was fourth, and the United States was fifth. Sweden ranked first in per-capita income in 1974.

A Limit to Taxation?

What might give concern to free-enterprise proponents and potential investors in these countries is the fact that the cost of these social services has made the Nordic countries, together with the Netherlands, undisputed leaders in the world in raising taxes. In 1974, tax receipts of the Netherlands, Sweden, Norway, and Denmark were around 50% of gross national product, versus slightly more than 30% in the United States. In Finland, the figure was about 38%.

With such high taxes, the question arises: What are the limits to which taxes can be raised without creating mass resistance or evasion by the taxpayers, and without seriously impairing personal endeavor and, thereby, economic growth?

The first rumblings of a tax revolt occurred in Denmark where a non-partisan candidate for political office named Mogens Glistrup proposed to abolish income taxes and social services. The government apparatus for administering social services had become so expensive, he argued, that the individual taxpayer would be financially better off if he paid no income taxes at all and took care of his own social services. The small government apparatus needed to provide other government functions could easily be financed through the sales tax, the candidate said. In their election in November 1973, the Danes elected Mr. Glistrup's

172

Scandinavia and Finland

Progress Party to the second spot among ten political parties. A new election in 1975 did very little to change the fragmented political situation. In November 1976, the Swedes voted their socialist party out of office.

World Trade Dependence

Another significant factor in the investment climate of the Scandinavian countries is their great dependence on world trade, making their economies subject to the business trends of their main trading partners — Western Europe and the United States. In exports of goods and services as a percentage of gross national product, Norway with 44% average between 1972 and 1974, was third among all countries of the world, closely behind the Netherlands and Belgium. Shipping services are Norway's main "export," with Norway having far more ships per capita on the Seven Seas than any other country. Denmark was fifth, with about 33% of its gross national product going into export, the largest exports being agricultural products. Sweden was sixth, with about 29%; the largest exports, about 48% of the total (excluding services), were machinery, automobiles, and other engineering products.

In view of Scandinavia's great dependence on foreign trade, it is surprising to find these countries somewhat isolated when it comes to an interchange of portfolio investments with foreign countries. (There are just as many restrictions on Scandinavian investments in foreign securities as there are on foreign investments in Scandinavian securities.) This seems to be partly the relic of strict foreign exchange controls imposed during the Depression and World War II, and partly an effort to prevent control of local industry by larger and financially stronger nations.

In 1976, only Denmark had relaxed its regulations. Foreign investors can buy Danish stocks and bonds without restrictions, and as of January 1, 1978, Danish investors will be allowed to buy foreign securities.

Danish Fixed-Income Securities

Bonds dominate the Copenhagen stock market because of their high yields and their far greater availability. The face value of all Danish domestic bond issues listed on the *Københavns Fondsbørs* in 1975 was about DKr. 195 billion ($33 billion) versus about DKr. 19 billion ($3.2 billion) for the total market value of all common stocks. (There is also an after exchange, where less seasoned equity issues are traded on the

173

floor of the exchange after the trading hours.) Total "nominal" trading volume in bonds in 1975 was DKr. 11.7 billion ($1.9 billion) as compared with DKr. 317 million ($53 million) of equity trading on the exchange and DKr. 15 million ($2.5 million) on the after exchange. More than 80% of the Danish bonds are sold by private bond-issuing mortgage credit institutions either as first mortgage credit bonds (DKr. 111 billion [$18.7 billion]) or second mortgage credit bonds (DKr. 62 billion [$10.5 billion]). The balance of some DKr. 23 billion ($3.9 billion) in 1975 consisted of state and local government bonds, shipping bonds, and general corporate bonds. Rates for first mortgage bonds in 1975 ranged from 12½% to 15%. Second mortgage bonds yielded about 0.25% more than first mortgage bonds.

The mortgage credit associations are peculiar to Denmark. They are non-profit organizations, comparable to cooperatives, and their profits are added to their reserves. They are owned by the borrowers — corporations and institutions developing, financing, and owning real estate. According to an act of the Danish parliament, a ceiling of 80% of the underlying property value has been established for loans raised through mortgage credit associations. Any additional mortgage must be guaranteed by the government or by an insurance company. First mortgage bonds are secured by up to the first 40% of the property value; second mortgage bonds by the second 40%, up to 80%. Bonds are available in denominations of DKr. 1000 ($170), 5000 ($850), 10,000 ($1700) and 20,000 ($3400), with maturities from ten to 40 years. Issues are actively traded on the Copenhagen stock exchange. There are seven bond-issuing mortgage credit institutions; the largest of them is *Kreditforeningen Danmark.*

In 1976, the Danish government, in order to finance its increasing budget deficit, introduced new one- and two-year discount bills at the going short-term interest rates, but at prices below par. They were of particular interest to individual investors because the capital gains at redemption are tax free.

The Danish government, government agencies, and private institutions are also heavy borrowers outside Denmark. In 1976, about 35 Danish Eurodollar bond issues were outstanding, plus several more in other Eurocurrencies, including issues of the Kingdom of Denmark, *Carlsberg-Tuborg*, the City of Copenhagen, and the *Denmark Mortgage Bank.*

Danish Common Stocks

In 1975, 148 equity issues of 115 companies were listed on the main exchange. Trading volume in most of them was small, although total volume has increased by about 60% over 1974. The stock most likely to strike a familiar chord among investors outside Denmark is that of the brewers of Carlsberg and Tuborg beer, *Førenede Bryggerier*. With 1975 sales of DKr. 2.7 billion ($459 million), the "united breweries" accounted for 80% of Danish beer production and for 90% of the country's beer exports. It is the largest brewer on the European continent and also owns a number of licensed breweries in several other countries.

Old Asia hands are familiar with the *Danish East Asiatic Co.* (*Ostasiatiske Kompagni*), a commodity trading company, operating its own shipping line and now also engaged in many manufacturing operations throughout the world. Originating in Thailand in the 19th century, it is today the largest Danish corporation, with 1975 sales of about DKr. 12.5 billion ($2.1 billion).

Among the more actively traded stocks are those of the three leading Danish banks — *Kjøbenhavns Handelsbank* with 1975 assets of DKr. 25 billion ($4.25 billion), *Den Danske Bank* (formerly *Den Danske Landmandsbank*) with 1975 assets of DKr. 18 billion ($3 billion), and *Privatbanken* with 1975 assets of DKr. 10 billion ($1.7 billion). The Danish banks are active in both commercial banking and the brokerage and investment business, but they do not own interests in Danish industry. The banks, in the 1970s, went repeatedly into the equity market for new capital to maintain their capital ratio at the legal minimum of 8% of deposits and guarantees.

Burmeister & Wain, Denmark's largest shipbuilders, with 1974 sales of DKr. 516 million ($88 million), has suffered from the sharp decline in tanker construction as a result of the oil crisis, but it is benefiting to some extent from North Sea oil exploration work.

Other Danish companies fairly well known outside their homeland are the Danish ceramic manufacturers *Bing & Grondahl* and *Kgl. Porcelainsfabrik* (Royal Porcelain Factory) and *Superfos*, a chemical and fertilizer company.

Danish shares are registered in the buyer's name, but a simple endorsement makes them negotiable for anyone who holds them. Coupons must be detached to collect dividends. For practical reasons, a foreign investor should leave his shares in the custody of a bank or broker. There is a withholding tax of 15% on dividends due non-resident investors, which is recoverable for United States taxpayers.

Danish Investors

In addition to the three leading banks mentioned above, another major factor on the investment scene is *R. Henriques jr. Bank* and its broker affiliate. All four are active participants in Eurobond syndicates and are prepared to be in the forefront of foreign investments as soon as Danish investors can again buy foreign securities in 1978. Denmark has four investment trusts and a number of insurance companies, but none of them have any sizable holdings of foreign securities.

Only officially licensed brokers can deal on the floor of the stock exchange. They also deal directly with the public, as do the banks. Banks can trade with each other or through brokers, but they cannot operate on the floor of the exchange.

Information on Danish stocks has improved with the new stock exchange legislation passed in 1972 and the new Danish Company Law passed in 1973. In addition, progress has been made to bring Danish disclosure practices in line with the EEC's European Company Law and proposed stock exchange legislation.

Danmarks Nationalbank, the central bank, publishes an annual report in English with a section on the securities market. Limited information on Danish stocks and investment funds is found in *Green's Danske Fonds og Aktier*. The two leading financial publications are the daily *Børsen* and the weekly *Finanstidende*.

Sweden Keeps Door Half Shut

Though Sweden is Europe's second wealthiest country in terms of per-capita income, it offers limited investment opportunities for the foreign investor and it is only a marginal market for foreign securities. Currency restrictions make it difficult for the Swedish investor to buy foreign securities. Foreign mutual funds are prohibited by law in Sweden.

In 1975, when Sweden for the second year in a row ran a payment deficit, the *Sveriges Riksbank*, the central bank, encouraged Swedish commercial banks to raise money abroad to stimulate Swedish industry, but these borrowings were limited to bank loans and bond issues, and did not affect the restrictions on equity investments by non-residents.

At the end of 1975, 101 stock issues were listed on the *Stockholms Fondbörs*, the stock exchange, with a total market valuation of SKr. 42 billion ($9.66 billion). The total number of bond issues listed was 1326, with a market value of SKr. 128 billion ($29 billion). Bond trading is relatively low — a total trading volume in 1975 of SKr. 780 million ($179 million), versus a trading volume of SKr. 2 billion ($460 million) for equity issues.

Scandinavia and Finland

Swedish Common Stocks

Sweden has a number of industrial companies of world-wide renown, among them the two automobile manufacturers *SAAB-Scania* and *Volvo*; the electrical appliances and electronics manufacturer of vacuum cleaner fame, *Electrolux*; the world-wide roller bearing manufacturer, *SKF*; and *L.M. Ericsson*. *Ericsson* is the only Swedish stock that can be bought in the United States, in the form of American Depositary Receipts traded over-the-counter. The company is a major supplier of telephone and other telecommunications equipment for the international market. It operates more than 120 subsidiaries and affiliates in about 100 countries. Its annual report in English is an outstanding example of good disclosure practices.

Purchases of other Swedish securities by a non-resident are extremely difficult. Unless the stock is already owned by a non-resident, such purchases must be approved by the *Riksbank*. Approval is not automatically given and depends to some extent on the industry involved. Shares of Swedish banks, insurance companies and defense products manufacturers are completely taboo to foreigners. Permission to buy shares of Swedish shipping companies, mining enterprises, other natural resources companies and real estate operations is rarely given to foreign investors. Foreign ownership in most Swedish companies is usually limited to 20% of the voting shares or to 40% of the total share capital. This ownership limitation is accomplished through the issuance of four types of shares — Class A "restricted" and "free" and Class B "restricted" and "free". Foreign investors can buy only "free" shares. "Restricted" shares can only be owned by Swedish nationals. Class A shares have one vote per share; Class B shares may have 1/100th vote per share or 1/1000th vote per share in older companies but not less than 1/10th vote in companies founded after 1944. Usually 80% or more of the Class A shares issued are "restricted". For all practical purposes Swedish bonds are barred to foreign investors.

Many Swedish securities can be bought in Sweden by foreign investors without special permission of the *Riksbank* if so-called "switch currency" is used — these are the proceeds of a sale of Swedish securities by a foreign investor. Switch currency is a "right" to buy Swedish securities and must be paid in addition to the purchase price of the shares. The money paid for rights is on deposit while the shares are held and will be recovered when the shares are sold. There is a 30% withholding tax on dividends paid to non-residents.

177

International Investing

Swedish Investors

A Swedish investor may buy a foreign security only if he sells an equal amount of other foreign securities first or he must acquire rights that result from the sale of a foreign security. This "switch currency" usually sells at a premium above the regular rate of exchange (about 16% in mid-1976). Thus, total holdings of foreign securities remain more or less constant, with their market value changing with the variations in the stock prices. There are no official figures on total foreign holdings by Swedish investors, but estimates range up to $500 million, with about 50% in United States securities.

This limitation has kept the Swedish investor active on the Stockholm exchange, with trading volume tripling between 1970 and 1975. About 9% of the Swedish population are active shareholders (almost as high a percentage as in the United States).

The largest Swedish investor is the *Swedish National Pension Fund*. As the contributions paid by companies are exceeding the disbursements, the fund is growing at a rate of about SKr. 10 billion ($2.3 billion) a year, and amounted to about SKr. 90 billion ($20.7 billion) at the end of 1975. Through intermediaries, the fund buys about 60% of all new issues of bonds and provides about one third of all loans to financial institutions and local authorities. Since 1974, through an investment subsidiary, it has also been able to invest in equity, with about SKr. 1 billion ($230 million) allocated in 1976. This may explain why the Swedish market since then has continued on a steady upward trend in spite of the recession and other economic problems of the country.

Both banks and brokers sell securities to the public, and both banks and brokers are members of the Stockholm exchange. Brokers, however, do not participate in underwritings. The four largest banks, accounting for about 80% of the total assets of all Swedish commercial banks, also dominate the securities business to about 80%. However, the banks cannot hold securities for their own accounts.

The largest Swedish bank, *PK-Banken*, resulting from a 1974 merger of the *Swedish Post Office Bank* and *Sveriges Kreditbank*, is government owned. The next two in size, *Skandinaviska Enskilda Banken* and *Svenska Handelsbanken*, are publicly-owned banks with their shares actively traded on the Stockholm stock exchange.

There are six mutual funds in Sweden — four linked to commercial banks, one sponsored by a savings bank, and one independent.

Scandinavia and Finland

Their total assets in 1975 were about $50 million, with only modest amounts of foreign securities in their portfolios.

Stock Transfer and Information

In 1971, Sweden instituted a new system of stock transfer based on a central computer file. Transfer of ownership can be registered there, without physical transfer of stock certificates. Owners also receive dividends automatically if their names are registered with the central depository, and there is no longer a need, as there was in the past, to send in a coupon to claim a dividend. An owner can appoint a nominee to be on the registry of the depository or he can have the shares registered in his own name in an "open deposit of a bank." The latter would be the most practical approach for a foreign investor. In 1976, a majority of public companies participated in this system.

Disclosure practices in Sweden are generally good. Several larger Swedish companies publish their annual reports, or a summary thereof, in English. *Svenska Aktiebolag* includes data on most Swedish stocks in its Swedish-language edition and also publishes an abridged English-language edition entitled *Some Prominent Swedish Companies*. Banks and brokers also publish information about Swedish securities. A daily stock market index is prepared by the brokerage firm of *Jacobson & Ponsbach*. The two leading financial publications are *Veckans Affärer* (which also publishes an annual volume, *Sweden's 200 Biggest Companies*, which contains tables and summaries in English) and *Affärsvärlden-Finanstidningen*.

Norway Restricted

Norway has caught the attention of international investors because of its major role in the North Sea oil exploration. The government encourages direct foreign investments, but restricts portfolio investments. All investments in Norwegian securities must be approved by the *Norges Bank* (the central bank), and in many cases approval of the company involved must also be obtained. Foreign ownership in banks is limited to 10% of the outstanding shares, in industrial and oil companies to 20%, and in shipping companies to 40%. Some other companies have their own limitations to foreign shares ownership. Investments by foreigners in companies involved in pulp and paper production, mining, and water power are barred. Permits to buy bonds are difficult or impossible to obtain. Moreover, there is a 25% withholding tax on dividends and interest payable to non-residents.

The one exception to these restrictions is *Norsk Hydro*, a 51% state-controlled public utility also engaged in fertilizer, chemical, aluminum, and oil production. Permission to buy *Norsk Hydro* shares is automatically granted by the central bank. The stock is also actively traded on the Paris and London exchanges. The company is an active borrower on the international capital markets. With 1975 sales of NKr. 4 billion ($720 million), it is Norway's largest enterprise.

Traditionally, shipping was Norway's main foreign currency earner, and the country's merchant fleet has been the fourth largest in the world for more than 100 years. Shares of the largest shipping company, *Kosmos*, are among the more actively traded on the *Oslo Børs*. The leading shipbuilder is *Kvaerner*, also publicly owned. Among other active stocks are those of the three leading banks — *Bergen Bank* (resulting from the 1975 merger of *Bergens Privatbank* and *Bergen Kreditbank*), *Kreditkassen*, and *Norske Creditbank*.

In all, about 160 stocks and 300 bonds were listed on the Oslo stock exchange in 1975, including six foreign stocks, among them one American, *I.U. International*.

Both banks and brokerage houses are members of the *Oslo Børs* and both can deal with the public.

Norwegian investors can buy foreign securities only with the proceeds from the sale of foreign securities, "switch currency," which usually sells at a premium. Total holdings of foreign securities are thus limited and are estimated to be about $150 million, perhaps one half in United States securities. Casualty insurance companies may buy foreign securities with foreign premium income.

A widely-used reference book on Norwegian stocks is the *Handbok over Norske Obligasjoner og Aksjer*, published by a leading brokerage firm, *Carl Kierulf*. Another broker, *Gunnar Bøhn*, publishes a stock guide entitled *Aksjer Oslo Børs*. The only business news in English is published once a week in the daily commercial and shipping newspaper, *Norges Handels og Sjøfarts Tidende*.

Finland Very Limited

For all practical purposes, Finland offers extremely limited investment opportunities to the foreign investor in spite of healthy economic growth and a hard-working, intelligent population. Foreign investments in Finnish companies are in most cases limited to 20% of the outstanding shares, but there is no restriction on portfolio investments in banks and insurance stocks. About 60 stock issues were listed on the *Helsingin Arvopaperipörssi* in 1976. Some of them are quite inactive. Total annual trading volume on the Helsinki exchange is hardly more than FMk. 200 million ($50 million). Total nominal value of all listed stocks is about FMk. 3 billion ($750 million). The state has a direct ownership in many industries because after World War II few companies could finance themselves through private channels. Even today, financing is by debt rather than through the sale of common stock. Large share ownership by the *National Bank of Finland* and the *National Pension Institute* also limits the number of shares available for public trading. A limited bond market includes government, mortgage credit institutions, and corporate issues.

Britain's and Denmark's entry into the EEC has curtailed Finland's trade with two of its major trading partners. Finland has negotiated a free-trade agreement with the Common Market countries that provides for a graduated mutual tariff reduction over a period of 11 years. Trade with the nine members of the EEC accounted for about 45% of Finland's foreign trade in 1972. In 1976, the Finnish economy was suffering from high oil prices, recession, and inflation.

In the other direction, Finland is walking a tightrope in its trade relations with the Soviet Union and the Eastern bloc nations, regulated through the Comecon pact. About 15% of Finland's foreign trade is with Comecon nations and 12% with the Soviet Union, and this trade is not always strictly governed by the free play of supply and demand and market price.

There is apparently no information in English on Finnish stocks. Whatever investment information is available is published in Finnish by the banks and brokerage houses. Both banks and brokers can be members of the Helsinki exchange and deal in securities with the public. Finns cannot invest in foreign securities.

International Investing

Danish Stock Exchange

Københavns Fondsbørs / Nikolaj Plads 6 / Copenhagen

*Leading Danish Banks and Brokerage Houses
Doing Investment Business*

Andelsbanken A.m.b.A. / Vesterbrogade 25 / Copenhagen
Den Danske Bank Af 1871 / Holmens Kanal 12 / Copenhagen
Den Danske Provinsbank A/S / Kannikegade 4-6 / Aarhus
R. Henriques jr. / Nikolaj Plads 2 / Copenhagen
R. Henriques jr. Bank-Aktieselskab / Højbro Plads 9 / Copenhagen
Kjøbenhavns Handelsbank / Amagertov 24 / Copenhagen
Privatbanken A/S / Børsgade 4 / Copenhagen

Partial List of Actively Traded Danish Stocks

Aarhus Oliefabrik (foods)
Bing & Grondahl (ceramics)
Burmeister & Wain (shipbuilding)
Den Danske Bank
Danske Sukkerfabrikker (foods)
Førenede Bryggerier (brewery)
Førenede Papirfabrikker (paper)
Kjøbenhavns Handelsbank
Kgl. Porcelainsfabrik (ceramics)
Nordiske Kabel (wire and cable)
Ostasiatiske Kompagnie (trading and shipping)
Privatbanken
Superfos (chemicals)

Danish Mutual Funds

Almindelig Investeringsforening / Goldschmidtsvej 23 / Copenhagen
Bankforeningernes and *Investeringsforening* / Bredgade 32 / Copen-
hagen
Dansk Sparinvest / H.C. Anderson Boulevard 37 / Copenhagen
Investor / Ny Vestergade 17 / Copenhagen

Principal Source of Information

Green's Danske Fonds og Aktier (Directory of Funds and Shares) published by *Børsen's Forlag* / P.O. Box 2103 / Copenhagen

182

Scandinavia and Finland

Information on Mortgage Credit Associations

Kreditforeningen Danmark / Jarmers Plads 2 / Copenhagen

Danish Business and Financial Publications

Børsen / P.O. Box 2103 / Copenhagen
Danmarks Handels og Sjofartstidende / Valbygaardsvej 62 / Copenhagen-Valby
Finanstidende / St. Kannikestraede 16 / Copenhagen
Fund Guide International / Kompagnistraede 34 / Copenhagen
Tidsskrift for Industri / H.C. Anderson Boulevard 18 / Copenhagen

Danish Newspapers With Good Business Coverage

Berlingske Tidende / Pilestraede / Copenhagen
Politiken / Politikens Hus, Raadhusplads / Copenhagen
Jyllands-Posten / Vilby / Jutland

Swedish Stock Exchange

Stockholms Fondbörs / Källargränd 2 / Stockholm

Bank Members of the Stockholm Exchange

Götabanken / Box 40106, 103 43 Stockholm and 405 09 Göteborg
Östgötabanken / Box 328, 581 03 Linköping
PK-Banken / Box 7042, 103 81 Stockholm
Skandinaviska Enskilda Banken / S-106 40 Stockholm
Skanska Banken / Fack 201 10 Malmö
Skaraborgsbanken / Fack 541 01 Skövde
Sparbankernas Bank AB / Box 4049, 102 61 Stockholm
Sundsvallsbanken / Fack 201 10 Sundsvall
Svenska Handelsbanken / Box 12128, 102 24 Stockholm
Uplandsbanken / Box 276, 751 05 Uppsala
Wermlandsbanken / Fack 651 01 Karlstad

Broker Members of the Stockholm Exchange in Stockholm

Aktiebolaget Bankirfirman Langenskiöld / Hovslagargatan 5B
Aktiebolaget Fondkomission / Skeppsbron 8

International Investing

Bankirfirman E. Öhman J:or AB & Co. Kommanditbolag / Box 7061, 103 82
Fondkommissionärsfirman Berg Kommanditbolag / Box 16200, 103 24
Fondkommissionärsfirman Hägglöf Kommanditbolag / Box 16162, 103 24
Fondkommissionärsfirman Persson & Co. AB / Majorsgatan 9
Jacobson & Ponsbach AB / Box 16295, 103 25

Partial List of Actively Traded Swedish Stocks
*ADRs traded on the United States over-the-counter market

ASEA (electrical equipment; owns 23% of *Electrolux*, 32% of *Svenska Fläktfabriken*, and 49% of *Skandinaviska Elverk*)
Atlas Copco (pneumatic machinery)
Boliden (zinc, lead, copper)
Electrolux (electrical appliances, radios, televisions)
L.M. Ericsson* (telephone equipment)
SAAB-Scania (automobiles, aerospace)
Sandvik (steel)
Skandinaviska Elverk (electric utility)
Skandinaviska Enskilda Banken
Svenska Cellulosa (forest products)
Svenska Fläktfabriken (machinery)
Svenska Handelsbanken
SKF (roller bearings, steel products)
Svenska Tändstick (matches; owns 32% of *British Match*)
Tirfing (shipping)
Uddeholm (forest products, steel)
Volvo (automobiles)

Swedish Mutual Funds, All in Stockholm

Delta, Sesam, and *Skandifond* managed by *Skandinaviska Enskilda Banken* / S-106 40
Interfond managed by *Interfond Stiftelsen* / Nybrogatan 7
Kapitalinvest and *Sparinvest* managed by *Robur AB* / Box 4049, S-102 61
Koncentra / Arsenalsgatan 9

Sources of Information in Stockholm

Svenska Aktiebolag (an abridged English-language edition is available under the title *Some Prominent Swedish Companies*) published by

Scandinavia and Finland

Kungl. Boktryckeriet P.A. Norstedt & Söner / Box 2030, S-103 12
Stockholm stock exchange index and reports are published by *Jacobson
& Ponsbach* / V. Trädgardsgatan 11B

Swedish Business and Financial Publications in Stockholm

Affärsvärlden-Finanstidningen / Box 1760, 111 87
Dagens Industri / Box 3177
Vär Industri / Storgatan 19
Veckans Affärer (also publisher of *Sweden's 200 Biggest Companies*) /
Box 3188, 103 63

Swedish Newspapers With Good Business Coverage

Dagens Nyheter / Ralambsvägen 17 / Stockholm
Göteborgs Handels- och Sjöfartstidning (weekly) / Kopmansgatan 10 /
Göteborg
Svenska Dagbladet / Ralambsvägen 7 / Stockholm
Sydsvenska Dagbladet / Krusegatan 19, Box 145 / Malmö

Norwegian Stock Exchange

Oslo Børs / Tollbugaten 2 / Oslo

Leading Norwegian Banks and Brokers in Oslo
Doing Investment Business

Andresens Bank A/S / Torvgaten 2-4-6
Bergen Bank / Kirkegaten 23 and Postboks 826 / 5001 Bergen
Gunnar Bøhn & Co. A/S / Tollbugaten 2
Christiania Bank og Kreditkasse / Stortovet 7
Fellesbanken A/S / Kirkegaten 14-16-18
Fondsfinans A/S / Haakon VII's Gate 6
Carl Kierulf & Co. A/S / Ovre Slottsgate 17
Den Norske Creditbank / Kirkegaten 24
Tennants Fonds- og Aktiemeglerforretning A/S / Tollbugaten 27

Partial List of Actively Traded Norwegian Stocks

Bergen Bank
Borregaard (forest products, chemicals)
Hafslund (utility)

International Investing

Kosmos (shipping)
Kreditkassen (banking)
Kvaerner (shipbuilding, machinery)
Norsk Hydro (utility, chemicals, fertilizer, oil exploration)
Norske Creditbank
Sigmalm (shipping)

Norwegian Investment Trusts

A/S Investa / Olav Kyrresgate 7 / Bergen
A/S Securus / Fr. Nansens plass 9 / Oslo

Norwegian Sources of Information in Oslo

Aksjer Oslo Børs published by *Gunnar Bøhn & Co. A/S* / Universitatsgate 22
Handbok over Norske Obligasjoner og Aksjer published by *Carl Kierulf & Co. A/S* / Ovre Slottsgate 17

Norwegian Financial and Business Publications

Farmand (weekly) / R. Amundsensgate 1 / Oslo
Kapital (weekly) / Box 18 / 1345 Osteras
Naeringsrevyen (weekly) / Drammensvn. 30 / Oslo
Norges Handels og Sjøfarts Tidende (daily) / Sjøfartsbygningen / Oslo

Leading Norwegian Daily Newspaper

Aftenposten / Akersgate 51 / Oslo

Finnish Stock Exchange

Helsingin Arvopapieripörssi / Fabianinkatu 14A3 / Helsinki

Member Firms of the Helsinki Stock Exchange in Helsinki

Bensow Oy-Ab / E. Esplanadikatu 22
Pankkiiriliike Ane Gyllenberg Oy / E. Esplanadikatu 33
Helsingin Osakepankki / Aleksanterinkatu 17
Pankkiiriliike L. Hüsi Ky / Temppelikatu 21C64
Kansallis-Osake-Pankki / Aleksanterinkatu 42

186

Scandinavia and Finland

Lamy Oy / Dagmarinkatu 8
Pankkiiriliike S.A. Lundelin Ky / Mannerheimintie 124A12
Osuuspankkien Keskuspankki Oy / Arkadiankatu 23
Pohjoismaiden Yhdyspankki Oy / Aleksanterinkatu 30
Pankkiiriliike Erik Selin Ky / E. Esplanadikatu 22
Oy Suomen Pankkiirilaitos / E. Esplanadikatu 22
Säätöpankkien Keskus-Osake-Pankki / Aleksanterinkatu 46

Finnish Economic Publication

Talouselämä / Fredrikinkatu 34 / Helsinki

Finnish Newspapers With Financial Coverage

Helsingin Sanomat / Ludviginkatu 2-10 / Helsinki
Kauppalehti / Yrjökatu 13 / Helsinki

10. Spain and Portugal

During the eclipse of Wall Street from 1969 to 1973, Spain was an unexpected bright new star in the international investment sky — unexpected because the country had been in economic obscurity for almost two centuries. Between 1973 and 1976 the economic waters became troubled, but the peaceful transition in 1976 to a constitutional monarchy raised new hopes, politically and economically.

Like an impoverished noblewoman too proud to display her penury to the prying eyes of a money-minded mercantile world, Spain, after the loss of most of her empire during the Napoleonic Wars, went into virtual economic seclusion throughout the 19th century when other Western European countries developed their industrial wealth. She collapsed into a paroxysm of self-destruction during the Civil War of 1936-1939. For the next 20 years she lived a pariah existence because of her sympathy towards the Axis powers during World War II and her own protective shell against outside influences and opinions, often found in governments that have no freely elected opposition.

Note: 1 Peseta = $0.015

189

International Investing

Coming Out of Seclusion

It was not until 1959 that Spain decided to join the rest of Europe, at least economically, by removing most barriers on foreign trade and investments. The decision took until 1964 to show results, but then it was as if the sluice gates had been opened between higher and lower levels of water — between high and low labor and living costs and between a surplus of labor and a dearth of it. Tourists and foreign businessmen and their money began to pour into Spain, and Spanish workers and maids swarmed into the factories, farms, and households of other European countries and sent their money home.

It was not exactly by her own bootstraps by which Spain pulled herself up, but by the inflow of foreign exchange from tourism, workers' remittances, plant investments by foreign companies, United States military expenditures, and other unilateral remittances. These began to exceed $2 billion in 1970 and reached about $2.5 billion in 1972. This allowed Spain to run a considerable surplus of imports over exports to bring in capital equipment and raise the living standards of its people. Foreign reserves reached $5.2 billion at the end of 1972, exceeded $6 billion by the end of 1973, and recoiled somewhat to $5.9 billion at the end of 1975. However, this does not reflect the fact that, in 1975, Spain had a balance-of-payments deficit of $3.4 billion, which was covered by foreign loans, leaving the level of foreign reserves relatively unchanged.

Industrial Build-Up

United States direct investment in Spanish plant facilities is estimated at about $1 billion, and some 350 American companies now have operations in Spain. Other industrial countries have also made substantial investments. Not only has this raised consumption of manufactured products inside Spain, but it has also made Spain a significant exporter of industrial products, notably automobiles, chemicals, electrical equipment, steel, and ships. Industrial exports are now far ahead of the once dominant exports of agricultural products and minerals. Much of the early investment was attracted by cheap and plentiful labor and considerable protection from the forces of a free market economy. These attractions began to fade in the early 1970s.

After 1973, foreign direct investment slowed down, and the government decided in 1976 "to abandon the system of passive acceptance of foreign capital and actively acquire it in the world markets, especially North America." And this is likely to mean more foreign loans.

190

Spain and Portugal

Paradise Lost

The most dramatic rise in service "exports" was in tourism, which doubled between 1964 and 1972 from about 14 million to 29 million foreign visitors. In 1973, they reached an all-time high of 34.6 million (Spain's population is 35 million). In 1975, the number receded to 30 million. This tourist flood has been a mixed blessing. While it brought in by far the largest income of foreign currency among all Spanish industry ($3.4 billion in 1973) and gave a great boost to the construction industry, tourism has also impaired the natural beauty of some of the most attractive coast lines in Spain, such as the Costa Brava, Costa Blanca, and Costa del Sol. This has removed some of the attraction that Spain offered in the past as one of the best bargains in climatically and scenically pleasant retirement havens, especially on its Mediterranean coast and islands.

GNP Growth Arrested

During the second half of the 1960s, the Spanish gross national product grew at an average rate of close to 8% in real terms, and this rate continued in the early 1970s until 1973. The peseta, for a while, was a strong currency. It appreciated from 70 pesetas to $1 in 1960 to an all-time high of 58 in 1973.

The world-wide recession reached Spain somewhat later than most other countries so that it wasn't until 1975 that the growth of the gross national product in real terms came to a complete halt. Inflation ran at a rate of 14%. In February 1976, the Spanish government devalued the peseta by 10% to 66.60 to $1.

Spain is not a member of the EEC, but was looking wistfully at the massive financial help that Italy was receiving from its fellow members. In 1976, Spain was negotiating to become a member herself.

Stock Index Passes Peak

The Spanish stock market index reflected the economic revival. It grew about fivefold between 1960 and 1973. In 1972, it rose 42% above the previous year's average, and in 1973 and 1974 it reached a peak, from which it had receded nearly 40% by the end of 1976.

Initially, the market benefited from other developments besides the economic revival. It was opened in 1960 to foreign investors who began to buy selectively. Then Spanish investment funds were set up which added to the buying throughout the 1960s. Spanish savings banks were required to put 45% of their assets into public or government-guaranteed securities; and finally, Spanish resident investors no longer had to pay capital gains tax for securities held over one year.

Up to 1970, the stock market was only a minor source of new capital for corporations and public agencies. Through government incentive, however, new issues since 1971 became an important factor in financing Spain's economic growth. In 1972, about $1.4 billion of new issues were sold, and they accounted for about 22% of all new financing. New issues of listed stocks are usually offered to existing stockholders at par value, providing them with handsome profits. As a result, trading volume picked up considerably, from about Pta. 40 billion ($600 million) in 1971 to about Pta. 110 billion ($1.65 billion) in 1974. Since then it has declined again. Even though the number of listed companies reached 547 in 1975, the market remained relatively thin, with a total capitalization of about $21 billion, with the ten leading companies representing about 53% of the total.

Three Exchanges

There are three Spanish stock exchanges — Madrid, Barcelona, and Bilbao. Madrid is the largest, accounting for about 60% of all transactions and apparently gaining on the other two exchanges, with Barcelona perhaps accounting for 22% of the trades, and Bilbao for the rest. All transactions are executed by brokers, who are appointed, in a personal capacity rather than as firms, by the Ministry of Finance. All banks, mutual funds, and portfolio management firms handling investment business must deal through a broker. Transfer of stock is a rather formal business and must be attested either by a broker who is a member of one of the three stock exchanges, a notary public or a *corredor de comercio*, who is somewhat of a broker's representative in cities that have no stock exchanges. In addition to a stock certificate, a Spanish investor also receives a so-called *póliza de operaciones al contado*, serving as evidence of his ownership of the stock certificates. He may keep this *póliza* when he deposits his stock certificates with a bank, and this may be useful if the certificate gets lost or misplaced. Spanish stock certificates can be either bearer certificates, without the name of the owner, or certificates registered in the name of the owner. In the case of bearer certificates, the owner must detach a coupon to collect his dividend. Registration of certificates does not ensure automatic dividend payments, as in most other countries. The owner must present the certificate at a bank to collect the dividend, and the certificate is stamped as evidence of payment.

Foreign Investors Encouraged

Foreigners are fairly unrestricted in the purchase of Spanish securities as long as these are paid for in pesetas derived from the conversion of a foreign currency. Total foreign portfolio investments in a single Spanish company may not exceed 50%. Shares of some companies, notably those involved in national defense and public information, may not be bought by foreign investors. Foreign investments in some other industries are limited to varying degrees. These include mining, motion picture production, hydrocarbon prospecting and processing, banking, shipping, and insurance. Proceeds from the sale of foreign securities originally bought with converted pesetas, as well as dividends and interest income, can be freely taken out of the country.

There is no withholding tax on dividends received by foreign owners of Spanish shares, and foreign investors pay no capital gains tax irrespective of the length of time the securities were held. There is a 24% withholding tax on fixed-income securities, which cannot be recovered, but can be set off against taxable income on the IRS income tax return. There are no Spanish shares, or American Depositary Receipts of Spanish shares, actively traded in the United States.

Where to Buy Spanish Securities

About 70% of the portfolio investment business in Spain is handled by the commercial banks; and the balance by special portfolio management companies. From a practical point of view, the American investor should contact the United States representative office of a Spanish bank for information. The banks cannot transact investment business in the United States, but they will arrange for the investor to open a dollar investment account at their head office in Spain and forward the investor's instructions. They will also provide the investor with investment information available from Spain. The office in Spain acts as a custodian for the stock certificates and attends to all the necessary details of stock transfer, dividend collection, rights offerings, etc. When the American investor sells his Spanish stocks, his dollar account will be credited with the proceeds. If he wants to close out his account, the dollars can be taken out of Spain without problems.

International Investing

Spanish Common Stocks

For an investor wanting to invest in the Spanish economy, shares of one of the leading banks offer the simplest and probably the safest way. The five or six leading commercial banks reportedly control between them almost 50% of Spanish manufacturing. A new government regulation in 1971 lifting some credit restrictions and offering tax rebates on new industrial investment further strengthened the position of the banks, since much of the new money is raised by the commercial banks. An effort by the government to separate the commercial and investment banking activities of the banks resulted in the formation of subsidiaries in one or the other type of banking so that the over-all scope of the business of the controlling bank remained unchanged.

The largest commercial banks, roughly in the order of the size of their deposits, are *Banco Español de Crédito, Banco Hispano Americano, Banco Central, Banco de Bilbao, Banco Exterior,* and *Banco de Santander.* All of them have had excellent stock market records during the years 1960 to 1973, with most of their prices rising tenfold or better, and they suffered in the retreat since 1974. Electric utilities are also publicly owned in Spain, and their operations are somewhat more in public view than those of manufacturing companies. Their stock market performance has not been as spectacular as that of the banks, and they have suffered more in the recession. The leading ones are *Fuerzas Eléctricas (FECSA), Iberduero, Hidroeléctrica Española, Union Eléctrica,* and *Sevillana Eléctricidad.*

Construction and real estate operations have been growth industries, but with more risk and cyclical factors. Actively traded stocks include *Dragados y Construcciones, Portland Valderrivas, Vallehermosa,* and *Imobiliaria Urbis.*

The steel industry greatly benefited from the boom. The largest integrated steel company, 25% owned by *U.S. Steel,* is *Altos Hornos Vizcaya.*

Spain's leading automobile manufacturer is *SEAT (Sociedad Española de Automotive de Turismo),* but its stock was one of the poorest performers in 1974 and 1975.

The chemical industry, in the mid-1970s, was on a strong expansion move, with heavy infusion of foreign capital. The leading company, partly foreign owned, is *Union Explosivos Rio-Tinto.*

Fixed-Income Securities

The bond market in Spain is very limited and hardly of interest to indi-

194

vidual investors. Yields in 1974 and 1975 were far below the inflation rate, and since the individual investor also pays a tax, straight bond issues are usually placed with a captive clientele — savings banks, insurance companies, and pension funds. Convertible bonds were more popular, and they accounted for more than 50% of all bond issues in 1975.

Investment Funds

Spanish investment funds are of recent origin. Initially, through a decree in 1958, closed-end investment funds received the green light to operate. Through a second decree in 1964, open-end funds were created, and at the same time foreign investment in these funds was stimulated by guaranteeing foreign investors repatriation of their money on redemption of the fund shares including tax-free dividends and capital gains. Since February 1973, Spanish investment trusts can invest up to 10% of their assets in foreign securities listed on a recognized stock exchange. Nevertheless, with 90% in Spanish securities, a Spanish investment trust represents a good vehicle for a smaller investor to invest in the Spanish economy on a diversified basis.

The total number of open-end funds in 1975 was 24, with total assets in the neighborhood of Pta. 20 billion ($300 million). Bank shares in 1974 accounted for about 25% of total holdings, with electric utilities second at about 13% of total assets. Fixed-income securities represented about 7% of total assets. The popularity of open-end funds decreased sharply with the receding stock market.

Closed-end funds are far larger in number — close to 500 in 1975, with assets of about Pta. 23 billion ($345 million) — but many of them are controlled bank funds, investment management funds, and family funds set up for tax reasons rather than public trading.

Foreign Investments

Except for the 10% allowed to investment trusts, Spanish investors in 1976 could not invest in foreign securities. This may change if Spain becomes a member of the EEC.

Sources of Information

Spanish companies are very uncommunicative by American standards,

195

and this is no doubt a deterrent to the foreign investor. With few exceptions, answering mail does not seem to occupy top priority with Spanish corporations and financial institutions. Even though the Madrid and Barcelona exchanges and most of the leading banks publish investment information, with reports on individual stocks, it takes time to get them if one is not on the spot. The American investor is largely confined to what he can get from the American offices of Spanish banks represented in the United States.

Portugal

Part of the Iberian Peninsula, and with a colonial history as glorious and far-flung as that of Spain, Portugal is nevertheless very different in character from Spain, There is practically no country in the world about which there is such unanimity of praise from visitors. The country's charm lies in its people, landscape, climate, and communities rather than in its historical treasures, although even these are attractive.

Portugal is beginning to follow Spain in the development of an industrial economy and it encourages foreign direct investments in production facilities. However, in 1976 it was not yet a country for foreign portfolio investment. All investments must be approved by the government, and in 1976 such approval was practically impossible to get unless it was requested to buy an interest in an operating company with the objective of instilling additional foreign capital and know-how. The small Lisbon stock exchange has been in a series of extreme gyrations.

There were also restrictions on the purchase by non-residents of income-producing property in Portugal, and mortgages for vacation homes bought by non-residents were difficult or impossible to get. With the tight-rope transition to a democratically elected government in 1976, the Portuguese stock market may eventually also open up to foreign investors, especially when the authorities recognize that a stock market can become a good source of new capital if it develops active and regular trading volume, including that from "speculators."

Spain and Portugal

Stock Exchanges

Bolsa Oficial de Comercio de Barcelona / Paseo Isabel II, Consulado 2 / Barcelona
Bolsa Oficial de Comercio de Bilbao / José María Olavarri 1 / Bilbao
Bolsa de Comercio de Madrid / Plaza de la Lealtad 1 / Madrid
Bolsa de Fundos de Lisboa / Praca de Comercio, Torreao Oriental / Lisbon

Partial List of Spanish Banks Doing Portfolio Investment Business

Banco de Bilbao / Alcalá 16 / Madrid. United States office: 767 Fifth Avenue / New York, New York 10022
Banco Central / Alcalá 49 / Madrid
Banco de Santander / Alcalá 37 / Madrid. United States office: 375 Park Avenue / New York, New York 10022
Banco de Vizcaya / Alcalá 45 / Madrid. United States office: 250 Park Avenue / New York, New York 10017
Banco Español de Crédito / Castellana 7 / Madrid. United States office: 375 Park Avenue / New York, New York 10022
Banco Exterior de España / Carrera de San Jeronimo 36 / Madrid. United States office: 46 West 55th Street / New York, New York 10019
Banco Hispano Americano / Serrano 47 / Madrid. United States office: 645 Fifth Avenue / New York, New York 10017

Sources of Information

All banks listed provide investment information. Also, the Madrid and Barcelona exchanges have information on listed companies on file.

Partial List of Actively Traded Spanish Stocks

Banks
Banco de Bilbao
Banco Central
Banco Español de Crédito
Banco Hispano Americano
Banco de Santander
Banco de Vizcaya

Utilities
Fuerzas Eléctricas (FECSA)

Iberduero
Hidroeléctrica Española
Sevillana Eléctricidad
Unión Eléctrica

Construction, Real Estate
Cros
Dragados y Construcciones
Portland Valderrivas
Vallehermosa

International Investing

Chemicals, Oil
Energía e Industria
Insular de Nitrógeno
Petroliber
Unión Explosivos Rio-Tinto

Automobiles
Citroën Hispania
FASA-Renault
SEAT

Retail
Galerías Preciados

Steel Processing
Altos Hornos Vizcaya
Nueva Montana Quijano
Ponferrada

Telephone Utility
Telefónica Nacional

Partial List of Spanish Investment Funds

Ahorrofondo / Alcalá 27 / Madrid
Bonserfond / Alcalá 37 / Madrid
Crecino / General Perón 27 / Madrid
Eurovalor / Cedaceros 11 / Madrid
Financiera Bansander S.A. / Paseo de Pereda 9-10 / Santander
Gesta / Lagasca 95 / Madrid
Gramco Iberia / General Sanjurjo 57 / Madrid
Inespa / Marqués de Valdeiglesias 6 / Madrid
Inrenta / Marqués de Valdeiglesias 6 / Madrid

Partial List of Spanish Investment Management
and Advisory Companies

AGECO / Miguel Angel 23 / Madrid
ANSA / Lagasca 118 / Madrid
Banif, S.A. / Juan Bravo 2 / Madrid
CEA / Alcalá 27 / Madrid
DACSA / Avenida Generalísimo Franco 474 / Barcelona
Finmacaya, S.A. / Núñez de Balboa 118 / Madrid
Finisterre, S.A. / Colón 2 / Valencia
Fondiberia / Paseo de Gracia 51 / Barcelona
Fondo Mediterraneo de Inv. / Ronda Universidad 9 / Barcelona
Fontisa / Paseo Castellana 7 / Madrid
Gesbancaya / Paseo Castellana 112 / Madrid
Gesbolsa, S.A. / Hortaleza 58 / Madrid
Gesfondo, S.A. / Buenos Aires 62 / Barcelona
Gesinca / Peligros 3 / Madrid
Geslevante, S.A. / Alcalá 21 / Madrid
Gesmo, S.A. / Balmes 196 / Barcelona
Gesnorte, S.A. / Valenzuela 8 / Madrid
Gestemar, S.A. / Goya 43 / Madrid
Gestimbao / Avenida Generalísimo Franco 538 / Barcelona

Spain and Portugal

Gestora de Títulos, S.A. / Paseo Castellana 7 / Madrid
SAECO / Avenida Generalísimo Franco 453 / Barcelona
SAFEI / Conde de Aranda 15 / Madrid
Serfiban, S.A. / Paseo Castellana 8 / Madrid
Sogeval, S.A. / Cedaceros 11 / Madrid

American Brokerage Offices in Spain

Barcelona
Merrill Lynch, Pierce, Fenner & Smith Inc. / Avenida Generalísimo
    Franco 534

Madrid
Bache Halsey Stuart Inc. / Alcalá 32
Baird, Patrick & Co., Inc. / Calle General Sanjurjo 55 (Bajo), Apar-
    tado 8254 Quintana
Merrill Lynch, Pierce, Fenner & Smith Inc. / Torre de Madrid 9-4
Shearson Hayden Stone Inc. / Avenida del Generalísimo 63

Spanish Daily Newspapers With Good Financial Coverage

ABC / Serrano 61 / Madrid
La Gaceta del Norte / Bilbao
Informaciónes / San Roque 9 / Madrid
La Vanguardia / Barcelona

Financial and Business Periodicals

Actualidad Económica (bi-weekly) / Padre Damian 19 / Madrid
Desarrollo (weekly) / Velázquez 61 / Madrid
El Economista / Conde Aranda 8 / Madrid
Información Comercial Española (monthly) / Goya 73 / Madrid

11. Italy

Italy for many years has been plagued by a flight of capital. Many Italians who want to build up a nest egg take their money across the border to Switzerland and have it invested on their behalf in foreign securities or other values. The Swiss border town of Chiasso and the nearby resort town of Lugano have thereby become two important international investment centers.

Thus, there is little reason for a foreign investor to do in Rome what most Romans do not do and invest his money in Italy — except perhaps for the man who wants to retire there (Italy, more than any other country, lures its citizens back after they have made their fortunes abroad). But even retirees don't always seem to invest their savings in Italy. If they have worked in a country with a relatively stable currency, they can leave their savings there and have the income transmitted, as needed; or they can stop in Switzerland on their way home and leave their money there to be invested safely.

Note: The lira exchange rate is not given because of its steadily declining value.

International Investing

Poor Investment Climate

The situation looked particularly bad during the first half of 1976, when it seemed that the communists might win the upcoming election. Capital flight became an avalanche. The lira declined precipitously. And the stock market, which had been in an almost steady decline since 1960, except for an upturn in 1973, followed suit. The elections of June 1976, with the communists just short of a total victory, left the political situation as unresolved as ever.

In spite of great efforts of the Milan stock exchange to upgrade the importance of the exchange and publicize its services, the underlying factors that make the Italian stock market weak have remained. In 1975, only 152 Italian companies and one foreign company were listed on the *Borsa Valori di Milano* — compared to about 500 in Germany and more than 800 in France, two other large industrial countries with relatively poorly developed stock markets. Total market capitalization of Italian shares in 1975 was about $11 billion — half that of Spain. Total nominal value of some 600 bonds and debentures was $65 billion. Average daily trading volume reported for stocks was about $6.6 million, and for bonds $3.4 million. But much of the trading is carried on outside the exchange among banks, and this trading volume and the prices of the transactions are not reported.

In June 1974, the Italian government passed a new law to regulate the securities market. It includes the establishment of an SEC-type supervisory body (*CONSOB*), the option for investors of a flat withholding tax on dividends and interest, regulations governing listing and trading of securities, the creation of special non-voting "saving" shares that provide anonymity to the shareholder, and other measures to develop a healthy capital market.

Foreign investors may invest in Italian securities, provide capital and loans to Italian enterprises, and repatriate their investments, provided these are registered with, and authorized by, the Ministry of the Treasury. Dividends and interest may be withdrawn subject to applicable withholding tax.

On the other hand, Italian investors are effectively discouraged from investing in foreign securities through regular channels in Italy. An Italian buying foreign securities must deposit, without interest, with the *Bank of Italy* or an authorized Italian commercial bank, an amount equal to 50% of the cost of his investment. The deposit is refunded on the sale of the foreign securities.

In spite of the new law, financial information on Italian companies, in 1976, still had to be taken with more than one grain of salt. Many publicly-owned Italian companies reportedly still adhered to the custom of keeping up to four sets of books — one for themselves, one for the tax collector, one for their bankers, and one for their shareholders. Moreover, even with all of these books, or because of them, many Italian companies have not been able to show an attractive earnings record over a period of years. For an outsider, it is difficult to know whether poor results are a bookkeeping matter or the reflection of genuine problems. A visitor to Italy is often struck by the efficient management and quality of products and services of many Italian business enterprises, which seem to belie the published figures of the Italian economy and of publicly-owned companies.

Cosa Nostra Tradition

It is, of course, easy to be contemptuous or condescending about the Italian economic and financial muddle. To understand Italy, one must understand the history of the Italian *cosa nostra* — the closely-knit family, tribal, and friendship associations that exist not only in the well publicized Mafia but actually in every other social strata in Italy. These associations were formed as a protection against foreign invaders and other exploiters of the hard-working peasants and artisans. In one way or another, Italy, throughout its history, until Garibaldi helped unite it as an independent state in 1860-1870, has been ruled or exploited by foreigners. Sicily has the oldest tradition of defense against foreign occupation. Several hundred years before Christ it was first occupied by the colonizing Greeks, then by Phoenician merchants, and later by the Roman militarists, who, with the sweat of slaves, made Sicily supply most of the grain they needed to give away to the welfare population of the City of Rome. The Romans, who started their military career by conquering the neighboring Etruscans, became, strictly speaking, alien rulers of the rest of Italy. When Rome fell in the 5th century, the Teutonic tribes ransacked the country. In 800 A.D., Charlemagne had himself crowned Emperor of the Holy Roman Empire of the German Nation, starting many hundreds of years of German robber baron expeditions into Italy, interrupted occasionally by French and Spanish forays. The dukes and *condottieri* of the Italian city states during the Renaissance were not exactly socialists when they carried on their intercity wars on the backs of the working population that had to pay for these ventures in blood, toil, and money. Nor were some of the more worldly popes, such as the Borgias, amateurs when it came to financial extortion of the faithful. In more recent history, Napoleon had a fling at Italy, and the Austrians ruled Venice and other areas until they were expelled in 1866. And neither Mussolini nor the democratic politicians since World War II can be called paragons of virtue and public ethics.

Thus, it is not surprising that the Italians, for sheer self-preservation, have developed a system of mutual self-protection against authority and of evading taxation and other extortions by dictatorial or corrupt government bodies. They operate a second underground economy that is beyond the reach of official government economic statistics and tax authorities. It is this underground family system that makes the economy function in spite of all government ineptitude and that preserves the atmosphere of prosperity in the face of official economic statistics that spell bankruptcy for the entire nation. It is a system that is not well suited for a conventional stock market, which depends on relatively honest disclosure practices. Nevertheless, here, for the record, are some of the largest Italian corporations.

Italian Common Stocks

Among the leading Italian companies in market capitalization and trading activity are *Assicurazioni Generali*, an insurance company with a good performance record; *SIP*, a telephone company with a stable growth in business volume; *FIAT*, producing excellent automobiles but poor financial results; and *Montedison*, a large chemical and synthetic fiber producer with an abysmal stock market record.

A number of holding companies also are among the leaders in market capitalization, notably *STET*, controlling several telecommunications companies; *Bastogi* (partly controlled by *Italcementi*, a producer of cement and other building products) holds a majority in *Beni Stabili*, a construction and real estate company, and has minority interests in other building materials and construction enterprises; and *Finsider*, which holds majority interest in *Italsider* and *Dalmine*, two leading steel companies. *Finsider* is 55% owned by *Istituto per la Ricostruzione Industriale* (*IRI*), a government agency that injects capital into, or takes over, industrial enterprises in distress. *IRI* also controls Italy's three largest banks, *Banca Commerciale Italiana*, *Banco di Roma*, and *Credito Italiano* — not among the actively traded stocks, but with fairly steady market prices.

Olivetti, next to *FIAT* probably the Italian company best known outside Italy, showed steadily declining results and stock market prices throughout the 1970s. The company nearly killed itself when, in the early 1960s, it acquired the bankrupt American typewriter manufac-

204

turer, *Underwood*, and only survived with the financial help of *FIAT*.

Pirelli, the largest Italian tire manufacturer, which joined forces with the British *Dunlop* in a 50/50 partnership, was a disaster case in the early 1970s, but had recovered somewhat in 1975.

The largest retailer in Italy is *La Rinascente*, but as with so much business in Italy its products and services are far more attractive than its stock market performance.

The 600-odd fixed-income securities listed on the Milan stock exchange are of no interest to foreign investors because of the weak Italian currency.

Italian Mutual Funds

Italian mutual funds offer a partial opportunity for investing in the Italian economy. Since 1970, 50% of their portfolios had to be invested in Italian securities; the balance could be invested in foreign securities. Since 1973, all new cash flow into the funds must also be invested in Italian securities, thereby further reducing the foreign content of the portfolios. Because Italy has no law governing mutual funds, all 12 Italian mutual funds existing in 1976 were registered in Luxembourg. Performance of the funds has been mediocre because of the commitment to the Italian economy and currency. About one-half of all the assets of Italian mutual funds are in the hands of the largest fund, *Fonditalia*, a survivor of the collapsed *IOS* mutual fund empire, and now owned by *Istituto Mobiliare Italiano* (*IMI*), a somewhat unique credit institution established to provide capital and make loans to private industry. In addition to *IMI*, Italy has a number of finance companies established to provide loans and credit primarily to companies that are not publicly owned, but in practice many of them seem to be closed-end security investment and venture capital companies run for the benefit of a relatively small group of shareowners.

Where to Buy Italian Stocks

Even though trading on the stock exchanges is the exclusive right of government-appointed brokers, and these brokers can do business with investors, in practice most of the investment business is handled by the banks. The banks have a national network of branch offices, all of which handle investment business, and it is difficult for brokers to compete on this scale. Some of the Italian banks are represented in New

York, but they are generally not equipped to do business with individuals.

The five largest banks in Italy with branch office networks are *Banca Nazionale del Lavoro, Banca Commerciale Italiana, Banco di Roma, Credito Italiano,* and *Banco di Napoli.* In general, they will not accept discretionary accounts, which means that each transaction must be authorized by the customer — not a practical procedure unless one lives in the country. A number of private banks will accept discretionary management of larger portfolios, leading among them *Banca C. Steinhauslin* and *Monte dei Paschi di Siena.* So will a relatively new, but substantial, mutual fund and portfolio management company, *SAFI* of Turin, with offices in Milan, which is half owned by *The Group Agnelli* (*FIAT*) and half by *Società Assicurazioni Industriali* (*SAI*), a large insurance company.

A number of regulations govern the purchase of Italian securities by non-residents, notably the one that requires that they be paid for with freely convertible foreign currency or from a foreign lira account. Stock certificates owned by non-residents must be deposited with an authorized Italian bank, or if they are to be taken out, registered with a special number and endorsed *circolante all'estero.* The latter is a time consuming and not very practical way; thus, it is advisable to leave Italian securities in the custody of an Italian bank.

Dividends and interest due can be transmitted to a non-resident up to a maximum of 8% per year of the invested capital. There is a withholding tax of 15% for United States residents.

Most trades on the Milan stock exchange are for "forward" settlement. Settlement day is a fixed date once a month — so that a trader can have up to 30 days before he settles a transaction. This encourages speculation and in-and-out trades.

Sources of Information

Information available on Italian stocks is limited and not very revealing, although there is a trend towards improvement. Pioneering work in this area is done by *Edizioni Sasip,* which publishes stock and bond guides on about 200 companies and is working on the development of security analysis methods for Italian companies. The two partners of the company were instrumental in the organization of an Italian security analysts society in 1972. *Sasip* has also started a joint venture with *DAFSA,* the French securities research firm, which is trying to develop unified security analysis methods throughout Europe.

Italy

Among the banks, *Banca Commerciale Italiana* and *Credito Italiano* publish the most comprehensive information on Italian securities and the Italian market, including some material in English.

A few brokers publish information on Italian stocks. One of the leading brokers, *Agente di Cambio Milla,* has published a guide on Italian convertible securities.

The leading financial newspaper is *Il Sole-24 Ore,* published in Milan.

International Investing

Principal Stock Exchange

Borsa Valori di Milano / Piazza degli Affari 6 / Milan

Partial List of Italian Banks Handling Investment Business

Bergamo
Banca Provinciale Lombarda / Via G. Sora 4

Florence
Banca C. Steinhauslin / Via Sassetti 4

Milan
Banca Commerciale Italiana / Piazza della Scala 6
Banca Lariano / Via Hoepli
Banca Morgan Vonwiller / Via Armorari 14
Banca Popolare di Milano / Piazza Meda 4
Banco Ambrosiano / Via Clerici 2. United States affiliate: *Ultrafin International Corporation* / 63 Wall Street / New York, New York 10005
Credito Commerciale / Via Armorari 4
Credito Italiano / Piazza Cordusio 2
Istituto Bancario Italiano / Via Manzoni 3

Naples
Banco di Napoli / Via Toledo 177

Palermo
Banco di Sicilia / Via Mariano Stabile 182

Rome
Banca Nazionale dell'Agricoltura / Via Loviano 16
Banca Nazionale del Lavoro / Via Vittorio Veneto 119
Banco di Roma / Via del Corso 307. United States affiliate: *EuroPartners Securities Corporation* / 1 World Trade Center / New York, New York 10048

Siena
Monte dei Paschi di Siena / Piazza Salimbeni 3

Turin
Cassa di Risparmio Torino / Via XX Settembre 31
Istituto Bancario San Paolo di Torino / Piazza San Carlo 156

Italy

Partial List of Finance and Investment Companies

Fideuram / Lungotevere Sanzio 15 / Rome
Istituto Mobiliare Italiano / Via delle Quattro Fontane 121 / Rome
IRI — Istituto per la Ricostruzione Industriale / Via Vittorio Veneto /
    Rome
SAFI / Corso Matteotti / Milan
SIGI / Piazza San Fedelo 2 / Milan

Independent Investment Research

Edizioni Sasip / Via S. Vittore al Teatro 1 / Milan

Partial List of Brokers in Milan

Agente di Cambio Milla / Via Morone 8
Agente di Cambio Tagi / Via Disciplini 9
Agenti di Cambio Foglia Alberto / Via della Posta 3
Ettore Fumagalli / Via Meravigli 16
Leonida Gaudenzi / Via delle Orsole 4B
Pietro San Martino / Via della Posta 8

A Representative List of Italian Stocks

Banks
Banca Commerciale Italiana
Banco Lariano
Banco di Roma
Credito Italiano
Mediobanca

Holding Companies
Bastogi
Breda
Finsider
IFI
La Centrale
Pirelli
STET

Insurance
Alleanza Assicurazioni
Assicuratrice Italiana

Assicurazioni Generali
Assicurazioni Milano
Fondiaria Incendio
Fondiaria Vita
RAS
SAI
Toro Assicurazioni

Real Estate
Beni Stabili
Generale Immobiliare

Manufacturing
ANIC (chemicals)
Cementir (cement)
Condotte d'Acqua (construction)
Cucirini (textiles)
Dalmine (steel tubes)
Erba (pharmaceuticals)

International Investing

Eridania (sugar)
Falck (iron and steel)
FIAT (automotive)
Italcementi (cement)
Italgas (gas)
Italsider (iron and steel)
Lepetit (pharmaceuticals)
Marelli (electrical engineering)
Mira Lanza (detergents, soaps)
Mondadori (publishing)
Montedison (chemicals)
Montefibre (synthetic fibers)
Motta (candies)

Olivetti (office machines)
Pierrel (pharmaceuticals)
Pirelli (tires and rubber)
Rumianca (chemicals)
SAFFA (matches, paper, chemicals)
SME (food and household goods)
Snia Viscosa (synthetic fibers)

Miscellaneous
Alitalia (airline)
La Rinascente (retailing)
SIP (telecommunications)

Partial List of Mutual Funds

Capital Italia S.A. / Via Carlo Marenco 26 / Turin

Fonditalia International / Lungotevere R. Sanzio 15 / Rome
Fondo di Investimento Interitalia / Via del Vecchio Politecnico 5 / Milan
Italamerica / Piazza della Scala 6 / Milan
Italfortune International Fund S.A. / Via Bigli 1 / Milan
Italunion S.A. / Via G. Sora 4 / Bergamo

Leading National Newspapers With Financial Coverage

Corriere della Sera / Via Solferino 28 / Milan
Daily American (English language) / Due Macelli 23 / Rome
Il Messagero / Via del Tritone 152 / Rome
La Stampa and Stampa Sera / Via Roma 80 and Galleria S. Federico 16 / Turin

Italian Financial Press

Espanzione / Via Bianca di Savoia 20 / Milan
L'Espresso / Via Cino del Luca 5 / Milan
Il Fiorini / Via Parigi 11 / Rome
Il Globo / Via Tomacelli 146 / Rome
Mondo Economico / Via Mercanti 2 / Milan
Ore 12 / Via Mozart 1 / Milan
Il Sole-24 Ore / Via Monviso 26 / Milan
Sucesso / Piazza Cavour 1 / Milan
Il Tempo Economico / Via Alberti / Milan

12. Austria

Austria today is the remnant of what was one of the largest and most powerful empires in the world. At the height of its glory, when the Hapsburg dynasty also ruled over Spain and its possessions, it was a realm over which the sun never set. But even during its sunset days before World War I — the days of Johann Strauss waltzes, Kaiser Franz Joseph, Mayerling, and *Der Rosenkavalier* — the empire was still the largest in Europe excluding Russia.

It came to a sudden end after World War I, when Austria was reduced to its present size. From 1938 to 1945, it was briefly incorporated into Hitler's Third Reich, but emerged afterwards as a neutral nation in its 1919 shape. All that remains of the past political glory is an oversized capital (where about 23% of the total population of about 7 million lives), an oversized bureaucracy, and tourist sights.

Nevertheless, Austria today represents a sound economy. Its currency is among the strongest in the world, having been revalued *vis-à-vis* the dollar almost as much as the Swiss franc and the German mark. Tourists who flock in from all parts of the world, including the Iron Curtain countries, are one of its main sources of foreign income. Traditions and memories of the old empire are what attracts them most —

Note: 1 AS = $0.055

the gigantic palace of Schönbrunn, the Belvedere and Hofburg, the Opera, the Riding Academy, the Ringstrasse (with its string of neo-something-or-other architecture), the Heurigen (the potent new wine served by the vintners in the villages on the slopes of the Vienna Woods), and the Prater, the amusement park with its giant wheel. And many tourists also enjoy the lovely scenery of the rest of Austria, ideal for both summer and winter vacations.

Fixed-Income for Retirement

Austria's beauty also makes it an attractive retirement haven. It is less crowded than Switzerland, and south of the Alps it offers a particularly pleasant climate — dry, warm summers and crisp winters ideal for skiing. It is for people with retirement in mind that Austria is of primary investment interest. The firm currency provides a safety feature against currency losses. The most advantageous investment vehicles are fixed-interest securities, which in 1976 paid a yield of about 9%. What is most important, however, is that Austrian residents, under certain conditions, can buy fixed-income securities with tax benefits, including tax-free interest. The regulations are somewhat complicated, and the counsel of an investment advisor of an Austrian bank is recommended.

A non-resident can buy Austrian fixed-income securities with foreign currency, and there is no withholding tax. A total of 995 fixed-income securities were traded on the Vienna stock exchange at the end of 1975, including 14 foreign issues. Total nominal value was AS 163 billion ($8.9 billion). The largest number of issues was mortgage and communal bonds, followed by industrial, bank, communal and utility notes, and government treasury bonds. New issues in 1975 amounted to AS 51 billion ($2.8 billion), up from AS 24 billion ($1.32 billion) in 1974.

Equity Investments Limited

Investment opportunities in Austrian common stocks are limited. Because of the preference for fixed-income securities, there has been very little equity financing. At the end of 1975, only 89 Austrian common stocks were listed, plus 27 foreign issues. The total market value of the Austrian shares at the end of 1975 was AS 23 billion ($1.27 billion). Total trading volume of listed stocks, including foreign issues, was AS 974 billion ($53.6 million) in 1975, of which AS 412 billion ($22.7 million) was traded on the floor of the *Wiener Börsekammer*, the balance out-

212

side the exchange. A large percentage of this represented trading in foreign stocks. Trading volume of foreign stocks has been increasing while trading volume in Austrian stocks has been on a downward trend in the 1970s.

By international standards there are practically no Austrian issues with enough float for anything but small institutional positions. Most of Austrian industry is controlled by banks, holding companies, or interlocking ownership. The large banks are controlled by the government. The largest Austrian bank, *Creditanstalt-Bankverein*, is 60% government owned, and so is the *Österreichische Länderbank*. Small float has led to some erratic price movements in the past, but throughout the 1970s, with the exception of a sharp rise in 1972, the index of the Austrian market has remained flat, unaffected by the bear markets in other countries during 1973 to 1975, or by the bull markets beginning in 1975.

Among the somewhat more actively traded issues, also found in portfolios outside Austria, are *Steyr-Daimler-Puch,* a manufacturer of automotive equipment and other capital goods; *Semperit,* a tire and rubber manufacturer; *Veitscher Magnesitwerke,* one of the world's largest manufacturers of refractory bricks used in steel making; *Felten & Guilleaume,* a copper and steel wire manufacturer; and brewery stocks, such as *Gösser* and *Österreichische Brau. Steyr-Daimler-Puch* and *Semperit* are also traded on the Frankfurt and Munich exchanges.

There are no restrictions on the purchase and ownership of Austrian shares by non-residents provided the shares are paid for in freely convertible foreign currency. There is a withholding tax of 20% on dividends due to non-residents.

Like several other European countries, Austria has a central depository and clearing agency for securities where change of ownership can be registered by simple bookkeeping entry. Most Austrian shares are bearer certificates. For practical reasons, a non-resident is well advised to leave his Austrian shares with a custodian bank.

Foreign Stock Trading

Because of the limited equity investment opportunities in Austria, Austrian institutional equity portfolios usually contain a high percentage of foreign securities — much higher than in any other country. Often 50% or more are in United States securities, depending on the trends in the United States market. Since the funds available in Austria for investments are relatively small, total foreign equity holdings in Austria are probably not much more than $100 million, perhaps half of which is invested in United States stocks. Most of the foreign stocks must be bought via foreign banks and brokers on foreign exchanges, but Austrian banks encourage listing of popular foreign stocks on the Vienna exchange. Most foreign issues listed are actively traded, including the three United States stocks: *IBM, IT&T,* and *Sperry Rand.* The Dutch have four listings. German shares, with 10 listings, represent the largest foreign contingent on the *Börsekammer.* Foreign listings must be sponsored by one of the large banks, and total costs of listing, including sponsor's fee, legal and auditing costs, preparation of registration statements, and supporting advertising and publicity may run up to $50,000 to $60,000.

Banks

In Austria, an investor can buy securities from any financial institution, whether it is a member of the Vienna exchange or not. Non-members place their securities orders through members and split the commissions. All major banks are members and can trade on the exchange on behalf of their customers and for their own accounts. In addition, there are government-appointed brokers (*Sensale*), operating like market-making specialists, and free brokers, trading on the floor as intermediaries as well as for their own accounts. These brokers do not normally deal with individual investors.

The three leading banks with well developed investment services are *Creditanstalt-Bankverein, Österreichische Länderbank,* and *Girozentrale.* The leading private bank providing investment services and portfolio management is *Schoeller & Co.* The banks charge commission plus fees for complete portfolio management and custodial services, but commissions only if stock certificates are delivered to the investor.

Investment Trusts

Four Austrian investment funds, managed by *Österreichische Investment-Gesellschaft,* a subsidiary of *Creditanstalt-Bankverein,* are traded on the Vienna exchange. They are *Allinvest* and *Selecta,* mixed Austrian and international equity funds; *Securta,* a foreign equity fund; and *Allrent,* a fixed-income fund. Their total assets at the end of 1975 were AS 928 million ($51 million). Four other funds, managed by *Sparinvest-Kapitalanlagegesellschaft,* a subsidiary of *Girozentrale,* are sold directly to investors, with their daily net asset value prices published in

214

the official stock exchange bulletin. They are *Sparinvest,* an equity fund with predominantly foreign stocks; *Atlasfond,* an exclusively foreign equity fund; *Combirent,* a domestic fixed-income fund; and *Intertrend,* a foreign fixed-income fund. Their total assets at the end of 1975 were AS 2.2 billion ($121 million). *Sparinvest* had the largest United States position with about $14 million. United States holdings in *Securta* were about $1.5 million, in *Selecta,* $750,000.

Four foreign investment funds are traded on the Vienna stock exchange — three German and the *Austro-International Fund* registered in Liechtenstein. The Dutch *Robeco* and *Rolinco* funds are also traded in Vienna, but they are considered equity issues.

Sources and Channels of Information

Investment information on Austrian securities in English is scanty, but all three of the large banks publish comprehensive stock exchange yearbooks in German, the most detailed one, including charts on Austrian stocks, being that of *Girozentrale.* A small Austrian security analysts society was founded in 1974, but most members are really portfolio managers. A good amount of information on foreign stocks is published by the leading banks. Information on United States stocks comes primarily from United States brokers.

Some international investment information services include reports on Austrian companies, notably *Capital International Perspective.* *Reuters* and *Telekurs* (Swiss) carry a number of Austrian securities on their instant stock-quote service.

In relation to the size of the country, Austria has an unusually large number of newspapers and periodicals, including almost 20 specialized business and financial publications. *Trend* is a popular business publication that also carries stock market news.

International Investing

Austrian Stock Exchange

Wiener Börsekammer / Wipplingerstrasse 34 / Vienna

Selected List of Bank Members of the Vienna Exchange

Allgemeine Sparkasse in Linz / Promenade 11-13 / Linz
Bank für Arbeit und Wirtschaft A.G. / Seitzergasse 2-4 / Vienna
Berger & Comp. Bankhaus / Rathausplatz 4 / Salzburg
Creditanstalt-Bankverein / Schottengasse 6-8 / Vienna
Erste Österreichische Spar-Casse / Graben 21 / Vienna
Genossenschaftliche Zentralbank A.G. / Herrengasse 1 / Vienna
Girozentrale und Bank der Österreichischen Sparkassen A.G. / Schubertring 5 / Vienna
Österreichische Länderbank A.G. / Am Hof 2 / Vienna
Österreichische Volksbanken A.G. / Peregringasse 3 / Vienna
Österreichisches Credit-Institut A.G. / Herrengasse 12 / Vienna
Schoeller & Co. / Renngasse 1-3 / Vienna
Spängler Carl & Co., Bankhaus / Schwarzstrasse 1 / Salzburg
Zentralsparkasse der Gemeinde Wien / Vordere Zollamtsstrasse 13 / Vienna

Some Actively Traded Austrian Stocks

Banks and Insurance
Creditanstalt-Bankverein
Internationale Unfall
Österreichische Länderbank

Construction
Perlmooser Zementwerke
"Universale" Hoch- und Tiefbau

Magnesite
Veitscher Magnesitwerke

Chemicals and Rubber
Semperit
Stölzle Glasindustrie
Treibacher Chemische Werke

Electrical
Felten & Guilleaume

Breweries
Österreichische Brau
Brüder Reininghaus Brauerei
Gösser Brauerei
Brauerei Schwechat

Foods
Leipnick-Lundenburger

Machine Tool and Metallurgy
Hutter & Schrantz
Jenbacher Werke
Steyr-Daimler-Puch
Wagner-Biró

Paper
Leykam-Josefsthal

Textiles
Vöslauer Kammgarn-Fabrik

Austria

Austrian Investment Management Companies

Österreichische Investment-Gesellschaft m.b.H. / Schottengasse 6 /
Vienna (Funds: *Allinvest, Allrent, Securta, Selecta*)
Sparinvest-Kapitalanlagegesellschaft m.b.H. / Schubertring 5 /
Vienna (Funds: *Atlasfond, Combirent, Intertrend, Sparinvest*)

Austrian Business and Financial Press

Bank und Börse / Strozzigasse 26 / Vienna
Finanznachrichten / Bankgasse 1 / Vienna
Trend / Marc-Aurel-Strasse 10-12 / Vienna
Wiener Börsen-Kurier / Biberstrasse 2 / Vienna

Viennese Daily Newspapers With Financial Coverage

Arbeiter Zeitung / Rechte Wienzeile 97
Die Presse / Muthgasse 2
Kronenzeitung / Muthgasse 2
Kurier / Lindengasse 52
Nö Volksblatt / Löwelstrasse
Wiener Zeitung / Rennweg 12a

13. Japan

Anyone who had picked a Japanese stock in 1968 would have had an excellent chance of tripling or quadrupling his money by 1972 if he had done only as well as the averages. The Tokyo Dow Jones average of 225 selected blue-chip stocks ranged between a low of 1266 and a high of 1851 in 1968 to reach a high of 5207 in December 1972, peaking out at 5359.74 on January 24, 1973. An American investor would have gained another 30% in terms of dollars as a result of the revaluation of the yen.

Many individual Japanese stocks did far better than the average — the best known among them that of *Sony*, the consumer electronics company that rose like a rocket from $77 million in sales in 1963 to $796 million in 1972, showering its excellent products on all parts of the globe. The *Sony* American Depositary Share traded on the New York Stock Exchange, which equals one *Sony* share on the Tokyo Stock Exchange, rose from the equivalent (after splits and rights issues) of about $1 in 1968 to above $18 in early 1973. Many other Japanese stocks have also performed far better than the average. The stock of *Nomura Securities*, the largest Japanese brokerage house, benefiting from the Japanese stock market

Note: Yen 300 = $1

219

boom, rose by 365% in a single year — year end 1971 to year end 1972. In the same year, *Nikko Securities*, the second largest brokerage house, saw its stock rise by 393%. And *Daiwa Securities* rose by 336%. The stock of *Sumitomo Bank*, the third largest bank, went up 129%, and that of *Sumitomo Marine and Fire*, a large insurance company, climbed 61%. *Nissan Motor*, which makes Datsuns, had a rise of 116%.

Seeing such dramatic results, foreign investors became keenly interested in Japanese common stocks. Net foreign purchases in 1971 amounted to $430 million and to $352 million in 1972. American investors participated only to a limited extent since they had to pay the Interest Equalization Tax on the purchase of foreign stocks before January 30, 1974, when it was removed.

Through the Trough

In early 1973, the Japanese stock market appeared to take a breather, receding from its all-time high for what appeared to be a level of consolidation. However, when towards the end of the year the Japanese economy seemed to be undermined by oil price rises to a far greater extent than any other industrial nation, the breather threatened to become a rout.

Suddenly economists and analysts discovered all the inherent weaknesses in the Japanese economy, foremost among them the lack of its own energy supplies and many vital raw materials. The economy was vastly overextended, they said. The small islands were bursting at their seams. There was no more room for the expanding population, housing, or production facilities. Traffic in Tokyo and other large cities was choked. Air and water were seriously polluted. Farmlands had been lost and fishing grounds were exhausted or unsafe.

Two Japanese business traditions were considered particularly onerous in a serious recession — the complex distribution system and the lifetime job security of Japanese employees. In distribution, centuries-old channels continue to exist which include up to four intermediaries between the producer and the ultimate consumer. Even department stores buy through a chain of wholesalers rather than directly from the manufacturers. The tradition of high-school-to-retirement job security saddles the Japanese manufacturer with a rigid labor cost that is difficult or impossible to reduce in times of recession. This puts him at a disadvantage *vis-à-vis* American corporations, for instance, which can lay off workers not needed for reduced production levels up to the executive suite.

Japan

Last but not least, most Japanese stocks are highly leveraged. This means that the percentage of net worth to total capitalization of Japanese companies is very low (14.3% in March 1976, for all companies). In times of business expansion this can produce a rapid earnings increase in relation to the total number of shares outstanding. In a recession, however, earnings can collapse even more rapidly.

With so much doom in view, foreign investors in 1973 and 1974 dumped practically all of the Japanese stocks they had bought in previous years. Net sales in 1973 were $638 million, and in 1974 (when it might have been wiser to buy) were $1.133 billion. The Tokyo Dow Jones index declined to a low of 3355 in October 1974, but the decline was not as sharp as might have been expected, and not out of line with the decline of other leading stock markets. By mid-1975, the index had recovered to the 4500 level.

The pessimism, shared by many Japanese investment professionals themselves, proved exaggerated. The Japanese and their economy showed an amazing resilience. Perhaps two of the secrets of the Japanese performance are the astonishing discipline of the Japanese, both as individuals and within their economic groups, and the homogeneity of purpose of the entire nation, with government, business, and labor, usually, if not always, cooperating with each other rather than being at loggerheads. This makes it possible for the government to shift economic gears overnight with guidelines that are to a large extent followed voluntarily by manufacturers, bankers, and labor.

In the two years prior to 1973, the Japanese government, embarrassed by an overwhelming foreign payment surplus, had encouraged every conceivable means for the Japanese to spend money abroad — to buy foreign securities, make direct investments abroad, lend to foreign borrowers, import, travel, and even to buy foreign art treasures wholesale. For a year or two, Japanese travellers with their cameras were the prominent feature on airplanes, in hotels, in business centers, and at tourist sights all over the world.

Following the Arab oil embargo, the Japanese government reversed itself overnight. No more foreign portfolio investments, except with proceeds from the sale of foreign securities; no more foreign borrowers admitted to the Japanese credit market; direct investments abroad sharply curtailed; foreign travel discouraged. At home, in the meantime, the population tightened its belt. The traditional high savings rate, which averaged about 20% of net take-home pay in the years 1964 to 1972, increased to 25% in 1974 and 1975. Manufacturers, trying to avoid layoffs, reduced work hours, and in some cases, with employee consent,

221

froze wages or even cut them by up to 10%. The rate of unemployment peaked out at 2.4% — traumatically high by Japanese standards, but low in comparison to all other industrial nations.

Exporters scrambled hard to develop new markets with the OPEC countries, Africa, Western Europe, and South America. Efforts were intensified to increase invisible exports from banking and other service industries and from manufacturing operations abroad.

The results: The trade balance, which had been running in the red in 1974 and 1975, turned positive in 1976. The foreign currency reserves, which had tumbled from an all-time high of $18 billion in 1972 to $12 billion in 1973, slowly moved up to $15 billion in early 1976. The growth of the gross national product in real terms, which had dropped to slightly below zero in 1974 from an average annual rate of 10% for an entire decade, recovered in 1975 and is expected to be at an annual rate of 6% in 1976. The Tokyo Dow Jones index seemed headed for 5000 again.

Suddenly, in early 1976, Japanese stocks were rediscovered as great investment opportunities, second only to United States securities. (Some of the smarter foreign money had already gone back in 1975, when Japanese security analysts still intoned a cautious tune.)

The Japanese Market

The Tokyo stock exchange is the first in the world in the number of shares traded and second only to New York in the total value of shares traded. Average share prices range from the equivalent of about 30¢ to $3. There are seven stock exchanges in addition to Tokyo, with only Osaka and Nagoya having some regional significance. For the foreign investor only Tokyo matters.

In April 1976, shares of 1400 companies were listed on the Tokyo exchange — 908 in the 1st Section and 492 in the 2nd Section. These 1400 issues represent about 170 billion shares. The 1st Section has somewhat stricter listing requirements than the 2nd Section and includes more seasoned companies. The difference is comparable to that existing between the listing requirements of the New York and American Stock Exchanges.

Average daily trading volume reached a peak of 338 million shares in 1972, representing a value of Yen 72 billion ($240 million). It receded to a low of 179 million shares in 1974, with a value of Yen 43 billion ($143 million). It wasn't much better in 1975. In January 1976, it sud-

Japan

denly spurted ahead to an average daily trading volume of 408 million shares, valued at Yen 109 billion ($363 million), the highest volume since January 1973.

There are no floor specialists on the Tokyo exchange. Markets are made by the Japanese brokerage firms. Banks cannot trade on the exchange. Stop-loss orders are not permitted, but Japanese investors can buy stocks on margin, which foreign investors are not permitted to do. Short sales are possible.

One of the attractions of the Tokyo market has been its liquidity. Individual investors in 1975 accounted for somewhat over 75% of the public trading volume; corporations for about 9%; and the balance was divided among mutual funds, insurance companies, banks, and foreign investors. What these figures hide, however, is the fact that individual holdings declined from about 46% of all listed stocks in 1963 to about 33% in 1975. Financial institutions increased their shares from about 22% to 35%, corporations from 17% to 26%. The balance of about 6% was shared by mutual funds, foreign investors, and other holders, whose holdings had declined on a percentage basis. Banks, insurance companies, and corporations trade only a small percentage of their holdings per year. Thus, even though individual Japanese investors maintained a high trading volume in relation to their total holdings, the market had become less liquid because of institutional positions held over longer periods of time. New listings and rights offerings, amounting to about Yen 1 trillion ($3.3 billion) in 1975, did not entirely offset this reduced liquidity.

New Issues

Only around 100 new stocks were listed between 1971 and 1975, and this includes 16 foreign stocks encouraged to list in 1973 and 1974, when the Japanese had an excess of foreign currencies to invest.

More new shares have become available through equity financing of already listed companies, In the past, many Japanese companies offered additional shares to existing shareholders at par value, which was usually well below market price. This gave shareholders a handsome profit. More and more companies, however, have gone over to issuing shares close to the market price. This, in many cases, found less enthusiastic response among shareholders. So as not to dilute its stock for existing shareholders, a company making an equity offering in the open market at market price compensates its existing shareholders by a free stock distribution.

223

International Investing

Equity financing through convertible debentures are hamstrung in Japan by the regulation requiring that corporate debentures must be secured by collateral. However, Japanese corporations went into the Eurobond market and into some foreign domestic markets, including the United States and Germany, where no such collateral was required, to sell convertible issues. This gave United States investors a convenient and attractive opportunity to participate in the Japanese stock market by buying convertible issues of popular Japanese companies, registered with the SEC, such as *Mitsui & Co., Matsushita Electric Industrial, Dai Nippon Printing, Kubota,* and *Komatsu.*

Foreign rights can be offered to United States shareholders only if the offering is registered with the SEC. Only a few Japanese companies with a great many of their American Depositary Receipts traded in the United States have registered their rights with the SEC, among them *Tokio Marine & Fire.* In other cases, an investor owning a Japanese stock for which rights are offered must take the initiative to exercise the rights if he finds out about them. If he does nothing, the rights will usually be sold on his behalf by the broker or bank handling his account and the proceeds will be credited to him.

Proxy and Custodian

In order to trade in Japanese shares, a non-resident must appoint a Japanese standing proxy — generally the Japanese broker. This proxy is authorized to act on the investor's behalf, as far as buying, selling, and dividend disposition is concerned. It is also advisable to appoint the broker custodian of the share certificates since it is impractical and risky to have them delivered outside Japan. Besides, the certificates are printed only in Japanese, and even foreign brokers usually leave their certificates in Japan since they usually are not able to read and handle them. There are no street name accounts in Japan in which a broker can hold the shares in his own name on behalf of his customers. If Japanese shares are bought through an American broker they are often left in the custody of an American bank established in Japan.

Dividends and Taxes

Dividends for non-resident investors are paid to the Japanese custodian who can either remit them or reinvest them. Most Japanese companies pay dividends twice a year — about three months after the record date.

Japan

Dividends on common stocks are generally expressed as a percentage of the par value of the stock, but stock tables published in the financial pages usually show the actual yen amount per share, plus the yield.

A 15% tax is withheld in Japan on dividends due non-resident investors. A United States resident may claim the tax against his own Federal income tax. There is no capital gains tax in Japan, but capital gains made by a United States resident on the sale of Japanese stocks must be reported on the Federal income tax form.

Japanese Brokers

As in the United States, the securities business in Japan is separated from the commercial banking business. Only brokers can deal in securities.

There are more than 250 securities firms in Japan, but the business is dominated by the Big Four — in the order of their size: *Nomura, Nikko, Daiwa,* and *Yamaichi.* Together they account for about 60% of all stock transactions, up to 80% of all bond trading, and for practically all of the underwriting management of new issues. All four are represented in the United States and in many other countries of the world. Four of the smaller ones have also opened offices in New York — *New Japan, Nippon Kangyo Kakumaru, Sanyo,* and *Wako.*

The Big Four have been enormously profitable in the past few years — partly a result of the rapid expansion of their business overseas, but partly also because they are efficiently operated. They can handle billion-share days without a hitch thanks to advanced computerization.

The leading Japanese securities firms are publicly owned and their shares are traded on the Tokyo exchange. ADRs of *Nomura, Nikko,* and *Daiwa* are traded in the United States over-the-counter.

After a banner year in 1973, the Japanese brokerage firms went through a year of retrenchment in 1974 as a result of the recession and sharply reduced trading volume. However, their profits increased in 1975 mainly because of an enormous volume of bond trading. Prospects in 1976 were bright.

Banks

The Japanese banks showed the effects of the recession later than the brokerage firms and, in 1976, seemed to take longer to recover. In the early 1970s, thanks to a rapid expansion outside Japan, the Japanese banks had been growing faster in terms of total assets than banks of any other country, but some overexpansion began to cut into their profits in 1975.

The largest among the Japanese banks are the so-called "city banks," headquartered in major cities but operating branch offices throughout the country. Most of them have also spread world-wide, financing the expanding foreign trade and investments of Japanese industry and participating in international financing operations, such as Eurodollar loans. In Japan they provide all regular commercial and private banking transactions, including savings accounts. Most of their funds are derived from deposits — demand, time, and saving.

The four largest Japanese banks are among the top 12 in the world, ranked by total deposits: *Daiichi Kango Bank, Fuji Bank, Sumitomo Bank,* and *Mitsubishi Bank.* For a while, the somewhat smaller *Bank of Tokyo,* which more than any other Japanese bank had concentrated on overseas business, grew fastest. It also managed to maintain an earnings growth in the recession. Other banks actively traded on the Tokyo exchange include *Sanwa Bank, Mitsui Bank,* and *Bank of Yokohama.*

Insurance Companies

Almost all life insurance companies are mutual companies — owned by policy holders and not by stockholders. However, casualty companies are publicly owned and their stocks are among the most actively traded. In addition to insurance writing, they also engage in loan and investment activities. The four largest, roughly in the order of their size, are *Tokio Marine & Fire, Yasuda Fire and Marine, Taisho Marine and Fire,* and *Sumitomo Marine and Fire.*

Industrial Stocks

Consumers world-wide are most familiar with the trade names of Japanese electronics products, such as *Sony, Pioneer Electronic,* and *Panasonic* (made by *Matsushita Electric Industrial*). *Sony* and *Matsushita* have been traded on the New York Stock Exchange for several years. *Pioneer Electronic* was listed on the New York Stock Exchange in December 1976, after having made a public offering of 4 million of its ADRs in the United States.

A security analyst researching *General Electric* in the United States, or *Siemens* in Germany, cannot ignore *Hitachi,* Japan's leading manu-

226

Japan

facturer of heavy electrical machinery, appliances, and electronics products. Its stock is represented in many international portfolios.

Japanese cameras and automobiles have left their mark world-wide — in quality, quantity, and price. Actively traded Japanese photographic industry stocks include *Fuji Photo Film, Canon,* and *Nippon Kogaku.*

The most actively traded Japanese automotive stocks are *Toyota, Nissan,* and *Honda.* A fourth, *Toyo Kogyo,* is heavily committed to the Wankel engine, which did not quite live up to the runaway success expected from it. *Honda* made a public offering of 2.3 million of its ADRs in the United States in December 1976, and was scheduled to be listed on the New York Stock Exchange in 1977.

One of the glamor stocks of the early 1970s was *Dai'Ei,* a discount chain which tried to cut through the cobweb of the Japanese distribution system and buy directly from manufacturers. It was partly successful in this, but by 1975 had run into overexpansion problems. A better stock market performance was produced by a competitor, *Ito-Yokado.* A number of Japanese department stores also recorded good stock market performances in the first half of the 1970s, including *Marui, Mitsukoshi,* and *Hankyu Department Stores.*

One of the peculiarities of the Japanese business world is the specialized trading company which sells everything from hairpins and sewing needles to bulldozers and entire industrial plants anywhere in the world. Among the leading ones are *Mitsui Co., Mitsubishi Corporation, C. Itoh,* and *Marubeni.* Their stock market performances suffered in 1973 and 1974 from the world-wide recession. *Mitsui* and *Mitsubishi* recovered in 1975 but *Itoh* and *Marubeni* did not.

Two Japanese printing companies have been popular with international portfolio managers — *Dai Nippon* and *Toppan.*

Steel companies and shipbuilders were popular in 1973. The steel industry was operating at maximum capacity and with such a large backlog that it was expected to remain profitable for a long time to come. But as so often is the case of investment consensus, it bet on the wrong horse. There were setbacks, but the steel industry in Japan is still considered modern and sound. Among the more actively traded Japanese steel stocks are *Nippon Steel, Nippon Kokan* (also shipbuilding), *Kawasaki Steel,* and *Sumitomo Metal Industries.*

The shipbuilding industry of Japan has built up a world-wide reputation for price and quality. In 1973, most shipyards had orders for many years in advance but this backlog was sharply reduced by 1976. Three shipbuilders actively traded are *Hitachi Shipbuilding, Ishikawajima-Harima,* and *Mitsui Shipbuilding. Kubota,* Japan's largest manu-

227

facturer of agricultural equipment, listed on the New York Stock Exchange in September 1976.

Zaibatsu

An investor who wonders about the frequent recurrence of the same name in companies in different industries (there is *Sumitomo Bank, Sumitomo Marine and Fire, Sumitomo Chemical, Sumitomo Metal Industries,* etc.) should know that these all originally belonged to huge family enterprises called *zaibatsu*, which engaged in practically every type of business activity in the country — manufacturing, trading, banking, shipping, mining, insurance, etc. Before World War II, about 80% of the Japanese economy was controlled by the *zaibatsus*. After the war the *zaibatsus* were dismantled and the individual units set up as independent companies, most of them publicly held. Over the years, however, the old family ties revived. There are now interlocking stock ownerships among many of the old family and the newly-formed companies, informal over-all policy meetings among the managements of the independent companies, mutual financial aid where needed, and reciprocal business transactions.

The largest of the old *zaibatsu* groups is Mitsubishi, which includes *Mitsubishi Bank, Tokio Marine & Fire, Mitsubishi Corporation* (trading), *Mitsubishi Heavy Industries* (aerospace, shipbuilding, industrial plants), *Mitsubishi Oil, Kirin Brewery, Nippon Yusen Kaisha* (the largest shipowners in the world), and about 40 others in different industries. *Mitsubishi Bank* holds shares in all of the publicly-owned Mitsubishi companies — usually less than 10%, but it provides often 20% and more of the commercial loans these companies borrow. Other large *zaibatsu* groups are Mitsui, Sumitomo, and Yasuda.

These groups have some positive aspects of conglomerates — financial resources can be directed wherever they are most effective, the interchange of business intelligence from various industries, and business referrals among the members. At the same time they have the advantage that each member has independent management exposed to the analytical eyes of investors and the harsh realities of the stock market. In foreign trade, they represent a powerful united front.

Investment Trusts

Practically all Japanese mutual funds are managed and sold by brokerage firms, and the name of the firm is usually identified in the name of the fund. Some Japanese trusts have a limited lifetime, with a fixed number of shares which, when redeemed, are retired. On maturity, the trust is liquidated and replaced by a new trust. Other Japanese investment trusts are comparable to American mutual funds and their shares are always redeemable. Foreign investors need approval from the Ministry of Finance to buy Japanese investment trust shares, but this is usually a formality undertaken by the management company. The foreign investor must also commit himself not to redeem the shares for at least six months.

Japanese investment trusts cover a variety of different investment objectives, including growth, balanced portfolio, and fixed income. A number of Japanese funds have international portfolios.

Total assets of Japanese investment funds grew from Yen 1.4 trillion ($4.6 billion) in 1970 to Yen 3.34 trillion ($11.1 billion) in 1975 — about 55% in equity funds and 45% in bond funds. However, equity funds in 1975 were about 25% in bonds.

In 1972 and 1973, Japanese investment funds were net purchasers of foreign securities — $166 million and $189 million respectively. In 1974 and 1975 they were net sellers — $61 million and $49 million. A large percentage of their foreign holdings was in United States securities.

Bond Market

Japan's Ministry of Finance has fluctuated in its policy on participation of foreign investors and foreign borrowers in the Japanese bond markets, depending on the country's payment balance. When Japan had a surfeit of foreign exchange, as in 1972, it closed its doors to foreign investments in Japanese bonds but opened the Japanese capital market to a limited extent to foreign borrowers. Two years later, when the country had a heavy payment deficit, it reversed itself on both scores.

In 1976, foreign investors could again buy Japanese bonds, and there was a certain interest in them on the part of sophisticated international portfolio managers because of the increasing strength of the yen. The three most widely traded bond types are government bonds (yields to maturity in 1976 from 8.5% to 9%), bank debentures (yields to maturity about 8.7%), and the bonds of *Nippon Telephone and Telegraph* (yields from 9% to 9.3%). There is only a limited supply of corporate bonds in the trading market. Many of them are owned by individual investors who usually hold them until maturity.

The yen market has been opened to foreign governments and international organizations. In 1976, there were 15 foreign bonds denominated in yen listed in Tokyo, among them several issues of the *World Bank* and the *Asian Development Bank*, as well as individual issues of Australia, Quebec, Mexico, Brazil, Finland, and New Zealand. Yields were slightly higher than those of comparable Japanese bond issues.

Where to Buy Japanese Stocks in the United States

There are more opportunities to buy Japanese stocks in the United States than stocks of any other foreign country except Canada. In November 1976, about 100 Japanese common stocks were available in the United States in the form of American Depositary Receipts or Shares. Many of them trade quite actively so that there is no problem buying and selling shares close to the quoted prices.

Practically all American brokers are willing to execute orders for ADRs, but for an ADR traded over-the-counter an investor might get a somewhat better price from a broker who is making a market in a specific ADR (market makers are listed in the so-called "pink sheets" published daily and available at all American brokerage offices).

Japanese ADRs are registered either under Form S-1 or S-12. Registration under Form S-1 conforms to American accounting principles and regulations of the SEC. Form S-12 is a simpler registration, accompanied by the latest financial report of the foreign company, and it is not registered with the SEC.

The easiest way to participate in the Japanese market on a broad, diversified scale under professional management is to buy shares of *The Japan Fund*, which are traded on the New York and Pacific Stock Exchanges. In 1976, the fund had an average of 60 Japanese securities in its portfolio, including several not available in the United States as ADRs. It publishes quarterly reports to shareholders with current portfolios and balance sheets, and its portfolio is a good guide to Japanese securities selection. *Nomura Capital Fund of Japan* was registered with the SEC and was offered to the American public in 1976. An open-end fund, its primary investment objective is long-term capital appreciation, with at least 80% of its assets in Japanese corporate securities.

An investor who wants to buy a Japanese stock that is not traded in the United States will have to go to one of the American brokers specializing in foreign stock trading (listed at the end of Chapter 1), or to a Japanese broker represented in the United States (listed at the end of this chapter). However, Japanese brokers established in the United States specialize in institutional business, and most of them are not equipped to handle small individual accounts. For large accounts, Japanese brokerage houses will offer complete international portfolio management through their investment management subsidiaries.

Listing Foreign Securities in Japan

Listing of a foreign stock on the Tokyo exchange may be effective in arousing investor interest and developing trading volume. A number of legal and technical problems initially delayed the listing of foreign securities in Tokyo, but in the latter part of 1973 and in 1974 a total of 16 foreign securities were listed — 14 United States stocks and two French. Average daily trading volume of all listed foreign shares on the Tokyo exchange at the end of 1973 was about 36,000 shares, with a value of Yen 468 million ($1.56 million). In 1974 and 1975, the average daily trading volume went down to about 8,000 shares. It picked up again to about 12,000 shares in January and February of 1976, but declined in subsequent months.

One of the conditions of listing is that there be at least 2,000 Japanese shareholders of 100-share round lots in the price range of $10 to $100. This means that the sponsoring brokerage house must get a sufficient number of foreign shares into the hands of Japanese investors before a stock can be listed. Sponsorship is always by one of the Big Four brokerage houses. Total listing costs may run up to $200,000 including an advertising and public relations program to publicize the listing. Detailed information on listing requirements are available from any of the Big Four brokerage houses represented in the United States.

How to Communicate with Japanese Investors

The cost of listing in Japan makes little sense unless a company is prepared to conduct a continuing communications program in Japan, including announcement of financial results and other important corporate developments and publication of annual and interim reports in Japanese, or at least translations of key sections of the annual report into Japanese. The sponsoring brokerage house should also maintain information flow to Japanese investors. For any company not listed in Japan, the most practical way to reach Japanese investors is through the Japanese brokerage houses represented in the United States.

International Investing

Sources of Information

Some Japanese companies, especially those involved in international business, are publishing annual reports in English, but most Japanese annual reports are in Japanese and thus not accessible to the foreign investor who does not read the language. Moreover, Japanese accounting principles vary greatly from those applied in all other countries. For instance, Japanese corporations do not consolidate their financial statements, reporting earnings of only the parent company, excluding those of wholly- or partly-owned subsidiaries. This often understates true earnings. However, Japanese companies will report on a consolidated basis from the financial period beginning April 1977. The leading Japanese brokerage houses have increased their investment information tremendously, and a great deal of it is available in English. The research units of the leading Japanese brokerage houses are far larger than those of their United States counterparts of comparable size. The largest among them, *Nomura Research Institute*, is organized into three subdivisions, employing together about 300 security analysts. *Nikko*, the second largest brokerage house, has formed *Nikko Research Center*, serving customers throughout the world. *Daiwa Securities* publishes prolific reports under its own name.

Why Invest in Japan?, published by *Nomura Securities* in July 1976, presented the most complete overview of the Japanese market available at that time.

Among American brokerage houses, *Drexel Burnham Lambert* offers the most complete reports on the Japanese market. And in Europe, *Vickers, da Costa* (London) is recognized for its special expertise on Japan and Southeast Asia.

The leading reference work in English on the larger Japanese publicly-owned companies is *Diamond Japan Business Directory*, which includes financial data on each company. *The Oriental Economist*, a monthly magazine, publishes a yearly *Japan Company Directory* as well as *Japan Economic Yearly*. Two Japanese financial weeklies are published in English and an investor anywhere in the world can subscribe to their air mail editions — the *Japan Stock Journal* and *Japan Economic Journal*. The *Japan Securities Research Institute* publishes annually an English-language review of the Japanese stock market, *Securities Market in Japan*. It has published a standard reference work in English: *Securities Regulations in Japan*.

Japan

Principal Stock Exchange

Tokyo Stock Exchange / Kabuto-cho, Chuo-Ku / Tokyo

Japanese Brokerage Houses in the United States

Daiwa Securities Co. America, Inc. / 1 Liberty Plaza / New York, New York 10005 and 250 East First Street / Los Angeles, California 90012

New Japan Securities International Inc. / 80 Pine Street / New York, New York 10005 and 235 East Second Street / Los Angeles, California 90012

Nikko Securities Co. International, Inc. / 140 Broadway / New York, New York 10005 and 555 California Street / San Francisco, California 94104 and 250 East First Street / Los Angeles, California 90012

Nippon Kangyo Kakumaru Securities Co. Ltd. / 1 State Street Plaza / New York, New York 10004

Nomura Securities International, Inc. / 100 Wall Street / New York, New York 10005 and 523 West Sixth Street / Los Angeles, California and 555 California Street / San Francisco, California 94104 and 190 South King Street / Honolulu, Hawaii 96813

Sanyo Securities Co. Ltd. / 100 Wall Street / New York, New York 10005

Wako Securities Co. Ltd. / 1 World Trade Center / New York, New York 10048

Yamaichi International America, Inc. / 1 World Trade Center / New York, New York 10048 and 321 East Second Street / Los Angeles, California 90012

Japanese Stocks Traded in the United States in the Form of American Depositary Receipts
* ADRs traded on the New York Stock Exchange

Registered with Form S-1
Canon (photographic equipment)
Hitachi Ltd. (electrical and electronic equipment)
Honda Motor* (automobiles)
Kansai Electric Power (utility)
Komatsu (earthmoving and construction machinery)
Kubota* (agricultural and industrial machinery)
Kyoto Ceramic (industrial ceramic products)
Matsushita Electric Industrial* (radios, televisions, appliances)

233

Mitsubishi Heavy Industries (aerospace, shipbuilding, industrial plants)
Mitsui Co. (trading company)
Nippon Electric (electronic equipment)
Pioneer Electronic* (audio equipment)
Sony* (radios, televisions, appliances)
Tokio Marine & Fire (insurance)
Tokyo Shibaura Electric (electrical and electronic equipment)

Registered with Form S-12
Ajinomoto (foods)
Akai (tape recorders)
Asahi Glass (glass, chemicals)
Ashikaga Bank
Bank of Kobe
Bank of Tokyo
Bank of Yokohama
Banyu Pharmaceutical
Bridgestone Tire (tires and rubber)
Brother Industries (sewing machines, appliances, typewriters)
Calpis Food (soft drinks)
Casio Computer
Dai'Ei (retailing)
Dai-Ichi Kangyo Bank
Dai Nippon (printing)
Daiwa House (prefabricated houses)
Daiwa Securities (brokerage house)
Eidai (plywood, prefabricated houses)
Eisai (pharmaceuticals)
Fuji Bank
Fuji Photo Film (film and Xerography)
Fujita Corporation (construction and engineering)
Fujitsu (telecommunications equipment and computers)
Hitachi Koki (industrial machinery)
Hochiki (fire alarms and extinguishers)
Hokuriku Bank
Industrial Bank of Japan
Ito-Yokado (retail)
Japan Air Lines
Kajima (construction and civil engineering)
Kanebo (textiles, fibers, cosmetics, food)
KAO Soap
Kashiyama (textiles, apparel, shoes)
Kawasaki Steel
Kirin Brewery
Kumagai-Gumi (engineering and construction)

Japan

Kyowa Bank
Makita (electric tools)
Marubeni (trading company)
Marui (retailing)
Matsushita Electric Works (lighting equipment and wiring devices)
Meiji Seika (confections, canned foods, pharmaceuticals)
Mitsubishi Bank
Mitsubishi Corporation (trading company)
Mitsubishi Electric (electrical machinery and appliances)
Mitsubishi Estate (real estate)
Mitsubishi Kakoki (plant engineering)
Mitsubishi Trust & Banking
Mitsui Bank
Mitsukoshi (retailing)
Nagoya Railroad
Nikko Securities (brokerage house)
Nippon Mini Bearing
Nippon Optical (cameras)
Nippon Shimpan (financial services)
Nippon Suisan (fishing and fish processing)
Nissan Motor (automobiles)
Nomura Securities (brokerage house)
Omron Tateisi (electric components and business machines)
Ricoh (office machines)
Saitama Bank
Sanko Steamship
Sanwa Bank
Sekisui Prefab Homes
Sharp (radios, televisions, appliances, calculators)
Shiseido (cosmetics)
Shizuoka Bank
Sumitomo Bank
Sumitomo Electric (cables)
Suruga Bank
Taisei (construction)
Taisho Marine and Fire (insurance)
TDK Electronics (magnetic tapes, ferrites, magnets)
Teijin (synthetic fibers)
TOA Harbor Works (civil engineering and dredging)
Tokai Bank
Tokyu Land (real estate)
Toray (synthetic fibers)
Toto (sanitary equipment)
Toyota Motor (automobiles)
Yamazaki (baking and confections)

International Investing

Yasuda Trust & Banking

Other Active Stocks Not Available as ADRs

Asahi Breweries
Asahi Chemical (synthetic fibers and chemicals)
Chubu Electric Power (utility)
Chugoku Electric Power (utility)
Ishikawajima-Harima (shipbuilding)
Mitsui Shipbuilding
National Cash Register Japan
New Japan Iron & Steel
Nippon Musical (pianos and organs)
Nippon Univac (computers)
Toppan Printing
Toyo Kogyo (automobiles)
Yamaha Motors (motorcycles)

The Ten Most Actively Traded Stocks in 1975 in Tokyo

		Million Shares
1.	*Nippon Steel*	1006
2.	*Hitachi Ltd.*	868
3.	*Teikoku Oil*	683
4.	*Hokkaido Colliery & Steamship*	626
5.	*Konishiroku Photo*	594
6.	*Matsushita Electric Industrial*	574
7.	*Komatsu*	545
8.	*Ishikawajima-Harima*	543
9.	*Daiwa House*	540
10.	*Fujitsu*	495

Sources of Information

The leading Japanese brokerage houses provide investment information in English, including stock guides. *Nomura Securities* publishes an annual *Manual of Securities Statistics. Industrial Groupings in Japan* is published by *Dodwell Marketing Consultants* / CPO Box 297 / Tokyo 100-91. The English-language *Diamond Japan Business Directory* includes financial information on each company. It is available from *Diamond Lead Co.* / 4-2 Kasumigaseki 1-chome, Chiyoda-ku / Tokyo and *OCS America Inc.* / 27-08 42nd Road / Long Island City, New York

Japan

11101. *Japan Company Directory* is published by *Oriental Economist* / Nihonbashi / Tokyo. *Securities Market in Japan* is published annually by *Japan Securities Research Institute* / Tokyo Shokenkaikan 1-14, Kayaba-cho, Nihonbashi Chuo-ku / Tokyo. The institute is also the publisher of *Securities Regulations in Japan* by Misao Tatsuta.

United States Brokerage Houses in Tokyo

Drexel Burnham Lambert / Suite 430, Fuji Building / 2-3 Marunouchi 3-Chome, Chiyoda-Ku

Goldman, Sachs & Co. / No. 704 Yurakucho Building / 5 Yurakucho, 1-Chome, Chiyoda-Ku

Loeb, Rhoades & Co. / P.O. Box 5428

Merrill Lynch, Pierce, Fenner & Smith Inc. / Toranomon-Mitsui Building / 8-1 Kasumi Gaseki, 3-Chome, Chiyoda-Ku

Paine, Webber, Jackson & Curtis Inc. / 5th Floor, AIV Building / 1-3 Marunouchi, 1-Chome, Chiyoda-Ku

English-Language Financial Periodicals

Japan Economic Journal / 9-5 Otemachi, 1-chome, Chiyoda-ku / Tokyo

Japan Stock Journal / CPO Box 702 / Tokyo

14. Hong Kong and Singapore

In 1971 and 1972, the Hong Kong and Singapore stock markets shot up like Roman candles and came down just as fast in 1973 and 1974. It was strictly a game for local crap shooters, and for a few not so local ones, most of them headquartered in "the City" of London. Since that time, the situation has calmed down. The world-wide recession has sobered many of the would-be millionaires. The authorities instituted a few controls to protect investors. The two cities are vying with each other as serious financial centers to act as international bankers and international portfolio managers for investors throughout Southeast Asia and to offer local portfolio investment opportunities to stouthearted investors from all over the world.

Hong Kong

Hong Kong is an anachronistic leftover from the colonial days when the British carried the "white man's burden" to all corners of the earth. The

Note: 1 HK$ = $0.20 and 1 S$ = $0.40

32-square-mile island of Victoria, on which downtown Hong Kong is located, was ceded by a weak, isolation-minded China, not entirely voluntarily, to the British at the end of the Opium War in 1842. A much larger, 360-square-mile area on the mainland was leased by the British in 1898 for 99 years. For reasons of their own, the Chinese communists left both the island and the mainland portion of Kowloon unmolested when they drove the Nationalist Chinese into the sea in 1949. Hong Kong is still a Crown Colony ruled by the Queen of England through a governor. Hong Kong became a key refugee haven and transient point for Chinese who escaped the communist regime. Its population increased from about 3 million in 1961 to 4.38 million in 1976. Hong Kong also became a focal banking and trading point for overseas Chinese and others doing business in the Far East. It became a major producer of light industrial products made with low-cost labor, as well as an important traffic hub for air and shipping lines. Foreign visitors — tourists and businessmen — reached a peak of 1.3 million in 1973. One of the best indicators of economic growth are exports, which increased 600% between 1960 and 1974, from HK$ 2.867 billion (US$ 573 million) to HK$ 23 billion (US$ 4.6 billion).

About one-third of Hong Kong's trade is with North America, one-third with Western Europe, and the balance with the rest of the world. Exports represent almost 70% of the gross domestic product, which was HK$ 35 billion (US$ 7 billion) in 1974, while imports are often equal to the domestic product. This makes Hong Kong's economy extremely vulnerable to those of its trading partners, as reflected in the serious business contraction in 1973 to 1975, with unemployment reaching levels of 15% and a sharp decline in real wages. By the same token, Hong Kong quickly responded to the pick up of the United States economy in 1975.

Because of the complete impracticability of controlling and recording the beehive-like economic and financial activities of more than 4 million people — many of them operating only with an abacus and a few brush strokes, if they keep records at all — Hong Kong is almost the only remnant of a classic Adam Smith type of free economy.

In fact, there is not even a central bank. During the 1973-1974 recession, the money supply decreased sharply in Hong Kong and prices, imports, and wage rates declined. However, savings increased, and total bank deposits at the 74 licensed banks rose from about HK$ 24 billion (US$ 4.8 billion) in 1972 to about HK$ 35 billion (US$ 7 billion) at the end of 1975. In addition, substantial amounts of undeposited money are believed to be in the hands of merchants, unlicensed bankers, and the general public — some of it in the form of other store values such as gold. (Hong Kong had become the main gold market in Eastern and

Hong Kong and Singapore

Southeastern Asia.) Under Hong Kong's free enterprise system one can do whatever one wishes with one's money without reporting one's transactions to any authority — receive it from anywhere, send it anywhere, exchange it into any other money or value, or buy anything from anywhere in the world. This lack of government interference has also kept the tax rates low — 16.5% for corporations and a maximum of 15% for individuals, with no capital gains tax.

Stock Exchanges

Even though the Hong Kong Stock Exchange had been around since 1891, it did not really come alive until the end of the 1960s to start a freewheeling existence that had almost no equal in recent stock market history. The Hang Seng Index rose from below 100 in 1970 to an all-time high of 1711 early in 1973. By the end of 1974, it was down again to 150. By mid-1976 it had recovered to the 400 level, with trading activity picking up sharply at the beginning of the year.

Before reaching its peak, the trading boom got so out of hand that the Hong Kong Stock Exchange could no longer handle all of the activity. Three competitive exchanges sprang up — the Far East Exchange, the Kam Ngan Stock Exchange, and the Kowloon Stock Exchange — which traded many of the same issues that were traded on the Hong Kong Stock Exchange as well as new, unseasoned stocks that could not find a place on the Hong Kong Stock Exchange.

The situation became so chaotic, with many malpractices being reported, that the Legislative Council of Hong Kong, in 1973, passed a Securities Bill and a Protection of Investors Bill that required the registration of brokers and investment advisors and established a securities commission with statutory powers to police the market. The total number of stock exchange members remained high — about 130 brokers being registered. In 1976, efforts were underway to combine the four markets into one.

About 160 companies are listed on the Hong Kong Stock Exchange with a total market capitalization in 1975 of about HK$ 30 billion (US$ 6 billion). Reported trading volume in 1975 had declined to about HK$ 2 billion (US$ 400 million) from a high of HK$ 12 billion (US$ 2.4 billion) in 1973, but it was picking up again in 1976. Most of the market capitalization represents banks, trading companies, and real estate operators rather than the leading manufacturing industries of Hong Kong — textiles, plastics, electronics, etc. The most actively traded stock is that of *Hong Kong and Shanghai Banking*, which for all practical purposes acts as Hong Kong's central bank and prints most of Hong Kong's bank notes. It also does about 60% of all of Hong Kong's commercial and private banking business. The bank's earnings growth was uninterrupted by the 1973-1974 recession.

Another prestigious Hong Kong enterprise with roots in the preWorld War I old-China-hand days is *Jardine, Matheson*, a trading company also involved in banking and finance and many other ventures, including distribution, transportation, and real estate. Other former trading companies now highly diversified include *Swire Pacific* and *Wheelock Marden*. A fourth, *Hutchison International*, was on the verge of bankruptcy at the end of 1975 when *Hong Kong and Shanghai Banking* came to the rescue with a capital infusion.

During the stock market boom, real estate developers and property managing firms were popular, the leading among them were *Hong Kong Land, Hong Kong Realty and Trust*, and *Realty Development*. With space so obviously limited for a rapidly growing economy and population, real estate prices are expected to go only one way — up. The recession put a damper on some of this enthusiasm, especially in connection with hotel building. Closely linked to Hong Kong's worldwide shipping activities is *Hong Kong and Kowloon Wharf*, involved in docks, warehousing, container facilities, and transportation.

Fixed-income securities found no interest in the Hong Kong bull market when everybody wanted to get rich quickly, but a few bond and convertible issues were beginning to appear in 1976.

Sources of Information

Information published by Hong Kong-based firms is still scanty. However, other sources are available, notably the foreign investment firms doing business in Hong Kong and the Hong Kong Stock Exchange, which publishes a monthly *Gazette* and a *Year Book* with financial information on some 150 stocks. *Far East Data Service* provides data sheets on all listed companies. Hong Kong also has a number of specialized business and financial magazines. The leading daily newspaper is the *South China Morning Post*.

An investor wanting to take a shot at the Hong Kong market can also consider a Hong Kong-based investment fund managed by one of the reputable local financial houses, such as *Jardine Securities*. They have a close-up view of what is going on in a fast-moving game.

Hong Kong and Singapore

Investments from Hong Kong

Hong Kong has become an important investment center for world-wide portfolio investments by its own residents as well as by overseas Chinese throughout Southeast Asia. Net purchases of United States securities, for instance, amounted to $83 million in 1975 — about equal to Belgium's purchases. This business is handled by United States and other foreign brokerage houses established in Hong Kong. About 20 foreign companies were listed on the Hong Kong Stock Exchange in 1975, most of them Japanese, including *Hitachi, Matsushita Electric Industrial,* and *Sony.* The Dutch *Robeco* and *Rolinco* funds were also listed, but United States stocks were still absent. The *Asian Wall Street Journal* provides daily stock reports of the American and European markets for Hong Kong investors.

Singapore

In spite of the same roller-coaster stock market action, the investment scene appears somewhat more solid in Singapore than in Hong Kong, based as it is on more diversified manufacturing and banking activities.

For anyone but the romantic armchair traveler, Singapore, in the pre-World War II colonial days, was known as the dullest city in the Far East by far. Founded in 1819 as a British naval outpost on a 225-square-mile tropical island fringed by mudflats and mangrove swamps, it had no history and local color to build on. It was populated by a small band of British bureaucrats, naval men, and merchants, and by a much larger contingent of hard-working Chinese coolies, shopkeepers, and traders. The spirit was clean, honest, and puritanical, at least on the surface — ladies of easy virtue were kept under wraps — but the dullness of the place, according to W. Somerset Maugham, resulted in undercover diversions and dramas not unlike those encountered in the affluent American suburbia of today.

The spirit of hard work, honesty, and puritanism has carried into the modern island state of Singapore, making it one of the most reliable and rewarding places in Asia to build up industry and deposit, borrow, and invest money. The economic growth rate in constant terms, running at a clip of better than 10% in the years 1972 and 1973, still remained ahead in the recession years at a rate of 6.8% in 1974 and 4% in 1975. The budget remained balanced, a trade surplus was maintained, and currency reserves built up from about US$ 3 billion in 1970 to

US$ 7.5 billion in 1975 — one of the highest per capita of any nation in the world. Per capita income of the 2.2 million multiracial people — 76% Chinese, 15% Malay, 6% Indian, plus 3% others — is the second highest in Asia, following Japan.

In a world accustomed to a thousands-of-years old tradition of considering thriving cities desirable prizes to be conquered, Singapore has the unique distinction of having been peacefully expelled from the country to which it belonged. After the departure of the British Raj, Singapore, in 1963, became part of the Federation of Malaysia, which occupies the Malay peninsula south of Thailand and part of the island of Borneo. The Federation was to be peacefully multiracial, but friction soon developed between the Singapore Chinese and the Malays who made up the majority of the other parts of the Federation. Views on economics also diverged widely. The hard-working Singaporeans objected to the federal government's policy of handouts to the poorest in the Federation, clinging to the old-fashioned Chinese notion that it is better to teach a man to fish than to give him a fish. To avoid bloody clashes, Singapore was asked to leave the Federation in 1965. It became an independent nation under its energetic prime minister, Lee Kuan Yew, whose puritanism seems to match that of the British governors' wives of the past. (He banned long hair on young men as well as movies depicting excessive violence.) In office since 1959, he was reelected in 1972 to a new five-year term while his party gained all 65 seats of the legislature.

Booming Economy

On its own feet, Singapore quickly built up its economy and its ability to defend itself. Foreign investments increased steadily until it exceeded S$ 2 billion (US$ 800 million) in 1972. They amounted to an additional S$ 944 million (US$ 378 million) in 1973, S$ 822 million (US$ 329 million) in 1974, and, reflecting the world-wide recession, to S$ 400 million (US$ 160 million) in 1975. About one-third of the direct investments came from the United States, with other major contributions from the United Kingdom, Holland, and Japan. A large portion of the new capital goes into the petroleum industry, Singapore being in the fortunate position of having major offshore fields in its territorial waters. Other industries benefitting from foreign investments include electronics and electrical equipment, photographic apparatus, telecommunications equipment, textiles, and shipbuilding. Total exports in 1975 exceeded

244

Hong Kong and Singapore

US\$ 4.8 billion of which about half was in re-exports. The balance of payments remained positive, with a surplus of about S\$ 972 million (US\$ 389 million) in 1975. Inflation was kept down to about 3% in 1975.

Thriving Banking

One of the greatest boosts to the economy was the decision to make Singapore a leading banking center of Southeast Asia. Banking deposits were encouraged by guaranteeing bank secrecy and abolishing the withholding tax earned on deposits and other interest-producing investments made by non-residents. This brought in vast amounts of money from Chinese and others in neighboring states. Singapore banks also "invented" Asiadollar financing. Asiadollars are the same as Eurodollars, namely American dollars owned by non-residents of the United States. By amending tax and exchange control regulations, the Singapore government made it possible for Singapore and foreign banks setting up business in Singapore to conduct international financing operations from Singapore, thereby attracting to the city state an estimated US\$ 11 billion, in 1975, in Asiadollar capital. The major borrowers are multinational and domestic corporations which use the money to develop their operations throughout Asia; but Singapore banks are also participating in international Eurodollar and Asiadollar underwriting syndicates.

Stock Market

This booming economy reflected itself in the stock market of Singapore which, like the Hong Kong market, ran away in a speculative fever in 1972. In 1973, it came down again to more realistic levels. In 1972, Singapore dropped all restrictions against foreign portfolio investments, thereby putting it on the map of international investment markets. Income from portfolio investments can freely be taken out of the country, and the original capital can be repatriated if the securities are sold.

Formerly operated as a single exchange with the Malaysian Exchange, the Stock Exchange of Singapore, in 1973, severed these ties and adopted new and revised trading rules under The Securities Industry Act of 1973, which include new listing requirements and corporate disclosure directives. It is the government's policy to develop the market into a good source for new capital and to encourage both domestic and foreign listings on the exchange.

245

International Investing

At the end of 1975, 268 companies with a total market capitalization of S\$ 14 billion (US\$ 5.6 billion) were listed — 149 industrials, 30 rubber producers, 35 tin miners and processors, 17 financial institutions, 15 hotels, 14 property companies, and 8 palm oil producers.

The total number of listings includes 154 companies incorporated in Malaysia and 25 incorporated in other countries (but with their main operations either in Singapore or Malaysia). No United States stocks were listed in 1976.

Common Stock

The most active stock (115,248 shares traded in 1975) is that of *Sime Darby*, one of the old-time British trading and commodity firms. Still engaged in international and domestic trade today, the holding company has a stake in plantations and the manufacture of tractors and other heavy equipment. Another widely diversified trading, shipping, and manufacturing organization is *Inchcape Berhad*, also actively traded.

As in many other fast developing countries, the banks in Singapore offer one of the simplest and soundest opportunities to invest in the growing economy as a whole. All leading Singapore banks showed rapidly rising earnings in the years 1971 to 1973, including the *Development Bank of Singapore, Oversea Chinese Banking*, and *United Overseas Bank*, each with paid-up capital slightly in excess of S\$ 100 million (US\$ 40 million), with *Oversea Chinese Banking* having a slight edge over the other two. All three have major stakes in a number of publicly-owned industrial companies and financial institutions.

Natural rubber and tin represented the main wealth of Malaya in colonial days, and with natural resources becoming scarce in the 1970s, they may again play an important role. The British *Dunlop Holdings* has two subsidiaries listed on the Singapore exchange — *Dunlop Estates*, a rubber plantation company, and *Dunlop Malaysian Industries*, a tire manufacturer. Other rubber plantation companies listed in Singapore include *Batu Kawan* (also a large palm oil producer) and *Kempas*. Tin mines include *Aokam Tin* and *Berjuntai Tin* while *Straits Trading* is a tin smelter. Tin and rubber stocks were not among the actively traded issues in 1975.

Following *Sime Darby*, the second most active issue in 1975 was *Faber Merlin Malaysia*, a hotel operator. Another active hotel stock is *Far East Hotels Development*. Among active industrial stocks were *Pan Electric Industries* and *United Engineers*.

A number of government and corporate bonds are also traded.

246

Hong Kong and Singapore

Where to Buy Singapore Stocks

All investment business in Singapore is handled by brokers who trade on the exchange and deal directly with the public. In 1975, there were no Singapore brokers represented in the United States. An American investor must go either to one of the American brokers handling foreign business (see Chapter 1 listings), or communicate directly with a Singapore broker. Some London brokers as well as some Japanese brokers also have expertise in Singapore stocks.

Dividend Tax

Singapore companies pay a 40% tax against current and future dividends. The investor receives a tax credit with his dividend check, and this credit can be offset against his Singapore income tax. A United States resident can offset the tax against his taxable income reported on his Federal income tax return. There is no withholding tax on interest earned by a foreign investor from Singapore fixed-income securities.

Investments from Singapore

With its recent growth as a financial center, Singapore has also become an international portfolio investment center for the island and neighboring countries. Major institutional investors are banks, investment funds, and insurance companies, but individuals, both local residents and foreign nationals working in the area, are quite active. The largest institutional portfolio is that of *Great Eastern Life Assurance*, managed by *Oversea Chinese Banking*. Another major factor on the international investment scene is the Monetary Authority of Singapore, established in 1970 to take over most of the functions of a central bank. Institutions and individuals buy foreign securities through branch offices of foreign brokerage houses established in Singapore, which are also the main sources of information on foreign securities.

Singapore has also authorized the establishment of foreign-owned merchant banks which provide corporate finance services as well as investment advice and portfolio management.

The *Development Bank of Singapore* is a major borrower in the Asiadollar and Eurodollar bond market. Owned 49% by the government and 51% by private interests, it stimulates industrial development through medium- and long-term financing.

International Investing

Sources of Information

The leading daily newspaper, the *Straits Times*, provides a certain amount of corporate news as well as daily quotations on the local and American stock markets. The *Business Times* is more specialized in economic and business news. The *Asian Wall Street Journal*, published in Hong Kong, is available on the same day in Singapore, with world-wide stock market reports.

The Stock Exchange of Singapore has a number of informative publications, including the daily and weekly *Financial News* covering market activities and corporate news, the monthly *Singapore Stock Exchange Journal* (with financial information, semi-annual company reports, and feature articles), a *Company's Handbook*, an annual *Fact Book*, and manuals on listing, by-laws, etc.

Information on direct investment is found in the *Investor's Guide* published by the Singapore Chamber of Commerce, which also issues the monthly *Economic Bulletin*.

Hong Kong and Singapore

Principal Hong Kong Stock Exchanges

Hong Kong Stock Exchange, Ltd. / 21st Floor, Hutchison House
Kam Ngan Stock Exchange / 7th Floor, Connaught Centre

Hong Kong Stock Exchange Foreign Brokerage House Members

Astaire & Co., Far East / 20th Floor, Prince's Building
James Capel & Co. / Room 608, Hong Kong Hilton
W.J. Carr, Sons & Co. (Overseas) / St. George's Building
Cazenove & Co. (Far East) / Hutchison House
Daiwa Securities International (HK) Ltd. / Hang Chong Building
Hoare & Co., Govett (Far East) Ltd. / 14th Floor, Connaught Centre
The Nikko Securities (Asia) Ltd. / 19th Floor, St. George's Building
Nomura International (HK) Ltd. / 14th Floor, Connaught Centre
Richardson Securities of Canada (Pacific) Ltd. / Bank of Canton
    Building
Vickers, da Costa & Co. Hong Kong, Ltd. / 1211 Connaught Centre
Yamaichi International (HK) Ltd. / 9th Floor, Hutchison House

United States Brokers Not Members of the Stock Exchange

Bache Halsey Stuart Inc. / Shell House
Merrill Lynch, Pierce, Fenner & Smith Inc. / 15th Floor, St. George's
    Building

Partial List of Hong Kong Investment Management Companies

Asian European Investment & Securities (Crédit Lyonnais) Ltd. / 8th
    Floor, Solar House
Asian International Acceptances & Capital Ltd. / 11th Floor, Hutchi-
    son House
G.T. Management (Asia) Ltd. / 13th Floor, Hutchison House
Bank of America International S.A. / 13th Floor, Hutchison House
James Capel (Far East) Ltd. / 6th Floor, 123 Wyham Street
Jardine Fleming & Co., Ltd. / 46th Floor, Connaught Centre
Orion Pacific Ltd. / St. George's Building
N.M. Rothschild & Sons (HK) Ltd. / 17th Floor, Connaught Centre
Schroders and Chartered Ltd. / Chartered Bank Building
Wardley Ltd. / Hutchison House

249

International Investing

Partial List of Actively Traded Hong Kong Securities

Associated Hotels
China Engineers (contractors)
China Light & Power (utility)
Eastern Asia Navigation (shipping)
Hang Seng Bank (51% owned by *Hong Kong and Shanghai Banking*)
Hong Kong Electric (utility)
Hong Kong and Kowloon Wharf (diversified)
Hong Kong Land (real estate)
Hong Kong and Shanghai Banking
Hong Kong Telephone
Hong Kong and Whampoa Dock (shipbuilding)
Hutchison International (industrial and real estate holding company)
International Pacific Securities (investment trust)
Jardine, Matheson (trading, banking, transportation, real estate)
Jardine Securities (investment trust)
New World Development Ltd.
Swire Pacific (holding company)
Wheelock Marden (holding company, shipping, real estate, trading,
    finance)
Wheelock Maritime (shipping)
Winsor (textiles, apparel, shoes)

Company Data

Far East Data Service / Lane Crawford House

Stock Market Publications

Hong Kong Stock Exchange Gazette (monthly) and *Year Book* (with
    company information) published by *Hong Kong Stock Exchange
    Ltd.* / 21st Floor, Hutchison House
Kam Ngan Stock Exchange Journal (monthly and bilingual) published
    by *Kam Ngan Stock Exchange* / 7th Floor, Connaught Centre

Hong Kong Financial Publications

Asian Finance / Suite 9A, 223 Gloucester Road
Asian Money Manager / 57-59 Lockhart Road, 11/f, Block C
Wall Street Journal / Morning Post Bldg. Tong Chong St., Hong Kong

Hong Kong and Singapore

Hong Kong General Business Publications

Asian Business & Industry / 1908 Prince's Building, Des Voeux Road
Asian Sources Magazine, Trade Media Limited / 2nd Floor, David House, 37 Lockhart Road
Economic Information & Agency / 11th Floor, 342 Hennessy Road
Far East Economic Review / 4th Floor, Marina House
Modern Asia / Room 902, Jubilee Commercial Building

Hong Kong Daily English-Language Newspapers
With Good Business Coverage

Asian Wall Street Journal / 2-F, South China Morning Post Building, Tong Chong Street, Quarry Bay
Hong Kong Standard / News Building, 635 King's Road
South China Morning Post / Taikoo Sugar Refinery, Block D, Quarry Bay
The Star / 19-21 Pennington Street, Causeway Bay

Singapore Stock Exchange

Stock Exchange of Singapore Ltd. / 601 Clifford Centre, Raffles Place

Singapore Stock Exchange Members

Alliance Securities (Pte) / 4-D Far Eastern Bank Building, Cecil Street
Associated Asian Securities (Pte) / 7th Floor, Overseas Union Shipping Centre, Collyer Quay
J. Ballas & Co. (Pte) / 5th Floor, Straits Trading Building, 9 Battery Road
Cathay Securities (Pte) / G9-11 Central Building, Magazine Road
K.S. Foo & Co. (Pte) / 2nd Floor, 35/36 Philip Street
Fraser & Co. (Pte) / Maritime Building, Collyer Quay
Kay Hian & Co. (Pte) / 7th Floor, Tat Lee Building, 63 Market Street
Kim Eng Securities (Pte) Ltd. / 1501 Hong Leong Building, 16 Raffles Quay
Lee & Co. (Stock & Sharebrokers) (Pte) / 3rd Floor, Interocean House, 1 Finlayson Green
George Lim & Co. (Pte.) / 41A Robinson Road
Lim & Tan (Pte) / 34th Floor, Hong Leong Building, Raffles Quay
Lyall & Evatt (Pte) / 17th Floor, Hong Leong Building, Raffles Quay
Ong & Co. (Stock & Sharebrokers) Pte. Ltd. / 3rd and 4th Floors, Tat Lee Building, Market Street

International Investing

Pacific Union Co. (Pte) / 17th Floor, Shenton House, 3 Shenton Way
Phillip Securities (Pte) / 1st Floor, Grand Building, 17A Phillip Street
J.M. Sassoon & Co. (Pte) Ltd. / 11th Floor, UOB Building, 1 Bonham
  Street, Raffles Place
Summit Securities (Pte) / 96B Robinson Road
E.G. Tan & Co. (Pte) / Suite 801, Ocean Building, Collyer Quay
Tsang & Ong (Pte) / 16th Floor, UOB Building, 1 Bonham Street,
  Raffles Place

United States Brokers in Singapore

Bache Halsey Stuart Inc. / Suite 12A, Yen Seng Building, Orchard
  Road
Merrill Lynch, Pierce, Fenner & Smith Inc. / Yen San Building

Merchant Banks and Investment Managers in Singapore

Asia Pacific Capital Corporation / 8th Floor, UIC Building, 5 Shenton
  Way
Asian and Euro-American Merchant Bank Ltd. / 12th Floor, Shing
  Kwan House, 4 Shenton Way
Associated Merchant Bank Ltd. / 13th Floor, Straits Trading Building,
  9 Battery Road
Brandts Ltd. / 1606/8 Tower Block, Goldhill Plaza, Newton/Thomson
  Road
Chartered Merchant Bankers Ltd. / 1701/7 Straits Trading Building,
  9 Battery Road
Citicorp Financial Ltd. / UIC Building, Shenton Way
D.B.S.-Daiwa Securities International Ltd. / Podium 517, DBS Build-
  ing, 6 Shenton Way
Dresdner (South East Asia) Ltd. / Podium G128, DBS Building, 6 Shen-
  ton Way
First Chicago (S) Merchant Bank Private Ltd. / 49 Robinson Road
Haw Par Merchant Bankers Ltd. / 900 Cathay Building
Indo-Suez & Morgan Grenfell (S) Ltd. / Podium 120 DBS Building,
  6 Shenton Way
Jardine Fleming (S.E.A.) Pte. Ltd. / 16th Floor, Shing Kwan House,
  4 Shenton Way
Lewis and Peat Merchant Bank Ltd. / 2nd Floor, Finlayson House,
  Raffles Quay
Morgan Guaranty and Partners Ltd. / Podium 402, DBS Building,
  6 Shenton Way
New Court Merchant Bankers Ltd. / 11th Floor, International Build-
  ing, Orchard Road

Hong Kong and Singapore

Singapore International Merchant Bankers Ltd. / 19th Floor, Straits Trading Building, 9 Battery Road
Singapore-Japan Merchant Bank Ltd. / 11th Floor, SIA Building, 77 Robinson Road
Singapore Nomura Merchant Banking Ltd. / 16th Floor, Straits Trading Building, 9 Battery Road
Temenggong Merchant Bankers Ltd. / 3rd Floor, Cathay Building
United Chase Merchant Bankers Ltd. / 12th Floor, Straits Trading Building, 9 Battery Road

Partial List of Singapore-Based Stocks Actively Traded

Aokam Tin
Batu Kawan (natural rubber and palm oil)
Berjuntai Tin
Bukit Sembawang Estates (real estate)
Central Properties (real estate)
Chemical Company of Malaysia (fertilizer and agricultural chemicals)
Cold Storage (refrigerated foods, dairy products, soft drinks)
Development Bank of Singapore
Dunlop Estates (natural rubber)
Dunlop Malaysian Industries (tire and rubber manufacturing)
Faber Merlin Malaysia (hotels)
Far Eastern Hotels
Fraser & Neave (food)
Goodwood Park Hotel
Great Eastern Life (insurance)
Inchcape Berhad (trading, shipping, manufacturing, distribution)
Island & Peninsular (real estate)
Kempas (natural rubber)
Malayan Banking
Malayan Breweries
Malayan Tobacco
National Iron & Steel
North Borneo Timbers (forest products)
Oversea Chinese Banking
Overseas Union Enterprise (real estate)
Pan Electric (electrical machinery)
Robinson (retailing)
Shangri-La Hotel
Shell Refining (petroleum refining)
Sime Darby (trading, distribution, manufacturing)
Singapore Land (real estate)
Straits Trading (tin smelting)
Tasek Cement
Times Publishing (newspaper)

International Investing

Tractors Malaysia
United Engineers (machinery and engineering)
United Overseas Bank
United Plantations (palm oil)
Wearne (automobile assembly)

Stock Exchange of Singapore Publications

Companies Handbook, Company Statex Service (weekly financial reports on listed companies), *Fact Book* (annual), *Financial News* (daily and weekly), *Listing Manual and By-Laws, Singapore Stock Exchange Journal* (monthly), all available from the exchange at 601 Clifford Centre, Raffles Place.

Singapore Chamber of Commerce Business Publications

Investor's Guide and *Economic Bulletin* (monthly) published by Singapore Chamber of Commerce / Denmark House

Other Useful Publications

Singapore as an International Financial Center published by *Price Waterhouse & Co.* / 1251 Avenue of the Americas / New York, New York 10020
Singapore — The Financial Centre published by *J.M. Sassoon & Co. (Pte) Ltd.* / 11th Floor, UOB Building, 1 Bonham Street / Singapore

Principal Newspapers with Financial Coverage

Business Times / Times House, River Valley Road
Straits Times / Times House, River Valley Road

15. Australia

From the end of World War II to 1973, Australia was one of the most promising countries for immigrants keen to start new lives, for venture capital to seed the development of great resources, and for canny portfolio investors to make handsome capital gains. Then, between 1973, when a Labor Party government took office, and its ignominious removal in December 1975, the country's economy and its stock markets went through the most traumatic experience in their history. A statement made in the earlier edition of this book concerning the new Australian Labor government proved to be an understatement: "No matter where an investor's personal sympathies lie in the choice between a government labeled socialist and one labeled conservative, he must allow for the fact that the former often has a dampening effect on stock prices." The Sydney Stock Exchange "All Ordinaries" index fell from a high of 637 at the beginning of 1973 to a low of 256 in September 1974. It has been recovering slowly but fairly consistently since then, and by mid-1976 had climbed to about 475.

Note: A$1 = US$1.05

255

International Investing

Opening the Doors

Discovered relatively late in the course of European exploratory travels after Columbus, Australia was first settled towards the end of the 18th century by small numbers of Britishers. It is now governed as a Federation of States with a constitution fashioned after the British parliamentary system.

Until World War II, Australia, limiting its immigration mostly to Anglo-Saxons, remained glaringly underpopulated in an increasingly overcrowded world. As Japan started its expansionary thrust in the 1930s, Australians became increasingly concerned about their relative population vacuum and the 10,000 miles between themselves and the arms of their mother country, England. They began to form closer ties to the United States, and throughout World War II, the Korean War, and the Vietnam War, Australia remained the United States' staunchest ally and supporter in the Pacific political and military theater.

After World War II, Australia opened its doors wide. Its population grew at an annual rate of about 2% per year, including some 100,000 immigrants, to a total of about 13 million in 1973, with plenty of space and resources to continue growing. The continent is in the fortunate position of having many natural resources far in excess of domestic needs, and some of them are in short supply elsewhere. The country is a leading exporter of wool, wheat, meat, sugar, coal, iron ore, nickel, bauxite, and other minerals. From being almost completely dependent upon imports of crude oil, Australia, in 1973, became about 65% self-sufficient in crude oil production. Together with huge coal and uranium deposits, these new oil reserves have made Australia relatively immune to the energy crisis.

Americans have played an important role as direct investors in Australia's industrial and natural resource developments. American investments accelerated greatly in the late 1960s and the early 1970s, until, by 1973, they were about US$ 5 billion, or 42% of an estimated total of US$ 12 billion in foreign direct investments. This put British investments, for the first time, in second place, a few percentage points behind the United States. In 1976, about 50% of the Australian mining industry was foreign owned, and around 30% of the manufacturing industries.

Buy Back Australia

In 1973, the economic advance came to a grinding halt. The Labor Party, after 23 years out of power, had run on the election promise to

Australia

"buy Australia back for the Australians." Foreign direct investments decreased to a trickle. The budget deficit increased by 1260% from A\$ 293 million (US\$ 366 million) in fiscal 1973-1974 to A\$ 3.6 billion (US\$ 4.5 billion) in fiscal 1975-1976. Inflation ran rampant, with an increase in the consumer price index of 15.1% in 1975 as compared to 6.2% in 1972. Immigration almost ceased, with only a few professionals admitted. A slew of economic policy changes threw all business planning into confusion. Stock prices and trading volume declined precipitously.

The tide was reversed with the installation of a new government in December 1975. Confusion and uncertainty about direct foreign investment was dispelled with a new policy statement in April 1976. Foreigners are again encouraged to make direct and portfolio investments in Australia, with traditional restrictions still in force for basic sectors, such as banking, radio and television, daily newspapers, and certain areas of civil aviation. Foreign real estate investments are subject to review to prevent speculation in Australian property. Foreign companies are encouraged to raise capital in Australia through equity issues rather than bank credits or debt issues. There are no restrictions for foreign portfolio investors to buy Australian securities with the exception of uranium stocks and the government is keenly interested in revitalizing the Australian stock markets.

Stock Exchanges

The two leading Australian stock exchanges are Melbourne and Sydney. There are smaller exchanges in Adelaide, Brisbane, Hobart, and Perth. All of them operate under the same trading procedures established by the Australian Associated Stock Exchanges. Following a decision in January 1972, to adopt common listings, many listed Australian companies can be traded on several exchanges.

At the end of the fiscal year June 30, 1975, listings on the Stock Exchange of Melbourne comprised 1,111 industrial stocks, 378 mining issues, 265 preference (preferred) stocks, and 2,378 fixed-income securities with a total market valuation of A\$ 28 billion (US\$ 35 billion), down from A\$ 37 billion (US\$ 46 billion) in 1972. On the Sydney Stock Exchange, 1,046 industrial stocks and 297 mining and oil stocks were listed, most of them duplicated on the Melbourne exchange. Total trading volume on the Melbourne exchange in the 1974-1975 fiscal year was A\$ 863 million (US\$ 1 billion), about one-half in equity and one-half in fixed-income securities, down from A\$ 1.3 billion (US\$ 1.6 billion) in

257

1972. Total trading volume on the Sydney exchange was A\$ 838 million (US\$ 1 billion).

By United States standards, the Australian stock markets are very narrow. Only about 50 of the common stock issues are traded actively enough to be of interest to the foreign investor who is not actually on the scene.

Where to Buy Australian Stocks

Most of the investment business in Australia is handled by brokerage houses which deal directly with individual and institutional investors and banks and trade with each other on the floor of the exchanges. Banks cannot be members of the stock exchanges. Australian banks, however, provide investment advisory and portfolio management and custodial services for investors. Probably the most active in this area are *The National Bank of Australasia* and *The Bank of New South Wales.* Both offer excellent booklets on portfolio investments in Australia. Their New York offices cannot directly execute investment orders but will refer an interested investor to their Australian offices and provide published information. Other Australian banks with representative offices in New York are *Australia and New Zealand Banking Group* and *Commercial Banking Company of Sydney.*

In 1976, there were no Australian brokers established in the United States, but several maintain regular contacts with American brokers and institutional investors. A few Australian brokers have offices in London. Many Australian shares, especially mining issues, are actively traded on the London exchange.

Australian Stocks Traded in the United States

Between 1974, when the Interest Equalization Tax on the purchase of foreign securities was removed in the United States, and mid-1976, the number of Australian shares traded in the United States over-the-counter in the form of American Depositary Receipts increased from four to more than 20. The original four were *Woodside-Burmah Oil,* a mining company, *G.J. Coles* and *Myer Emporium,* two retail operations, and the largest of all Australian companies, *Broken Hill Proprietary.* Other sizable companies added since then include *MIM Holdings* and *Comalco,* nonferrous metal producers, *Dunlop Australia,* a rubber products and textiles manufacturer, and *Thomas Nationwide,* a road and rail transportation company. ADRs can be bought through any United States brokerage office.

With 1975 sales of A$ 1.8 billion (US$ 2.25 billion), *Broken Hill Proprietary* is the largest Australian corporation and probably offers one of the best over-all investments in the Australian economy. Originally a mining company, it now makes practically all of the steel used in Australia; in a joint venture with Exxon, it produces a large portion of the oil and natural gas consumed in Australia; it mines all of the iron ore, manganese, and coal it needs for its own operations; it owns bauxite deposits and has access to other minerals; it does heavy manufacturing, including shipbuilding and the fabrication of mining equipment. *Broken Hill Proprietary* is likely to remain a leading factor in the development of Australia's industry and natural resources.

Oil Production

After many decades of search, Australia finally made sufficient oil discoveries in the late 1960s to reduce its dependence on foreign crude oil supplies from 90% in 1969 to about 35% in 1976. Refinery capacity has also been increased to such an extent that practically no petroleum products are imported in refined form. In addition to *Broken Hill Proprietary, Ampol Petroleum* is an Australian-owned oil company with a sales volume in 1975 of A$ 248 million (US$ 310 million). It has an interlocking ownership with *Ampol Exploration,* an oil exploration company with about A$ 5 million (US$ 6.25 million) reported revenue. The two *Ampol* stocks are available in the United States as ADRs. The other listed petroleum distributor, *H.C. Sleigh,* is 23% owned by *Caltex Petroleum* of the United States. Other Australian oil activities are carried on by foreign oil companies.

Mining Stocks

Australian mining stocks have always caught the attention of the more speculative investors, but between 1971 and 1975 the Metals and Minerals Index of the Australian stock exchanges has been on a steady decline, and not many investors could have made much money in such shares. One of the most notorious of Australian mining stocks, *Poseidon,* caused a world-wide investment sensation when, in 1968, its price shot up from A$ 1 to above A$ 250 on the news of large nickel discoveries. It came down almost as fast when operating losses piled up and, interrupted by a few erratic swings, it slid back to A$ 1.50 by 1976.

259

International Investing

When a new, hot mining issue appeared on the scene in 1975 — *Pancontinental Mining*, engaged in uranium prospecting — investors were a little more cautious. They drove up the stock from A$ 1 to A$ 20, and by mid-1976 it had dropped to A$ 15.

No doubt many Australian mines harbor riches that will be much in demand in the years to come, but to evaluate their returns in terms of stock prices is a specialist's game. Among the larger Australian mining enterprises are *Conzinc Riotinto* (iron ore, aluminum, lead, zinc), 81% owned by the British *Rio Tinto-Zinc; MIM Holdings* (silver, lead, copper, coal mining); *Australian Mining and Smelting* (lead, silver, zinc); and *BH South* (copper).

Banks and Bank Stocks

Australian banks occupy a particularly strong position in the economy. Like the banks in Canada, but unlike United States banks, they are not restricted in their geographical range of operations. They may have nation-wide branch systems. This resulted in the formation of only six publicly-owned Australian "trading" banks, plus one government-owned commercial bank, *Commonwealth Bank*. Together, the seven handle more than 90% of the country's commercial and checking account deposits and about 75% of the savings accounts. The largest of the publicly-owned banks, *Bank of New South Wales*, has more than 1200 branch offices inside and outside Australia. The other five are *Australia and New Zealand Banking Group, National Bank of Australasia, Commercial Bank of Australia, Commercial Banking Company of Sydney*, and *Bank of Adelaide*. Australian banks offer a wide range of services, including commercial and private deposit and savings accounts, commercial and consumer finance, merchant banking, mutual fund management and sales, portfolio management, investment services, and even travel services. Their generally increasing earnings are even better than reported because Australian banks have developed the practice of allocating substantial unspecified amounts to reserves every year. Five of the major bank stocks are also traded in London. There are no restrictions for portfolio investments in banks by foreigners, as distinct from buying a controlling interest.

Industrial Stocks

Australian industrial stocks represent over 75% of the market value of all Australian common shares. The growth of the population has enlarged the market for industrial products to such an extent that it has become economical to manufacture products locally that were once imported. There are about 64,000 plants in Australia in 200 different industries. Manufacturing contributes approximately 25% of the gross national product and employs about 25% of the working population. Distribution and service industries also perked up. Many of the industrial and consumer companies are actively traded, among them: *Allied Mills* (flour milling, bakeries, edible oils), *Australian Consolidated Industries* (glass, plastics, engineering), *Carlton and United Breweries, G.J. Coles* (retail), *F&T Industries* (building materials), *Hooker Corporation* (real estate, building, unit trusts, hotels), *Myer Emporium* (retail), *Pioneer Concrete,* and *Thomas Nationwide* (freight transportation).

Investment Trusts

Although somewhat limited in their portfolio selections because of the narrowness of the Australian stock market, both closed-end and open-end funds (unit trusts) have achieved a certain success in Australia. While operated by management companies, many of the investment trusts are associated with Australian trading banks, which actively sell the shares. Unit trusts have a particular attraction for Australian investors because income, including capital gains, is not taxable in the hands of the trust, which can thereby distribute the maximum of earnings. The unit trust shareholder must, of course, pay taxes on the dividends received. There is no capital gains tax in Australia on any securities held longer than the tax year, which runs from July 1 to June 30. Many of the unit trusts have substantial portfolios of high-yielding fixed-income securities.

Fixed-Income Securities

Among the more interesting features of the Australian bond market, especially for the smaller investor, are Commonwealth bonds whose rates of interest and redemption prices rise at stated intervals during the life of the issue. Rates are usually marginally better than the current short-term bond rates. An investor is limited to a maximum holding of A$ 100,000 per issue. Such bonds are excellent protection against inflation for anyone living in Australia or wanting to settle there. Australian fixed-income securities, in 1976, offered interest rates up to 12%, which made them attractive to anyone believing in the renewed strength of the Australian economy and currency.

Regulations and Taxes

A non-resident of the Sterling area must have approval from the Australian Exchange Control Authority before he can buy an Australian security. This is, in most cases, a formality which takes about 24 hours, and is generally handled by the broker or bank serving the investor. The permit number is usually endorsed on the stock certificate. All Australian stock certificates are registered in the name of the owner and sent by the registrar directly to the owner, not the broker. Thus, there can be no street name accounts, as in the United States, where an investor can leave his certificate in the hands of his broker and borrow money on it for purchases on margin. An investor in Australian stocks can, however, appoint a nominee — a bank or a custodial service — for safekeeping of his securities. For a non-resident investor this is, no doubt, the most practical thing to do. A custodian will take care of all necessary formalities in buying, selling, and registering the shares; and he will collect the dividends and interest due and exercise or sell rights in accordance with standing instructions from the investor. When a non-resident of Australia wants to repatriate the proceeds from the sale of Australian securities, a permit from the Exchange Control Authority is needed; but again, this is a formality in most cases, attended to by the broker or the custodian.

There is a withholding tax on both dividends and interest on Australian securities held by non-residents. The tax on dividends is 15% for residents of countries with which Australia has a double taxation agreement — the United States, Canada, New Zealand, the United Kingdom, Singapore, and Japan. For residents of all other countries the withholding tax on dividends is 30%. On interest received by non-residents from Australian fixed-income securities the tax is 10%. Certain government bonds are exempt from withholding tax.

Australian Investments Abroad

Until 1972, Australians were not able to invest in foreign securities. Since then, the individual investor may invest up to A$ 10,000 (US$ 12,500) a year in foreign stocks and the institutional investor up to A$ 1 million (US$ 1.25 million). They may not buy foreign fixed-income securities. The initial reponse by Australian investors was cautious, but has been gradually increasing, particularly among major institutional investors. Many Australian individual investors have remained conservative, however, in staying with their own securities, which they know. Information on foreign securities is difficult for them to obtain.

Sources of Information

Disclosure by Australian companies is a good deal more limited than that by American companies, but improvements are in progress. The Sydney and Melbourne exchanges publish information sheets on many listed companies. Other worthwhile publications available from these two exchanges include *Australian Shareholders Guide, Jobson's Yearbook of Public Companies, Jobson's Mining Digest Yearbook,* and *Australian Securities Markets.* Most brokers and some of the trading banks publish information on specific Australian securities and the market in general.

The leading financial publications are the *Australian Financial Review* (daily) and the *Bulletin* (weekly) and the *National Times* (weekly). Other publications of interest to investors include the *Australian Stock Exchange Journal* (monthly), *Rydges Digest* (monthly), and the *Australian Miner* (weekly).

Several Australian daily newspapers have good business coverage, including *The Australian,* the *Daily Telegraph,* and the *Sydney Morning Herald,* in Sydney; and *The Age* in Melbourne.

International Investing

Principal Australian Stock Exchanges

The Stock Exchange of Melbourne / 351 Collins Street / Melbourne
The Sydney Stock Exchange / 20-22 O'Connell Street / Sydney

Some Members of the Melbourne Stock Exchange

E.L. & C. Baillieu / 459 Collins Street
Clarke & Co. / 365 Little Collins Street
Davies & Dalziel / 408 Collins Street
A.C. Goode & Co. / 395 Collins Street
May & Mellor / 351 Collins Street
McCaughan, Dyson & Co. / 412 Collins Street
Wm. Noall & Son / 85 Queen Street
Potter Partners / 325 Collins Street
Simon, Lidgett, Collingwood & Co. / 406 Collins Street
Wallace H. Smith & Co. / 351 Collins Street
Vinton Smith, Dougall & Co. / 351 Collins Street
J.B. Were & Son / 379 Collins Street

Some Members of the Sydney Stock Exchange

Bain & Co. / 3-10 O'Connell Street
Hattersley & Maxwell / 105 Pitt Street
Jackson, Graham, Moore & Partners / 56 Pitt Street
Ralph W. King & Yuill / 33 Bligh Street
Ross McFadyen & Co. / 17 O'Connell Street
Meares & Philips / 33 Bligh Street
Ord Minnett T.J. Thompson & Partners / 1 New York Street
Pring, Dean & Co. / 20 O'Connell Street
William Tilley, Hudson, Evans & Co. / 15-19 Bent Street
A.B.S. White & Co. / 82 Pitt Street

Leading Banks Handling Investment Business

Australia and New Zealand Banking Group Ltd. / 351 Collins Street / Melbourne. United States office: 63 Wall Street / New York, New York 10005
The Bank of New South Wales / 60 Martin Place / Sydney. United States office: 270 Park Avenue / New York, New York 10022
Commercial Banking Company of Sydney Ltd. / 343 George Street / Sydney. United States office: 450 Park Avenue / New York, New York 10022

264

Australia

The National Bank of Australasia Ltd. / 271-285 Collins Street / Melbourne. United States office: 375 Park Avenue / New York, New York 10022

Most Active Australian Industrial Stocks Listed by Value
*ADRs traded in the United States

*Broken Hill Proprietary** (steel and diversified production)
Bank of New South Wales
The National Bank of Australasia
*Myer Emporium** (retailing)
*G.J. Coles** (retailing)
CSR (sugar, building materials, minerals)
EZ Industries (zinc, uranium)
Carlton & United Breweries
Commercial Bank of Australia
Lend Lease (construction and real estate)
IAC (Holdings) (financial services)
*Thomas Nationwide** (transportation)
Australian Guarantee (financial services)
Waltons (retailing)
Tooth & Co. (brewery)
Thiess Holdings (construction and coal mining)
Allied Manufacturing (tobacco products, processed foods, packaging)
*Australian Consolidated** (packaging, building products, other services)
*Woolworths Ltd. Australia** (retailing)
Pioneer Concrete (building materials)
*Hooker Corporation** (construction and real estate)

Additional Australian ADRs Traded in the United States

W.R. Carpenter (merchandising)
Courtaulds (chemicals, synthetic fibers)
Dunlop Australia (rubber products, textiles)
Philip Morris Australia (tobacco)
Santos (gas)
Union Carbide Australia (chemicals)

Most Active Oil and Mining Securities
*ADRs traded in the United States

*Western Mining**	*Utah Mining*
Bougainville Copper	*Woodside-Burmah Oil**

265

International Investing

MIM Holdings*	Hamersley Holdings
Australian Mining & Smelting	Robe River
Associated Australian Resources	Westralian Sands
BH South*	Cudgen
Conzinc Riotinto	Weeks Natural Resources
Pancontinental Mining	Poseidon
North Broken Hill	Emperor Mines
Peko-Wallsend*	Gold Mines of Kalgoorlie (Australia)

Additional Oil and Mining Australian ADRs

Ampol Exploration	Consolidated Gold Fields of Australia
Ampol Petroleum	Interstate Oil
Comalco	Mayne Nickless

Partial List of Australian Investment Management Companies

AFT Ltd. / 16 O'Connell Street / Sydney
The *Australian Fixed Trusts* group, which in 1936 pioneered unit trusts in Australia, markets through the branches of *AFT Ltd.* units in trusts managed by *AFT Ltd., AFT Property Co. Ltd.,* and *AFT Woolworths Realty Ltd.* As of March 1, 1975, the group managed over 100 unit trusts with investments valued at more than A$ 100 million (US$ 125 million).

ANZ Managed Investments Ltd. (a wholly-owned subsidiary of *Australia & New Zealand Banking Group*) / GPO 5174AA / Melbourne
As of March 1, 1975, the company managed five unit trusts, two public superannuation funds, and various investment portfolios with a total value of A$ 156 million (US$ 195 million).

Australasian Financial Management Ltd. (incorporated in the Bahamas) / Level 40, Australia Square, George Street / Sydney

CBA Managed Investments Ltd. / 316 Flinders Lane / Melbourne

CitiNational Capital Corporation Ltd. / 84 Pitt Street / Sydney

CKT Managers Pty. Ltd. / 303 Collins Street / Melbourne

CNF Managers Ltd. / 379 Collins Street / Melbourne

Cowan Fund Management Pty. Ltd. / 377 Little Collins Street / Melbourne

Darling Management Ltd. / 15 Bent Street / Sydney

Delfin Investment Services Ltd. / 16 O'Connell Street / Sydney

EPM Ltd. / 6-10 O'Connell Street / Sydney

Financial Planning Corporation Pty. Ltd. / 220 George Street / Sydney

International Pacific Investment Management Ltd. / 56 Pitt Street / Sydney

Share Australia Management Company Ltd. / 40th Level, Australia Square, George Street / Sydney

Australia

Telford Property Fund Ltd. / 300 George Street / Sydney
Tjuringa Management Ltd. / Norwich House, 6-10 O'Connell Street / Sydney
Trevia Management Ltd. / 34 Hunter Street / Sydney
Universal Flexible Trusts Ltd. / 25 Elizabeth Street / Melbourne
Wales Financial Services Ltd. (a wholly-owned subsidiary of the *Bank of New South Wales*) / The Wales House, 66 Pitt Street / Sydney
As of September 30, 1975, the group managed 26 trusts with investments valued at more than A$ 56 million (US$ 70 million), a public superannuation fund with investments of A$ 67 million (US$ 84 million), and various other portfolios with a total value for managed investment funds exceeding A$ 550 million (US$ 687.5 million).

Australian Financial Publications

Australian Financial Review (daily) / Broadway / Sydney. United States office: 1501 Broadway / New York, New York 10036
Australian Miner (weekly) / 36 Carrington Street / Sydney
Australian Stock Exchange Journal (monthly) / PO Box 3186, GPO / Sydney
Bulletin (weekly) / PO Box 4088 / Sydney
The National Times / Jones Street, Broadway / Sydney
Rydges Digest (monthly) / 74 Clarence Street / Sydney

Australian Newspapers With Good Business Coverage

The Age / 250 Spencer Street / Melbourne
The Australian / 2 Holt Street / Sydney
The Daily Telegraph / 168 Castlereigh / Sydney
The Sydney Morning Herald / 235 Jones Street, Broadway / Sydney

16. Mexico

Until the Mexican government devalued the peso on September 1, 1976, and set it afloat, Mexico combined the attractions of a popular retirement haven for many Americans with opportunities for what appeared to be safe fixed-income investments providing unusually high yields of 10% or more net per year after Mexican taxes. Many Americans had built up their Mexican nest eggs long before they actually took the final step to retire. Many other foreign investors with no Mexican retirement in mind were sufficiently attracted by the investment potential to put part of their money there.

As this book went to press, it was too early to say what effect devaluation and a floating Mexican peso would have on future foreign portfolio investments and bank deposits in Mexico. The immediate effect for those who had not withdrawn their money before devaluation was a currency loss equivalent to three to four years of interest income. It appeared, however, that there would be no currency controls, that the peso would remain fully convertible into other currencies, and that foreign investors would be able to withdraw dividends and interest payments as well as capital if they decided to liquidate their investments.

Note: Because of the peso devaluation in 1976 from $0.08 to about $0.04 per peso, no dollar equivalents are given.

269

International Investing

Rumors Won Out

The Mexican peso had been pegged to the dollar since 1954 at the official rate of $1 = 12.50$ pesos. The peso remained linked to the dollar during the latter's decline *vis-à-vis* other, stronger world currencies. For many years the peso was considered the strongest currency of all developing nations. It was admitted as a reserve currency to the International Monetary Fund and to futures tradings on the Chicago Mercantile Exchange, which makes a futures market for some of the leading currencies of the world. The latter may have been a curse in disguise.

Rumors of a possible devaluation of the peso had popped up with regularity in the past only to be found unfounded every time. The devaluation rumors in the first half of 1976 were particularly pronounced, based on a whopping budget deficit, a high inflation rate, and a large foreign trade deficit. The rumors were fanned by a barrage of newspaper articles in the United States and the fact that the peso began to trade at a substantial discount for future delivery on the Chicago Mercantile exchange. The rumors were hotly denied by Mexican authorities and the Mexican banking and investment community. Nevertheless, the Mexican peso became a classic case history of a currency having become sufficiently weak on its own that investors' panic and cold speculators' calculation could push it over the brink.

Investments Easy

Assuming that the devalued peso will remain freely convertible and find a relatively stable base, investments in Mexico at the new currency level may become as attractive as they had been in the past — and retirement opportunities and tourism have become more attractive at the new exchange rate. For a United States resident it is much simpler to invest in Mexico than in practically any other foreign country, and it is much easier to keep informed about investments. All leading Mexican banks and brokers handle foreign investment accounts, and a number of them publish informative investment newsletters. All will correspond and send regular statements in Spanish and quite a few banks will correspond in English, although their statements will be in Spanish. Brokers specializing in handling United States and Canadian clients, on the other hand, correspond in English, and their booklets, brochures, and accounting statements are in English.

A foreign investor can ask his Mexican bank or brokers to send his statements to any address of his choice, or he can give instructions for his statements to be held until he can pick them up. The foreign investor can also leave standing instructions for the reinvestment of interest and dividends earned. In order to do this, as well as to execute buy and sell orders, Mexico's banks and brokers almost always require a limited power-of-attorney making them *mandatarios,* or authorized representatives of their investment clients. This is simple to arrange, involves no legal fees, and can be revoked at any time without penalty.

Economic Growth

The visible evidence of economic growth has been overwhelming for anyone who has visited Mexico at regular intervals during the past 20 years. Mexico City grew almost overnight from a sedate Spanish colonial capital into a huge, modern metropolis which, like a rapidly growing octopus, continues to sprawl over the central plateau and up the surrounding mountains. Skyscrapers, housing developments, industrial plants, government buildings, hotels, schools, arenas, subways, new roads — all were built with a dynamic speed that belied the traditional image of the sleeping peon under a huge sombrero with his chin drooped to his chest. The automobile population grew by leaps and bounds, filling the streets and air to the choking point and creating one of the worst cases of pollution found anywhere in the world. Highways fanned out from Mexico City, and a road system grew to link even the remotest villages via a highly efficient bus system. Sleepy towns grew into industrial centers, market places, traffic hubs, and tourist meccas. Fishing villages and deserted beaches developed into modern seaside resorts with luxury hotels and marinas. Even the most isolated Indian hamlets in the highest mountains shared in the economic progress with government-built water systems, granaries, and schools.

In cold figures, this meant that between 1960 and 1973, the Mexican gross national product, in constant 1960 prices, grew at an average annual rate of 7%. In 1974, the growth rate was 5.9%, and it was 4% in 1975. Until 1972, successive Mexican governments had been able to accomplish this surprising growth rate with a minimum of inflation. Then, in 1973, spurred by deficit spending, the inflation rate rose to 15.7%. It reached a high of 22.5% in 1974, and was 10.5% in 1975. Whether the declining economic growth rate is coincidental with the rising inflation or its consequence remains a moot point. It had been the government's objective to spur the economy through deficit spending.

The spectacular economic growth spread its benefits to large sectors of the upper and middle classes, but it left the majority of the poor

271

untouched — not because the government did not make every effort to improve their lot but simply because the birthrate among the poor rose as fast as the economy. The Mexican population has been growing at an annual rate of 3.5%, but the birthrate among the poor was much higher than among the well-to-do. President José López Portillo, with a six-year term expiring in December 1982, has family planning high on his priority list. Whether he is able to overcome the Mexicans' traditional attitude towards families remains to be seen. At the same time, Portillo, in his previous position as finance minister, reduced the public works and welfare spending of his predecessor and he increased tax collection significantly by cracking down on tax evaders. Increasing oil exports at world market prices and a revived tourist traffic, which had been badly hurt by the boycott of those who support Israel in 1975, also promised an improved balance-of-payments in 1976. Thus, there were good reasons to expect a revival of Mexico's traditional economic growth rate.

Stable Government

Mexico's long-term economic growth proves one thing: no developing country can improve its economic lot unless it has a stable government that encourages the productive efforts of the individual. Mexico has had a stable one-party government since 1929, when a party which later became the Revolutionary Institutional Party was founded under a democratic constitution. Other parties exist, but their influence within the government is minimal. Mexico is, for all intents, a one-party state.

Democracies come in all shapes and sizes. The Russians say they have a democracy, so do the Americans, and so do the Mexicans. To Anglo-Saxon purists, a one-party system is not a democracy. Yet the Mexicans have had the same party in power for almost 50 years. It is indeed surprising that such a system has not degenerated into a dictatorship. The Mexicans have preserved all key features of a democracy: free movement of people inside the country and across its borders, a relatively free press, free admission of all foreign news media, free flow of money in and out, and a rule of law, even if its application may sometimes appear harsh or capricious.

Probably the secret to the Mexican political system is the fact that a balance of power exists within the ruling party, which includes representatives of major national interests, such as labor unions, business, and the military. The presidential candidate of the party is nominated by an internal election process within the party. Once nominated, his election by the voters is assured. Nevertheless, he appears to run as hard for office as any American presidential candidate. For several months before the election he visits almost every hamlet from Yucatán to the Rio Grande. This campaign does not change the election results, but it serves the useful purpose of giving the president a face-to-face acquaintance with many of his people and their problems.

The president is elected for one term of six years. He cannot run for reelection. Each president and his cabinet implant a special stamp on the economy. President Luís Echeverría Alvarez, whose term expired on November 30, 1976, believed that economies are stimulated by huge government spending and raising the government debt, and he discouraged direct foreign investments, which had helped greatly to build Mexico's industry. His successor, Portillo, seems intent on swinging the pendulum back to fiscal conservatism and a climate that encourages productivity increases through private initiative.

The Mexican political system, instituted after 100 years of bloody turmoil, seems to be the most workable for the Mexican people. Like many living bodies, it shows signs of fatigue and indisposition from time to time, which manifested themselves in the student uprising and the provincial guerrilla activities in the early 1970s, but, on balance, the Mexican government so far has demonstrated strong regenerative powers, and there were no signs of sweeping change in 1976.

Nevertheless, changes even in democratically elected governments can result in major changes in the investment climate — a fact that sophisticated investors try to keep in mind.

Awakening Stock Market

Mexico's economic growth in the past offered investors no opportunity in growth stocks. The three stock exchanges — Mexico City, Monterrey, and Guadalajara — had very little practical significance as a source of new capital or for serious investment purposes. Traditionally, Mexican industry and business had relied on debt financing — primarily bank loans — rather than equity financing. The shares that were listed on the exchanges, with a handful of exceptions, had a very limited market or no market at all. Trading was controlled by banks, family groups, and other insiders, and much of it occurred outside the exchanges. Total daily trading volume averaged 100,000 shares, with a market value of less than $1 million.

The situation changed dramatically under the Echeverría administration, which tried to create a second domestic source for raising capital. The three exchanges were consolidated into one national organization called *Bolsa de Valores de México* with headquarters in Mexico City and branches in Monterrey and Guadalajara. The system is computerized to speed up trading and settlements. A public information campaign was launched to educate the Mexican public about securities investments and to encourage Mexican corporations to provide adequate disclosure for investment purposes.

The national securities commission (*Comisión Nacional de Valores*) was enlarged into an effective supervisory organization. No stocks, bonds, or notes (*pagarés*) may be offered to the public without registration with, and approval by, the commission, which also controls the registration and licensing of individuals and firms as stock brokers. No one may use the title *casa de bolsa* (broker) without meeting strict government standards for ability, integrity, and financial solvency. An approved brokerage firm displays the letters *CNV*, followed by its permit number, on its letterhead.

Under the new rules, all Mexican banks and brokers are required to execute all stock transactions through the *Bolsa de Valores*.

To top it all off, Mexico's central bank, *Banco de México*, in March 1976, issued a regulation requiring all Mexican banks to invest 8% of their total savings accounts reserves in an approved list of shares and mortgage bonds of Mexican corporations. An additional 4% may be made available to brokerage houses for loans to customers wanting to invest on margin in any of the approved securities. Total savings accounts are estimated at $2 billion. This means that about $240 million will be channeled into the Mexican stock market within less than two years.

The effect on the market was electrifying. The index, which plateaued at the 200-level during 1973 to 1975, had already risen to 250 by mid-March 1976. When the announcement was made it shot to 280. By June 1976, it had settled at the 270 level. Daily trading at times reached 300,000 to 400,000 shares.

If government education didn't do it, this dramatic rise of the index certainly managed to focus the public's attention on the stock market, and the news of a potential market miracle *à la Japonaise* spread beyond the Mexican border. The peso devaluation in September 1976 gave the market a further boost. However, it was apparent in 1976 that the market was still far too thin to absorb all of this new money — not a suitable playground for any but the most speculative investor.

In 1976, most of the Mexican stocks could not be purchased by foreign investors, but the situation was in flux, and new names were added to the approved list for foreign investors. To get up-to-date information on available Mexican common stocks, a foreign investor can contact the stock exchange or a licensed brokerage firm. He can also subscribe to *The Mexican Investor*, a bi-monthly investment advisory letter which

Mexico

publishes a list of actively traded stocks as well as a model portfolio.

Until 1973, all Mexican stocks were bearer shares. Since then, companies have also issued registered shares. For a while, these presented a tax advantage. Now, however, both registered and bearer common stock is subject to a 21% tax. Foreign buyers must register all of their Mexican stock holdings — including bearer shares — in a formality executed by the broker or bank dealing with the investor.

Investment Funds

One of the simplest methods for a foreign investor to participate in the Mexican stock market is to buy one of the four available investment funds: *FIMSA, FIRME, Fondo Banamex,* or *Multifondo Inversora Mexicana.* All are listed on the stock exchange but are usually purchased directly from the management companies at sales charges ranging up to 8%. Fund shares are redeemable on sight by their respective management companies at net asset value. The funds are operated under strict government regulation; they are exempt from Mexican income tax; and they involve no custodial charges.

Fixed-Income Securities

The Mexican businessman, as one Mexican investment counsellor has said, prefers to pay a high interest on debt to build his business rather than have stockholders poke their noses into his affairs and tell him what to do. The shoe may also be on the other foot. Investors may prefer a safe income to a speculation on the uncertain fate of shares in a company that does not tell them what is going on.

Whatever the case may be, the overwhelming majority of investment opportunities in Mexico in the past have been in fixed-income securities, and it remains to be seen whether the reforms of the stock market will bring about a change. Receiving average net yields of from 9% to 12% a year between 1968 and 1975, the investor in Mexican fixed-income securities has done considerably better than practically every amateur and professional investor in the United States market during the same time.

Very little expertise is needed. The leading banks and brokers offer a choice of sound investment opportunities and take care of all purchase details. Not all banks and brokerage houses, however, audit and collect interest for their foreign clients; nor do all send their foreign clients

275

monthly statements in English. In other words, some of the institutions act as straight commission sales agents only and, once the transaction is completed, it is up to the foreign investor to personally manage the details of his investment. Because of this, most United States investors in Mexico have found it convenient to select banks or brokerage firms which have administrative and custodial services and report in English.

High Liquidity Investments

Mexico offers the foreign investor two classes of highly liquid securities which, although legitimately called bonds actually function like call-money. By far the most popular of these are the *bonos financieros*, or liquid bonds. These are issued in minimum units of 100 pesos by all of Mexico's industrial development banks, and by *Nacional Financiera*, the large, government-owned, industrial development bank. Net interest in 1976, after Mexican taxes, was 7.5%. The bonds can be cashed by the investor, or his Mexican representative, in a matter of minutes. Furthermore, the investor may take out all, or part, of his investment at any time, with no questions asked, and will be paid full par value at all times. Interest in liquid bonds is paid quarterly.

Less popular, but still highly liquid, are *bonos hipotecarios*, which are a form of mortgage bond. In 1976, these paid 7.25% per year after Mexican taxes, with interest payable monthly. As in the case of liquid bonds, all or part of the investment can be withdrawn at any time without penalty and at par. Most banks and brokerage firms handle these bonds, or they can be purchased directly from the issuing mortgage banking institutions. The interest earned from both liquid bonds and mortgage bonds may be reinvested (compounded) for greater yield.

Bank Time Deposit Contracts

By far the most popular form of investment with both foreigners and Mexicans is the bank deposit contract, equivalent to a certificate of deposit in the United States. As in the case of liquid bonds, time deposit contracts are issued by all Mexican industrial development banks (*financieras*) and by *Nacional Financiera*. They can be purchased for three months, six months, one year, and two years, with interest payable monthly. They can be bought in either pesos or dollars. Net interest, after Mexican taxes, on peso certificates in 1976 ranged from 8.5% on three-month certificates up to 11.5% on one- or two-year certificates;

276

Mexico

on dollar certificates from 7.5% on three-month certificates to 8.5% on one- or two-year paper. The exact return depends on the maturity and the size of the certificates. If monthly interest payments are reinvested, the yearly net yields after Mexican taxes may amount to 12.25%. To open an account with a brokerage house for time deposit contracts most brokerage houses require a minimum initial investment of $2,000.

Minimum Risk Plus a Raffle Chance

Among Mexicans, one of the most popular long-term, fixed-income securities is Mexican government bonds (*Bonos del Ahorro Nacional*), which are comparable to United States Savings Bonds. Their popularity stems partly from the fact that the government holds a raffle every three months with every number of every bond sold participating. There is one winner for each series of 4,000 bonds, and each winner receives, tax free, ten times the amount he paid for his bond. An investor who buys all of the 4,000 bonds in a single series can, therefore, increase his income by 1%. Without the winnings, an investor will receive exactly double his investment after ten years, when the bond matures. If he cashes it in before expiration, he receives about 7% interest, prorated for each three months the bond was held. Redemption values of the bonds are printed on the back of the certificate. Mexican government bonds cannot be purchased by Americans from within the United States, but once in Mexico they may invest any amount in these securities without getting into trouble back home.

Corporate Bonds

Mexico also offers a few attractive opportunities for investing in corporate bonds. *Telmex* (*Teléfonos de México*) has issued a series of mortgage bonds (*obligaciones hipotecarias*) with maturities up to 20 years. These issues of 50 million pesos each are redeemed through a drawing at the rate of 3.33 million pesos per year beginning at the end of the fifth year from the date of the issue. Since they are usually selling below face value, they combine a high net yield with a built-in capital gains, provided the investor holds them to redemption.

Celanese Mexicana, on July 1, 1976, offered an issue of 200 million pesos in straight debentures at an interest rate of slightly above 15% which, after deducting the 21% withholding tax, represents a net yield of better than 12%. The bonds sold at a slight premium after issue. They will be redeemed in one payment after five years.

International Investing

No Investor Losses

It is well worth noting that although Mexico has no equivalent of the United States' Federal Deposit Insurance Corporation, no depositor in a Mexican bank, or investor in debt obligations (such as time deposit contracts) of a Mexican bank, has lost a dime over the last 45 years. Banks have failed, of course, just as they have in other parts of the world. But when this happens in Mexico, the Mexican National Banking Commission takes over the institution, reorganizes it, and gets it back on its feet. During this time the stockholders of the bank may lose money, but the depositors and investors in the bank's debt securities are protected to the last cent, and the bank's doors are never closed.

Mexican Investment in Foreign Securities

There are no official restrictions for Mexicans or foreign residents in Mexico to invest in foreign securities. However, Mexicans are discouraged from investing in foreign securities as an unpatriotic act and, judging by official statistics, they seem to be patriotic. The *United States Treasury Bulletin* does not isolate Mexico in its statistics on purchases of United States securities by foreigners, but almost all of the total purchases from Central and South America are accounted for by such tax havens as the Netherlands Antilles and the Bahamas. The investments from all other countries must be minimal.

At least two American brokerage houses — *Merrill Lynch, Pierce, Fenner & Smith* and *E.F. Hutton & Co.* — are represented in Mexico. They cannot sell directly to the public but have affiliations with Mexican commercial and development banks that also act as brokers and underwriters.

Sources of Information

Because of the great influx of United States and Canadian tourists and retirees into Mexico, information in English on how to invest and retire in Mexico is prolific. The two most widely read books on the subject are: *How You Can Invest or Retire in Mexico* by Carl D. Ross and *Invest and Retire in Mexico* by Sidney Wise. Mr. Wise also publishes a widely-read bi-monthly market letter, *The Mexican Investor*. Other popular investment letters are *Mexletter* and *Lloyd's Mexican Economic Report*, the latter published by Mexico's largest brokerage house, *Allen W. Lloyd y Asociados, S.A.*

278

Mexico

Principal Stock Exchange

Bolsa de Valores / Uruguay 68 / Mexico City

Major Mexican Commercial Bank Headquarters in Mexico City

Banco Comercial Mexicano, S.A. / Uruguay 55. New York office: 450 Park Avenue / New York, New York 10022
Banco de Comercio, S.A. / Venustiano Carranza 44. New York office: 540 Madison Avenue / New York, New York 10022
Banco Internacional, S.A. / Reforma 156
Banco de Londres y Mexico, S.A. / Bolívar and 16 de Septiembre
Banco del Pais, S.A. / Torre Latino Americano
Banco Mexicano, S.A. / 5 de Mayo 35. New York office: 44 Wall Street / New York, New York 10005
Banco Nacional de Mexico, S.A. / Isabel la Católica 44. New York office: 45 Wall Street / New York, New York 10005

Development, Investment, and Trust Banks (Financieras)
All in Mexico City unless indicated otherwise

Credito Minero y Mercantil / Reforma 144
Financiera del Atlantico, S.A. / Venustiano Carranza 51
Financiera Banamex, S.A. / Isabel la Católica 39
Financiera Bancomer, S.A. / Venustiano Carranza 44
Financiera Colón, S.A. / Reforma 185
Financiera Comermex, S.A. / Uruguay 55
Financiera Industrial, S.A. / Monterrey, Nuevo Leon
Financiera Intercontinental, S.A. / Insurgentes Sur 453 P.B.
Financiera Internacional, S.A. / Reforma 156
Financiera del Norte, S.A. / Morelos 110 (corner Reforma)
Nacional Financiera, S.A. / Isabel la Católica 51
Sociedad Financiera de Industria y Descuento, S.A. / Avenida Francisco 1

The Five Largest Mortgage Banks, All in Mexico City

Banco de Cédulas Hipotecarias, S.A. / Reforma 364
Banco Hipotecaria Azteca, S.A. / Reforma 107
Banco Nacional de México, S.A. / Isabel la Católica 44
General Hipotecaria, S.A. / Reforma 195-1er piso
Hipotecaria Bancomer, S.A. / San Juan de Letran 13

279

International Investing

Mexican Investment Trusts in Mexico City
Comparable to closed-end mutual funds

Fondo Industrial Mexicano, S.A. (FIMSA) / Venustiano Carranza 48-101
Fondo de Inversiones Banamex, S.A. / Isabel la Católica 44
Fondo de Inversiones Rentables Mexicanas, S.A. (FIRME) / Venustiano Carranza 54
Multifondo Inversora Mexicana, S.A. / Monte Pelvoux 110

Government Savings Bonds (Bonos del Ahorra Nacional)

Information office: Reforma 77 / Mexico City
Nacional Financiera, S.A. (liquid bonds and time deposit contracts) / Isabel la Católica 51 / Mexico City

Approved Brokers
All in Mexico City unless otherwise indicated

Acciones y Valores de México, S.A. / Isabel la Católica 38-705 y 707
Asesoria y Promoción Bursatil, S.A. / Isabel la Católica 52-602
Bursatil de México, S.A. / Isabel la Católica 43-801
Casa de Bolsa del Atlantico, S.A. / Venustiano Carranza 48-1er piso
Casa de Bolsa Bancomer, S.A. / Isabel la Católica 45-1o piso
Casa de Bolsa Madero, S.A. / Isabel la Católica 24-22
Casa de Bolsa Serfin, S.A. / Juarez 14
Curbelo, Madrigal y Cia., S.A. / Uruguay 68-7o piso
James E. Day y Asociados, S.A. / Sector Juarez Calle 14 No. 411 / Guadalajara
Invermexico, S.A. / Campos Eliseos 385 Edif. A-4o piso
Inversora Bursatil, S.A. / Isabel la Católica 38-106 y 107
Allen W. Lloyd y Asociados, S.A. / Prisciliano Sanchez 220 / Guadalajara
Operadora de Bolsa, S.A. / Isabel la Católica 24 Desp. 202
Fernando Pesqueira y Cia., S.A. / Fco. y Madero 42-4o piso
Procorsa, S.A. / Hamburgo 190-A
Promotora de Operaciones Bursatiles, S.A. / Juarez 4-503
Victor M. Rubio y Cia., S.A. / Reforma 292-601
Sociedad Bursatil Mexicana, S.A. / Chapultepec 246-201
Tecnica Bursatil, S.A. / Isabel la Católica 38-107
Carlos Trouyet, S.A. / Juarez 14-2o piso
Valores Banamex, S.A. / Isabel la Católica 39-1er piso
Valores Bursatiles, S.A. / Reforma 444-5o piso

Mexico

Active Issues of the Bolsa de Valores de México

Altos Hornos (steel)
Aluminio (aluminum)
Anderson Clayton (foods)
A.P. Green (refractories)
Apasco (cement)
Aviamex (airline)
Bacardi (liquors)
Banamex (bank)
Campos (tools)
Cannon (hosiery)
Carbide (chemicals)
Cechisa (cellulose)
Celanese (synthetics)
Cenmalt (malt)
Eaton (automotive)
Ecatepec (steel)
Fibanco (bank)
Frisco (mining)
Fundidora (steel)
General Electric (appliances)
IEM (appliances)
Indetel (telecommunications)
Ind. Resistol (chemicals)
Kimberly (paper)

Lamosa (building products)
Liverpool (retail)
Loreto (paper)
Metalver (tanks)
Moctezuma (brewery)
Moderna (tobacco)
Moresa (automotive)
Nafin (government bank)
Negromex (chemicals)
Palacio Hierro (retail)
Paris Londres (retail)
Peñoles (mining)
Reynolds (aluminum)
Sanborn (retail)
San Cristobal (paper)
San Luís (silver)
San Rafael (paper)
Spicer (automotive)
Tabacalera (tobacco)
Tamsa (steel pipe)
Telmex (telecommunications)
Tepeyac (steel)
Tolteca (cement)
Tremec (automotive)

Sources of Information

Business Mexico published by American Chamber of Commerce of Mexico / Department X, Lucerna 78 / Mexico City

Business Trends / Homero 136 / Mexico City

Establishing a Business in Mexico published by United States Government Printing Office / Washington, D.C. 20025

Lloyd's Mexican Economic Report published by Allen W. Lloyd y Asociados, S.A. / Prisciliano Sanchez 220 / Guadalajara

The Mexican Investor published by Mexican Financial Advisory Service / Reforma 398-203 / Mexico City

Mexletter, S.A. / Hamburgo 159 / Mexico City

Ross, Carl D. How You Can Invest or Retire in Mexico. Business Reports, Inc. / 1 West Avenue / Larchmont, New York 10538

Samuels, Donovan P. The Basic Facts for Investing in Mexico. Ammex Asociados, S.A. / Lago Silverio 224 / Mexico City

Wise, Sidney T. Invest and Retire in Mexico. Doubleday & Company / Garden City, New York 11530

17. Brazil

Except possibly for Mexico, Latin America at this stage would not appear to be a suitable area for the portfolio investor. Most Latin American countries are plagued by political instability, and for most of them much agony is likely to lie ahead before they reach a political climate that permits a healthy and stable economic growth from which all of their people can benefit, not just a privileged few. The unfortunate feudal heritage and attitudes left by Spain at its departure in the early 19th century still survives today in many of the Latin American countries. Cuba, on the other hand, demonstrates that radicalism in the other extreme is not a road to riches either; rather a scaring away of the geese that can lay edible eggs. Unless an understanding is reached between those who have the know-how and money and those who must learn to use the modern tools of production there is not much hope for a country to improve the economic lot of all its people and enjoy living in peace. So far, in most countries, the tradition of the upper few to take their earnings to Switzerland rather than reinvest them in their own homeland continues. Why, then, should a foreign investor — either directly or through portfolio investments — put his money into such countries?

Note: The cruzeiro exchange rate is not given because of its steadily declining value.

International Investing

Rich in People and Resources

The one exception — and the one country to watch — is Brazil. Of Portuguese tradition and attitude rather than Spanish, the Brazilians have shown a great tolerance towards other races and creeds, and they have kept their doors wide open to immigrants from all parts of the world. Portuguese, Africans, American Indians, Italians, Germans, Japanese, and others have come to blend into a nation of more than 100 million in a country that is larger than the continental United States without Alaska, a country that has more farmland than the whole of Europe, more forests than any other nation except Canada and Russia, a third of the world's known iron ore deposits, and many other natural resources, including bauxite, manganese, limestone, diamonds, gold, silver, nickel, and chromium.

In the course of its history Brazil has gone through a number of economic boom periods based on single commodities, notably cotton, rubber, and coffee. These were usually accompanied by erratic production and price swings, so typical for most commodities, and ended in depressions. In the late 1950s and early 1960s, Brazil was a country in economic chaos that couldn't pay its bills and had a runaway inflation which sometimes reached almost 100% a year.

In the late 1960s, a radical change took place. A new economic boom started — but this one was based on solid industrial development. Manufacturing and mining passed agriculture as the main contributor to the gross national product. Almost overnight Brazil became an important producer of steel, automobiles, chemicals, pharmaceuticals, cement, and paper. Automobile production increased from 225,000 vehicles in 1967 to over 524,000 in 1975, many of them made for export. In addition, 65,000 tractors and 405,000 trucks, buses, and other vehicles were produced in 1975. Brazil became practically self-sufficient in manufactured consumer goods.

Foreign investments poured in from all parts of the world, for a total of about $10 billion, with the United States leading, followed by West Germany, Canada, Japan, and Switzerland. The Japanese, who over the past century had settled there as farmers, came as big investors, planning to build steel mills and other heavy industry for which they can no longer find suitable locations in their crowded homeland.

Gross national product in real terms was increasing at an average annual rate of around 10% in 1971 through 1974 — one of the highest rates in the world. Employment was rising at a rate of almost 1 million new jobs a year, and per capita income had almost doubled from about $360 in 1969 to more than $600 in 1973.

Brazil

A Faltering Spell

This heady growth has come to a sputtering halt since the Arab oil embargo. Oil is the one key natural resource lacking in Brazil. Intensive searches so far have not produced enough discoveries to reduce the country's oil bill significantly ($3 billion in 1975). Foreign debt increased from about $10 billion in 1973 to $22 billion in 1975, and it was still rising in 1976. Inflation, which had been brought down to what for Brazil was a reasonable level of about 20% per year, was 34.5% in 1974 and 30% in 1975 and was heading for 50% in 1976. The high rate of inflation, in spite of indexing, has severely reduced the real income of most wage earners, and with a rapidly rising population, real wealth has not trickled far down from the managerial and money classes to everyone else. Economic growth in real terms had slowed down to 4% in 1975. The economy showed severe organizational and managerial strains as well as disturbingly large government ownership and bureaucratic fetters.

In addition, the question of long-range political stability did not seem fully answered in 1976. The current military regime, which came into power in 1964, elected its third president, General Ernesto Geisel, in 1974, to a five-year term. The election process is comparable to that of Mexico — one candidate, elected for a single term, and selected by an unrevealed process within the ruling party. At the outset, the military regime had made some vague promises of eventual restoration of civilian rule. In 1976, there was no evidence of such civilian rule. It remained to be seen whether the Brazilian system would mature into a viable system, return to a multi-party democratic system, or eventually collapse under economic, social, and political stresses.

Stock Exchanges

The Brazilian government has moved to develop the two leading stock exchanges — in Sao Paulo and Rio de Janeiro — into useful sources for new capital by providing a number of incentives to Brazilians to invest in stocks and bonds. As a result of this policy, there was a wild speculative fever on these exchanges in 1971, sending stock prices to giddy heights. By 1974, they had returned to their 1970 levels if calculated in terms of constant cruzeiros.

No official figures on market capitalization are published, but according to an estimate by the British brokerage firm *Vickers, da Costa,* capitalization of all quoted Brazilian shares is about $20 billion. About two-thirds of this is in "firm" hands — government ownership or minority interests of foreign corporations. Individual investors, by far the most active traders on the exchanges, account for perhaps 27% of the holdings, with the balance distributed among institutional investors and investment funds.

In 1975, about 600 companies were listed on the *Bolsa de Valores do Sao Paulo* and *Bolsa de Valores do Rio de Janeiro* — about 300 only in Sao Paulo, about 130 only in Rio de Janeiro, and the balance on both exchanges. In addition, there were some 60 smaller companies listed on 11 regional exchanges, which together accounted for only about 3% of total market value of all listed Brazilian companies.

Combined annual trading volume of the two leading exchanges was between $1 and $1.5 billion in 1974 and 1975. Because of Brazil's tradition of very high inflation, stock market statistics in cruzeiros are meaningless unless they can be converted into constant terms in relation to a base year. For instance, the Sao Paulo *Bovespa* index in inflationary terms rose from 100 in 1968 to a peak of 2500 in 1971 and declined to about 1500 by mid-1975. In constant terms, the index rose from 100 in 1968 to a peak of 1200 in 1971, and was about 350 in mid-1975.

For this reason, indexed treasury bills (*ORTN*) are by far the most popular fixed-income security in Brazil. In 1975, some $5 billion worth of these were in circulation, as compared to about $2 billion of non-adjustable treasury bills (*LTN*). Index treasury bills have their capital value adjusted monthly in line with the inflation index. Income also rises with inflation. Private fixed-income securities consist primarily of commercial paper, bank certificates of deposit, and mortgage notes — a total of about $12 billion in circulation. A small number of convertible corporate bond issues have been sold. Most of the trading of fixed-income securities is outside the exchanges, and no statistics on trading volume are available.

Trading on the exchanges is through licensed brokerage firms which deal directly with the public. In addition, there are investment banks acting as underwriters and investment fund managers and security dealers (*distribuidoras*) acting primarily as dealers and distributors of securities for their own accounts or as agents.

How to Invest in Brazil

In 1976, foreign portfolio investors could not buy Brazilian securities without undergoing many bureaucratic difficulties. However, since May 1975, foreign investors have been able to participate in the Brazilian market through special investment funds managed jointly by Brazilian investment banks and foreign fund managers and distributors. These funds cannot be actively offered in the United States unless registered with the SEC (none were in 1976), but an American investor, at his own initiative, can buy these shares from foreign sources. Only non-resident foreign investors may own shares in these funds, and a number of other restrictions apply to encourage long-term rather than hit-and-run investments. Repatriation of the capital invested can start only after three years at the rate of 20% each six months. There is no withholding tax as long as the capital and dividends remain in Brazil. On withdrawal from Brazil, a withholding tax applies to both dividends and realized capital gains at a complicated sliding scale starting with a basic rate of 15%. At least 50% of the portfolio must be invested in common stocks or convertible issues of Brazilian companies that are not controlled by a Brazilian government agency or by foreign interests. The balance can be invested freely in all other vehicles, including treasury bills, new issues, and foreign or government controlled companies. Investment in a single company is limited to 10% of the voting stock or 20% of total capital.

In 1976, four Brazilian funds for foreign investors were sold through foreign managers and others were in their infancy, including those sold through *Barclays Bank* and *Crédit Commercial de France*.

Another way to participate in Brazil's economic development is to buy shares of *Brascan*, a Canadian holding·company heavily invested in Brazil and trading on the American Stock Exchange.

In 1976, Brazilian investors could not invest in foreign securities.

Sources of Information

One of the most comprehensive reviews of the Brazilian stock markets has been published by *Vickers, da Costa* of London. In addition, all managers of Brazilian funds for foreign investors provide reports on the fund performance and the Brazilian investment scene in general.

Bank of Boston International publishes a Brazilian economic newsletter. Among Brazilian institutions publishing economic and investment news in English are *Banco Lar Brasileiro, Banco do Investimento do Brasil,* and *Lara. Journal do Brasil*, a daily newspaper available on some newsstands in New York City, reports on the stock markets. *Deltec Securities* of New York specializes in trading Latin American securities, including Brazilian issues. *Goldman, Sachs & Co., White, Weld & Co,* and *Drexel Burnham Lambert* are among other brokerage houses keeping an eye on the Brazilian scene.

International Investing

Principal Stock Exchanges

Bolsa de Valores do Rio de Janeiro / Praca XV de Novembro 20 / Rio de Janeiro

Bolsa de Valores do Sao Paulo / Alvares Penteado 151-65 / Sao Paulo

Security Firm Specializing in Latin American Stocks

Deltec Securities Corporation / 1 Battery Park Plaza / New York, New York 10004

Brazilian Funds for Foreign Investors

The Brazil Fund. Brazilian manager: *Banco do Investimento Brasileiro.* Foreign managers: *Vickers, da Costa Ltd.,* London; *Murray, Johnstone & Co.,* Glasgow; *Foreign & Colonial Trust,* London; *Touche, Remnant & Co.,* London; *Scottish United Investors,* Edinburgh.

Brazilian Investments. Brazilian manager: *Banco Bozano Simonsen.* Foreign manager: *James Capel & Co.,* London.

Brazilvest. Brazilian manager: *Banco do Investimento Brasileiro.* Foreign managers: *White, Weld & Co.,* London; *Laurence Prust & Co.,* London.

Robrasco. Brazilian manager: *Banco do Investimento Brasileiro.* Foreign manager: *Robeco,* Rotterdam.

Some Actively Traded Stocks

Acesita (steel)
Alpargatas (textiles, apparel)
Banco do Brasil
Belgo Mineira (steel)
Brahma (brewery, soft drinks)
Light (utility)
Petrobras (oil production, refining)
Pirelli (tires)
Siderugica Nacional (steel)
Souza Cruz (tobacco, supermarkets)
Vale do Rio Doce (iron ore)
Varig (airline)

Sources of Information

BIB International (monthly) published by *Banco do Investimento do*

Brazil

Brasil, Divisao do Investimentos / 28th Floor, Rua Direita 250 / Sao Paulo

The Brazilian Economy: Trends and Perspectives (monthly) published by *Banco Lar Brasileiro S.A.* / Rua do Ouvidor 98 / Rio de Janeiro

Darst, David. "Flying Down to Rio: Brazil is Opening its Stock Markets to Foreign Investors." *Barron's,* April 21, 1975.

Lara S.A. Monthly Letter published by *Lara S.A.* / 4th Floor, Rua do Carmo 17 / Rio de Janeiro

Newsletter Brazil published by *Bank of Boston International* / 2 Wall Street / New York, New York 10005

18. Israel

Just before the Yom Kippur War in 1973, Israel seemed one of the bright new stars in the international investment firmament. Immigrants had come at the rate of 40,000 to 50,000 a year, bringing the population to a total of 3 million to help make the desert bloom. Money flowed in to the tune of $1 billion a year in the form of loans, investments, and one-way restitution payments from West Germany. The gross national product rose from 5% to 10% per year in constant terms to reach per-capita levels several hundred times higher than those of its Arab neighbors. The stock market index had doubled in two years and many Israeli stocks had become the hot issues of the day.

But a man keeping his nose to the grindstone, outperforming everyone in sight, usually does not endear himself to his less competent neighbors, especially if he sometimes forgets political sensitivities, as hardworking people are apt to do. Whatever else the Yom Kippur War was intended to accomplish in terms of political goals, it crippled the Israeli economy.

Note: 1I£ = $0.12

International Investing

Defense spending increased from $840 million in 1972 to $4.2 billion in 1976, or about one-third of the gross national product. Foreign investments were reduced by half. Immigration dried up to a trickle. Gross national product in constant terms declined. Inflation ran rampant, reaching levels of above 30% per annum in 1976. The Israeli pound was devalued from 4.20 to the dollar to about 8 in July 1976, with a scheduled continuing devaluation of 2% per month. The balance of payments deficit had reached $3.7 billion in 1975. The total foreign debt at the end of 1975 was $9 billion. There seemed no end in sight.

Indexed Bond

Before the 1973 war, when inflation was running at more modest rates, the Israeli government and major banks had issued bonds that were linked to the cost-of-living index to protect the investor against inflation, or tied to the dollar to protect him against devaluation. As inflation accelerated, investors were less and less inclined to buy anything else but indexed bonds which, by 1975, accounted for almost 90% of the daily trading volume of about $720,000 on the Tel Aviv Stock Exchange. Foreign investors until then had been able to buy these bonds, but are now restricted to a few issues denominated in dollars and sold outside Israel.

Indexed bonds during a galloping inflation skyrockets the budget deficit and the public debt. To reverse the tide, the government, in 1975, reduced the indexing of new bonds to only 90% of the cost-of-living increase, and within three years this percentage is to be lowered to 70%. New bond issues indexed to the dollar were suspended for a while, but a few became available again in 1976. In addition, the government began to levy a 1.5% turnover tax on debenture sales, it abolished bearer debentures for new issues, and it froze the bond investment portfolios of provident (mutual) funds, savings plans, and life insurance schemes. This resulted in a selling wave on the fixed-income market and to a sharp decline in prices. Sales of new issues to the public came to a halt.

Equity Market

Perhaps because of the clamp down on indexed bonds, and perhaps because of rays of hope of economic revival, the Israeli equity market began a modest revival in 1976, with the general share index rising from

292

112, in June 1975, to 135 in June 1976, about in line with inflation. Trading volume also perked up.

A number of Israeli stocks are actively traded in the United States over-the-counter, notably *Bank Leumi le-Israel* and various issues of *IDB Bankholding* and its subsidiary, *Industrial Development Bank of Israel*. *Elscint*, making radioisotope scanning and image storing equipment, made a public offering of 400,000 shares in the United States in 1972. These are traded over-the-counter. For a time, the stock was popular as a high technology issue.

Three Israeli issues are actively traded on the American Stock Exchange: *Alliance Tire and Rubber*, Israel's only tire manufacturer, *American Israel Paper Mills*, the country's largest paper manufacturer, and *Etz Lavud*, a wood products manufacturer.

Among Israeli shares traded only in Tel Aviv that found investor interest in the United States are *Electric Wire and Cable*, a manufacturer of power and telephone wire and cable, *Property and Building Corporation*, a large real estate development firm, and *Koor*, an industrial holding and development company.

In May 1976, there was a flurry in stocks related to oil exploration and production on the basis of rumors that oil had been found in Sinai. Stocks particularly affected were *Jordan Exploration and Investment*, *Delek Fuel*, *Piryon*, *Paz Investment*, and *Lapidoth Prospectors*.

Investment Companies

An investor who wants to have a diversified participation in the Israeli economy can buy shares of one of the bank investment and holding companies. Leading among them are *Bank Leumi Investment* and *Discount Bank Investment*, both traded on the Tel Aviv Stock Exchange. In addition, *Bank Leumi* manages eight open-end investment funds with different investment objectives, and *Israel Discount Bank* manages six.

In the United States, two American-based funds with Israeli security portfolios can be bought: *Israel Development* and *Israel Investors*, both closed-end funds. *Israel Development* is part of *AMPAL American Israel Corporation*, a group of financial companies founded in 1942 to help finance the development of Israel. *AMPAL* debentures and preference shares are traded over-the-counter in the United States. *AMPAL's* annual report includes capsule reviews of the results of those Israeli corporations in which the group has major investments.

293

International Investing

Investment Channels

It is simple to invest in Israeli securities from the United States, even those traded only in Israel. Any American broker will handle orders for Israeli securities traded on the American Stock Exchange or on the over-the-counter market. Securities traded only in Israel are available through *Leumi Securities,* a subsidiary of *Bank Leumi le-Israel,* the largest Israeli bank, and through the brokerage houses of *Brager* and *Oscar Gruss.* In Israel itself, 70% of the brokerage business is in the hands of the banks that are members of the Tel Aviv Stock Exchange, but these banks cannot sell securities in the United States. The balance of the brokerage business is done by other members of the exchange.

Before 1973, investment clubs buying Israeli securities mushroomed in the United States. The war put a damper on these clubs, but a good number of them continue in existence. Information on these clubs and good guidelines on how to form a club are available from the *Zionist Organization of America.*

Sources of Information

Leumi Securities distributes investment information prepared by *Bank Leumi,* including *What's New,* an investment publication, and *Economic Review.* The firm does not itself make any stock market recommendations. Other Israeli banks also prepare information. Two consulting firms in Tel Aviv provide independent investment information: *Stock Exchange Information Service* of *Halevi & Co. Economic Counselling,* which publishes data on individual companies similar to the *Standard & Poor's* sheets, and *National Consultants.* Three financial newspapers with stock market information are published in Tel Aviv: *Shaar, Yom-Yom* and *Mabat.*

Two Israeli investment information services are published in the United States: *Israeli Securities Review* and *Israeli Investor's Report.* General information on the Israeli economy is available from *Israel Investment and Export Authority.*

The larger Israeli companies, and especially the banks and investment companies, produce excellent annual reports in English. However, many of the smaller companies are less informative and provide no information in English. Annual reports are often not published until six months after the end of the fiscal year, and the Tel Aviv exchange, in 1975, did not require that listed companies release quarterly earnings.

294

Israel

Stock Market

The Tel Aviv Stock Exchange Ltd. / 113 Allenby Road / Tel Aviv

*United States Brokers Accepting Orders for
Israeli Securities Traded Only in Israel*

Brager & Co. / 12 East 80th Street / New York, New York 10021
Oscar Gruss & Son / 80 Pine Street / New York, New York 10005
Leumi Securities Corporation / 18 East 48th Street / New York, New
York 10017

Israel Investment Companies and Funds Traded in the United States

AMPAL American Israel Corporation / 30 East 42nd Street / New
York, New York 10017 (traded over-the-counter)
Israel Development Corporation / 30 East 42nd Street / New York,
New York 10017 (traded on the American Stock Exchange)
Israel Investors Corporation / 850 Third Avenue / New York, New
York 10022 (traded over-the-counter)

Israeli Securities Traded on the American Stock Exchange

Alliance Tire and Rubber "A"
American Israel Paper Mills ADRs
Etz Lavud
Israel Development Corporation

Israeli Securities Traded Over-the-Counter in the United States

AMPAL
Bank Leumi le-Israel ADRs
Elscint
Israel Discount Bank "A"
IDB Bankholding Ord.
IDB Bankholding Pref.
Industrial Development Bank of Israel "C"
Industrial Development Bank of Israel "CC"
Industrial Development Bank of Israel "D"
Industrial Development Bank of Israel New Cap Nts.
Israel Bank of Agriculture Pref.
Israel Investors Corporation

Isras
PEC Israel Economic Corporation
Rassco Ord.
Rassco Pref.
Real Estate Participation
Tourist Industry Pref.

Mutual Funds Traded in Israel

Managed by *Bank Leumi le-Israel*
Bedolach: 31% common stocks, 22% convertibles, 47% indexed bonds
Gavish: 25% common stocks, 55% indexed bonds, 20% foreign currency-linked bonds
PIA: 34% common stocks, 32% indexed bonds, 34% foreign currency
Shamir: 100% indexed bonds
Tarshish: information not available
Topaz: 75% foreign currency-linked bonds; 25% foreign securities
Yigdal: 70% common stocks, 26% convertibles, 4% indexed bonds
Zamid: 66% indexed bonds, 34% foreign currency-linked bonds

Managed by *Discount Bank Investment Corporation*
Alon: 76% indexed bonds, 17% foreign currency-linked bonds, 7% stocks and convertibles
Brosh: 41% indexed bonds, 59% stocks and convertibles
Dekel: 100% stocks and convertibles
Dolev: 77% foreign currency-linked bonds, 23% indexed bonds
Eshel: 88% indexed bonds, 12% stocks and convertibles
Oren: 89% indexed bonds, 11% stocks and convertibles

Selected Israeli Securities Listed on the Tel Aviv Exchange

Finance, Insurance, and Investment
Bank Hapoalim
Bank Leumi le-Israel
Bank Leumi Investment (closed-end)
Discount Investment (closed-end)
General Mortgage Bank
Hassneh (insurance)
IDB Ord. (bank)
Mizrachi Bank
Tefahot (mortgage bank)
Union Bank

Israel

Industry and Service Companies
American Israel Paper Mills
Alliance Tire and Rubber "B"
Argaman (textile dyeing)
Ata Textile (apparel)
Clal Industries (holding company)
Delek Fuel (oil)
Dubek (cigarettes)
Elco I.L. 1 (electromechanics)
Elco I.L. 2.5
Electra (electrical goods)
Electric Wire and Cable
Elite (chocolates)
Elron (computers)
Polygon (textile dyeing)
Taal Plywood (furniture and boxes)
Teva (pharmaceuticals and chemicals)

Land and Building Companies
Africa Israel (real estate)
ILDC (real estate)
Mehadrin (citrus groers)
Property & Building (real estate)

Sources of Information

Israel Investment and Export Authority / 850 Third Avenue / New York, New York 10022
Israel Investor's Report / 110 East 59th Street / New York, New York 10022
Israel Securities Review / 557 Beach 129th Street / Belle Harbor, New York 11694
National Consultants Ltd. / Hadar Dafna Building, 39 Shaul Hamelech Boulevard / Tel Aviv
Stock Exchange Information Service of *Halevi & Co. Economic Counselling Ltd.* / 54 Haneviim Street / Jerusalem
Investment club information is available from *Zionist Organization of America* / ZOA House, 4 East 34th Street / New York, New York 10016

Financial Newspapers

Mabat / Tel Aviv
Shaar / 15 Hatzfire Street / Tel Aviv
Yom-Yom / 34 Itzchak Sade Street / Tel Aviv

19. Gold

Except for wedding rings and fillings for their teeth, gold was a dead issue for most Americans for many decades until suddenly, one day in August 1971, the United States declared that it was no longer willing to exchange gold for dollars owned by foreigners. Gold became headline news and it has stayed in the news ever since. The price of gold shot up from its fixed rate of $35 an ounce in 1971 to an all-time high of $197.50 on December 30, 1974, and then went on an erratic, well-publicized decline to about $112 in mid-1976. Gold mining shares became hot issues for the more adventurous investors. Gold coins of old and new vintage and of all denominations became keenly promoted collectors' items. Americans were again allowed to buy gold bullion on December 31, 1974. Gold futures trading was instituted by the Chicago Mercantile Exchange.

Why all the hubbub? The simple explanation is that gold, while not ideal, is by far the most practical yardstick by which to measure the true value of things and money — an uncomfortable censor of governments that debase their currencies.

What is Money?

Money, after all, is only a standardized token by which the value of goods and services can be measured and which can be used to pay for these goods and services. Throughout history, many different things have been used as monetary tokens and yardsticks — cowrie shells, axheads, grains, animal skins, various metals and metal coins, printed paper, and even cigarettes (in the post-World War II era in occupied Germany). The ideal money is one that remains in fairly constant supply relative to the goods and services available. If the supply of money increases faster than the production of goods and services, it loses its value in relation to those goods and services, and prices go up. This is then called "inflation."

Paper money is a perfectly acceptable monetary yardstick as long as its supply is strictly controlled and remains in balance with the available goods and services. However, in the 37 years from 1934 to 1971, money supply in the United States (cash in circulation plus demand and time deposits at banks) rose about three times faster than the gross national product (measured in constant dollars). This meant that the purchasing power of one dollar, as measured by the consumer price index, sank to about 30¢ between 1934 and 1971. During the same time, the price of gold remained artifically fixed at $35 per troy ounce (slightly heavier than the regular ounce). When, on August 15, 1971, the United States declared that it would no longer pay gold for the dollars it owed foreigners, the long-established confidence in the dollar as an international standard of exchange vanished and people turned to what had been a more dependable measure of value since antiquity — gold. Its price tripled within two years, reflecting almost exactly the decline in the purchasing power of the dollar to one-third of its 1933 value. In fact, the average price of a man's suit remained practically unchanged between 1934 and 1973 in terms of gold — about one troy ounce — worth $35 in 1934 and about $100 in 1973, and $130 in 1976. When gold was at $197 it was obviously overpriced in relation to a man's suit.

The dollar disaster had been looming throughout the second half of the 1960s. It had been predicted for several years by some Cassandras to whom nobody listened, including some of the now famous gnomes of Zurich. It arrived with some delay. People just couldn't believe that the economically strongest country in the world could be brought to such a pass through fiscal irresponsibility. But then, few Romans realized that currency debasement was a major contributor to their empire's collapse.

Gold

For most of its last 400 years until its demise in 475 A.D., Rome so inordinately debased its coinage and raised taxes that its productive citizens found it less and less rewarding to produce. With a declining gross national product, population began to decline, and finally there were not enough people and resources left to defend the empire against the invading barbarians.

What is the Gold Standard?

Ever since the time when man learned to produce and work gold and silver these precious materials have proved to be the most stable and reliable monetary tokens — gold more so than silver because silver has had more erratic production and consumption rates than gold. This made the value of silver less reliable in relation to other goods and services. Gold has the additional advantage of not seriously deteriorating even after centuries of storage under the most unsuitable conditions.

Byzantium, which became the successor to Rome in 324 A.D. under Constantine the Great, was one of the longest-lasting empires on the strength of a sound gold currency that retained its face value for 800 years. When debasement started in 1100 A.D., the empire went downhill until Constantinople, defended by another Constantine, was conquered by the Turks in 1452.

The economic advance of the 19th century was based on the gold standard, which practically all countries of the world had adopted. This meant that they minted gold coins of a specified weight or agreed to exchange paper money for gold at a fixed rate of exchange. In most countries this "golden age" came to an end with World War I; in the United States it lasted a little longer.

The United States went on a *de facto* gold standard in 1834; it fixed the price of gold at $20.67 per troy ounce; and it made the gold standard official in 1900 with the Gold Standard Act. Treasury goldback notes bore the message: "Redeemable in gold on demand at the United States Treasury or in gold or lawful money at any Federal Reserve Bank." Silver also was legal tender in the form of silver coins or silver certificates redeemable in silver dollars.

In 1934, the United States devalued the dollar for the first time in terms of gold — from $20.67 to $35 per troy ounce, and citizens could no longer ask for gold in exchange for paper money or own gold bullion. Foreign central banks, however, could still ask for their dollars to be redeemed in gold.

International Investing

In 1964, the United States stopped putting silver in coins. The price of silver had risen above the face value of coins and people started hoarding the coins as fast as the government could mint them until the huge government stock of 2 billion troy ounces of silver was completely exhausted. The Federal Reserve also stopped printing on its notes the message that they are "redeemable in lawful money at the United States Treasury or at any Federal Reserve Bank." One-dollar and five-dollar bills with the inscription "One (or five) silver dollar(s) payable to the bearer on demand" were also withdrawn. In other words, Americans could no longer exchange paper money for real money.

Surpassing the Peak

In August 1971, the United States declared that it was no longer prepared to exchange gold for dollars held by foreigners, and in December 1971, it established a new parity of $38 per troy ounce of gold, raised on February 10, 1973 to $42.22. This was completely meaningless since neither the Federal government nor any foreign central bank was willing to exchange gold for paper dollars at any price, and the free market price of gold at the end of 1971 was already well above $40 and rose to $65 by February 1973. It reached its peak of close to $200 at the end of 1974, driven up by speculative buying in anticipation of the fact that, as of December 31, 1974, United States residents would again be allowed to own gold bullion. To cushion a potential strong buying demand from its citizens, the United States government, in January 1975, auctioned off 2 million ounces of its own gold. However, most of this gold was bought by foreign institutions. The idea of owning gold bullion seemed to be too alien an idea to most Americans. The gold price receded throughout 1975 and 1976, and in mid-1976 the metal dropped to a new low of $107. On June 2, 1976, the International Monetary Fund began regular auctions at six-week intervals of 780,000 troy ounces of gold each. The first of these auctions had a dampening effect on the price of gold, but by early 1977 gold had recovered to about $150 in spite of continued auctions by the IMF.

The Future of Gold

It is impossible to predict the future price trend of gold. A great many factors come into play, chief among them the emotional and speculative buying of gold for hoarding and investment purposes. A new monetary panic or political crisis may send the price of gold up to new heights.

302

Gold

Unloading by disillusioned investors may send it into an abyss. Other factors coming into play are the rate of production, industrial consumption (almost equal to free-world production in 1975), Russian sales to pay for imports, and continued auctions in the Western world by government agencies. Riots in South Africa that would close the mines could make the price of gold bullion skyrocket while rendering the shares of South African gold mines worthless. Only one factor influencing the price of gold can be measured — the rate of inflation.

When discussing inflation confusion sets in. Most people, including learned economists, identify all rises in prices with inflation. There are really three main causes for rises in prices, and only one can properly be called inflation. When a monopoly, such as the oil-producing countries, artificially raises the price far above its production cost, it is really redistributing money — from the pockets of the hapless users to its own. It is not putting more money into circulation. This is not inflation. The same happens, of course, when manufacturers form a cartel to keep prices up or when labor unions manage to negotiate wage increases higher than their increase in productivity.

A second cause for higher prices is the increasing scarcity of a product in demand. The most obvious example is land. The supply of land available is rigidly fixed. As the population increases, the amount of land available for each one of us decreases. We all are getting poorer in terms of land. And this expresses itself in rising real estate prices. This is not true inflation. We just have to do with less land and smaller living quarters. The same happens when a raw material, such as whale oil, gets in short supply. But so far, man has usually found a substitute for a raw material that is being exhausted and priced out of the market.

Genuine inflation occurs only when the supply of money grows faster than the amount of goods and services produced. This has happened very strikingly in the United States. Between 1933 and December 1975, the M2 (cash in circulation plus demand, time, and savings deposits in commercial banks) supply of money rose from $45 billion to $664 billion, or 14.75 times. Gross national product in terms of constant 1958 dollars rose from $141 billion to $821 billion, or 5.92 times. In other words, the money supply rose 2.5 times as fast as the supply of goods and services. The gold price rose from $35 to $125, or 3.5 times.

Money inflation makes it appear that goods and services are getting more expensive, but what it really means is that people are getting poorer because their money is worth less; and their money is worth less because they pay indirectly for government expenditures that should normally be paid in taxes. When they run out of money and borrowing power, the government simply puts more money into circulation by selling government securities and increasing bank credits. Putting more money into circulation is a complex operation, obscured to the public eye, and it can vary from country to country. In the United States the principal way this is done is for the Federal Reserve to "buy" securities of the Federal government and its agencies. Every such security bought by the Federal Reserve creates new money and every government security sold by the Federal Reserve reduces the money supply. The Federal Reserve can also create more money by allowing banks to lend more through a reduction in bank reserve requirements.

Modern politicians and bureaucrats have received additional fuel for their inflationary policies from the theories of the renowned British economist, Lord Keynes, who maintained that the best way to stimulate the economy in a slow period is to increase the money supply, i.e., create inflation; while in boom periods, you deflate, i.e., decrease the money supply. Unfortunately, practically all political leaders have used only the first part of the prescription — even in times of boom — like the psychopath who takes a little alcohol to calm his nerves and then just keeps on taking more and more because it is so effective, until he is an incurable alcoholic. Throughout history there is no example of inflation having cured economic ills; healthy economies in the long run have existed only in periods of sound currency when people had an incentive to work and save.

The United States is not isolated in its inflationary binge. In the 1960s, when it ran up some $100 billion in debt with foreigners without supplying goods and services in return, it fueled inflation in many other countries. But the majority of countries have become quite skilled in their own right, running up budget deficits balanced by the printing presses. Many of the underdeveloped nations, appealing to the guilty conscience of the richer nations or blackmailing them by threats of unrest, have been able to raise money from international bank syndicates with guarantees from international government agencies, while deriving very little concrete productivity in return. Much of this money looks like footloose inflationary money unlikely to be paid back or to be matched by production of goods and services.

Thus, a gold bug has every reason to believe that inflation will continue to play into his hands, and if he is convinced that gold is the only solid value to hang on to in the quicksand of phantom money, he will, as Frenchmen have done for many generations, cling to gold.

How to Buy Gold

A gold bug has several ways to be in gold — bullion, coins, the gold futures market, or gold mining shares. Bullion represents a major investment and presents a storage problem. Not everyone feels comfortable with gold bullion in the house. Banks and others who sell it will provide storage at a cost. Together with the fact that bullion does not pay any interest, the negative cost of owning gold must be weighed against the available interest rates on safe income securities in relation to inflation. An interest rate on a British gilt edged bond of 14% while inflation runs at 16% costs the investor 2% per year, not allowing for the currency risk and taxes. An interest rate of 4% on a Swiss bond, with the inflation rate running at 2%, earns the investor 2% a year plus the possibility of a currency gain. Ownership of gold may cost more than 2% a year for safekeeping, and there is the unpredictable risk of price fluctuations and no interest income.

Gold coins are easier to keep. There are two types of gold coins: those that are no longer minted (such as the French 20-franc piece which usually sells at a premium of about 100% above the bullion price) or gold coins that continue to be minted to satisfy the demand of gold bugs, such as the South African Krugerrand, the Austrian Corona, and the Mexican 50-peso piece, which sell fairly close to the bullion price. Any financial publication, such as *Barron's*, carries advertising that offers a vast array of literature on the subject.

Relatively new is the possibility to invest in gold futures on the Chicago Mercantile Exchange and the Commodity Exchange in New York. An investor who believes in the long-range rise of gold can buy, for a down payment of only 10% (on margin), a contract for the future delivery of gold. He doesn't have to take delivery, but can sell it during the course of the contract, and buy a new contract on margin. This makes it possible to be invested in a substantial amount of gold at relatively small cost. But if the price turns against the investor, it also makes it possible to lose large amounts of money for a relatively small stake. As the Chicago Mercantile Exchange itself points out: "The gold futures market is not for the faint-hearted, nor should anything but risk capital be used for speculating in it." Anyone interested can write for a very informative booklet to the International Monetary Market of the Chicago Mercantile Exchange.

How to Buy Gold Stocks

In a book on foreign securities, gold mining stocks are worth special mention.

Gold stocks, both domestic and foreign, are easy to buy in the United States. Most of the important South African gold stocks are actively traded in the United States in the form of American Depositary Receipts and they can be bought from any American broker. However, an investor might get a better price if he buys a gold stock traded over-the-counter from a broker who makes a market for it. Information is readily available. The selection of individual gold stocks is tricky, however, and a specialist in gold stocks is preferable to a generalist as an advisor.

Two key questions about a gold mine are: What are its ore reserves and how rich are its ores? A number of gold mines and holding companies are also in other mining ventures, including platinum, uranium, silver, copper, and lead, and these elements of the operation may have major bearings on earnings and balance the results from gold mining. Since many gold mines, like other metal mines, have a relatively short life span, the yield from the investment must repay the invested capital before the mine is exhausted, plus a worthwhile profit to the investors. Finally, it should be observed that gold mining stocks are subject to wide price swings that are exploited by traders. It requires a good deal of insight and restraint, if not inside trading information, to catch a gold stock at the bottom of the swing rather than at the top.

Gold Investment Funds

An investment in a single operating mine has a high element of risk because a mine disaster from fire, flood, explosion, or rock burst can close down a mine for a time. Thus, a seasoned investor will spread his investment over several mines. An investor who cannot afford to buy several gold mining stocks, as well as any beginner, is wise to buy shares of an investment fund specializing in gold stocks. The two leading ones are *International Investors* and *ASA*.

International Investors is a United States-managed fund based in New York. Its asset value increased from a low of $4.48 (adjusted for a 3:1 stock split) in November 1971, to an all-time high of $23.04 on April 3, 1974, and had settled back to about $8.00 at the end of 1976. The buyer pays a front-end load commission of 8.5% which is reduced for large orders. In 1976, about 86% of its portfolio was in gold-mining shares; the balance in silver and other mining and foreign industrial shares. The list of its holdings can serve as an investor's guide to gold stocks.

ASA is a South African investment fund (formerly *American-South African Investment Company Ltd.*) which can be bought on the New York Stock Exchange. The shares are also traded on the leading Euro-

Gold

pean stock exchanges. The policy of the fund is to invest between 50% and 80% of the assets in South African gold mining companies and up to 20% in companies outside South Africa engaged in mining or related activities or in the holding and development of real estate. In mid-1976, about 75% was in gold, most of the balance in diamonds in the form of *DeBeers* stock.

A second important South African gold investment fund, traded in the United States over-the-counter in the form of ADRs, is *AMGOLD* (*Anglo American Gold Investment Company*). It has the broadest and most carefully selected portfolio of gold securities in the world; yet it usually sells at a sharp discount of net asset value (whereas *ASA*, in the past, has sold at a high premium). With a pure portfolio of gold stocks, it is an excellent vehicle for participation in the gold sector.

Mining Finance Houses

AMGOLD is controlled by *Anglo American Corporation of South Africa*, the largest mining finance house. Mining finance houses were established in South Africa to finance and underwrite mining and industrial developments. They control most of the gold mines. However, mining finance houses are generally diversified and they reinvest a good portion of their income in new ventures. Their dividend payout is usually lower than that of gold mining stocks or gold investment trusts. *Anglo American Corporation of South Africa*, for instance, derives only about 25% of its income from gold mining; the balance comes from diamonds, copper, platinum, real estate, coal, and steel. A giant organization, it controls about 40% of South Africa's gold production and practically the entire world's production of diamonds (through its control of *DeBeers*). Because of the diversification, price movement of its stock has been less erratic than that of pure gold stocks. Other well-known mining finance companies include *Gold Fields of South Africa* and *Consolidated Gold Fields*.

Individual Mining Stocks

An investor who wants to take a greater risk in trying to beat the "averages" of a gold stock investment fund or a finance house has more than 30 ADRs of *kaffirs* to choose from. (The South African word *kaffir*, an old term used for the blacks of the country, is a generic term for gold mining stocks, probably because the *kaffirs* are doing all of the physical

307

work.) Shares not available in the United States can be bought in Johannesburg or in London.

All South African gold mines must sell their output to the South African government at a fixed price. The government then sells the gold that it does not need as a monetary reserve on the free world market. Profits derived from these free market sales are distributed to the mines on the basis of their deliveries. Thus, the mines benefit from rising gold prices. It must be pointed out in conclusion that some seasoned investors will not buy South African gold stocks, or any other South African stock, because they consider the risk of riots substantial under the *apartheid* system of the country. The effect of riots on South African gold mining shares became painfully apparent in June 1976.

Canadian Gold Stocks

Canada produces about 4% of world production. Production has been declining steadily over the past few years. Until the recent sharp rise of the gold price, many Canadian gold mines needed government subsidies to stay in business. As in South Africa, the higher gold price has not re-sulted in higher gold production, but profits have improved. Stock prices of the leading gold stocks rose sharply. *Dome Mines*, listed on the New York Stock Exchange, traded around $17 to $19 in 1970 and 1971 and was at about $64 in April 1974. In December 1976, it had sold at $43. Its affiliate, *Campbell Red Lake Mines*, also listed on the New York Stock Exchange, more than tripled in price from about $20 to $70 between 1970 and November 1973, and it sold for $24 in December 1976.

The choice among Canadian gold stocks is limited, and the United States investor will find it more convenient to confine himself to those traded on United States markets.

In addition to the two companies listed on the New York Stock Exchange, two Canadian gold mining issues are listed on the American Stock Exchange — *Giant Yellowknife Mines* and *Pato Consolidated Gold Dredging*. The latter is a Canadian company operating in Colombia, a country that adds an additional element of risk.

Even though it does not belong in a book on foreign stocks, the only significant United States producer of gold, *Homestake Mining*, deserves some mention. Only about 5% of its sales are derived from gold, but a much higher percentage in earnings when gold prices are good. Its stock price responds to the price of gold bullion, having risen from about $9 in November 1971 (adjusted for a 2:1 stock split) to a high of $67 in August 1974, and receded to about $37 by the end of 1976.

Gold

Sources of Information

With the renewed interest in gold came a veritable flood of information on gold and gold stocks, mostly in the form of investment letters, articles and seminars. There is no way of doing justice to them all here. But a good deal of material is available from a few leading United States brokerage houses. Good information is also available from leading British brokerage houses.

The classic book on the subject is *How to Invest in Gold Stocks* by Donald J. Hoppe. It makes highly informative reading even for someone who is not an investor in gold stocks or any other stocks. For those who are, Mr. Hoppe also reviews all major gold mining stocks of the world.

All gold stocks listed on the New York and American Stock Exchanges, and several of those traded over-the-counter, are covered at regular intervals by *Standard & Poor's* service.

Weekly charts on South African *kaffirs* are available in the United States from *Indicator Chart Service*.

The *Mining Journal* in London publishes an excellent *Quarterly Review of South African Gold Shares* and covers the entire gold scene extensively in its editorial pages. The daily *Financial Times*, also in London, publishes detailed annual and interim reports on South African gold mining stocks and an index of share prices. Canadian mines are covered in *The Northern Miner*, published in Toronto, as well as in the (Toronto) *Financial Post* investment information service.

Most South African gold mines and finance companies produce outstanding, informative annual reports which are sent to investors on request. In addition, the South African *Financial Mail* and *Financial Gazette* cover gold and gold shares in depth.

International Investing

Gold Investment Funds

Anglo American Gold Investment Co. Ltd. / 44 Main Street / Johannesburg, South Africa and 40 Holborn Viaduct / London
ASA Ltd. / 545 Marshall Street / Johannesburg, South Africa (traded on the New York Stock Exchange)
International Investors Inc. / 122 East 42nd Street / New York, New York 10017

South African Mining Finance Companies and Gold Investment Trusts Available as ADRs

Anglo American Corp. of South Africa
Anglo American Gold Investment
Consolidated Gold Fields
Free State Development & Investment
General Mining & Finance
Gold Fields of South Africa
International Mining
Rand Selection
Sentrust Beperk
Southvaal Holdings
U.C. Investments
Union Corporation
Zandpan Gold Mining

South African Gold Mining Companies Available as ADRs

	Mine Life in Years at $130/oz.*
Blyvooruitzicht	11
Bracken	6
Buffelsfontein	19
Doornfontein	24
Durban Deep	4
East Driefontein	34
ERPM	3
Free State Geduld	19
Grootvlei	7
Harmony	12
Hartebeestfontein	22
Kinross	19
Kloof	29
Leslie	5

Gold

*Drexel Burnham Lambert estimate

Investment Information and Advisory Services

Financial Post (on Canadian mining) published by *Maclean-Hunter Ltd.* / 481 University Avenue / Toronto and 625 President Kennedy Avenue / Montreal

Kaffir Chart Service published weekly by *Indicator Chart Service* / Indicator Digest Building / Palisades Park, New Jersey 07650

Quarterly Review of South African Gold Shares published by *The Mining Journal Ltd.* / 15 Wilson Street / London

Books

Hoppe, Donald J. *How to Invest in Gold Stocks. Arlington House* / New Rochelle, New York 10801

Moog, Rees. *The Crisis of World Inflation. William Baxter* / 51 Weaver Street / Greenwich, Connecticut 06830

Other Publications

Financial Mail / Carlton Center, Box 9959 / Johannesburg

The London Financial Times / Bracken House, Cannon Street / London (Daily except Sunday, by airmail; next-day delivery may be arranged through their office at 551 Fifth Avenue / New York, New York 10017)

Mining Journal (weekly, by airmail) / 15 Wilson Street, Moorgate / London

International Investing

The Northern Miner (weekly) / Circulation Department, 77 River Street / Toronto, Ontario, Canada

South African Financial Gazette / 8 Empire Road Extension / Auckland Park, Johannesburg

Information on gold futures trading is available from the International Monetary Market of the Chicago Mercantile Exchange Inc. / 44 West Jackson Street / Chicago, Illinois 60606

Partial List of Investment Advisory Letters Covering Gold From Time to Time

American Institute for Economic Research / Great Barrington, Massachusetts 01230

Dines Letter / 18 East 41st Atreet / New York, New York 10017

T.J. Holt & Co. / 277 Park Avenue / New York, New York 10017

International Reports / 200 Park Avenue South / New York, New York 10003

Investment Guideline / *McConnell Craig Capital Advisors Ltd.* / Suite 408, 200 Bay Street / Toronto, Ontario, Canada

Lynch International Investment Survey / 120 Broadway / New York, New York 10005

Powell Monetary Analyst / *Reserve Research Ltd.* / 63 Wall Street / New York, New York 10005

World Market Perspective / 144 Mason Street / Greenwich, Connecticut 06850

20. Eurobonds

Since the elimination of the Interest Equalization Tax in 1974, the American investor can avail himself of an international fixed-income vehicle that has appealed to many foreign investors since its inception in 1963 — Eurobonds.

By generally accepted definition, a Eurobond issue is a bond offering underwritten by an international syndicate and sold outside the country of the currency in which it is denominated. A Eurobond denominated in United States dollars, for instance, taps the dollars owned by investors who are not residents of the United States.

Eurobonds have a number of special features that make them of interest either to issuers or investors:

1. They are not subject to regulations of government or government agencies such as the SEC.

2. There is no withholding tax on interest payments.

3. Yields are often higher than those of comparable domestic issues.

4. Maturities are relatively short (five to ten years for 1975 and 1976 issues), even for high-quality issuers.

5. Sinking fund features are often attractive.

International Investing

Because Eurobond issues are not registered with the SEC, they cannot be offered in the United States at issue time. Only after an issue is considered sufficiently matured — usually after 90 days — will an American broker sell a Eurobond to an investor living in the United States. Since Eurobonds are issued in bearer form, they are particularly popular with investors who do not trust the stability of their own government or the leniency of their tax collectors. Many Eurobond holders go on annual pilgrimages to Luxembourg to cash their coupons or redeem their bonds.

Origins

Eurobonds owe their origins to three events in the early 1960s — the dollar drain, which put increasing amounts of United States dollars into the hands of institutions and individuals outside the United States, the Interest Equalization Tax imposed in 1963 on the purchase by Americans of foreign stocks and bonds in a short-sighted effort to stem the outflow of dollars, and the Federal government's regulation requiring United States multinational companies to raise capital abroad for their overseas expansion.

Until 1963, the United States had been the most important foreign capital market for governments and other borrowers wanting to raise money outside their homelands. These foreign borrowings, even though a short-term dollar drain, were a major source of foreign income for the United States. A foreign borrower of $100 million at 5% for ten years paid back $150 million in the course of the loan.

The IET stopped the immediate outflow of new loan capital and the inflow of interest income in the United States. It did not stop the over-all outflow of dollars, which was the result of other ill-conceived government policies, chief among them the Vietnam War and the general debasement of the currency. By the early 1970s, more than $100 billion were in the hands of non-residents, and the amount may have tripled since the Arabs raised the price of oil. The foreign borrowers — national governments, government agencies, municipalities, and international organizations — who formerly came to the United States to borrow money, began, in the early 1960s, to tap these Eurodollars as a source of capital. London merchant banks pioneered the concept of the Eurobond issue and London became the primary marketplace for these bonds. In 1965, American corporations joined the flock of foreign borrowers of Eurodollars. At that time, the United States government began to limit the amount of money American corporations could transfer abroad to finance overseas operations. These corporations then turned to the Eurodollar pool and raised money outside the United States by selling both straight debt as well as issues convertible into the common stock of the parent company.

Other currencies held outside their homelands joined the Eurodollar market. A new term was coined to describe this homeless money — Eurocurrency. The most widely used currencies, in 1975, besides the United States dollar, were the Deutschmark, Canadian dollar, Dutch guilder, and the French franc. The borrower's choice of currency depends on its availability and its relative current and potential future strength. In addition, artificial currency units were created, such as the European Unit of Account, which is a composite of all the currencies of the nine European Economic Community countries, and the Special Drawing Rights (SDRs) of the International Monetary Fund, a weighted composite of IMF-member currencies, with the United States dollar accounting for more than 30% of the "weight." Such issues reduce the currency risks by spreading it over many different currencies.

More than $40 billion in Eurobond issues (including issues denominated in other currencies) have been sold between 1963 and 1975. There was a low point in new issues in 1974, but this was caused more by the recession than the elimination of the Interest Equalization Tax or the lifting by the Federal government of curbs in the transfer of capital abroad by United States corporations. In 1975, the total of new issues rose to an all-time record of $7 billion, up from $1.8 billion in 1974. During the first eleven months of 1976, the total was $11 billion. Foreign borrowers were slow to come back to the United States capital market and preferred to stay in the Eurobond market, where they do not have to cope with SEC registration and undergo ratings procedures. Moreover, American investors, estranged from foreign investments during the duration of the IET, were slow in going back into international issues.

Types of Issues

More than 1400 Eurobond issues were outstanding at the end of 1976, ranging from a $500 million 7½% issue of the European Economic Community to an 8 million Kuwaiti dinar issue of the Spanish *Autopistas*, and including convertible issues of major American corporations such as the $75 million issue of *Xerox*. In earlier years, sizes of issues were in the $10 to $15 million range, with final maturities of 14 years, and a call protection of at least five years. In the 1970s, maturities have gone down to the five to ten year range, but the size of the issues has been creeping up, and issues of $25 to $50 million, or the equivalent in other currencies, were quite common by 1976. The number of United States issues (usually in the name of a foreign subsidiary and guaranteed by the American parent company) went down sharply during 1974 and 1975 when United States corporations were no longer forced by the Federal government to finance their overseas expansion abroad. This slack has been taken up by French, Japanese, and Canadian issues.

Eurobonds of foreign governments and government agencies, including those of Australia, Canada, Japan, New Zealand, and Norway, usually sell at a higher yield than comparable United States government obligations. Issues of supranational organizations sell at approximately the same yield as the best single foreign government issues. They include the European Economic Community, European Steel and Coal Community, European Investment Bank, World Bank, and Asian Development Bank. Particularly high yields may sometimes be found in bonds selling at a discount because of a nation's temporary economic problems. Anyone who believed in the recovery of Great Britain early in 1976 could have bought Eurodollar bonds of several British cities at yields to maturity of above 10%.

Many large American corporations have issued Eurobonds, including *Chrysler, duPont, Exxon, Ford, General Electric, Rockwell International, Standard Oil of Indiana, TRW, Textron, Carrier, Eaton,* and *W.R. Grace.* Often, yields of the Eurobond issue are somewhat better than those of the domestic bond issues of the same companies. Maturities of Eurobond issues are usually shorter, and in many cases they have sinking funds that the domestic issues do not offer.

The most popular United States Eurobond issues are the convertibles, especially those of corporations that do not have domestic convertible issues outstanding. They include *American Can, Firestone, Ford, General Electric, General Foods, Revlon, Sperry Rand, Xerox,* and, as the first one again after a lapse of two years, *Raymond International.* Yields are often higher than those of the underlying common stocks, and they offer opportunities to convert whenever the conversion premium is attractive.

Many foreign corporations have also sold convertible Eurobond issues, thereby offering the investor a relatively safe opportunity to participate in foreign equity markets. Of particular interest are the French *Michelin* issues; many Japanese issues, including two of *Hitachi Ltd.,* several of *Mitsubishi* companies, and two of *Mitsui & Co.;* the Dutch *Amro Bank, Hoogovens,* and *Philips Lamp;* and the *Union Bank of Switzerland.*

316

Eurobonds

Investors seeking a hedge against their own weak currencies have looked to issues in Deutschmarks, Dutch guilders, and the European Units of Account. After a lull in Deutschmark issues in 1973 and 1974, there was a resurgence of new issues in 1975 and 1976, including large issues of the European Coal and Steel Community, European Investment Bank, World Bank, Asian Development Bank, Ireland, and New Zealand. Euroguilder issues include those of the leading Dutch banks, New Zealand, Norway, *Norsk Hydro*, and *Unilever N.V.* European Units of Account issues showed a predominance of cities and municipal agencies of various European countries.

Where to Buy Eurobonds

Most Eurobonds are listed on the Luxembourg exchange or some other recognized exchange such as New York to make them eligible for inclusion in the portfolios of institutions that can buy only listed securities. However, very little trading takes place on the floor of the stock exchanges. Secondary market trading is done primarily over the telephone between dealers in the various financial markets of the world. While in the earlier years trading was somewhat spotty and many issues were not traded at all, the Eurobond aftermarket has become more orderly and systematized with the formation, in 1974, of the Association of International Bond Dealers, which publishes a directory of its members and monthly market quotations and yields for Eurobond issues. These are reprinted in the *Financial Times* of London. Recognized among the most active dealers, in 1976, were *Kredietbank* in Luxembourg, *White Weld, Kidder Peabody,* and *Merrill Lynch.* (A selected list of dealers can be found at the end of this chapter.)

Eurobonds are usually sold in 1000 denominations of the currency in which they are issued — *e.g.* $1000 or DM 1000. The most popular issues can usually be traded in up to 100-bond lots. DM issues have developed a fairly good trading volume on the Frankfurt exchange in lots of up to DM 25,000. Larger transactions are usually made outside the exchange. Most Euro-DM issues, and some issues in other denominations, have a mandatory redemption feature requiring retirement of the whole issue in equal annual installments, usually after a grace period of five years. Thus, a 15-year issue would be retired in ten equal installments between the sixth and fifteenth year.

Two clearing agencies for Eurobond trading have been established — *Euro-clear* in Brussels, operated by *Morgan Guaranty Trust Company of New York,* and *Cedel,* established by a group of banks in

317

Luxembourg. Both agencies also have clearing arrangements with several of the continental stock exchanges, notably Frankfurt, on which Eurobonds are traded.

How to Float a Eurobond Issue

Competition among investment bankers for the lead role in Eurobond issues is keen. Two qualifications are of particular importance: placement ability and creativity in designing an issue. The two are not necessarily found in one investment banker in equal strength. Some of the London merchant banks, notably *S.G. Warburg*, have an excellent reputation for pioneer work and originality in Eurobond issues. But the investment premium has reduced their market potential in the United Kingdom. And the Arabs in their inimitable righteousness have tried to impair the placement ability of Jewish bankers by refusing to be on the same underwriting syndicate with them. *Kredietbank S.A. Luxembourgeoise*, jointly owned by a number of European banks with the Belgian *Kredietbank* in the lead, has come up to the top of the list of Eurobond issuers thanks to an astounding placement ability, largely among Flemish investors. It has also demonstrated ingenuity in launching Euro Unit of Accounts and SDR issues. *Deutsche Bank* has shown particular clout in the placement of Euro-DM issues. For Eurodollar issues, the combine of *Crédit Suisse-White Weld* and the two other large Swiss banks head up the parade in total placement volume. In France, *Banque Nationale de Paris*, for size, and *Paribas*, for merchant banking abilities, share the lead.

Co-management is prevalent in Eurobond issues. When establishing rank lists, one method gives full and equal credit to each co-manager. Another method gives full credit only to the lead manager who "keeps the books" and does most of the work on a new issue. The rank list for 1976 below offers both methods side by side.

Eurobond issues are sold more easily if the borrower is well known by investors. This is no problem for borrowers who tap the Eurobond market at regular intervals, such as governments and supranational agencies. For a newcomer to the market, special marketing efforts are required. It is customary for an underwriter to take a first-time borrower on a whirlwind sales tour through the financial centers of Europe.

The success of a new issue and the coupon rate often hinge on this brief encounter with investor groups which may or may not be fully representative of their community on any given day. A safer way is to prepare the ground well in advance with a continuing investor relations program in Europe. A taboo: A sales tour through Europe without mentioning financing plans, followed immediately by the announcement of a new Eurobond issue.

Eurobonds

1976 Eurobond Underwriting Ranking
Full Credit to Each Manager

1975	1976		$ Volume (Millions)	Number of Issues
4	1	Credit Suisse White Weld	5,980.5	110
3	2	Union Bank of Switzerland	5,671.1	105
5	3	Swiss Bank Corp.	5,611.8	106
2	4	Deutsche Bank	4,301.6	76
1	5	Kredietbank Luxembourgeoise	3,121.0	74
8	6	Paribas	2,924.8	49
12	7	S. G. Warburg	2,723.4	51
7	8	Westdeutsche Landesbank	2,710.3	65
13	9	Amro Bank	2,705.0	36
10	10	Commerzbank	2,356.3	46
9	11	Societe Generale de Banque	2,082.0	44
14	12	Societe Generale	1,952.7	31
17	13	Banque Nationale de Paris	1,816.0	35
—	14	Wood Gundy	1,785.3	40
6	15	Dresdner Bank	1,741.0	47
19	16	Morgan Stanley	1,720.4	36
18	17	Credit Lyonnais	1,451.0	34
—	18	Kidder, Peabody	1,337.4	23
—	19	Manufacturers Hanover	1,264.7	29
21	20	Banca Commerciale Italiana	1,189.2	17
15	21	Banque Bruxelles Lambert	1,159.8	33
16	22	Algemene Bank Nederland	1,150.1	19
—	23	Orion	1,065.7	29
20	24	Merrill Lynch	958.4	28
—	25	BAII	955.8	15

Source: *Institutional Investor*

1976 Eurobond Underwriting Ranking
Proportionate Credit to Each Manager

1975	1976		Volume (Millions)	Number of Issues
8	1	Credit Suisse White Weld	$1,239.0	110
4	2	Union Bank of Switzerland	876.8	105
5	3	Swiss Bank Corp.	774.8	106
1	4	Deutsche Bank	557.6	76
7	5	Morgan Stanley	453.0	36
25	6	Wood Gundy	394.1	40
3	7	Kredietbank Luxembourgeoise	372.4	74
13	8	S. G. Warburg	353.0	51
11	9	Westdeutsche Landesbank	333.2	65
6	10	Paribas	335.9	49
9	11	Amro Bank	318.4	37
10	12	Banque Nationale de Paris	315.3	35
12	13	Commerzbank	285.8	46
2	14	Dresdner Bank	256.8	47
14	15	Societe Generale de Banque	225.1	44
19	16	Societe Generale	191.9	31
17	17	Credit Lyonnais	189.2	34
—	18	Kidder, Peabody	178.4	23
—	19	Orion	164.8	29
21	20	Merrill Lynch	143.6	28
—	21	Manufacturers Hanover	134.9	29
18	22	Banque Bruxelles Lambert	132.8	33
22	23	BAII	132.6	15
—	24	A. E. Ames	126.4	18
—	25	Hambros Bank	123.9	22

Source: *Institutional Investor*

320

Eurobonds

1976 Eurobond Underwriting Ranking
Full Credit to Lead Manager*

1975	1976		$ Volume (Millions)	Number of Issues
1	1	Deutsche Bank	1,904.1	18
2	2	Morgan Stanley	1,129.7	22
22	3	S. G. Warburg	984.2	19
10	4	Credit Suisse White Weld	849.4	19
4	5	Westdeutsche Landesbank	509.4	15
15	6	Union Bank of Switzerland	493.0	6
18	7	Wood Gundy	382.1	14
6	8	Kidder, Peabody	360.0	10
24	9	Orion	326.0	8
5	10	Dresdner Bank	316.7	9
20	11	First Boston	305.3	9
7	12	Commerzbank	299.4	7
9	13	Paribas	270.6	7
—	14	Hambros Bank	265.0	7
—	15	Kuhn, Loeb	220.0	4
8		Banque Nationale de Paris	220.0	4
—	17	European Banking Co.	215.0	4
—	18	Smith Barney	205.0	7
11	19	Amro Bank	185.5	5
—	20	Goldman, Sachs	141.1	4
—	21	Swiss Bank Corp.	135.0	2
—	22	Caisse des Depots	125.0	2
—	23	Societe Generale	117.5	4
21	24	Daiwa	105.0	3
—		Salomon Brothers	105.0	2

*Lead manager is defined as the organization "running the books."
Source: *Institutional Investor*

International Investing

Because of the problems involved in establishing these rank lists, the footnotes which appeared in the *Institutional Investor* [*II*] are reprinted here:

"Who gets credit for the deal? Because of a longstanding dispute about what is the 'fairest' way to allocate credit, *II* has chosen to present each of its compilations in three ways. First, each table is presented giving full credit to each of the managers, which is the most widely used formula for determining leadership. The second gives proportionate credit to each member of the managing group, by dividing the total amount of the deal equally. This is an accepted procedure even though it would be an unusual deal indeed in which the underwriters actually underwrote equal amounts. The third gives full credit for each deal only to the lead manager, since presumably the borrower being brought to market really is this banker's client: he runs the books, masterminds the deal and brings in other organizations as support. We believe our readers will find it illuminating to see how each of these approaches can change the rankings within individual categories.

"A few words should be said about *II*'s own effort. (We) found inconsistencies and inaccuracies in the data bases used by almost every organization we have studied (they ranged from listing medium-term credits as bonds to using the wrong lead managers). And while we have checked and cross-checked with as many as 20 different sources and organizations to produce these rankings, we suspect there will likely be some mistakes in our own effort. But we do not believe they would affect the rankings we present here in any dramatic fashion. It should be noted, too, that we have included bonds, notes and debentures (including convertibles) here and have used the annual average value of each currency, published by the U.S. Federal Reserve Board of Governors, to convert the value of non-dollar transactions into U.S. dollars."

Eurobond Issues by Currency

(U.S. $ million equivalent)

	1972	1973	1974	1975	1976
U.S. Dollars	3,288.0	1,850.9	857.0	3,115.50	8,038.00
Deutsche Marks	1,149.6	937.5	228.4	1,727.50	2,077.50
Canadian Dollars	—	—	60.1	560.39	1,394.63
Dutch Guilders	392.9	191.9	360.8	586.78	411.19
European Units of Account	—	98.9	171.0	381.13	102.51
French Francs	465.3	152.1	—	286.51	27.97
Austrian Schilling	—	—	15.0	—	18.70
Special Drawing Rights (SDR's)	—	—	—	173.62	—
Belgian Francs	—	—	—	77.43	—
Norwegian Kroner/Deutsche Mark	—	—	—	45.01	—
European Currency Units	30.0	—	—	36.88	—
Euro	—	64.8	67.9	—	—
Luxembourg Francs	142.8	91.8	—	—	—
Sterling/Deutsche Mark	99.0	32.6	—	—	—
£ Sterling	26.1	—	—	—	—
Australian Dollar/Deutsche Mark	35.7	—	—	—	—
Danish Kroner/Deutsche Mark	32.2	—	—	—	—
TOTALS	5,661.6	3,419.6	1,760.2	6,990.75	12,070.50

Source: *Crédit Suisse-White Weld*

323

Eurobond Issues by Type of Borrower

	1972	1973	1974	1975	1976
			(U.S. $ million equivalent)		
Central Governments	573.6	136.0	236.9	787.94	2,356.96
Government Agencies	701.6	474.2	343.9	1,831.49	1,523.91
Municipalities	431.3	458.1	135.1	567.11	374.24
International and European Agencies	401.2	427.7	222.4	393.26	1,695.22
Industrial and Financial Companies:					
Straight Debt	2,443.1	1,327.8	736.9	3,128.52	5,375.32
Straight Debt with Warrants	60.0	125.8	—	—	40.00
Convertibles	1,050.8	470.0	85.0	282.43	704.85
TOTALS	5,661.6	3,419.6	1,760.2	6,990.75	12,070.50

Source: *Crédit Suisse-White Weld*

324

Eurobonds

Selected List of Eurobond Market Makers

United States
Arnhold & S. Bleichroeder, Inc. / 30 Broad Street / New York, New York 10004
Kidder, Peabody & Co. Inc. / 10 Hanover Square / New York, New York 10005
Merrill Lynch, Pierce, Fenner & Smith Inc. / 1 Liberty Plaza / New York, New York 10006
Salomon Brothers / 1 New York Plaza / New York, New York 10004
Shields Model Roland Inc. / 44 Wall Street / New York, New York 10005
UBS-DB Corporation / 40 Wall Street / New York, New York 10005
White Weld & Co. Inc. / 91 Liberty Street / New York, New York 10006

United Kingdom (All in London)
Bankers Trust International Ltd. / 56-60 New Broad Street
Brown Harriman & International Banks Ltd. / 41 Eastcheap
Continental Illinois Ltd. / 14 Moorfields Highwalk
Daiwa Europe N.V. / 8-14 St. Martins-le-Grand
Deltec Trading Company Ltd. / 11 Copthall Avenue
Dillon, Read Overseas Corp. / 1 Hill Street
European Banking Company Ltd. / 40 Basinghall Street
First Boston Corp. / 16 Finsbury Circus
First Chicago Ltd. / P&O Building, Leadenhall Street
Goldman, Sachs International Corp. / 40 Basinghall Street
Kidder, Peabody Securities Ltd. / Bucklersbury House, Cannon Street
Manufacturers Hanover Ltd. / 8 Princess Street
Merrill Lynch, Pierce, Fenner & Smith Ltd. / 3 Newgate Street
Nesbitt, Thomson Ltd. / 1 Union Court, Old Broad Street
Salomon Brothers International Ltd. / 1 Moorgate
Samuel Montagu & Co. Ltd. / 114 Old Broad Street
Scandinavian Bank Ltd. / 35 Leadenhall Street
Strauss, Turnbull & Co. / 3 Moorgate Place
S.G. Warburg & Co. Ltd. / 30 Gresham Street
Westdeutsche Landesbank Girozentrale / 21 Austin Friars
White Weld·Securities / P&O Building, Leadenhall Street
Wood Gundy Ltd. / 30 Finsbury Square
Yamaichi International (Europe) Ltd. / St. Alphage House, 2 Fore Street

Switzerland (All in Zurich)
Crédit Suisse / Paradeplatz 8
Swiss Bank Corp. / Paradeplatz 6
Union Bank of Switzerland / Bahnhofstrasse 45

International Investing

Luxembourg
Banque Générale du Luxembourg S.A. / 27 avenue Monterey
Banque Internationale à Luxembourg S.A. / 2 boulevard Royal
Deeway Luxembourg S.A. / 47 boulevard Royal
Kredietbank S.A. Luxembourgeoise / 37 rue Notre-Dame

Association

Association of International Bond Dealers / c/o Allgemeine Treuhand
A.G., P.O. Box 1057 / 8022 Zurich

Newsletters

AGEFI International Bond Letter & Eurocurrency Financing Review
published by *AGEFI Press Ltd.* / 156 High Street / Sevenoaks,
Kent, England
Institutional Capital Markets Newsletter published by *Merrill Lynch,
Pierce, Fenner & Smith Ltd.* / 3 Newgate Street / London
International Bond Letter published by *Crédit Suisse-White Weld
Ltd.* / 125 Leadenhall Street / London

Publications

Euromoney / Tallis House, Tallis Street / London
Financial Times / Bracken House, Cannon Street / London
Institutional Investor International Edition / 488 Madison Avenue /
New York, New York 10022
The Hambro Euromoney Directory / 20 Tudor Street / London EC4Y
OJS

21. Offshore Investment Centers

The term "offshore" was first used in the investment world in the 1960s for United States mutual funds that established legal seats of business outside the United States to escape the jurisdiction of the SEC and to benefit from tax advantages that offshore havens offered.

Today the term is applied to any financial and investment operation specifically established in a location other than the main seat of business of an organization or the residence of an individual to reduce or defer tax obligations and to retain complete freedom in the movement of funds.

In addition to investment funds or trusts, individuals, banks, and corporations are making wide use of offshore investment centers. An offshore haven does not necessarily have to be an island in the middle of the ocean, as are the Bahamas or Bermuda, but can be located on a continent as, for instance, Luxembourg and Panama are. Even traditional investment centers, such as the United Kingdom and the Netherlands, may offer certain offshore privileges to non-resident investors. The most widely used "pure" offshore investment centers in 1976, roughly in the

327

order of the total volume of their traceable non-resident bank transactions, were the Bahamas, Hong Kong, Bermuda, Panama, Cayman Islands, Singapore, Liberia, the Netherlands Antilles, and the New Hebrides. Beirut has lost its important role as an offshore center in the Middle East as a result of the civil war, but other Arab countries, including Bahrain, the United Arab Emirates, and Jordan, are vying to take its place. The Channel Islands, the Isle of Man, and Gibraltar are of particular attraction to British financial institutions and individuals because of their special status under the British tax and currency regulations. Luxembourg has become the official stock exchange and interest disbursement center for Eurobond issues (which are free from withholding tax) and it is also used as a legal seat by many investment funds, leading among them Belgian and Italian funds. Smaller independent legal and financial havens in Europe include Monaco, Liechtenstein, Andorra, and San Marino. New mini-havens in the Seven Seas are Nauru, in the Pacific Ocean, and St. Vincent in the Caribbean.

Individuals

Individuals use offshore havens illegally to avoid taxes and escape currency controls of their home countries or legally to defer or level-out tax obligations and to retain greater flexibility in the use of their funds. Legal use of offshore investment centers are of particular interest to authors, performing artists, and other professionals who have widely varying incomes from many different countries, as well as to employees of multinational companies who may either be frequently transferred from one country to another or employed for a stretch of duty in so-called "hardship" countries, where housing, food, and medical care are provided by the employer and few cash needs arise.

A frequently-used method for self-employed individuals is to set up an offshore company which sells the individual's services to the ultimate employer or customer, much in the same way as a management consulting firm or law office will sell the time and expertise of its partners and employees to its clients. The offshore company pays the individual a fixed annual salary to cover his living expenses, while all excess income accumulates in the offshore company. The individual initially pays income taxes only on the salary. The offshore company can invest the excess income and collect interest and dividends from the investments and make capital gains without paying taxes. Eventually, when the individual withdraws the funds from the offshore company or dissolves it, he becomes liable for taxes in his country of residence and/or citizenship — but if his other income has ceased, he may pay a much lower rate than he would have paid at the time of peak income.

Such offshore companies usually involve expensive services of multinational tax experts and lawyers and are thus only of interest to individuals in the highest income brackets. On a more modest level, the Internal Revenue Service in the United States provides comparable advantages to self-employed individuals with fluctuating incomes by allowing them to average their incomes for tax purposes over five-year periods and to put away 15% (up to $7500 a year) of their annual income tax free in a self-employed retirement plan (Keogh). United States citizens always remain subject to United States tax laws no matter where they live, but taxes paid in other countries can be offset against United States income taxes.

Offshore tax havens are widely used by residents of politically unstable countries to preserve their nest eggs. Panama and Nassau are favorite offshore havens for Latin Americans who may have to leave their countries when a political regime changes — a frequent threat in many of them. Indians and Pakistanis expelled from East Africa were better able to readjust to a new life in a new country if they had been able to salt away some funds in an offshore tax haven.

Corporations

Corporations use offshore havens in many different ways — to maintain greater flexibility in the transfer of international funds, to defer or reduce tax obligations in different countries, to facilitate international borrowing, to finance international trade or other business transactions, to invest temporarily unrepatriated surplus funds, and to manage multinational pension funds. American corporations, for instance, establish Netherlands Antilles finance subsidiaries to raise money in the Eurobond market. This makes it possible to pay interest to foreign investors without withholding tax as they would have to do on domestic bond issues.

Today, no corporate chief financial officer of a multinational company can ignore offshore financial centers if he wants to minimize his tax obligations, protect his company against currency fluctuations, raise money at the most advantageous terms, and manage international funds at maximum efficiency. Specialized international accounting firms, tax lawyers, the leading international commercial and investment bankers and investment managers provide the expertise.

International Investing

Banks

Banks use offshore centers to service offshore customers as well as for a number of reasons of their own. In offshore centers they can often escape reserve requirements, interest rate controls, and other regulations imposed by their own governments. They may reduce their tax obligations or defer them. And most importantly, offshore centers facilitate participation in the Eurodollar, Asiadollar, and other Eurocurrency bank loan business.

Offshore Funds

Offshore funds are set up primarily to avoid withholding taxes on dividends and interest and capital gains tax, as well as to be free of foreign exchange controls, such as those which prevail in the United Kingdom. Completely free to make investments and disbursements in any part of the world, and usually outside the jurisdiction of any government regulatory body, offshore funds have considerable flexibility in their management, investments, and sales. The offshore fund business received a black eye with the collapse of the *IOS* fund empire of Bernard Cornfeld in 1969 and some other questionable fund operations; but in 1976, offshore funds offered by reputable banks or investment managers in many parts of the world fill a legitimate need for certain types of investors — notably those who themselves live in tax havens or low-tax countries, where taxes withheld on dividends, interest, and capital gains would be an outright loss to them, not recoverable in their own tax returns. Offshore fund shares cannot be offered in the United States.

Offshore funds are rarely managed in the country of their legal seat. Many of them are managed by British merchant banks, brokers, and investment companies; investment firms in many other countries also operate offshore funds. Because of the higher costs of operating offshore funds, their initial sales charges and management costs are often higher than those of domestic funds.

Sources of Information

All offshore operations are subject to a highly complex set of factors and regulations, including laws, taxes, currency and investment regulations, and interest rates in many different countries. Moreover, these factors

330

may change rapidly, as many countries, including the United States, try to make it increasingly difficult for their nationals to evade taxes or even reduce their tax obligations in legal ways. Thus, anyone interested in offshore investment operations needs highly expert advice. The best sources of information are the banks and investment firms that have for a long time provided international portfolio management, notably those in the United Kingdom, Switzerland, Belgium, the Netherlands, and France (and listed at the end of the respective chapters), as well as international accounting firms and tax lawyers specializing in international tax laws.

Glossary

This glossary covers primarily those technical investment terms used in this book, plus a few other commonly used terms. More complete glossaries can be found in New York Stock Exchange literature and various stock market and investment handbooks.

American Depositary Receipt (ADR): Certificates issued in the United States in lieu of original foreign securities deposited with a bank abroad. ADRs are actively traded in the United States in the same way as common stock.

arbitrage: The simultaneous buying and selling of a security on two different stock exchanges to take advantage of the price differential; or the buying of one security convertible into another, and the selling of the other, to take advantage of the price differential.

arbitrager, arbitrageur: A security trader making arbitrage deals.

Asiadollars: The same as Eurodollars — dollars owned by non-residents of the United States. If the dollars are in the hands of residents or banks in the Far East they are often called Asiadollars.

asset value (of an investment trust or fund): The market value on any specific day of all the securities held by an investment trust or mutual fund plus cash on hand, generally expressed on a per-share basis.

bargain: A transaction on The Stock Exchange, London.

bearer certificate: A certificate for a stock or bond not registered in the owner's name. Anyone holding the certificate can collect the dividends or interest due (usually by detaching a coupon) and can sell it without having endorsed it. In other words, a bearer certificate is comparable to cash.

beneficial owner: The ultimate owner of a stock certificate who receives the "benefits," such as dividends, associated with stock ownership. The term is often used when the apparent owner is a custodian who holds the stock certificate in trust for the "beneficial" owner.

blue chip: Stock of a well-known, large company, implying maximum safety of investment.

blue sky laws: Laws passed by individual states of the United States to protect the investor from fraud.

bond: A certificate of long-term, interest-paying debt issued by a corporation, government, or other organization to raise money.

broker: An individual or firm who buys and sells securities on behalf of an investor on a commission basis.

call (call option): A contract to buy a certain number of shares at a specific price within a specific period of time.

call of bonds: A redemption of bonds by the issuer before maturity, usually at a previously specified price that is higher than the redemption price at full maturity.

call protection: The time limit after the sale of a new bond issue during which the issuer cannot call any of the bonds for redemption.

capital gain (loss): Profit or loss from the sale of a security or other capital asset.

central bank: A government or quasi-government bank usually responsible for the money supply, foreign exchange reserves, and financial dealings of a country.

clearing bank: A British commercial bank which "clears" checks but also conducts almost every other conceivable banking business.

clearing house: A firm or agency that facilitates the receipt and delivery of stock certificates via bookkeeping entries to reduce the physical movement of stock certificates.

closed-end investment trust or fund: An investment trust with a limited number of shares which are traded in the same manner as other securities and often listed on stock exchanges. The price of the shares is determined by supply and demand and often varies from the per-share net asset value of the trust.

common stock: A share ownership in a publicly-owned company, usually entitling the owner to a vote during shareholder meetings and to the receipt of a dividend if the company pays a dividend (which is not necessarily the case even if a company earns money).

convertible bond: A bond that a holder, under specified conditions, may exchange into common stock.

coupon: A small piece of paper attached to "bearer" bonds or shares that must be detached and presented to a paying agent to collect a dividend or interest payment due.

334

Glossary

custodian: A bank, broker, or trust agency that holds an investor's securities for safekeeping and will usually attend to any action necessary in connection with the ownership, such as collecting dividends and interest due, exercising rights, or voting at shareholders meetings (if so instructed by the owner).

debenture: A long-term debt certificate, paying interest, and secured by the general credit of the issuer rather than a specific property.

demand deposit: A bank deposit that a depositor can withdraw at any time without notice.

dilution: An increase in the number of outstanding shares, thereby reducing the value of each share held by existing shareholders.

discount: 1. The amount under face value for which a bond is selling; 2. the amount under asset value for which the shares of a closed-end investment fund are selling; 3. the amount under conversion value for which a convertible bond is selling.

discretionary account: The broker has the authority to buy and sell securities on behalf of the customer without consulting him.

dividend: That part of the earnings of a company that is distributed to shareholders on a per-share basis. Dividend distribution is usually not automatic even if a company makes money. Each dividend is "declared" by the board of directors, usually on a quarterly basis in the United States; on a semi-annual or annual basis in most other countries of the world.

equity: 1. The ownership interest of a common or preferred stockholder in a company, i.e. the number of shares he holds. If a company sells "equity" this usually means that it raises money through the sale of common stock or bonds convertible into common stocks. 2. The excess value of securities over the debit cash balance that a customer has in a margin account with his broker.

Eurodollars: Dollars owned by non-residents of the United States.

Eurocurrency: Any European currency owned by a non-resident of the country issuing the currency.

ex-dividend: A stock trading without giving the buyer the right to collect a recently declared dividend (which the previous owner collects).

ex-rights: A stock that trades without recently issued rights to buy additional shares of the company. The rights may either have been exercised by the previous owner or sold separately.

fixed-interest security: A bond or debenture on which a fixed rate of interest is paid.

flat earnings: Earnings that remain more or less unchanged.

float: The number of shares of a securities issue that is freely available for trading, in contrast to the shares closely held by insiders or others unlikely to trade their shares.

335

front-end load: A sales commission charged by a mutual fund at the initial sale of shares to the investor.

gilt edged: A British expression for securities of greatest safety, usually government or government-guaranteed bonds.

holding company: A company that controls others without itself conducting any business.

index: A statistical average of the prices of a certain number of stocks traded on a stock exchange used to measure the average price action on the exchange.

institutional investor: An organization, such as a bank, insurance company, investment trust, pension fund, etc., making substantial investments, often on behalf of others.

investment banker: A firm that raises money for corporations by selling new public issues of securities or placing private debt commitments with lenders.

investment company or trust: A firm that invests money of participating shareholders in a diversified portfolio of securities.

jobber: A dealer on The Stock Exchange, London, who makes a market in a certain number of securities, dealing with brokers or other jobbers but not with the public.

Kaffirs: South African gold stocks.

leverage: This usually refers to borrowings of a company that are heavy in relation to the number of outstanding shares. Such a company is often called "highly leveraged." The per-share prices of the stocks of highly leveraged companies tend to rise more quickly in profitable years than the shares of less highly leveraged companies, and they also decline much faster in poor years.

linked bonds or debentures: A security whose price is linked to the cost-of-living index or a fixed exchange rate for a foreign currency or gold.

listed securities: Corporate stocks or bonds admitted to a stock exchange for trading.

liquidity: Active trading on a stock exchange, making it easy to buy and sell securities within a narrow price range.

margin, margin account: A margin account permits an investor to buy a security by paying only a limited percentage of the purchase price (the margin) and borrowing the balance from his broker.

market maker: A security dealer ready to buy or sell securities of a certain company, usually not listed on a stock exchange.

marking: The recording of a transaction on The Stock Exchange, London.

maturity: The date on which a bond or other long-term fixed-income security comes due and is redeemed.

Glossary

merchant bank: A British banking house engaged in corporate financing, investment banking, portfolio management, and other banking activities, except checking and savings accounts.

mutual fund: An open-end investment fund (q.v.).

NASD: The National Association of Securities Dealers Inc., an American organization of over-the-counter securities brokers and dealers.

NASDAQ: A computerized information network that provides brokerage offices throughout the United States with price quotations of most securities traded over-the-counter.

new issue: Shares offered to the public for the first time either of a company that has never offered shares to the public before or that is offering additional shares to those that have been issued before.

no load (fund): An investment fund that charges no sales commission for the sale of its shares (usually closed-end, q.v.), but if traded on an exchange or over-the-counter, the usual brokerage commission is paid by the investor.

odd lot: A stock transaction for fewer shares than the normal trading unit (usually 100 shares).

open-end investment trust or fund: An investment fund that continually issues new shares as it receives new capital or redeems shares of owners who want to sell them. Shares are usually sold at net-asset value, minus sales commission, which can be quite high.

offerings: Public sale of a parcel of securities at a fixed price, usually by a group of underwriters (q.v.).

option: The right, purchased at a certain price, to buy or sell a specific number of securities at a specific price on a specific day.

over-the-counter (OTC): An open market for securities not listed on a regular stock exchange.

par value: The nominal or face value of a stock, usually far below the market price.

pink sheets: Sheets published daily in the United States and printed on pink paper listing all the brokerage houses that make markets in over-the-counter stocks, including American Depositary shares for foreign stocks. Pink sheets are available at practically every American brokerage office.

portfolio: The different securities held by an individual investor, or an institution, such as an investment fund.

preferred stock: Stock taking precedence over common stock of the same corporation in the case of dividends and liquidation payments.

price/earnings ratio: The market price of a stock divided by its reported or anticipated earnings per share.

puts and calls: Options that give the right to buy or sell a fixed number of securities at a specified price within a specified period of time.

registered certificates: Stock certificates registered in the owner's name.

rights: A claim given to existing stockholders to buy additional shares of the company at a specific price within a specific time. Rights not exercised can usually be sold on the open market before expiration.

Securities and Exchange Commission (SEC): A United States government agency that regulates and polices security trading and information disclosure of publicly-owned companies.

security: In investment language, a certificate that gives the owner a share in a publicly-owned company or that certifies a loan to the lender. The term usually applies to common and preferred stock, bonds — interest bearing as well as bonds convertible into common stocks — and warrants and rights for the future purchase of a security.

security analyst: An investment professional who collects information on companies and industries to "analyze" the value of particular securities for investment purposes.

shares: Used interchangeably with common stock to denote a part ownership in a publicly-held company, issued to raise capital for the company, and traded on stock exchanges and other security markets.

specialist: A member of a stock exchange who makes a market for a number of stocks by buying all shares offered and selling all shares wanted. He is usually expected, in the United States, to buy and sell within a narrow price range to "maintain an orderly market."

stock dividend: The payment of stock in lieu of a cash dividend. A 5% stock dividend means that a holder of 100 shares receives five additional shares. If no cash dividend at all is paid by the company, the shareholder gets really no value. All that has happened is that the same size pie — the net worth of the company — is split into 105 slices rather than 100, and earnings per share are correspondingly diluted (q.v.). A stock "dividend" of 20% or more is really in the nature of a stock "split" (q.v.).

stock split: The issuance of one additional share for each share held by a shareholder without making him pay for it, as is the case when rights (q.v.) to buy additional shares are offered to shareholders. Sometimes splits are made by a different formula — 3:1, or 3:2, etc. Sometimes such stock "splits" are called stock "dividends" (q.v.). Stock splits are usually made to increase the number of outstanding shares and keep the price within the range that is most popular with investors. If the cash dividend remains unchanged for both old and new shares, a stock

Glossary

split or dividend represents an increase in the cash dividend. For instance, a 3:2 stock "split" or a 50% stock "dividend" is then an effective increase of 50% in the cash dividend.

stop order: An order to buy at a price above the current market price of a stock or sell below the current market price.

street name: Registration of shares in the name of the broker, without the owner taking physical delivery of the shares.

time deposit: A bank deposit that a depositor can withdraw only after a specified period of time.

transfer agent: A bank or other institution which transfers shares from one owner to another on behalf of the company that has issued the shares.

troy ounce: A weight used for gold and silver = 1.09714 regular ounces.

underwriter: A securities firm which commits itself, usually together with a group of other firms, to buy a new issue of securities for resale to the public.

unit trust: The name for open-end mutual funds in England and some other countries.

warrant: A certificate authorizing the holder to buy a specified number of shares of a company at a specified price within a specified period of time. The time limit is much longer, often by several years, than that for "rights" to buy shares.

yield: The annual income in dividend or interest which an investment returns, expressed in percentage of the market price of the security.

Charts

The charts in this section were produced by
Capital International Perspective
and are reproduced by permission of the publisher
Capital International S.A., 15 rue du Cendrier,
Geneva, Switzerland

For all charts, 1 January 1970 = 100.

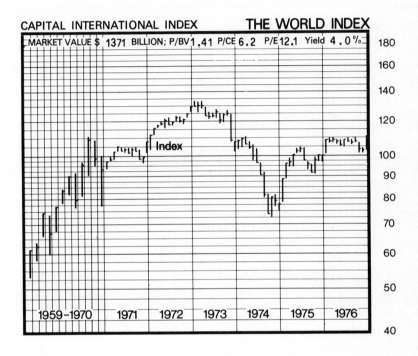

CAPITAL INTERNATIONAL INDEX **THE WORLD INDEX**

MARKET VALUE $ 1371 BILLION; P/BV 1.41 P/CE 6.2 P/E 12.1 Yield 4.0%

343

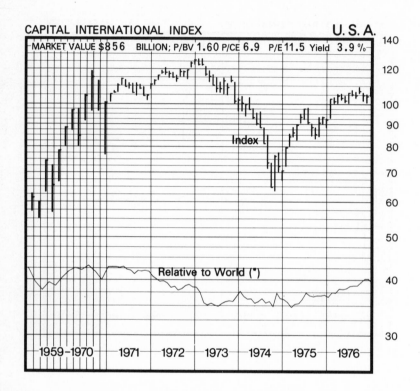

CAPITAL INTERNATIONAL INDEX .... U.S.A.

MARKET VALUE $856 BILLION; P/BV 1.60 P/CE 6.9 P/E 11.5 Yield 3.9 %

Index

Relative to World (*)

140
120
100
90
80
70
60
50
40
30

1959–1970   1971   1972   1973   1974   1975   1976

(*) All "Relative to World" curves take into account exchange gains and losses relative to the US dollar.

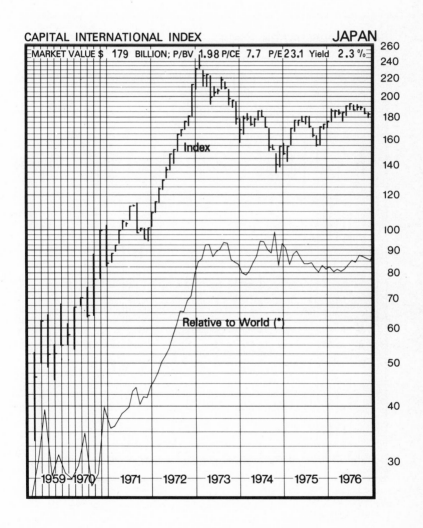

CAPITAL INTERNATIONAL INDEX — JAPAN

MARKET VALUE $ 179 BILLION; P/BV 1.98 P/CE 7.7 P/E 23.1 Yield 2.3 %

Index

Relative to World (*)

1959 1970   1971   1972   1973   1974   1975   1976

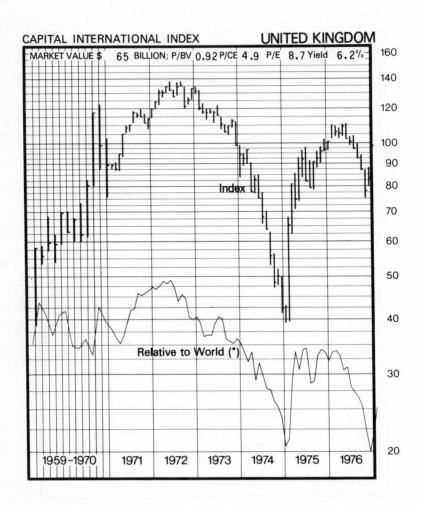

CAPITAL INTERNATIONAL INDEX   **UNITED KINGDOM**

MARKET VALUE $ 65 BILLION; P/BV 0.92 P/CE 4.9 P/E 8.7 Yield 6.2%

Index

Relative to World (*)

1959-1970   1971   1972   1973   1974   1975   1976

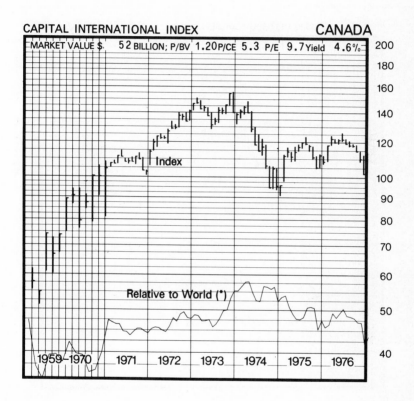

CAPITAL INTERNATIONAL INDEX — CANADA

MARKET VALUE $. 52 BILLION; P/BV 1.20 P/CE 5.3 P/E 9.7 Yield 4.6%

Index

Relative to World (*)

1959–1970 1971 1972 1973 1974 1975 1976

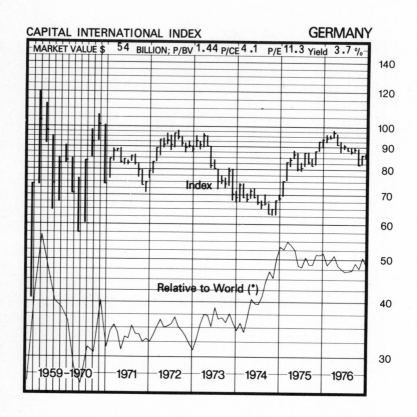

CAPITAL INTERNATIONAL INDEX   GERMANY

MARKET VALUE $ 54 BILLION; P/BV 1.44 P/CE 4.1 P/E 11.3 Yield 3.7 %

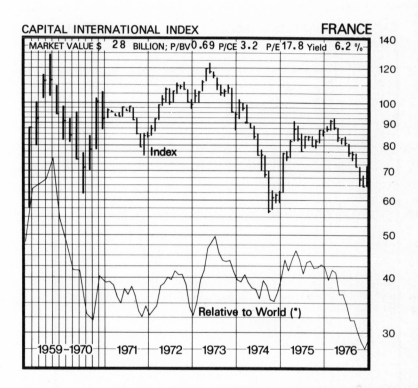

CAPITAL INTERNATIONAL INDEX   **FRANCE**

MARKET VALUE $ 28 BILLION; P/BV 0.69 P/CE 3.2 P/E 17.8 Yield 6.2 %

Index

Relative to World (*)

1959–1970   1971   1972   1973   1974   1975   1976

349

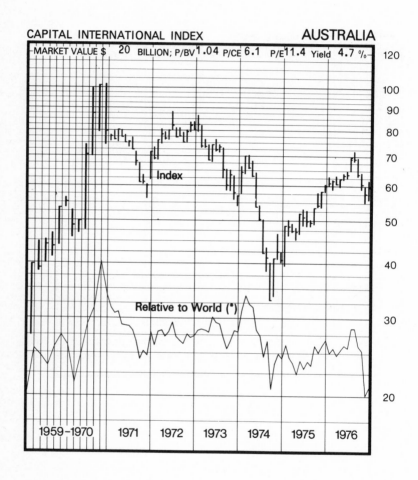

CAPITAL INTERNATIONAL INDEX • AUSTRALIA

MARKET VALUE $ 20 BILLION; P/BV 1.04 P/CE 6.1 P/E 11.4 Yield 4.7 %

Index

Relative to World (*)

1959–1970 1971 1972 1973 1974 1975 1976

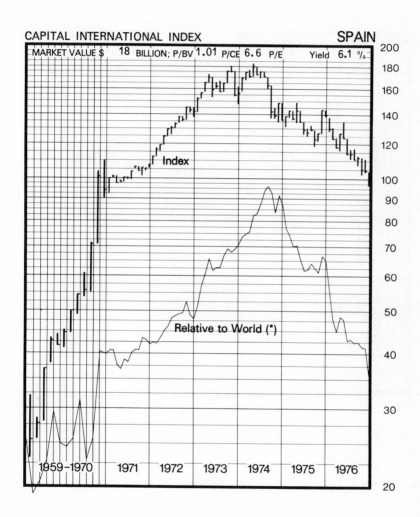

CAPITAL INTERNATIONAL INDEX   SPAIN

MARKET VALUE $ 18 BILLION; P/BV 1.01 P/CE 6.6 P/E   Yield 6.1 %

Index

Relative to World (*)

1959-1970   1971   1972   1973   1974   1975   1976

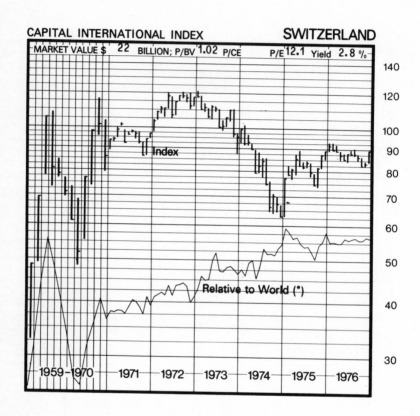

CAPITAL INTERNATIONAL INDEX   SWITZERLAND

MARKET VALUE $ 22 BILLION; P/BV 1.02 P/CE   P/E 12.1 Yield 2.8 %

Index

Relative to World (*)

1959—1970   1971   1972   1973   1974   1975   1976

140
120
100
90
80
70
60
50
40
30

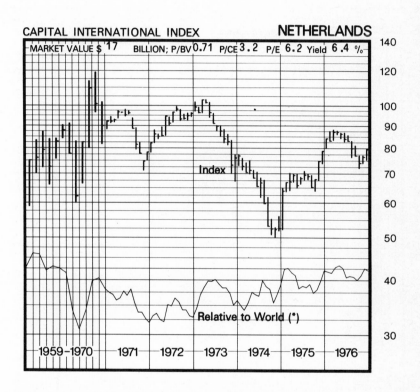

CAPITAL INTERNATIONAL INDEX — NETHERLANDS

MARKET VALUE $ 17 BILLION; P/BV 0.71 P/CE 3.2 P/E 6.2 Yield 6.4 %

Index

Relative to World (*)

1959–1970 1971 1972 1973 1974 1975 1976

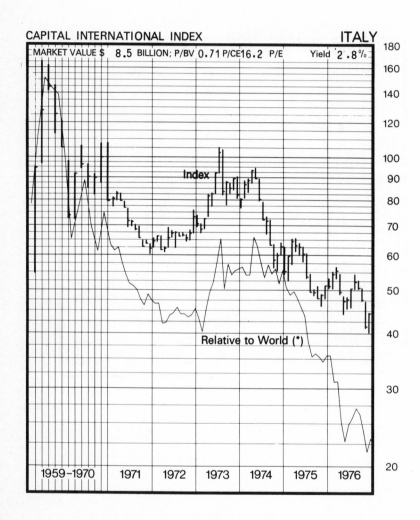

CAPITAL INTERNATIONAL INDEX   **ITALY**

MARKET VALUE $ 8.5 BILLION; P/BV 0.71 P/CE 16.2 P/E   Yield 2.8%

Index

Relative to World (*)

1959–1970   1971   1972   1973   1974   1975   1976

CAPITAL INTERNATIONAL INDEX   **SWEDEN**

MARKET VALUE $ 9.8 BILLION; P/BV 0.72 P/CE 3.2 P/E 8.3 Yield 5.1 %

Index

Relative to World (*)

1959–1970   1971   1972   1973   1974   1975   1976

160 140 120 100 90 80 70 60 50 40 30

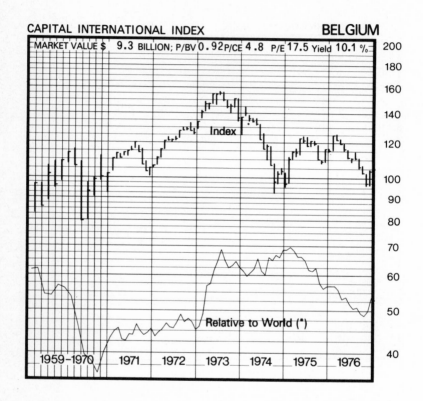

CAPITAL INTERNATIONAL INDEX   **BELGIUM**

MARKET VALUE $ 9.3 BILLION; P/BV 0.92 P/CE 4.8   P/E 17.5 Yield 10.1 %

Index

Relative to World (*)

1959–1970   1971   1972   1973   1974   1975   1976

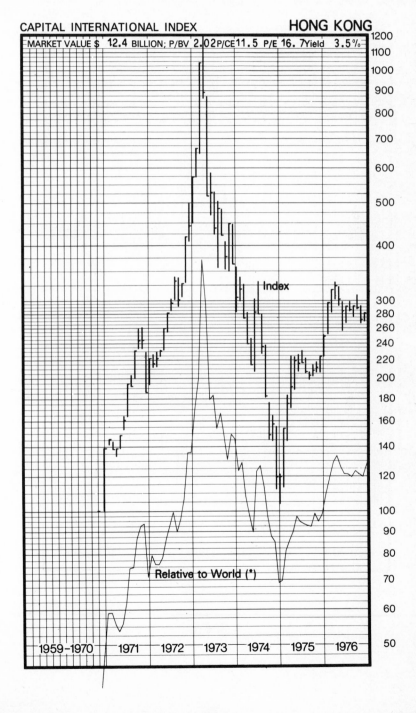

CAPITAL INTERNATIONAL INDEX   **HONG KONG**

MARKET VALUE $ 12.4 BILLION; P/BV 2.02 P/CE 11.5 P/E 16.7 Yield 3.5%

Index

Relative to World (*)

1959–1970   1971   1972   1973   1974   1975   1976

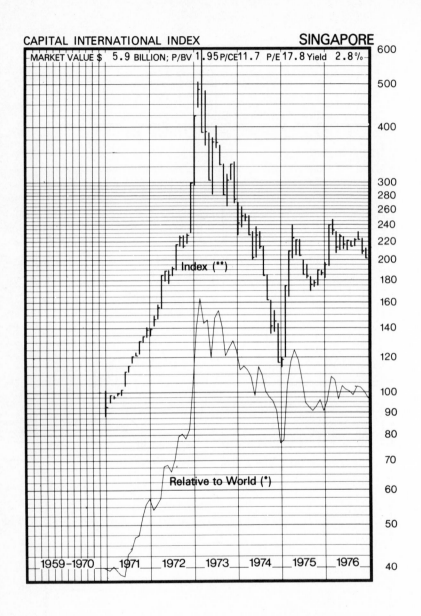

CAPITAL INTERNATIONAL INDEX   **SINGAPORE**

MARKET VALUE $ 5.9 BILLION; P/BV 1.95 P/CE 11.7 P/E 17.8 Yield 2.8%

Index (**)

Relative to World (*)

1959-1970   1971   1972   1973   1974   1975   1976

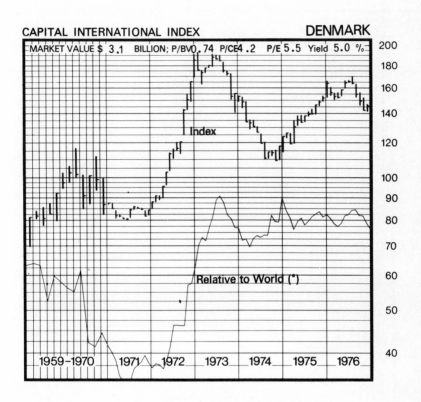

CAPITAL INTERNATIONAL INDEX   **DENMARK**

MARKET VALUE $ 3.1   BILLION; P/BV 0.74   P/CE 4.2   P/E 5.5   Yield 5.0 %

Index

Relative to World (*)

1959–1970   1971   1972   1973   1974   1975   1976

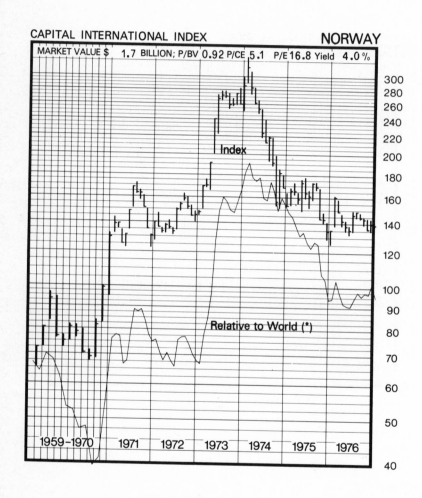

CAPITAL INTERNATIONAL INDEX NORWAY

MARKET VALUE $ 1.7 BILLION; P/BV 0.92 P/CE 5.1 P/E 16.8 Yield 4.0%

Index

Relative to World (*)

1959–1970   1971   1972   1973   1974   1975   1976

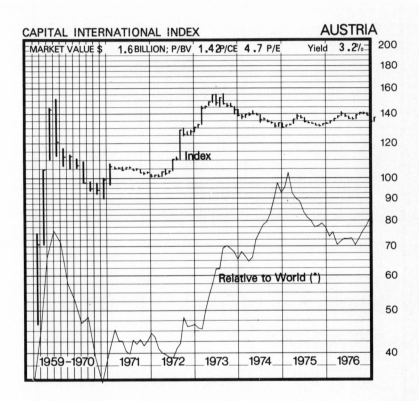

CAPITAL INTERNATIONAL INDEX   AUSTRIA

MARKET VALUE $ 1.6BILLION; P/BV 1.42P/CE 4.7 P/E   Yield 3.2%

Index

Relative to World (*)

1959–1970   1971   1972   1973   1974   1975   1976

GOLD MINES

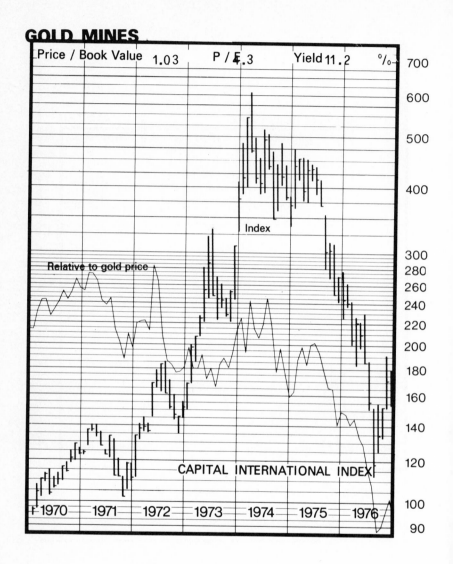

Price / Book Value 1.03   P / E .3   Yield 11.2   %

- 700
- 600
- 500
- 400

Index

- 300
- 280

Relative to gold price

- 260
- 240
- 220
- 200
- 180
- 160
- 140

CAPITAL INTERNATIONAL INDEX

- 120
- 100

1970   1971   1972   1973   1974   1975   1976

- 90

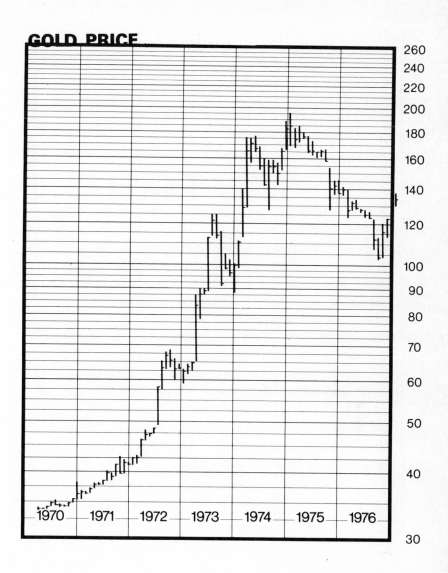

GOLD PRICE

NOTES

The gold mining section covers 28 mines operating in South Africa and North America and 11 South African finance and investment houses. Share prices of South African issues are all London prices, ex investment premium, expressed in UK pence. The Capital International index of gold mines is based on those prices and also includes the North American mines. For complete list of companies included in the index, see page 27. Company graphs are displayed by order of market value and include annual adjusted price ranges from 1959 to 1970 and monthly high and low ranges as of January 1971. Small horizontal bars indicate yearend or monthend closing prices. In addition to operating and financial data, the milling grade is shown whenever available.

Index

Index

Index

367

Index